THE KING'S SERJEANTS
& OFFICERS OF STATE

THE KING'S SERJEANTS
& OFFICERS OF STATE
WITH THEIR CORONATION SERVICES

BY

J. HORACE ROUND M.A., LL.D.

BARNES & NOBLE, Inc.
NEW YORK
PUBLISHERS & BOOKSELLERS SINCE 1873

First published 1911 by James Nisbet & Co. Ltd.
This edition published 1970 by
The Tabard Press Limited, London

© 1970, this edition, The Tabard Press Limited

First published in the United States, 1970
by Barnes & Noble, Inc.

ISBN 389 04033 9

Made and Printed in Great Britain by
Redwood Press Limited
Trowbridge & London

CONTENTS

CHAPTER I

INTRODUCTION

The class of whom these pages treat were those who held their lands ' by serjeanty, ' that is, by the performance of some specified service, either at all times or in time of war. In that work which has superseded all that went before it—I speak of the *History of English Law*—its learned authors tell us that in the days of which they write, " tenures are classified thus :— they are either free or not free : the free tenures are (1) frankalmoin, (2) military service, (3) serjeanty, (4) free socage ; in this order we will speak of them. " [1] It is needful to insist on the position here assigned to serjeanty, because the misconception on the subject is widespread and of old standing. [2] It was a persistent delusion that tenure of grand serjeanty was so noble as to rank above knight-service, and to include, even, all peerage dignities. [3]

[1] *Op. cit.* (1895), I, 218. So also Prof. Maitland wrote of " that scheme of holdings—frankalmoign, knight's service, serjeanty, socage, villeinage —which [in the 13th cent.] was becoming the classical, legal, scheme." *(Eng. Hist. Rev.,* V. 625).

[2] See my *Peerage and Pedigree,* I, 118-128, where the matter is fully discussed in my comments on Mr. Haldane's argument in the Lord Great Chamberlain case.

[3] This does not apply to that eminent antiquary, Madox, who knew better than to hold these fantastic views.

This singular error is at least as old as 'Lyttelton,' whose *Tenures* is doubtless responsible for its persistence to our own time.

His name is still sacred in Westminster Hall; and his celebrated work, *The Treatise on Tenures*, which Coke describes as "the most perfect and absolute work that ever was written in any human science," and for which Camden asserts that "the students of the common law are no less beholden than the civilians are to Justinian's Institutes," will ever prevent its being forgotten. [1]

What Littleton wrote was this :—

Tenure by Grand Serjeanty is where a man holds his lands or tenements of our Sovereign lord the King by such services as he ought to do in his proper person to the King : as to carry the banner of the King, or his lance, or to lead his army, or to be his marshal, or to carry his sword before him at his Coronation, or to be his sewer at his Coronation, or his carver, or his butler, or to be one of his chamberlains of the receipt of his exchequer, or to do other like services, etc. And the cause why this service is called Grand Serjeanty is, for that it is a greater and more worthy service than the service in the tenure of escuage. [2] For he which holdeth by escuage is not limited by his tenure to do any more especial service than any other which holdeth by escuage ought to do : [3] but he which holdeth by Grand Serjeanty ought to do some special service to the King, which he that holds by escuage ought not to do. [4]

By the time of Henry VIII the lawyers had gone further and so confused the subject that they pro-

---

[1] Foss' *Judges*, IV, 439.
[2] *i. e.* knight-service.
[3] *i. e.* the service due from a knight's fee was *uniform*.
[4] *Tenures*, sec. 153.

claimed " Grand Serjeanty " to *be* Knight-service. [1]

Serjeanty, on the contrary, was originally but one tenure ; its division into ' grand ' and ' petty ' serjeanty was of subsequent introduction. *All* serjeanty ranked below knight-service (*servitium militare*) and above socage. There were certain rules by means of which " tenure by serjeanty was kept apart from tenure by knight's service on the one hand and tenure by socage on the other, and even in the middle of the thirteenth century it still had an importance which is but faintly represented by the well known sections of Littleton's book. " [2]

It is admitted in the same work that " the idea of a serjeanty as conceived in the thirteenth century is not one that can be easily defined.......... we find it difficult to mark off serjeanty from knight's service on the one hand and from socage on the other. "

This difficulty is due to the fact that while knight-service was a fixed uniform duty, serjeanty varied infinitely in kind. But in all these matters we have a sure touchstone : the fiscal test cannot fail. I hope to show that at the close of the twelfth and in the earlier portion of the thirteenth century the exchequer recognised serjeanty as a separate and distinct tenure and found no difficulty in obtaining returns of serjeanties as a tenure standing by itself.

It is easier, however, to say what serjeanty was

---

[1] " In grand Serjeantry is included Knight Service... Grand Serjeantry is true service of chivalry [*i. e.* knight service] and no diversity between them, saving in the relief. " (See *Peerage and Pedigree*, I, 158).
[2] *History of English Law*, I, 271.

not than to give an exhaustive definition of what
it was.   In their brilliant section on serjeanty from
which I have already quoted, the authors of the
History of English Law write thus :—

Now it may be impossible to bring all these very
miscellaneous tenures under one definition which shall
include them, but exclude knight's service and socage.
However the central notion seems what we may call
'servantship'..... Obviously in many cases the tenant
by serjeanty...... is a servant *(serviens)* ; he is steward,
marshal, constable, chamberlain, usher, cook, forester,
falconer, dog keeper, messenger, esquire ; he is more or
less of a menial servant bound to obey orders within the
scope of his employment...... The notion of servantship,
free servantship..... seems to be as a matter of history the
notion which brings the various serjeanties under one
class name,..... one of the tributaries which swells the
feudal stream is that of menial service. [1]

This view may claim support, no doubt, from
the language of Domesday, where the tenants by
serjeanty are styled " servientes. "   But it seems
to me to cover serjeanty " in many cases, " but not
in all.   In such great divisions of the subject as
" the King's household " or " the King's sport, "
the definition of " servantship " may, one admits,
apply ; but it is a straining of that definition to
apply it to the large class of military serjeanties.
Indeed its authors admit that " when a tenant by
serjeanty is bound to go to the war as a *serviens*
with horse, purpoint, iron cap and lance, [2] the dif-

[1] *Op. cit.*, I, 267.
[2] There is an example of this service in the tenure of the manor of Hoo
Hall (or Martells) in Rivenhall, Essex. Felicia Martel was found, in
1252, to have held it " by serjeanty of finding a moiety of an esquire in
the King's army, within England, with doublet, lance, and iron cap,

ference between his tenure and knight's service seems to resolve itself into a mere difference between one kind of armour and another or one position in the army or another. " [1]   It is also admitted that " we find many men who are said to hold by serjeanty and are bound by their tenure to do other services which are not so distinctly menial, that is to say, are not so closely connected with the King's household. " [2]

But even services " connected with the King's household " present a problem of their own.   In name, indeed, they may savour of servantship, but in practice they, or many of them, have been always posts of honour, posts held by gentlemen and even by great nobles.   As early as the close of the tenth century Duke Richard of Normandy would have none, Wace tells us, but gentlemen in his household.

> Ne vot mestier de sa meisun
> Duner si a gentil home nun.
> Gentil furent li chapelein,
> Gentil furent li escrivain,
> Gentil furent li cunestable,
> E bien puissant e bien aidable ;
> Gentil furent li senescal
> Gentil furent li marescal
> Gentil furent li butteiller,

for 40 days. " (*Cal. of Inq.*, I, No. 239).   " Doublet " here rightly translates the Latin word formed from the French "pourpoint."   Morant wrongly combined it with lance, producing the phrase " purple lance," which is reproduced in Hazlitt's edition of Blount's *Tenures*, (p. 259), with the delightful suggestion that " A *purple lance* was perhaps one with a banner or pennon of that colour attached to it." (p. 431).

This serjeanty affords a clear example of partition (see below).

[1] *Op. cit.*, p. 268.
[2] *Ibid.*, p. 263.

6   INTRODUCTION

Gentil furent li despensier.
Li chamberlence e li ussier.
Furent tuit noble chevalier,
Chascun iur orent liurisuns [1]
E as granz festes dras [2] e duns. [3]

Although, in this case, we may make some allowance for tradition, I should be the last to rely on Wace for an epoch so remote from his own.   But he is, of course, good authority for the days in which he wrote (the reign of Henry II), and those immediately preceding them, and his list, in which we recognise the well-known officers of state, is of value if it does but reproduce the ideas of that period.

The fact that, even at the present day, the Royal household still contains, not only—of the officers named by Wace—a Lord Steward, a Lord Chamberlain, and Gentlemen Ushers, but Women of the bedchamber, Grooms-in-waiting, and Grooms of the bedchamber, all of them aristocratic posts, [4] illustrates the difficulty one has in apprehending the status of " the King's serjeants " (*servientes*) in the eleventh and twelfth centuries.   At times described as the King's ministers (*ministri*)—their office was always a *ministerium*—they have developed, in administrative history, into the " ministers " of to-

[1] These were the "liberationes," reckoned *per diem* ("Chascun iur"), of the *Constitutio domus regis*, to which we shall come below.
[2] These were the 'robes' and fees to which we find the officers of the King's household entitled.
[3] Roman de Rou.
[4] See *The Royal Household*, 1837-1897, by W. A. Lindsay Q. C., Windsor Herald, described as "an account of those who have had the honour to wait upon Her Majesty's person," and including Reports of Ceremonies.

day, who are, technically, still the King's 'secretaries' for the various administrative departments. For all power radiated, in theory, from the person of our Lord the King. In constitutional practice, as we all know, the administration passed out of the hands of the great household officers ; but this change was gradual.

Though the real work of governing the realm has fallen to another set of ministers, whose offices are not hereditary, to the king's justiciar, chancellor and treasurer,[1] still the marshal and constable have serious duties to perform. [2]

Even in actual Court duties there was a similar development. The hereditary holder of a household office delegated to a deputy with the same title the actual discharge of its functions, which he himself assumed more and more rarely until at last he officiated only at the great solemnity of a Coronation. As early as 1236, at the coronation of Queen Eleanor, we already find that this process had for its result the co-existence of a chief butler, assistant butler, and deputy assistant butler.[3] At the present day we see it illustrated by the simultaneous existence of a Lord Great Chamberlain, a Lord Chamberlain, and a Vice-Chamberlain. The office of Lord High Steward has, from an early date, been only revived for special occasions, such as a coronation, the Lord Steward having taken his place as the permanent officer. How early this

---

[1] But the chancellor and treasurer were, both of them, members of the King's household under the Norman Kings (J.H.R.).

[2] *History of English Law*, I, 263.

[3] See the section on the butler's office in this work.

process began it is not easy to say, but it extended, from at least the thirteenth century, to inferior offices in the household. For we find tenants by serjeanty then already returned as bound to perform their service at a coronation only. The tenant of Addington by kitchen service 'finds' a cook to perform it. In later days, under Edward III, the lady of the manor of Sculton Burdeleys still holds " by service of coming to the King's coronation with a knife and axe to perform the office of larderer, " but at other times, we may be sure, the larder knew her not.

The keen and persistent contest for this office of larderer [1] illustrates the eagerness to claim a comparatively menial office, and so does the assertion, to the last of the coronation banquets, of the right, in virtue of tenure, to act as towel-horse to the sovereign. [2]

There were not even fees to act as an attraction. Dukes and Earls have claimed, and mostly claimed in vain, to act as " Serjeant of the silver scullery, " but in that coronation office they had at least the privilege of making off with the plate.

The atmosphere of a Court has always tended to foster a servile spirit. Even the saintly bishop Andrewes, a man sprung from the trading class, did not hesitate to say of James, that " most high and mighty prince " who was perhaps the most unseemly monster that has ever sat upon the English throne, James, under whom his " rise was rapid, " [3]

---

[1] There were three claimants at the coronation of George IV and one at that of Edward VII (see the section on ' the King's larderer ').

[2] See the section on ' Basin and towel serjeanties.'

[3] See his life by his panegyrist, Canon Overton, in the *Dict. Nat. Biog.*

that he was "inspired of God." [1]   It was something, surely, of the same spirit that led men to fight for the privilege of holding the King's basin while he washed his hands. [2]   " We observe, " say the learned authors of the *History of English Law*, " that all these offices, if we regard only their titles, have something menial about them, "......

It may be long since the predecessors in title of these men really cooked the King's dinner or groomed the King's horses : but they glory in titles which imply, or have implied, that their duties are of this menial kind ; nor is it always easy to say when or whether the duty has become honorary.   When the Conqueror gives half a hide of land in Gloucestershire to his cook (D.B. 162b), it were bold to say that this tenant did not really roast and boil (I,263).

The illustration is not a happy one.   Far more striking would have been the fact that members of the mighty Norman houses of Bigod and of Giffard held, in succession, an Essex manor by the service of scalding the King's swine. [3]

My real criticism, however, is that, when we refer to the passage vouched, we find that Domesday speaks, not, as alleged, of the King's gift, but of the gift of *Earl* William. [4]   If we would find the Conqueror's cook and the lands given him by his

---

[1] This is one of those awkward facts to which Green's *Short History* has given a wide circulation, to the mingled rage and despair of the party that appeals to Andrewes.

[2] It led the Chamberlain of Normandy, under Henry II, to employ, as will be shown below, physical violence.

[3] See the section on ' the scalding serjeanty.'

[4] " Hanc dedit W(illelmus) com(es) cuidam coquo suo. "   This was the great William Fitz Osbern, earl of Hereford, who held a quasi-palatine position in the West of England.

master, we must seek him, not in any of the cooks
named as such in Domesday—for it is not proved
that they were the King's—but in a pre-Domesday
record, which enables us to trace our man.

We have the actual charter of the Conqueror
which tells us how he made provision for one of his
cooks, not indeed by carving a serjeanty out of the
lands at his disposal, but at the cost, Alas ! of a
bishop and his monks.   Surrounded by men bearing
great names of the Conquest, he informs Osmund,
Bishop of Salisbury, E(dward) the sheriff, and all
the thegns *(tainis)* of Wiltshire, that, at his entreaty
and in his presence, the bishop of Winchester has
granted to William Escudet, his cook *(coco meo)*,
for his life, the land which Wulfward Belgisone had
held in ' Alwoditon. ' [1]   We turn to Domesday and
there find, under ' Awltone ' (Alton Priors)—which
was, as the charter states, " de victu monacho-
rum, "—that in that manor William ' Scudet ' holds
three hides of the bishop.[2]

It is rare indeed that a Domesday entry can be
explained by means of a pre-Domesday charter ;
and to find William naming and providing for the
future of his cook is of some human interest.   We
are also now enabled to identify the William Scudet
who is entered among the King's serjeants *(servientes
regis)* in Wiltshire, as holding a substantial manor
at Westbury, with his cook.   Nor was even this
the limit of this favoured cook's possessions.   He
was provided for, it is to be feared, at the cost not
only of the monks of Winchester, but of the nuns

---

[1] *Calendar of Charter Rolls*, III, 345.
[2] This would date the charter 1078-1085.

of Romsey. For we detect him in a Romsey charter granted by Henry I, at a great Westminster crown-wearing early in his reign.[1]

The cook has placed two of his daughters in that aristocratic abbey, and the King informs the Wiltshire authorities that he confirms their father's 'restoration and grant' of the lands given with them to the abbey.[2] What is the meaning of these terms? We learn it on turning to Domesday Book, where we find that on both the Abbey's Wiltshire manors a 'William' was holding land which should not have gone out of its demesne.[3] There had been an act of reparation when his daughters took the veil. [4]

There may yet, possibly, come to light records of the actual creation of serjeanties before Domesday. In any case it is clear from the great record that there were many in existence when the survey was made. As this is a point of some importance in its bearing on the early origin of the system, it seems desirable to adduce definite cases in which the serjeanties of later days can be identified in Domesday. Somewhat capricious though it is in its method, the great survey evidently intends to distinguish serjeanty as a thing apart. The King's serjeants (*servientes regis*) are so classified under

---

[1] There were present Count Eustace of Boulogne and David. (of Scotland) the Queen's brother *(fratre regine)*. The latter is wrongly given and indexed as " fratre Reginaldi " (*Ibid.*, II, 103).

[2] " Habere in dominico suo terras illas quas Willelmus Escuet *(sic)* de eadem ecclesia tenuit et quas ipse Willelmus predicte ecclesie reddidit et concessit cum filiabus suis ; et quicunque aliquid tenet de predicta terra, precipio ut ad ecclesiam redeat " (*Cal. of Charter Rolls*, II, 103).

[3] " Non poterant ab æcclesia separari."

[4] The charter of Henry I was confirmed by Henry II. (*Ibid.*, p. 10).

Hampshire, Wiltshire, Dorset, Somerset, Devon, Leicestershire, and Warwickshire. Under Oxfordshire they are grouped as the King's ministers [1] (*ministri*). I cannot agree, however, with the authors of the *History of English Law*, that " when elsewhere we meet with ' Famuli Regis ' we may suppose that this is but another name for the *Servientes* and *Ministri* " (I, 269). On checking their references, which are to the second (the Eastern counties) volume of Domesday, I find that the tenants by serjeanty are not grouped as ' famuli,' and that the word denotes only individual Crown officers of a subordinate kind. In the Eastern counties, as in others where they are not formally grouped apart, we can usually distinguish the true serjeants, where any existed, towards the end of the survey.

Another group, which is found just before or after them, is that of the King's thegns (*taini*). The meaning of this phrase has been sometimes misunderstood, as by Eyton [2] and by Professor Maitland. The latter scholar, dealing with ' the thegns ' and the ' nature of thegnship, ' held that, according to Domesday,

the relation between thegn and lord is no longer conceived as a menial, ' serviential, ' or ministerial relation. The *Taini Regis* are often contrasted with the *Servientes Regis*. The one trait of thegnship which comes out clearly on the face of our record is that the thegn is a man of war. [3]

[1] Under Wiltshire they are grouped partly as *ministri* and partly as *servientes*, which proves that these terms were indifferently used.
[2] See my Domesday Introduction to the *Victoria History of Somerset*.
[3] *Domesday Book and Beyond*, pp. 162-163.

But when the vocations are named, we find 'King's thegns' who are priests, huntsmen, foresters, goldsmiths, reeves, bedels, falconers, chamberlains, and interpreters.   It is even possible, we shall see, to find among them a cook whose lands were afterwards held by kitchen serjeanty, and a goldsmith whose manor, in later days, was associated still with his craft.   Indeed, it is by no means clear that Domesday did intend to contrast the 'serjeants' with the 'thegns.'   The Surrey schedule has at the end the entry " Oswoldus, Teodricus, et alii *servientes* regis, " but the corresponding heading in the text is " Terrae Oswoldi et aliorum *tainorum.* " The real distinction I take to have been that by " taini " were meant men of English birth, or at least of English domicile before the Normans came. In the case of Hertfordshire the heading in the text " Terra *Tainorum* regis " is actually equated in the schedule by the entry " Derman et alii *Anglici* regis. " And a study of the whole record confirms this view.

We may now turn to those serjeanties which can be traced back to the time of the Domesday Survey.   Several of them will be dealt with, in detail, in this volume.   After the name of each tenant I have placed in brackets the tenure by which his land was subsequently held.

SURREY :— Odard the crossbowman (*balistarius*) of Moulsey (crossbow service) ; Tezelin the cook (kitchen service).

HAMPSHIRE :— William the archer (*arcuarius*) of Bentley (archer service) ; Geoffrey the marshal of East Worldham (marshalsea) ; Miles the porter (porter service at Winchester castle)[1].

DORSET : Osmund the baker (baker service).

SOMERSET [2]:—John the usher (usher service).

DEVON :—William the porter (porter service at Exeter Castle).

CAMBRIDGESHIRE :—Erchenger the baker (baker service).

ESSEX :—Walter the cook (kitchen service).

SUFFOLK :—Ralf the crossbowman (*balistarius*) of Burgh (crossbow service).

These, it must be remembered, are cases in which Domesday happens to name the vocation of the tenant, which is contrary to its practice. There are also cases in which it is possible, without this help, to trace back the serjeanty to 1086, but that is, of necessity, a difficult and laborious undertaking.

The principle of serjeanty was, no doubt, the grant of land in return for service, when the lack of ready money made the payment of wages in cash a matter of comparative difficulty. Great escheats to the crown under the Norman kings provided abundance of land from which fresh serjeanties were created ; but the process seems to have slackened under their successors and probably died out about the end of the twelfth century, or, at latest, in the reign of John. Grants of land were still made as rewards for service to the Crown, but

---

[1] See also my Domesday introduction to the *Victoria History of Hampshire*. (I, 429-432).

[2] Also in Dorset and in Wilts.

it was no longer a condition of tenure that the grantee should continue to serve in the same capacity. For instance, the crossbowman would no longer be required to render crossbow service.[1]

We may glance at two examples in illustration of this statement. The first is that of Master Urri (or Orri) 'the engineer', the second is that of Adam de Gurdon. The former is of interest as having the charge of the siege-train of John. When John crossed to Normandy in 1201, he wrote from Bonneville (8 June) to Geoffrey Fitz Piers bidding him assign to "our beloved Master Urri" (*Urricus*) as much land in Wickford and Canewdon, Essex, as had been forfeited there by Henry of Essex, and give seisin to his attorney, as Urri was accompanying him to construct his siege engines (*ingenia nostra*), so that he could not leave the King.[2] In view of this record evidence it is difficult to accept the *Red Book* statement that Wickford was given him (as "balistarius") by Richard I; but a plea roll of 6 Ric. I[3] (1194-5) records Urri 'Arbelaster' as impleaded for Wickford, and a plea of 24 Hen. III (1239-40) shews us the King's advocate stating that

quando manerium de Kanewodena cecidit in manum Dom. Regis Ricardi...... dedit idem Dom. Rex manerium illud...... cuidam Magistro Orry ingeniatori suo, et post mortem ipsius Magistri Orry habuit Alanus Orry manerium illud. [4]

---

[1] It may here be mentioned that there was usually some ambiguity in the word 'balistarius,' which was used both for a crossbowman and for one who worked siege engines (*balistæ*).

[2] *Rot. de Lib.*, 3 John, p. 14.

[3] Cited by Morant.

[4] *Bracton's Note Book*, case 1275.

The point, however, is that Urry and his heirs held, not by serjeanty, but by knight-service. [1]

John took Master Urri with him on his expedition to Ireland in 1210, where the ' engineer ' accompanied him to the siege of Carrickfergus in the north-east of the island, with a small body which formed the precursor of the corps of royal artificers, afterwards the Royal Engineers. It consisted of Master Osbert ' Petrarius,' with three comrades, in charge of the *Petrariae* or stone-throwing engines for battery, Master Pinel with six miners, and Master Ernulf with five more, Aubrey the sapper (*fossator*), Nicholas and four other foreign carpenters, and Ralf of Prestbury with eight English ones. [2]

Adam de Gurdon, who was provided for by a grant of lands at East Tisted, Hants, was also — although the fact seems to have escaped notice — an officer in John's host. Early in 1204 he is found in command of the crossbowmen, as William de Vernon was of the archers.[3] It is interesting to find that John obtained crossbows from Genoa, for at Crecy, it will be remembered, the crossbowmen of the French host were Genoese.[4]

---

[1] See the *Red Book* entries and the *Inq. p. m.* on Richard ' Orricus ' (31 Hen. III) and on his sisters Isabel (33 Hen. III) and Maud (34 Hen. III).

[2] *Rot. de Prest.* It must be remembered that mining operations at that time consisted of undermining an angle of the walls and then firing the timber supports which supported the roof of the mine.

[3] " Ade de Gordon *(sic)* et sociorum suorum balistar' et Willelmi de Vernun et sociorum suorum archer'." (*Rot. de Lib.*, 5 John, p. 78). The grant to him of lands at Tisted worth £12 a year terms him Adam "de Gurdun ' balist(ario) nostro " (*Ibid.*, p. 89). It will be remembered that John pledged himself, in the Great Charter, to banish, as soon as peace was restored, " omnes alienigenas milites, balistarios," etc.

[4] " Liberate de thesauro nostro Johanni balistario de Genua iiij^{or} *m.*

Mr. Joseph Bain, in his learned paper on Sir Adam Gurdun of Selborne,[1] could only suggest that " he was probably one of John's mercenary soldiers from France, as the surname is not unknown in Gascony. " He was certainly holding land in Hampshire as early as 1207,[2] and may have done so earlier still.[3] His estate at Tisted was held by serjeanty till 1254, when the service was changed to that of half a knight, but there seems to be no description of the serjeanty beyond that of supplying a serjeant in the host for forty days.

A great change was effected in the serjeanties in or about the year 1250, when Robert Passelewe, the deputy treasurer, conducted, at the head of a commission, an enquiry throughout the country, into the performance of their services and the alienation of their lands. The result of this enquiry was the great " arrentation " of which the record is largely preserved in the pages of the *Testa de Nevill* and forms one of our most valuable sources of information on the serjeanties.

The system adopted for dealing with the state of things which had arisen was to set out clearly the alienated portions of the lands (which were liable, in strictness of law, to forfeiture) and then to allow their holders to compound, either by paying a money rent, by way of " fine ", or by rendering a

---

pro balistis quas nobis portavit de Genua." *(Ibid.)*: Roger " de Genua, balistarius noster, " was being paid 4½d. and afterwards 6d. a day in 1204, and Roger " archerius de Genua " was given 40 marcs to compensate him for his losses in coming to the King. *(Ibid.,* p. 100).

[1] *Genealogist*, (N.S.) IV, 1 *et seq.*
[2] *Rot. de Fin.*, 9 John, p. 449.
[3] *V. C. H., Hants*, III, 30.

fractional quota of knight-service. Then the lands which had *not* been alienated either remained charged with the old service of the serjeanty or had it changed into knight-service. In the latter case, of course, the serjeanty came to an end. All this requires to be made very clear, because it led, we shall find, even the learned Madox into supposing that land could be held, at the same time, by serjeanty and by knight-service. It is to Blount's credit that he noted, the previous century, in his *Tenures*, that this " arrentation " had extinguished many serjeanties. It seems to me, however, that this was overlooked in certain cases where it was desired to claim, at a later date, that the old service had survived.

The authors of the *History of English Law* describe the " arrentation " thus :—

Robert Passelew was sent through England to "arrent" the alienated serjeanties, that is to say, to change the tenure from serjeanty into knight's service or socage. One instance out of a very large number will serve to show what was done. Walter Devenish held land by the serjeanty of finding three arrows when the king should hunt on Dartmoor ; he had alienated parts of the tenement to sub-tenants, his services were now changed into a rent of three shillings, one third of which was to be paid to him by his sub-tenants (*Testa de Nevill*, 197). [1]

Both statements are erroneous. Walter's services were *not* changed, but remained those of the serjeanty, [2] and the annual three shillings was the ' fine '

[1] *Op. cit.*, I, 315-316.

[2] " Et dictus Walterus faciat servicium prenominatum pro parte sua que non est alienata." This was the regular formula where the service was not changed. A real case of change (to knight service) at Aston Clinton, will be found in the next section.

for the *alienated* portions. Nor did their tenants
contribute one third of that fine : what they paid
(to Walter) was a third of the annual value of their
holdings, namely 3s. 5d.,[1] which actually exceeded
the fine. That is how the system worked. It is
almost incredible that a record can have been so
carelessly read.

It is a rather interesting little serjeanty. There
is the usual duplicate version of the ' arrentation '
on p. 198, from which we learn that Roger de
Mirabell' had forfeited it for homicide, and Henry III
had then transferred it to Walter with the same
service. This is absolutely accurate. Henry's
charter is duly found in the *Calendar of Charter
Rolls*[2] (16 March 1229) and we find that Walter
le Deveneis was no other than the ' physician ' of
Hubert de Burgh. The ' Skyredon ' of the *Testa*
becomes ' Skiledon ' in the charter, so one cannot
wonder that it baffled the Record Office editor. It
is, I have ascertained, Skirradon in Dean Prior, on
the south-eastern edge of Dartmoor. It was held
in 1212 (and *circ.* 1218) by David de Scyredun,[3]
whose ' ancestors ' were then alleged to have held it
' since the Conquest.' In a legal sense they may
have done so, for among the Devon ' thegns ' in
Domesday we find Alvric (*Aluricus*) holding a
virgate and a half in ' Siredone ' and ' Essaple, '
which latter is clearly the ' Sapesleg ' held with
Skirradon by David. Alvric may well have been

---

[1] " Ita quod dicti tenentes respondeant eidem Waltero de tercia parte
valoris ten' sui *(sic)* quilibet eorum secundum porcionem suam."

[2] Vol I, p. 92.

[3] *Testa*, pp. 195, 196.

one of the English huntsmen retained by William.

It should be observed that this was an absolutely typical case of ' petty ' serjeanty, which John defined in the Great Charter (1215) as the service " of supplying us with knives, arrows or the like." [1] Yet as late, at least, as 1250 it remained, we have seen, a serjeanty and had not sunk into socage.

[1] *History of English Law*, I, 304.

CHAPTER II

SERJEANTY
AND KNIGHT-SERVICE

It has been urged above that the distinction between these two tenures is one on which insistence must be laid. For, although the works of Maitland have made that distinction clear, the confusion on the subject is so persistent that it will not easily be dispelled.

The most striking instance, possibly, of that confusion was Mr. Haldane's argument, before the Committee for Privileges, in the Great Chamberlain case :—

if they were services of a higher degree, of a military nature, then you had knight's service, and it was petty serjeanty (serjeanty, of course, really comes from *serviens*), the work of a knight. [1]

But, apart from this example of ' clear thinking,' we have the statement in what is now the standard work on *Magna Carta*, that grand serjeanties were not liable " *as a rule* to payment of scutage. " [2] This is a relatively trifling slip, but if *any* serjeanty had been liable to scutage, the tenure would have been thereby proved to be, not serjeanty, but

[1] See my *Peerage and Pedigree*, I. 119.
[2] McKechnie's *Magna Carta*, p. 68.

knight-service.[1]   More surprising is the classification, under the head of ' serjeanties,' in a Record
Office Publication, of such services as " to maintain
5 knights in the King's army for 40 days "[2] or " to
provide two horsemen [3] at his own charge in time
of war " or " to find three knights with horses,
arms," etc.[4]   If this classification were right, there
would be an end of my case.   But, when we refer
to the text, we find no mention of serjeanty.   In
the first entry (abbot of Sherborne) the words
are :—" De feodis militum...... baroniam suam, pro
qua baronia faciet servicium f[eod'] duorum m[ili-
tum]. "[5]   In the third (abbot of Glastonbury) the
words are, " per baroniam, " and it is notorious that
both abbots held by knight-service.[6]   The intermediate entry relates to William of Higford, one
of Fitz Alan's tenants by knight-service.[7]

The touchstone by which, in practice, the two
tenures were distinguished was the payment of
scutage.   As is justly observed in the *History of
English Law*,—

Bracton's rule is clear, namely that if the tenant owes but
one hap'orth of scutage *(licet ad unum obolum)*, his tenure
is military, and this rule is fully borne out by pleadings
and decisions.   This point is important ;..... the small
yeoman often holds his little tenement by a tenure which

----

[1] See below.
[2] *Feudal Aids* (1900), II, 624.
[3] The word is *equites* (*i. e.* knights). *Ibid.* IV, 226.
[4] *Ibid.* (1906), IV, 604.
[5] What makes the error the more extraordinary is that on the oppo-
site page we have a precisely similar entry on the abbot's knight service,
which is carefully separated from the heading " de serjauntiis " lower
down.
[6] *Lib. Rub.*, pp. 213, 222.
[7] See *Testa*, p. 49 b.

is nominally and legally the same tenure as that by which the knight holds his manor. [1]

If a tenant was liable to scutage, his tenure could not be serjeanty, and if conversely, it was serjeanty, he was not liable to scutage.

The three leading cases illustrating this point are those relating to the tenure of Addington, of Langton, and of Comberton. The Addington serjeanty will be dealt with in its own place,[2] but the point here is that, in 1234, its tenant, William Aguillon, was charged with scutage in arrears, and pleaded that he did not owe it, as he held by serjeanty. A jury of twelve knights found that his plea was true, and he was thereupon pronounced to be not liable to scutage. For this case we are dependent on the Pipe Roll of 1234, the relative extract from which is printed in Madox' *Exchequer.* This I place below on the left, and on the right the version printed in the *Red Book of the Exchequer*, where the editor accepts the date " 1236 " (20 Hen. III). This version is obviously corrupt, as will be seen on attempting to parse it from the word " utrum. " It is only given in the *Red Book* to lead up to the jest that the Pipe Roll of 1161 ought to be thrown into the Fleet Prison.[3]

But I print it here because it has been appealed to as " a most decisive statement " against me, and as a " legal decision " that the roll of 1161 records " the Scutage of Toulouse. " [4]

---

[1] *Op. cit.,* I, 257.

[2] See the section on ' the *Maupygernoun* serjeanty.'

[3] " Quod rotulus Regis Henrici projiceretur in Gaiolam de Flete, tanquam convictus per XII."

[4] " " A most decisive statement in the course of an important case that

Surreia. Willelmus Aguilon, qui habet heredem Bartholomei de Cheney in uxorem, debuit unam marcam de scutagio de Kery, sicut supra continetur, et xx*s* de finibus et scutagiis sicut continetur ibidem, et xx*s* de scutagio Pictaviæ sicut continetur ibidem, et x*s* de scutagio de Elveyn sicut continetur ibidem. Sed non debet summoneri ; quia recognitum est per preceptum Regis coram Baronibus de Scaccario per sacramenta xij militum ejusdem comitatus quod non debet servicium militare de terris quas tenet in hoc comitatu de hereditate dicti Bartholomei de Cheney in Adintone, sed serjanteriam, scilicet inveniendi unum cocum in coronatione Regis ad faciendum cibum, qualem senescallus Regis preceperit, in coquina Regis (Madox, from P.R. 18 H.III).

Anno xx Regis Henrici, filii Regis Johannis, præcepit Rex attingere rotulum regis Henrici vij^m per xij milites juratos, utrum Willelmus Agulun qui habuit unum (*sic*) heredem Bartholomei de Cheym (*sic*) ; licet in eodem rotulo continetur, in comitatu Surreiæ, quod dictus Bartholomæus respondet de una marca pro militi (*sic*) cum scutagium esset Tolosæ assisum ad duas marcas ; propter quod videbatur ipsum facere servitium dimidii militis. Venit jurata et dicit quod Bartholomæus et predecessores sui et successores nunquam fecerunt militare servitium, sed servitium serjanteriæ, videlicet, inveniendi unum cocum in coquina domini Regis die coronationis suae ad faciendum quod Senescallus præciperet, etc. etc. (*Red Book*, p. 754).

It will be seen that the actual record, the one printed on the left, does not contain a word about the scutage of Toulouse and that the "legal decision" had nothing in the world to do with the purpose

was argued before the Barons in the 20th (*sic*) year of Henry III......
no one on this occasion seems to have doubted that the Scutage entered on the Roll was the Scutage of Toulouse, and this legal decision may be fairly regarded as establishing the fact beyond dispute." (*Lib. Rub.*, d. clxxxiii).

of the scutage on the Roll of 1161. Swereford's careless version on the right, merely repeats his own assertion that this was the scutage of Toulouse. [1]

Such is Mr. Hall's " legal decision " that Swereford's assertion was right.

The Langton case is thus stated by Madox in his *Exchequer* :— [2]

> There were also some serjeanties which paid Escuage. ....Joan, late wife of Thomas de Ludelawe was charged for the manor of Langeton with several Escuages of the armies of Scotland, assessed in the 28th, 31st, and 34th years of King Edward I, as if it had been holden of the King by the fourth part of a Knight's Fee : she alleged that the Manor of Langeton was a member of the Manor of Scrivelby, and that the manor of Scrivelby with its members was holden of the King by Grand Serjeanty, and not by knights service : hereupon, the King by his writ commanded the barons that if it appeared to them that the manor of Scrivelby was holden of the King by Grand Serjeanty and that the manor of Langeton was a member of the manor of Scrivelby, and that Joan and her ancestors had not formerly paid escuage for the said manor of Langeton, then they should discharge her of the said demanded scutages.

One is very loath to correct Madox, that great and learned antiquary who deserves our gratitude and respect ; but he has seriously mistaken the issue. The question raised was whether (South) Langton, Lincs., was a member of the Manor of Scrivelsby, which manor (it was alleged) was held by grand serjeanty. We are not told the result, but Joan's claim was wrong. The *Testa* proves

---

[1] " Fuitque assisum ad ij marcas pro exercitu Tholosæ " (*Lib. Rub.*, p. 7.)

[2] Citing Mich. brev., 9 Ed. II, rot. 13 a.

that South Langton was held by knight-service of the Marmions, who held it of the Crown,[1] and in the " Inquisition " on Philip Marmion, the last of his line, it is dealt with as quite distinct from Scrivelsby.[2]

This was about a quarter of a century before Joan's claim, and in the interval (1303) it had been returned as held by knight-service,[3] as it was again in 1346.[4] It is clear, therefore, that Joan's claim failed. In 1401-2 Scrivelsby " cum membris " was returned as held by grand serjeanty, but South Langton, again, as held by knight-service.[5]

The Comberton case was derived by Madox from the same source.[6] This serjeanty will be dealt with under " Hawk and falcon serjeanties. "

Philip de Hastang being charged with escuage for the manor of Comberton in the County of Cambridge, showed to the King by his petition that the said manor was holden of the King by service of keeping the King's falcons and not by knights service. Hereupon the King by writ ordered the Barons, if they found it to be so, to discharge him of the escuage. "

In all this, it will be seen, there is nothing about a tenement being held by both tenures. The question was whether it was held by the one tenure or the other.[7]

---

[1] *Testa*, pp. 332, 338.
[2] See the section on " the King's Champion."
[3] *Feudal Aids*, III, 146.
[4] *Ibid.*, p. 235.
[5] " Heredes Philippi Marmion tenent in South Langton dimidium mil. de domino rege in capite." (See *Ibid.*, p. 246 for both entries).
[6] " Pasch. brev., 9 Edw. II."
[7] I am not prepared to say that a tenant by knight-service could not grant land to a man to be held of him by serjeanty, or conversely, a

It is the more strange that Madox should have thus erred because he immediately proceeds :—

But if lands were holden by serjeanty only (and no Knights Service was annexed) they were not to pay escuage.

And he then cites the Aguillon and other cases proving that tenure by serjeanty, when established, secured *ipso facto* immunity from scutage (' escuage ').

Madox's error is due to his misunderstanding of two distinct classes of records. We will take his deductions from those classes separately.

It is said above that Escuage was paid out of Knight's Fees. There were also some Serjeanties that paid Escuage. Simon Puncard paid half a mark Escuage (*sic*) for his Serjeanty. Robert de Orton paid xx*s*. Escuage (*sic*) for his Serjeanty. [1]

As it was actually the distinctive mark of serjeanties that they did *not* pay " escuage, " we turn to the writer's notes for the evidence on which he relied, and we there find that there is nothing about " escuage " in either case ! The fact is that Madox was here misled—precisely as Mr. W. H. B. Bird has been similarly misled [2]—by the heading of his records : in one case it was " De Finibus militum et scutagiis," and in the other, " De Finibus et scutagiis militum. " But the actual entries run only " dimidia marca de Simone Puncard qui tenet

tenant by serjeanty enfeoff a man to hold by knight-service. This would not affect the tenure *in capite*.

[1] *Exchequer*, I, cap. XVI, sec. 3.

[2] See *Peerage and Pedigree*, II, 67. Mr. Bird assumed that " one would not expect to find a tenant in thanage under the heading ' De finibus militum.' "

per serjanteriam, " and " Robertus de Orton debet
xxs. pro serjeanteria sua. " These payments are
not styled " escuage." [1]

Let us continue the quotation :—

But peradventure these Serjeanties were also holden
by military tenure. For sometimes Knights' Service was
annexed to a Serjeanty ; that is, lands were holden both
by Serjeanty and by the service of a knight's fee or part
of a knight's fee. For certain lands, parcel of the serjeanty of William de Paris in Ayston and Clinton, Richard
de Crokel the tenant was to do the service of the thirtieth
part of a knight's fee ; and for certain other lands,......
parcel of the same serjeanty, William de Paris was to do
the service of one knight's fee, and to provide for the
King in his army, whithersoever he should go, one
Serjeant with two horses for xl days at his own charges.
For certain land belonging to the serjeanty of Godfrey le
Fawkener in Hurst, the tenant John Hereberd, was to
do the service of the sixtieth part of a knight's fee.

The error of Madox in this case is more incom-
prehensible than in the other. For these are
simple instances of serjeanties " arrented " by
Robert Passelewe in 34 Hen. III,[2] from the records
of which year his evidence is taken. The arrentation of the serjeanty of Aston Clinton, Bucks,
occupies no less than two columns of the *Testa*
(pp. 254-5), and we there read that, as its lands had
been largely alienated, they were dealt with in three
portions thus :—   (A) William de Paris is to do
the service of one knight for the portion remaining

---

[1] An extremely striking instance of these misleading entries is found
on the Pipe Roll of 8 John, under Lancashire, where the heading is
" Fines et scutagia militum de VII° scutagio," though thegns, drengs and
serjants follow. (Farrer's *Lancashire Pipe Rolls*, pp. 204, 210.)

[2] See *Exchequer*, I, cap. II, sec. 5, and p. 17 above.

in his hands,[1] while (B) Richard de Crokele, for himself and several holders of small portions is to do the service of the thirtieth part of a knight's fee, and (C) William is to pay the Crown £5.11.0. a year for all the other alienated portions, the holder of each of which is to pay him a third of its annual value towards that sum. [2]

Again, in the case of the Hurst serjeanty, Robert the Falconer had held the land " by the serjeanty of keeping a cast.... of 3 falcons at the King's cost,"[3] but his son and successor, Godfrey, had his serjeanty arrented, [4] when John Herberd and his wife, who held thirty-five acres of it, compounded by fine to hold it by the service of the fiftieth (or sixtieth) of a knight's fee.

In these cases, which are very numerous, tenure by serjeanty was *exchanged* for tenure by knight-service. That land should be holden " both by serjeanty and by the service of a knight's fee " is a contradiction in terms.

We can now turn to another and most important aspect of the matter. This is the evidence that the Crown authorities treated the two tenures as distinct and obtained returns of them as such.

[1] William's mother, Nicia de Clinton, had died in 31 Henry III holding this serjeanty by the service described, but when William himself died in 40 Hen. III (*i. e.* after the arrentation), he is entered as having held " by service of 1 Knight's fee " (See the *Inq. p. m.* on each).

A generation later, Ela Countess of Warwick is entered as holding Aston Clinton as one knight's fee *(Feudal Aids,* I, 85); but in 1346 exemption is claimed for the Manor " quia tenetur per serjancyam." (*Ibid.,* p. 123). This illustrates the confusion caused by arrentation. (Compare p. 18 above).

[2] Compare p. 18 above.

[3] *Cal. of Inq., Henry III,* No. 835 ; *Testa,* p. 217.

[4] *Testa,* p. 216.

My first instance is the carucage of 1198, for which the serjeanties received separate treatment, as being distinct from the knight's fees[1]. A separate enquiry into the holders of them, and their payments, followed[2]. As I have observed of the King's serjeants, " occupying as they did an intermediate place between those who held by military service and those who did not, they were not strictly within the scope of the taxes which affected either."[3] The result was a composition (*finis*).

My next example is the great Inquest of 1212.[4] For this we have the actual writ, quoted under Staffordshire, in the *Testa* (p. 54) :—

precipimus tibi quod sine dilacione... diligenter inquiri facias, sicut melius inquiri poterit, de omnibus feodis militum et omnimodis tenementis... que de nobis tenentur in capite, in balliva tua *per militare servicium vel per serjantiam qualemcunque, et qui ea teneant, et per quod servicium.*

This writ is immediately followed by returns headed :— 1. " Isti tenent per servicium militare " 2. " Isti tenent per serjantiam " (*Testa*, p. 54).

The third and most important example is afforded by the writs and returns of 1236. It is the most important, because it distinguishes serjeanty,

---

[1] " sergenteriæ vero domini regis, quæ non erant de feodis militum, excipiebantur, sed tamen imbreviabantur et numerus carucatarum terræ et valentiæ terrarum, et nomina servientium." (Hoveden, IV, 47). See my paper on "The Great Carucage of 1198" in *Eng. Hist. Rev.* (1888), III, 501-510, cited in *Hist. of Eng. Law*, I, 270.

[2] De serjentariis domini regis, quis eas habet, et per quem, et qui finem non fecerint ad auxilium domini regis et qui fecerunt, et finis capiatur." (*Ibid.*, IV, 62).

[3] *E. H. R.*, III, 509.

[4] See, for this, my paper on " The Great Inquest of Service, 1212," in *The Commune of London and other studies*, pp. 261-277.

not only from knight-service above it, but also from socage below it, and for the further reason that it proves the distinction at this later date to be still well defined. I have not dealt with this return before, and the point may have escaped notice.

In 1235, the King had been granted an " aid " for the marriage of his sister Isabel of two marcs from every knight's fee. Owing to the scattered nature of fiefs he did not feel satisfied that everyone had paid, and on 20 May 1236 he issued a writ to the Sheriffs commanding a searching enquiry. Its terms are known to us from its recital by the Sheriffs of Norfolk and Suffolk[1] and of Northumberland[2] to whom, as to other Sheriffs, it had been addressed. The Sheriff was first required to send on to the " barons " whose honours had their *caput* within his county the King's letters calling for detailed returns from them, and was then directed to prepare a triple return himself. This return was to comprise (1) All those who held only a single knight's fee or any fraction of one, and (2) all those who held (A) by serjeanty or (B) by socage,[3] with full particulars of the localities of these tenements and of the nature of the serjeanties.

---

[1] *Testa*, p. 282.

[2] *Ibid.*, p. 388.

[3] " Et quum plures alii sunt in comitatu tuo qui singularia feoda et minora de nobis tenent in capite, quibus non scribimus, tibi praecipimus quatinus, in fide qua nobis teneris, nomina singulorum illorum qui talia feoda de nobis tenent in comitatu tuo et in quibus villis feoda illa sint, per literas tuas patentes citra predictum terminum significes prædictis baronibus nostris de scaccario et similiter nomina omnium illorum *qui de nobis tenent per serjantiam vel socagium* et ubi et in quibus villis sint *dicte serjantie et socagia*, et quales sint ille serjantie, distincte et apte, ita curiose, et diligenter premissa omnia exequens quod ad te propter negligentiam tuam capere non debeamus."

This writ is followed, for East Anglia, by the
Sheriff's return giving the particulars demanded and
carefully divided into three sections : (1) Knight's
fees ; (2) socage tenements ; (3) serjeanties. When
the nature of these returns has once been grasped,
we can detect them under other counties. Thus
we have the corresponding Sheriff's return for
Staffordshire.[1] For Northamptonshire we can detect the corresponding return on pp. 27-8 of the
Testa, for the Sheriff expressly says at the end that
he had directed the bailiff of the Soke of Peter-
borough (which he could not deal with) to supply
the particulars required.[2] Again we detect the
sheriff's returns for Oxfordshire on pp. 117-8 of
the *Testa* :—

Viris venerabilibus et discretis dominis baronibus de
scaccario domini Regis Vic' Oxon' salutem. Mitto vobis
nomina illorum qui singularia feoda vel minora tenent in
capite de domino Rege in com' Oxon'.

Mitto etiam vobis nomina omnium illorum qui de
domino Rege tenent in capite *per socagium vel per serjantiam*,
et quales sint serjantie et in quibus villis sint dicta
socagia et serjantie.

The formula, it will be seen, is reproduced with
precision.

Here then we have definite evidence that even
so late as 1236 the three tenures were still well

---

[1] " Inquisito facta per vic' Stafford' (1) de militibus qui tenent singularia et minora feoda de domino Rege in capite et (2) de tenentibus (A)
per socagium et (B) per serjantiam, et ubi et in quibus villis." *Testa*,
p. 52.

[2] " Preterea mandatum est ballivo abbatis de Burgo Sancti Petri quod
nobis significet nomina omnium tenencium de domino Rege in capite in
balliva sua tam per servicium militare quam *per serjantiam et socagium*
secundum formam precepti domini Regis quod inde suscepit."

recognised as distinct, although the severance by John's Charter (1215) of serjeanty into two classes was alleged to have rendered petty serjeanty 'socage in effect.'

It may perhaps be thought that I have unduly laboured the point that tenure by serjeanty was a thing wholly apart from tenure by knight-service, but I have already demonstrated the inveterate confusion on the subject ; and as final and amazing illustration of the fact, I will cite a passage from Prof. Oman's *Art of War in the Middle Ages* (1898). After vainly attempting to reinstate the old theory of knight-service, which had been exploded by myself,[1] showing that he did not even understand such a well-known phrase as *vetus feoffamentum*, and betraying further confusion,[2] the present Chichele Professor tried his hand at serjeanty.

A sub-tenant with a few hundred acres of land would probably have been called by a chronicler of the time of Henry I a " miles," by a chronicler of the time of John or Henry III a " sergeant," and by a chronicler of the time of Edward III a squire (*armiger* or *scutifer*). The condition of the three men would have been much the same, but the name changed thrice (p. 365).

To this is appended an illuminating note as follows :—

That sergeant originally means... a landed military dependent who is not a knight, is well shown..... we are dealing with sub-tenants and not merely small tenants in chief.

Those who have followed me as far as this must

---

[1] See *History of English Law*, I, 238-239.
[2] See my *Commune of London and other studies*, pp. 57-60.

by now be aware (1) that the " landed " serjeants they have met with were *not* sub-tenants ; (2) that these " landed " serjeants *were* " small tenants in chief ; " (3) that they were not always, or even usually, military ; (4) that a tenant by serjeanty was from the first distinct from a tenant by knight-service, and that the latter was still a " miles " under John and Henry III as he was under Henry I.

We have here, obviously, not merely ignorance of the fact that it depended on the *tenure* of the " few hundred acres " whether a man held them as a *miles* or a *serviens*, and whether he owed the service of the former or of the latter, but also confusion between the tenant by serjeanty, bound to perform certain service in respect of his land, and the soldier (*serviens*) hired at a penny a day when the knight was hired at eightpence.   This hired *serviens* is found on the rolls from the early years of Henry II's reign precisely as he is in the chronicles of the reign of John. [1]

One should not perhaps expect accuracy from so fecund a writer, but when an Oxford historical professor betrays such confusion as this, it cannot be needless to insist that the tenures of the " knight " and of the " serjeant " were not only wholly distinct, but involved also distinct services, which the touchstone of scutage kept apart at the time of which he here treats.

[1] See my *Feudal England*, pp. 271-272, 283.

CHAPTER III

SOME FEATURES OF SERJEANTY

Owing to the diverse character of its service it was not possible to apply to serjeanty the same uniform system of taxation that was applied to knight-service. It was not, we have seen, liable to scutage, nor did it contribute to the three aids that were so distinctive of military tenure (*servicium militare*). But to certain feudal incidents it was no less liable. Relief, for instance, had to be paid on succession to a tenement held by serjeanty, and the burdens of wardship and " marriage " affected it no less than the knight's fee.

The relief, at first arbitrary, came to be limited by custom to one year's value of the tenement : it was the wardship that gave trouble. If a dead man had held a small tenement in chief by serjeanty, and a considerable estate, as an under-tenant, by knight service, the king claimed rights of wardship over the whole in virtue of the former tenement. This claim, which affected the overlord of the other land, was explicitly abandoned by the Great Charter, so far at least as affected a certain class of serjeanties, which became thence known as holdings by " petty " serjeanty. The clause was this:—

Nos non habebimus custodiam heredis vel terre alicujus, quam tenet de alio per servicium militare, occasione alicujus parve serjanterie quam tenet de nobis per servicium reddendi nobis cultellos vel sagittas vel hujusmodi.

It is justly observed in the *History of English Law* (I, 304) that " The term 'small serjeanty' seems one which is not yet technical, and the nature of those serjeanties which are too trivial to justify the royal claim is indicated in the rudest manner." The point, however, which I wish to make, and which, so far as I know, has not been made before, is that we have here an instructive parallel to that cleavage of the *barones* into the " greater " and the " lesser " which had its origin, similarly, or at least its recognition, in a clause of the Great Charter. By that clause " a rough division was drawn somewhere in the midst, but the exact boundary was necessarily vague ; " [1] " the line between great and small has been drawn in a rough empirical way, and is not the outcome of any precise principle." [2] I wish to emphasise this point because of the wellknown difficulty that has been experienced by those who have striven to discover the real distinction between a ' greater ' and a ' lesser ' baron.[3] It is the old difficulty of the lawyer striving, as ever, to substitute a date and a fixed line for a gradual differentiation.

It is doubtful if even the great Bracton really

[1] McKechnie's *Magna Carta*, p. 295.
[2] *History of English Law*, I, 260.
[3] See my *Peerage and Pedigree*, I, 359, and *The Commune of London*, pp. 252-3, where I quote a charter of 1190, which speaks of the greater barons *(majores barones)* of the City of London, in illustration.

understood the working of the new distinction in practice. [1] Littleton certainly did not, and has misled all who have followed him ; but by his time the lawyers had contrived to introduce their confusion. His classification is this :—

Tenure by Petit Serjeanty is where a man holds his land of our sovereign lord the King by giving to him yearly a bow, or a sword, or a dagger, or a knife, or a lance, or a pair of gloves of mail, or a pair of gilt spurs, or an arrow, or divers arrows, or other small things belonging to war. [2]

And such service is but socage in effect, because such tenant by his tenure was not obliged to go, or do anything, in his proper person, touching the war ; but to render and pay, yearly, certain things to the King, as a man paid his rent. [3]

It is justly observed of this in the *History of English Law* that " we cannot say that ' petty serjeanty ' has necessarily any connexion with war, or that petty serjeanty is ' but socage in effect. ' " (I, 262).

For legal historians serjeanty presents two points of great interest in the alleged inalienability and impartibility of tenements held by this tenure. As to the former one can add little to what has been so well explained in the *History of English Law*, [4] and I will only supplement it by a very notable allusion, in 1203, to the custom of England, as the

---

[1] See his *Note Book*, and Prof. Maitland's comments on Case 743. As I read the case, the point at issue seems to have been whether the tenure was " petty " serjeanty or not. There is no need to question the name " Waveringe, " for the serjeanty is found in *Testa*, p. 219.

[2] *Tenures*, Lib. II, cap. 9, Sec. 159.

[3] *Ibid.*, sec. 160.

[4] See Vol. I. (1895), pp. 270, 315-6, and *cf. Plac. Abb.*, p. 48.

ground for this restriction. The serjeanty is that of Robert Falconer.

et si quid predictus pater ejus de predicta terra aliena-verit, id juste et *secundum consuetudinem Angl[ie]* revocari faciatis. [1]

The alleged impartibility is a more difficult question and one which is by no means only of academic interest. In the famous contest for the office of Lord Great Chamberlain, at the opening of the late reign, this doctrine was the very essence of Lord Ancaster's claim.[2] Expressed in syllogistic form, the proposition would run :—

> Serjeanties are impartible.
> The Great Chamberlainship is a serjeanty.
> Therefore the Great Chamberlainship is impartible. [3]

The major premiss I doubt, and the minor I deny. Let us, however, see what impartibility means. It is alleged that in the case of a tenement held by serjeanty it is not inherited by co-heirs, jointly, but passes to the eldest daughter (or sister) [4] as an undivided whole. This eldest co-heir is sometimes spoken of as having the *æsnecia* (*droit d'aînesse*).

The authors of the *History of English Law* appear, at first sight, to accept this contention as

---

[1] *Rot. de Lib.*, 3 John, p. 72.

[2] See *Peerage and Pedigree*, I, 118, 122-124.

[3] The above passages prove, I think, that I here fairly reproduce the argument of Lord Ancaster's leading counsel (Mr. Haldane) ; but in the Printed Case it was urged, more cautiously, that " the law relating to Grand Serjeanty applied "... " the office of Great Chamberlain, though an office in gross, is held by the tenure of Grand Serjeanty. "

[4] Or other senior co-heir.

valid, at least for early days. But their language is guarded :—

> We find that a tenement held by serjeanty is treated as inalienable and impartible... We have pretty clear proof that so late as John's reign it was thought a serjeanty could not be partitioned among co-heiresses ; the eldest daughter would take the whole....
>
> Of the serjeanties he [Glanvill] here says nothing ; of them it were needless to speak, for a serjeanty is the most impartible of all tenements, impartible (so men are saying) even among daughters.
>
> It is Bracton's opinion that a tenement held by serjeanty ought not to be divided, and this opinion seems to have been warranted at all events by the practice of an earlier age.[1]

We have, it may at once be said, evidence that this contention was advanced, this allegation made. But was it so *held* ?

When we scrutinise the cases on which the learned authors rely, we find them practically reduced to one, that of the Beaksbourne serjeanty.[2] This was a case in which the senior co-heir and her husband claimed a carucate of land in Livinge-bourne,[3] Kent, in 1201, against William de Bec, who held it, but was only the representative of a junior co-heir.[4] The former claimed the *whole* land as serjeanty, descendible to the eldest daughter.[5]

---

[1] *Op. cit.*, I, 270 ; II, 266, 273.

[2] *Plac. Abbrev.*, pp. 34, 39 ; *Select Civil Pleas* (Selden Soc.), 112. It was also cited as proof of the eldest daughter's right in the Great Chamberlain case.

[3] Now Beaksbourne.

[4] The pedigree *appears* to be that Avice was eldest co-heir of the eldest co-heir, and William de Bec heir of a junior co-heir.

[5] " Ipsi totum petunt et... dicunt quod terra illa est serganteria Domini Regis,...... et ipsa Avicia de primogenita est."

Early in 1203 they returned to the attack, but it seems to have been overlooked that they now shifted their ground.   They no longer claimed the whole, nor did they mention serjeanty.   They claimed only forty acres, as the lady's rightful share of the inheritance, though repeating that she was the senior co-heir. [1]

It was now their opponent's turn to plead that the land was held by serjeanty, and therefore impartible—and to produce a charter of Henry II granting the serjeanty to his father, husband of the junior co-heir. [2]   This, it will be seen, was exactly parallel to the determination, in later times, of the abeyance of a barony by the prerogative of the Crown.   This point is new.

It is clear that the plaintiffs again failed, even in their modified claim, for William de Bec ('Bethe') is found holding the whole subsequently [3] and Richard de " Bek " after him, [4] and the place retains their name (Bek's [Beaks] Bourne) to this day.   This, then, is hardly the case one would select to prove that " the eldest daughter would take the whole. " [5]

---

[1] " Sicut jus et racionabilem porcionem Avice... in Limingeburn sicut eas que eam contingunt ex racionabili porcione sua de terris que fuerunt Rogeri de Burnes avunculi... et desicut A. fuit primogenita, et ipse Willelmus de postnata " (*Plac. Abbrev.*, p. 39).

[2] " Et Willelmus dicit quod terra illa est de sergeanteria Domini Regis et non debet partiri, et profert cartam Domini Regis Henrici patris, in qua continetur quod ipse concessit et dedit Hugoni de Becco ministerium... et precepit quod idem Hugo habeat et teneat, et heredes sui, ministerium illud cum terris " etc.

[3] *Testa*, p. 219.

[4] *Ibid.*, p. 216.

[5] There is another leading case, of much later date, against the right of the eldest co-heir.   This is that of the King's Champion.   The

But, it may be urged, the case at least supports the view that a serjeanty could not be divided. It is doubtful, however, if this view is borne out by the early evidence of records. We have, at the same period, the instance of a Herefordshire Serjeanty at Marden, where the husband of the eldest daughter has to pay forty shillings (1204) to avoid partition being made [1]. The Givendale serjeanty of crossbow service [2] affords a clear instance of partition between co-heiresses, and so does the Northumbrian serjeanty of hereditary coroner, and the Rivenhall serjeanty referred to above. [3]

In later days (1442), a striking instance is afforded by the curious Kentish serjeanty of holding the king's head when he crossed the channel. This was adjudged to be Grand Serjeanty (*servicium Magnæ Serjantiæ*), and the two daughters and co-heirs of John Baker, who had held it, were alike charged with relief on their succession. [4]

The Serjeanty of Runham, Norfolk, with its unique render, seems to afford a clear case of partition. Walter de Evermue held it by the service of two *muids* of wine and 200 pearmains. [5] An *Inq. p. m.* on Walter de Evermue in 1 Edw. I

senior co-heir, in that case, vainly urged *æsnecia*, it being decided that the manor of Scrivelsby, held by the junior co-heir, carried the office.

[1] "Rannulfus de Mahurdin debet xl*s*. ne partitio fiat de terra quæ fuit Willelmi de Mahurdin, quam ipse tenet de Rege per serjanteriam, eo quod ipse in uxorem habet primogenitam filiam ejusdem Willelmi" (Pipe Roll, 6 John, rot. 2 d.).

[2] See below.

[3] See p. 4.

[4] See the relative record cited in Madox' *Baronia Anglica*, p. 245.

[5] " per servicium duorum modiorum vini et cc de permeyns"... " per duo modia vini et cc piromagii" (*Testa*, pp. 283, 294) ; "per duo modia vini et cc piromagnis" (*Lib. Rub.*, p. 459).

(1271-2) records that his heirs are the three daughters of Jolland de Evermue, and gives the service as " two measures (*mutarum*) of wine and 200 pears called ' pearmains' yearly at the Exchequer. " [1] This version is repeated a few years later. [2] In 1327 Walter de Billingeye, representative of one of the three co-heirs, is found to have held a third of the manor " by service of a third part of two measures of wine and of 200 *pirarum de Permeyns*." [3] And in 1335 a lady is similarly found to have held a third of the manor " by petty serjeanty, " *viz.* a third of the above service. [4] The partition, therefore, of the service as well as of the land is clearly established.

In all cases of serjeanty we have to keep in view the double character of the inheritance, namely, the land itself and the service or office by discharge of which the land was held. These two factors are the " ministerium et terra " of the Pipe Roll of 1130. In the case of the Marshalship of the Hawks [5] it seems very doubtful whether John's charter did not sever that office from the land and make it an hereditary office in gross. In that of the marshalship held by Juliane, wife of William Fitz Audelin (*temp.* Hen. II), it is certain that the lands of her serjeanty [6] were divided between her co-heirs. Again, in that of the forestership of Gillingham Forest, which was held in chief by

[1] *Cal. of Inq.*, II, No. 32.
[2] *Ibid.*, No. 160.
[3] *Ibid.*, VII, No. 59.
[4] *Ibid.*, No. 712.
[5] See below.
[6] See " A marshalship at Court " below.

serjeanty early in the 14th Century, the holder left
as his heirs four daughters, [1] between whom the
lands were equally divided by the King's order,
though the actual office went to the eldest alone.

There is another aspect in which the problem
may be viewed. When the lands held by performance of the service are found (from whatever
cause) in the hands of two or more holders, who
should perform the service? This was the issue
raised in the Duke of Buckingham's case, which
has been much discussed and which I have dealt
with fully in another place. [2] The Duke (*temp.*
Hen. VIII) held two out of the three manors
which it was alleged (though wrongly) were held
by the service of acting as Constable of England.
This position should be deemed akin to those
arising before Courts of Claims when portions of
one original *serjanteria* were in more hands than
one. At the Coronation, for instance, of George IV,
the right to serve as larderer was allowed in respect of three of the old manors then in three different hands, and from the time of Richard II holders
of various portions of the barony of Bedford have
been jointly found entitled to serve as almoner. [3]
In such cases the selection was left by the Court
to the King, a virtual revival of early practice. [4]

This brings us to the point of transition. Can

---

[1] Amice, wife of William de Bogelegh, Elizabeth, wife of John Cley,
Alice, wife of William Chonnesone, and Michaele, wife of John de
Rondes. (See for details of this case my paper in *Ancestor*, I, 252-254).

[2] *Peerage and Pedigree*, I, 147-166.

[3] See below. The Office of Chief Butler presents some analogy in so
far as claimed in respect of one of the Norfolk manors, but in the case
of that office there has been no allowance of joint right.

[4] See p. 40 above.

we distinguish, from an early date, between offices in gross, inheritable as of fee, and offices attached to certain lands, which lands were held by the service of discharging them ?

Investigation proves that there has always been a tendency to assume that, if the holder (by inheritance) of an office in gross also held certain lands, the lands were held by discharge of that service. Where it can be shown, as it sometimes can, that the lands were held by knight-service before the office was acquired, or conversely that the office was held before the lands were acquired, we can, with absolute certainty, disprove that assumption.

There are two instances in point. It is known that the hereditary office of Great Chamberlain was first bestowed on the De Veres by Henry I towards the close of his reign, and that it was unconnected with the tenure of land. It is also known that their barony (with its *caput*, Hedingham Castle) had been held by them from the Conquest and was held by knight-service. Nevertheless, it was clearly shown in the Great Chamberlain case that this office was found in " Inquests after death " to be attached to their barony, [1] the *reductio ad absurdum* being reached when Richard Harlackenden—whose father, the earl's steward, had purchased Earl's Colne on the dissipation of their estates,—was found, under Charles I, to have held that manor by the grand serjeanty of being Chamberlain of England. [2] The other instance illustrates the converse state of

---

[1] As early as 1264 this was found of Castle Hedingham and several other of their manors on the death of Hugh, earl of Oxford.

[2] " Per magnam serjantiam essendi magnus Camerarius Angliæ."

things. The Duke of Buckingham's case rested
on the assumption that three manors were held
jointly by the service of acting as Constable of
England, but I have been able to show that two of
these manors had been acquired by his ancestors at
a later period than that at which they obtained the
office. [1]

With regard to another officer of state, the
Marshal, Coke states that the Marshalship ever
passed by the grants of the King, and never belonged to any subject by reason of tenure, as the
stewardship and constableship of England sometime
did. [2] He is mistaken in his illustration, for the
two great offices he cites were not, as a fact, so
held. The marshalship, however, was certainly
believed, at least as early as 1243, to be connected
with the tenure of Hampstead Marshal. But this
belief also was, in my opinion, wrong, on the
ground that the Marshals held the office before they
can be actually proved to have held this manor. [3]

It was very candidly stated in Lord Ancaster's
" Case " (1901) that " the offices of Steward, Constable, Chamberlain, and Marshal were all granted
in fee," though this would remove them (according to the authors of the *History of English Law*)
from the category of serjeanties. It was also
admitted that, in spite of definite allegations,—

It is, however, very doubtful whether the great offices
of State were really attached to manors except in the
sense that manors were granted as maintenance. Such a

---

[1] *Peerage and Pedigree*, I, 151, *et seq.*
[2] *Institutes*, 128.
[3] See the section on the Marshal below.

tenure has often been alleged and occasionally found by
juries. No mention of manors occurs in the grants of
the offices, though certain manors have always descended
to the persons who succeeded to the offices and came to
be considered as appurtenant thereto.

On the subject of these offices of state the authors
of the *History of English Law* speak with some
caution.

Some of the highest offices of the realm have become
hereditary, [1] the great officers are conceived to hold their
lands by the service or serjeanty of filling these offices.
It is so with the offices of the King's steward or seneschal, marshal, constable, chamberlain, etc. (I, 263).

If this passage may be construed as implying that
such conception was wrong, there is nothing to be
said ; but we are left in some doubt as to what their
meaning was. I cannot find that they dealt, explicitly at least, in any portion of the work, with
such offices as apart from land : under " Serjeanty "
alone are they mentioned. And the authors, we
must remember, recognise " serjeanty " only in
connexion with the tenure of land.

One had not, therefore, the advantage, in 1902,
when the question was raised as to the descent of
an hereditary office in gross, that of the Great
Chamberlain, of any direct expression, on their
part, of opinion on the subject. They name it
only in connexion with land, and it was common
ground with the claimants that it had no such
connexion. All that can be said is that, at least,

---

[1] This phrase is not a happy one ; it implies that these offices were
hereditary in the blood, though the authors' meaning, evidently, is that
they were annexed to the tenure of certain lands.

they do not countenance the view so confidently advanced, on behalf of Lord Ancaster, that the office, or its tenure, was serjeanty. [1]

In default of such guidance, recourse was had to the descent of analogous offices of state. "The history of these offices," it was urged, " is extremely relevant. " [2] This, no doubt, is so, if only it were kept apart from the law, or alleged law, of descent in the case of tenure by serjeanty. [3] What we have to remember is that these great offices were not held by serjeanty, and that, even if they were, the law that such tenure involves descent, without partition, to the eldest alone of the co-heirs is by no means established as fact.

In this Volume it is not proposed to deal at great length with the history of these offices, but rather to treat them in relation to the true serjeanties and to examine the view generally, but, I think, wrongly held that they were annexed to the possession of certain fiefs or manors. It is probable that this view was suggested or supported by the fact that deputies or subordinates of these officers, whose

[1] The only relevant passage would seem to be that in the section on " Incorporeal things, " where we read, under " Offices as things," that " If ' offices ' are to fall within the pale of private law at all, if they are to be heritable and vendible, perhaps we cannot do better than treat them as being very like pieces of land " (II, 134). To this, however, it might be replied that the Great Chamberlainship, though heritable, was not "vendible. " It was, indeed, the essence of Doddridge's famous " opinion " on the descent of the office, under Charles I, that, though held in fee simple, the office could not " be transferred over to any other blood." (Collins' *Precedents*, p. 188).

[2] Lord Ancaster's " Case."

[3] The offices of steward, constable and marshal were those selected as parallel, but that of chief butler was omitted. One must point out, therefore, that insomuch as it did not descend to the eldest co-heir, its evidence was unfavourable.

services are described by the same names, did undoubtedly hold lands by the performance of such
services. But the great offices, on the contrary,
appear to have been held in fee. With one of
them, the office of chief butler, I shall deal somewhat fully, because the right to it was keenly
disputed barely ten years ago, while its origin and
descent appear to stand in need of historical
treatment.

A few remaining points may here be touched
on. In the first place, the serjeant had no power
to alter the character of his service. In Wiltshire,
for instance, Richard Danesy was charged with
converting his larder service into a military serjeanty without warrant. [1] But with the King's
permission more than this could be done. Tenure
by serjeanty could be converted into knight-service,
and *vice versa*. [2]

Again, there is a point of some consequence for
coronation claims. If, it may be asked, a pur-
chaser can acquire a tenement conferring the right
to render a Coronation service, how can the Crown
protect itself against an unwelcome claim ? In
early days, at least, the restraint on alienation
afforded an efficient bulwark ; but even now it is
amply protected. In the first place, a long series of
precedents proves its right to appoint a deputy,
acceptable to itself, by whom the service may be
actually performed ; in the second, it can fall back

---

[1] " Dictus Ricardus mutavit servicium suum predictum (custodire lardarium domini Regis) in aliud sine warranto ad inveniend' domino Regi
unum servientem equitem et armatum " etc. (*Testa*, p. 146).

[2] See the cases cited by Madox in *Baronia Anglica*, pp. 32-33, and
compare that of Wigan the marshal.

on its absolute dispensing power. In the " Duke of Buckingham's case " (*temp*. Henry VIII), the judges, when deciding that the office of Constable " should have continuance in the Duke " (in virtue of two manors), held also that " the King at his pleasure may refuse the service of the Duke in exercising of the said office. "[1] In this decision they were clearly right, as is proved by a series of precedents extending from the coronation of Edward III (as I shall show) to the present day. I am now able to produce evidence that Edward dispensed, at his coronation, with the service even of the King's champion, while, as to the present, the action of the Crown in dispensing with the Coronation banquet, for the last eighty years, has swept away, in practice, most of the " services, " although reserving, in theory, all rights and privileges.[2] Nor is the change limited exclusively to those services which had to be performed outside Westminster Abbey. The claim of the Barons of the Cinque Ports to carry the canopy over the King in the procession[3] extended to the nave of the Abbey, and their rights were keenly discussed in the Court of Claims for the Coronation of Edward VII.[4] Asked by the President :—

Suppose it should not be His Majesty's pleasure to

[1] *Peerage and Pedigree*, I, 165.

[2] The ' Proclamation,' now issued, contains the words " And we do further by this Our Royal Proclamation... dispense, upon the occasion of this Our Coronation, with the services and attendance of all persons who do claim and are bound to do and perform any services which, according to ancient custom or usage, are to be performed in Westminster Hall or in the Procession. "

[3] See the section on "The Canopy bearers " in this work.

[4] See Wollaston's *Court of Claims*, pp. 39-46.

have a canopy ; do you say your right goes to the extent
that he must have a canopy in order that you may perform
your duty ?

their Counsel replied that " if it is not His Majesty's
pleasure to have a canopy, we do not desire to press
that part of our claim, though we say that it is part
of our right that a canopy should be provided. "
The Court gave judgement " that if it is His
Majesty's pleasure to have a canopy, then the
Barons of the Cinque Ports are entitled to bear it."
Legally the point involved is whether a claimant
has " a right as against the King." [1]   It is clearly
the correct view that such right is " subject to His
Majesty's pleasure.[2]   This point will arise again
when I come to deal with "The Glove and sceptre
serjeanty, " and suggest that the Sovereign, in the
hour of his crowning, is not bound to accept
" support " from any mortal man.

Lastly, there is a small point arising from the
fact that great lords, such as the Counts of Boulogne
and of Eu, could and did create serjeanties on the
lands of their English fiefs.[3]   The services from
these lands would be rendered to themselves, but
when the widespread Boulogne fief escheated to the
Crown, and its tenant held of the King *ut de honore*,
the case of these serjeanties might present some
difficulty. A chamberlain, for instance, of the
Count of Boulogne would not become a chamber-

[1] Compare *Ibid.*, p. 58.
[2] *Ibid.*, p. 59.
[3] Littleton asserted that " a man cannot hold by Grand Serjeanty,
or by Petit Serjeanty, but of the King " (*Tenures*, sec. 161). This,
however, is wrong. " One may well hold by serjeanty of a mesne lord.
Bracton speaks clearly on this point " (*Hist. of Eng. Law*, I, 265).

lain of the King.   In such a case the service due might be, and apparently was, changed to another.

The two Primates also, and even some bishops and abbots, had tenants holding of them who were under the obligation of rendering certain services; and the former, at their enthronizations, imitated to some extent coronation ceremonies.   But in a work devoted to the King's serjeants, these services can only be dealt with by way of illustration.

CHAPTER IV

THE KING'S HOUSEHOLD

It is, no doubt, owing to the fact that he wrote as a scholar for scholars, whether in his *Constitutional History* or in his great Prefaces to the series of Chronicles and Memorials,[1] that the true greatness of Stubbs is not more widely known. It may be that this is not the place for insisting on the vastness of his learning, the soundness of his judgment or the supreme merit of the work he did for English history ; but those who have realised this for themselves, and who have even been privileged to receive instruction at his hands, cannot readily forego any opportunity of expressing their sense of the debt due to him and of its somewhat imperfect appreciation.

There could be no better introduction to the subject of this chapter than that wonderful passage in which he brings before us the King's palace of Westminster as the centre of the work of government, as the home of that court (*curia*) from which developed all administration, all justice, and all finance. At the risk of mutilating that passage I quote from it what follows :—

When the palace and the abbey had grown up together,

[1] in the Master of the Rolls' Series.

when Canute had lived in the palace and Hardicanute
had been buried in the abbey, and when the life and
death of the Confessor had invested the two with almost
equal sanctity, the abbey church became the scene of the
royal coronation, and the palace the centre of all the work
of government. The crown, the grave, the palace, the
festival, the laws of King Edward, all illustrate the perpe-
tuity of a national sentiment typifying the continuity of
the national life. There the Conqueror kept his summer
courts,[1] and William Rufus contemplated the building
of a house of which the great hall which now survives
should be only one of the bedchambers.

After observing that the reign of Edward I
"saw the whole of the administrative machinery
of the government permanently settled in and
around the palace," the historian proceeds :—

The ancient palace of Westminster...... must have presented a very apt illustration of the history of the Constitution which had grown up from its early simplicity to
its full strength within those venerable walls...... As the
administrative system of the country had been developed
largely from the household economy of the King, the
national palace had for its kernel the King's court, hall,
chapel, and chamber :...... the chamber became a council
room, the banquet hall a court of justice, the chapel a
hall of deliberation ; but the continuity of the historical
building was complete, the changes were but signs of
growth and of the strength that could outlive change......
It was a curious coincidence certainly that the destruction
of the ancient fabric should follow so immediately upon
the great constitutional change wrought by the reform
act, and scarcely less curious that the fire should have
originated in the burning of the ancient exchequer tallies,
one of the most permanent relics of the primitive simplicity of administration.[2]

[1] *i.e.* the Whitsuntide crown-wearings (see below).
[2] *Constit. Hist.* (1878), III, 382-5. A foot-note points out that " the
tallies had been in use until 1826. "

It is, precisely, " the primitive simplicity of administration " under the Norman Kings that will most impress the reader. In the document to which we are now coming, " The establishment of the King's Household, " we are struck at the very outset by the fact that the first officer named, the (Lord) Chancellor, who receives the then large salary of five shillings a day, is entitled to a fixed daily allowance of candle-ends, as are the lesser officers of the Household. This ' Establishment, ' indeed, is of so early a date that it practically stands alone. It is partly in consequence of this that it presents some difficulties ; for we do not possess contemporary records to assist us in its elucidation. Except for the Pipe Roll of 1130, which affords little help, we are virtually dependent on such assistance as later evidence affords. It is to this document, however, that we must look for the origin of the great offices of state, and for the illustration of those services which were rendered in the King's household or in connection with his sport by those who held of him " by serjeanty."

What then is this document, and where is it printed ? It was printed by that industrious anti-quary, Hearne, in his *Liber Niger Scaccarii* (1774), from the text in the Little Black Book of the Exchequer, and again in the official edition of the *Red Book of the Exchequer* (1896), from the text in that volume. Stubbs, somewhat strangely perhaps, deals with it only in a footnote, as giving " the daily allowances of the several inmates of the palace ; " but in more recent years it has been critically discussed, with a knowledge of both texts, by an officer of the Public Record Office, Mr. Hubert Hall, firstly in his *Court Life under the Plantagenets* (1890), pp. 242-9, and then in his official edition of *The Red Book of the Exchequer*, pp. cclxxxviii-ccci, 807-813. As his text and observations are the source of information to which the student would naturally turn, it will be necessary to say something of them, the more so because he has described Hearne's notes as " clumsy and far-fetched " and brought against him the charge that he " did not always treat his MSS. texts with proper respect." [1]   " It is," he added, "both strange that historians should have been so long content with the printed version of Hearne, and most desirable that a perfect text should be provided at the first opportunity." [2]   A few years later his own was published.

Now a very good test of Mr. Hall's critical judgment, and indeed of his ability even to read the MS. before him, is afforded by his lengthy observations on its word *sal'*.

It will be only necessary to place side by side his assertions in 1890 and in 1896.

1890

The greatest stumbling-block experienced by Hearne in his annotation of the Black Book MSS.,.... was in respect of the word " Sal.," as it appears in this abbreviated form. Hearne, who did not always treat his MSS. texts

1896

In the *Constitutio* itself much difficulty has been experienced in the rendering of certain archaic terms and formulæ. A very good instance will be found in the case of the abbreviation *Sal'*, which appears in connection

[1] *Court Life*, p. 242.
[2] *Ibid.*, p. 244.

with proper respect, seems to have jumped at once to the conclusion that by this abbreviation, which appears in almost every entry in connection with an inferior sort of simnel, a *salted* loaf was implied, *i.e.* "simenellus salus" or "salinus." Unfortunately, however, the occasional extensions of "sal." in the two Exchequer MSS. scarcely warrant this conjecture, in spite of the immense amount of learning which has been expended thereon. In the Black Book the word is twice extended, once as "salu." and again as "salci."......

The Red Book also gives two extensions, both as "sal-ac." It has seemed to me, therefore, perfectly simple and probable to understand the word "salacii," dripping, or animal grease of some kind, in contrast to the more costly royal simnel, which may have been compounded with oil or butter. In fact, a simnel of this kind was probably very like a modern tea-cake, and I would even venture to suggest that the familiar "Sally Lunn" etc. etc. (pp. 242-3).

with a certain kind of simnel..... The simnel in question was probably the *pain de sel* or *panis de sala* supplied to the Hall, or Household, as contrasted with the *Payn demayn* or *Panis dominicus* reserved for the high table..... but there can be little doubt that, rightly or wrongly, the scribes of both Exchequer MSS. read the word as "salted," since in the Black Book it is twice extended as *salum*, and in the Red Book twice also as *Salatum*. At the same time it by no means follows that this is the correct form, for the MSS. have been transcribed with very scant intelligence. A "salted" or "seasoned" simnel, or possibly a cake compounded of salt dripping instead of oil, may have been served out as the accompaniment of a rather liberal allowance of wine, but the *pain de sel* is a more reasonable alternative.

The plain facts, it will be seen, are, when

stripped of verbiage, that Hearne read his MS. as meaning a "salted" simnel ; that for this he was charged by Mr. Hall with not treating his MS. "with proper respect" and with having "jumped at once to the conclusion" that " a *salted* loaf was implied," thus completely ignoring " a repeated reading ; " and that this charge rests solely on the misreading of the MSS. by Mr. Hall himself in three out of four cases !

This is not my own assertion ; it rests on Mr. Hall's own words, as given side by side above, and on his admission that " the scribes of both Exchequer MSS. read the word as ' salted '." But as he is there discreetly silent as to his previous statements, it is only when I print them side by side that their contradiction is revealed.

Mr. Hall, has, somewhat impertinently, spoken of my "hasty charge" against Swereford,[1] of which he claims to have cleared him " on the clearest possible evidence," but which, was made with full consideration and which as the point is historically important, I subsequently proved up to the hilt.[2] What shall we say of his own charge against the unfortunate Hearne ?

A further collation of Mr. Hall's statements illustrates the value of his critical judgment where texts are concerned.

1890	1896
The Black Book text is *considerably inferior* to that of	The text of the Black Book, which is otherwise

[1] Preface to *Red book of the Exchequer*, p. clxxxiv.
[2] See my *Studies on the Red Book of the Exchequer* (Printed for private circulation).

the Red Book of the Exchequer, which contains another
and a much more careful
transcript, and this text has
been chiefly followed in the
translation appended here...
(p. 242). [1]

the more correct, is defaced
by some gross blunders in
the rubrication of the initial
letters. (p. ccxcviii). [1]

The quotation on the right proceeds thus :—

Both MSS. are utterly at fault with 'Oinus Polcheard,'
for which the readings 'Dominus' or 'Omnis' have
hitherto been suggested. This officer can, however, be
easily identified with 'Oinus Polcehart' or 'Oinus serviens' of the Pipe Roll of 1130, his office being doubtless
that of the Poultry (Puletarius). *Cf.* the local names of
the Polecat.

Now, in the first place, the Black Book, so far
from being "utterly at fault," reads the name,
according to Mr. Hall himself, "Oinus Polechart"
(p. 810), which, we learn, is right. And why, in
the second, was his office "doubtless that of the
Poultry (Puletarius)"? The record places him at
the head of the officers of the Great Kitchen, but
Mr. Hall transfers him to another department and
makes him "Serjeant of the Poultry" (p. ccxci).
Why? Can it be possible that, because his name
began with 'Pol', Mr. Hall has "jumped at the
conclusion" that he was "the King's Poulterer"?[2]
It would seem, indeed, inconceivable were it not
that he actually renders his record's "Bernarius"
as "bear-ward" (p. ccxciii),[3] apparently because it

---

[1] The italics are mine.
[2] *Court Life*, p. 246.
[3] And *Court Life*, p. 249.

begins with ' Ber-' [1] One can hardly imagine that there is any other scholar, in or out of the Record Office, ignorant of the fact that a *bernarius* was a hunt-servant in charge of hounds. [2] Mr. Hall is evidently unaware that there was a man named ' Polcehard' who held a hide in Berks at the time of the Domesday Survey. As the Pipe Roll of 1130 proves that Oin ' Polcehart' held a hide in that county (p. 126), we have here clearly the origin of his possibly unique surname. [3]

I must point out that these criticisms are not on the work of an amateur, or even of an ordinary scholar. Mr. Hall has put himself forward, from among his fellow-officers, to teach others how MSS. should be edited and how records should be read. On these subjects he has lectured and he has written, and always, to quote the phrase he himself applies to Madox, with a " great show of learning." He has thereby challenged public criticism and investigation of his claims to instruct others. *The Red Book of the Exchequer* is no mere private enterprise ; it is the official edition of a famous public record, and the authority, for scholars, of that edition is matter of public interest.

I am compelled to deal critically with Mr. Hall's treatment of this document of " inestimable value,"[4] because it affects directly a work on " the King's serjeants. " I have, for instance, devoted sections

---

[1] The word for ' bear-ward' was *ursarius* (see *Pipe Rolls*, 2-4 Hen. II [1844], pp. 136, 149).

[2] See the chapter below on ' the King's sport.'

[3] Mr. Hall makes the wild suggestion that " this Owen was possibly a Welshman. "

[4] *Court Life*, p. 244.

to "the King's tailor" and "the serjeanty of the Hose," and, as the rendering "tailor" is opposed to Mr. Hall's conclusion in *The Red Book of the Exchequer*, I am relieved to find that his *Court Life*, on the contrary, supports it.

1890	1896
I have also ventured to suggest "tailor" as a better reading than "counter," who would have appeared as 'calculator,' if any such office existed apart from the exchequer. It will be seen that "hosiers" are mentioned in another place (p. 244).	Difficulties have also been experienced in connection with the offices of the *Hosarii* and of the *Tallator* of the Household, though such difficulties must have been of the commentators' own making. Probably, however, the confusion between the offices of hosiers of the Wardrobe and Buttery respectively is of old standing, but *Cissor* would certainly have been the title applied to the King's Tailor, and the official here referred to was doubtless the Tally-cutter in the suite of the Treasurer and Chamberlains (p. ccxcix).

So we first learn that the word *Tallator* must mean 'tailor,' because, if it meant 'counter,' *calculator* would be used, and then, on the contrary, that it meant 'Tally-cutter' (*i. e.* reckoner), because, if it meant 'tailor,' *cissor* would be used! And, while in 1890 the 'hosiers' are connected, we see, with the 'tailor,' in 1896, on the contrary, they are placed in the butler's department (p. ccxci).

Before we leave what I may term the 'Sally

Lunn' school of criticism, it may be well to note its verdict on the date of these " famous regulations. "[1] In 1890 they could " be distinctly referred to the reign of Henry II ; " in 1896 we read that the Establishment " has been commonly assigned to the time of Henry II, although it is actually dated in the reign of Henry I by the scribe who copied it into the Red Book of the Exchequer, " and that " Mr. Stapleton clearly proved long since that this Establishment refers to the reign of Henry I. "[2]

The exceptionally early date of this ' Establishment of the Household' (*Constitutio domus regis*) is seen, on careful study, in the names of some of the officers and in their classification. The *Escantiones*, for instance, were of sufficient importance to form a class by themselves, but their subsequent disappearance makes their functions doubtful, though they significantly appear on the similarly early Pipe Roll of 1130.[3] They appear to have been cupbearers. In France the *Grand Échanson* existed independently of the Chief Butler. The *Hosarii*, also, of our document have completely baffled enquirers,[4] though these also are named on the Pipe Roll of 1130. Another mark of antiquity is the prominence of the ' Dispensers '. There was a ' Master Dispenser ' of the bread, with others under him, a ' Master Dispenser ' of the Larder, with other Dispensers of the Larder, who served in turn, and ' Master Dispensers ' of the Butlery.

[1] *Court Life*, p. 242.
[2] *Red Book*, p. cclxxxviii.
[3] "Osmundus Escanceon" (Berks) ; "Turstinus Escanceon" (Middlesex).
[4] See the section below on ' The serjeanty of the Hose. "

The function of these officers has proved so obscure that they have sometimes been confused with stewards, [1] whose office was quite distinct.

Even the ' Master ' Dispensers only received about half the pay of the stewards and other officers of the first rank. As a lengthy section of this work is devoted to a family of "King's Dispensers," one may explain that theirs was virtually the issue department of the Household ; they " dispensed " the rations of bread and of wine with which the *Constitutio* is so largely concerned. The *expensa* of the record became, no doubt, on English lips, the ' spence ', and its officer the ' spencer ', and these renderings are now adopted in Record Office publications. But as a ' spencer ' would convey to a modern Englishman no meaning except, perhaps, that of an overcoat, I prefer the form ' dispenser ', which does at least convey a very similar meaning in connection with the verb 'dispense'. In French, the word *dépense* retained its meaning as buttery, larder, etc., as did the word *dépensier*, which long denoted also a ship's purser.

On the great officers of state the evidence of this record is, in my opinion, of high importance. The test of their position is their pay. The chancellor, who comes first as a cleric, receives five shillings a day, and the stewards, [2] who receive the same, become the units of wage for the other great officers. [3] This raises the question of the Marshal's

---

[1] *e.g.* in Hall's *Court Life*, pp. 245-7.

[2] The mention of "Dapiferi" is important as implying that there were then more Stewards than one (see the section on the Steward below).

[3] "Dapiferi sicut Cancellarius...... Magister Pincerna sicut Dapifer......

position at the time. The marshals follow immediately on the constables, and the sectional heading in the Red Book may be disregarded : [1] the text, therefore, runs :—" Rogerus de Oyli similiter. Magister Marscallus similiter, scilicet Johannes. " Now Roger, we find, only received two shillings a day, as against the five shillings of the *Dapifer*. It is true that the marshal seems to have had fees in addition (*preter hoc*), but the impression, certainly, is conveyed that he was then inferior to the constables. There is some reason to believe that this was the case abroad. [2]

We are dealing, in these officers of state, with an institution of high antiquity : their offices, it is well recognised, can be traced back to the Empire, long before the Normans set foot in England. The *Capitula Remedii*, Stubbs notes, " mention the camerarius, buticularius, senescalcus, judex publicus and conestabulus : the Alemannic law enumerates ' seniscalcus, mariscalcus, cocus, and pistor '. " [3] "The Karolingian Court," he adds, " had a slightly different rule : the four chief officers are the marshal, the steward, the butler, and the chamberlain." From the Empire this system passed into France, and thence into Normandy, and, in my opinion, it

Magister Camerarius par est Dapifero in liberatione. Thesaurarius, ut Magister Camerarius...... Constabularii liberationes habent sicut Dapiferi et eodem modo. "

[1] It is not found in the Black Book text.

[2] I do not know that anyone but Stubbs has touched upon this point. He pointed out in a foot-note that in (the Kingdom of) Naples the marshals were subordinate to the constable, but that " in England the marshal was not subordinate to the constable " (*Const. Hist.* [1874], I, 354).

[3] *Const. Hist.*, I, 343.

was Edward the Confessor who introduced it, with other Norman innovations, into England. [1]

Under our Norman Kings we become able to distinguish the Steward, Constable, Marshal, Chamberlain, and Butler. There is, however, extreme difficulty in determining the holders of these offices for a century after the Conquest. That admirable antiquary Madox, while careful to avoid error, was unable in the absence of records, on which alone he wisely relied, to satisfy himself on the subject. [2] Dr. Stubbs wrote as follows :—

The exact dates for the foundation of these offices cannot be given, nor even a satisfactory list of their early holders...... It is, however, to be noticed that each of these names appears to have been given to several persons at once ; there were certainly several *dapiferi* and *pincernæ* at the same time. These were honorary distinctions probably, although they may in some instances have been grand serjeanties. The dignity that emerges ultimately may be the chief of each order ; the *high* steward, the *great* butler, the lord *high* chamberlain. [3]

The offices, I think, of chamberlain and of butler are the first to emerge singly ; the chief marshalship had been determined before the year 1130 ; but the claims to the high stewardship and the constableship of England were still, apparently, conflicting at the date of the *Constitutio*, and, indeed, for many years afterwards.

[1] See my paper on " the officers of Edward the Confessor " in *Eng. Hist.Rev.*,vol. XXI. I do not think the earlier officers named by Stubbs as occasionally occurring in England belong to this definite system.
[2] See the chapter on " The officers of state " in his *History of the Exchequer*.
[3] *Const. Hist.*, I, 344-5.

We are again reminded that all administration developed out of the King's household when we find Stubbs writing, as before:—[1]

The great officers of the household form the first circle round the throne, and furnish the King with the first elements of a ministry of state. There is from the very first some difficulty in drawing the line that separates their duties as servants of the court from their functions as administrators.[2]

England is, perhaps, the one country in which the outward forms of government have been jealously and obstinately retained, however wide their separation from the facts of national life. It is still in the old Norman-French that the royal assent is given and would, in theory, be refused to the bills passed by Parliament. The King "who reigns, but does not govern," must still, at every coronation, " solemnly promise and swear to govern the people of this " kingdom. Parliament, it may be, now governs, or, it may be, the Ministry that Parliament has placed in power ; but in the great act of the King's crowning Parliament has no part; Parliament and Ministry are still ignored, as they were ignored of old. On that day the King's Ministers are the ministers of his Norman ancestors ; about him in the Abbey are the Steward and the Chamberlain, the Constable and the Marshal of England, [3] though the Steward and the Constable are now revived for the day only to complete the picture of a dead past.

[1] p. 53 above.
[2] *Const. Hist.*, I, 343.
[3] The Chief Butler, as such, has ceased to figure at Coronations since the banquet was abandoned by William IV.

In the Holy Roman Empire—where the coronations of the Emperors presented striking analogies to those of our own Kings—the distribution of the great offices, in the words of Stubbs, " was permanent, and was observed, with some modifications, down to the latest days of the Empire, in the electoral body, where the Count Palatine was high steward, the Duke of Saxony marshal, the King of Bohemia cup-bearer, [1] and the Margrave of Brandenburg [2] chamberlain." [3]   In France, also, at the crowning of its " most Christian King, " there were found two at least of the great officers of state, the Constable and the Great Chamberlain, though the Steward had disappeared at an early date. [4]   But with the Empire and the Kingdom their officers have passed away : in England only are they still found by the throne of the new-crowned King.

Before leaving the subject of the King's household, one may note the primitive aspect of its division into two great departments, the hall (*aula*) and the chamber (*camera*).   Perhaps it would be more correct to say that the house, rather than the household, was so divided.   But to understand the

---

[1] Otherwise " Arch-Butler. "

[2] Ancestor of the Kings of Prussia (now German Emperors.)

[3] *Const. Hist.*, I, 344.   See also Taylor's *Glory of Regality* pp. 101-3, and Bryce's *Holy Roman Empire* (1871), pp. 230-1, where he aptly quotes the lines from the *De Imperio Romano* of Marsilius of Padua :
" Est Palatinus Dapifer, Dux portitor ensis,
Marchio præpositus cameræ, pincerna Bohemus,
Hi statuunt dominum cunctis per sæcula summum. "

[4] Philip, Count of Flanders officiated at the coronation of Philip Augustus, and " the seneschal of France, as a coronation official, survived the accession of Louis the Ninth.   Ultimately the constable of France took his place. " (Harcourt's *His Grace the Steward*, p. 55).

household arrangements, this division must be kept in view. There were also, of course, on the one hand, the chapel and chancery, with the Chancellor at their head, and, on the other, the kitchen, larder, butler's department and so forth ; but the ' hall ' and the ' chamber ' were the kernel, as it seems to me, of the palace. We shall find, perhaps, the nearest equivalents in the ' state apartments ' and ' private apartments ' of a modern palace, while the phrase ' groom of the privy chamber ' seems to preserve the meaning of the medieval *camera*. In any case it was from the ' chamber ' that the chamberlain derived his name, and with it that his functions were connected. It was in the hall, on the other hand, that the marshal preserved order and that the steward, as *dapifer* (*discthegn*), set the dish upon the table.

The hall (*aula*) still denoted, in Norman as in classical times, [1] the palace as a whole. [2] But we are still reminded by Westminster ' Hall ' of the word's true meaning. It is, still, in theory, from his ' chamber ' that the King goes forth to be crowned, [3] and in the ' hall ' of his palace, Westminster Hall, that the coronation banquet is held, although it is now dispensed with. And I think that from the present we can feel our way to an even more remote past. For if we study the

[1] *Cf. aulici* (courtiers).

[2] See, for instance, the Conqueror's charter making a grant to the New Minster, Winchester, in return for the land he had taken from its cemetery for making his palace (" ad aulam meam faciendam ") in *New Minster and Hyde Abbey* (Hants. Rec. Soc.), p. 111.

[3] It was from " a certain chamber " in the " Old Palace of Westminster " that George II, " being clothed in his royal robes " proceeded to his Coronation, as did George IV after him.

historic fees claimed by the Great Chamberlain,
and those also of the Queen's Chamberlain, we find
them practically representing the contents of the
bedchamber alone.[1]   The original *camera*, therefore,
may have been the actual *thalamus*, in days when
even a king required little more than a ' chamber '
in which to sleep at night and a ' hall ' in which
he spent the day.

THE STEWARD

" The Steward of England still is, and, according
to popular tradition, always has been the first officer
of state in the kingdom. "   Such are the opening
words of the Preface to *His Grace the Steward*
(1907), that notable work by the late Mr. L. W.
Vernon Harcourt, which has made obsolete all that
had previously been written on the history and
functions of the office in this country.   There are
those, doubtless, who, in the usual fashion, would
condemn the author's outspoken criticism of the
errors and the fables which older antiquaries had
been indolently content to repeat.   For those of
whom I speak never ask themselves whether such
criticism is just, but only whether it is severe.
Mr. Vernon Harcourt was entitled to claim, as he
did claim on his title page, that his work was "a
novel inquiry...... founded entirely upon original
sources of information and extensively upon hitherto
unprinted materials. "   A scholar who had under-
taken the labour required for such a work was
entitled to speak with some scorn of the book-

---

[1] The velvet for robes was another matter altogether.

making writers who had followed one another in the repetition of error.

It has already been explained that 'the Lord Steward,' as 'Steward of the Household,' is distinct from 'the Lord High Steward.' But originally this was not so. For although Mr. Vernon Harcourt did not make the matter clear, he cited the document of 1221, in which the chief stewardship is styled " senescalcia hospicii nostri " (p. 77). The Montforts magnified this office into the Stewardship " of England " about the middle of the 13th Century, and a steward " of the household " (*hospitii domini regis*) appears subsequently as a distinct officer and develops into the Lord Steward.

One of the difficulties presented by this office is indicated by its double Latinisation as *dapifer* and as *senescallus*. A *dapifer*, as his name indicates, had for his duty to serve the king by placing the dishes on his table. He was, as Stubbs pointed out, the *discthegn* of days before the Conquest, the *infertor* of the Salian law. In this capacity he was represented in later days, among ourselves, by the " sewer, " who, in the days of Edward IV, " receveth the metes by (as)sayes and saufly so conveyeth it to the King's bourde...... and all that cometh to that bourde he setteth and dyrecteth. " [1] By this time he had been, sharply enough, differentiated from the Lord Steward (" Styward of Housholde "), who, under the king, had the governance of the Household. [2] Yet, as is cautiously observed by the judicious Madox, " whether there was anciently a

[1] *Household Ordinances.*
[2] *Ibid.*

notable difference, or any, between the *Senescallus* and the *Dapifer* in England, let others judge. " [1]

Mr. Vernon Harcourt, while admitting that the steward " is and was, " in England, " first officer of state, " contends that this position was an unauthorised development, and that his earlier position was comparatively humble. " The *original* sewer, or dapifer, " he writes " was, of course, the subsequent lord high steward " (p. 180). Under the Conqueror, the *dapifer*, he holds, was but " the dishthane and caterer " (p. 21) ; under John he had still no higher privilege than that " of serving at the royal table on special occasions, with perhaps the additional right of carrying a sword at coronations " (p. 76) ; even under Henry III, he dismisses the belief of Simon de Montfort that his office of Steward entitled him to most important functions as a delusion.

Henry may have found it difficult to convince him that the sole duty properly belonging to Simon de Montfort as hereditary steward was the business of chief sewer at particular state banquets. Nevertheless such was the case, and moreover there was nothing intrinsically strange in the matter. The strangeness lay rather in the circumstance that the French and other dapifers had soared to precedence over all other functionaries, than in the fact that the English dish-thegn was a dish-thegn still (p. 84).

For it is the essence of the writer's theory that the development of the *dapifer* and his functions began in France towards the close of the eleventh century and gave rise to the erroneous belief that he ought to possess similar powers and similar

[1] *History of the Exchequer* (1711), p. 33.

precedence in England. In the closing year of the eleventh century the French *dapifer* rose, we learn, to be " the first great officer of state ".... " his preeminence appears fully established " (pp. 1, 22). The force of continental example was increased under the Angevin kings by the facts that the *dapifer* happened to be the chief officer of Anjou (p. 35), and that Henry II's eldest son acted as *dapifer* to the French king, in 1169, as Count of Anjou. Thus it was that, from about the middle of the twelfth century, this office became, he holds, an object of ambition with great nobles in England.

But, even if we admit the justice of his main contention, especially his rejection of the view that the steward was originally justiciar, the writer was perhaps too eager to depreciate the steward's position. He may not, at first, have enjoyed precedence, but he was always one of the great officers. It is very doubtful, however, if it was one of his functions to bear the royal sword before the king at coronations, though it was so borne at the coronation of Philip Augustus; for, as we saw above, the phrase ' portitor ensis ' denoted, in the Empire, the marshal. The only case in which this privilege seems to have been exercised in England was at the coronation of Richard I, when the Earl of Leicester bore one of the swords. The other privilege, which was exercised by the steward as *dapifer*, was that of setting the first dish on the table at the coronation banquet and on similar great occasions. Henry, heir-apparent of England, so served the French King in Paris (1169),[1] and the Count of Flanders

---

[1] " servivit regi Franciæ ad mensam ut senescallus Franciæ. "

at the coronation of Philip Augustus.[1] Of the
great officers of the Empire, the Count Palatine,
as *dapifer*, carried " four dishes of meat " at the
coronation, and though we do not seem to have
direct evidence [2] of this function in England, there
can be little doubt that it was duly performed at
coronation banquets.

The point requires to be insisted on because, in
his *Glory of Regality*, Taylor, describing the Coronation Banquet, asserts that the bringing on of the
first course, which is preceded by the " sewers, "
" was anciently superintended by the *dapifer* or
grand sewer " (p. 220), whose office he treats as
wholly unconnected with that of the Steward
(pp. 124-5). But the " sewers " were themselves
preceded by three officers of state " mounted on
goodly horses, " *viz.* the Steward, with the Con-

---

[1] " in regiis dapibus apponendis. "

[2] We have such indirect evidence as the service of the earls of Devon,
as stewards, at the enthronization of the bishop of Exeter, when it was
part of their duties to place, personally, the first course *(totum primum
ferculum)* before the bishop at the banquet, receiving as fee four silver
dishes *(quatuor discos argenteos)* out of those used for the purpose. The
earls of ' Clare ' similarly received, as high stewards, at the enthronization
of archbishops of Canterbury, the dishes set before them at the first
course. I would also invite attention to the services of the Lords Willoughby d'Eresby as stewards to the bishops of Durham, for their palat-
inate made them almost petty sovereigns. In 1317 Robert, Lord
Willoughby, was found to have held Eresby by service *(inter alia)* of
" being steward to attend upon the bishops' dishes *(fercula)* on the days
of their consecration, and on Christmas Day and Whitsunday yearly. "
(Cal. of Inq. VI, p. 48). A similar return was made on the death of
his grandson in 1372, the service being then defined as " to carry the
messes of meat to the table upon the day of their consecration, as also at
Christmas and Whitsuntide " (Dugdale, *Baronage*, II, 84). This service
is not mentioned by Mr. Lapsley in his valuable monograph on *The
County Palatine* (Harvard Historical Studies, 1900) though he deals fully
with the steward under " officers of state " (pp. 76-80).

stable on his right and the Marshal on his left
(p. 219). At the coronation of George III, a
private letter states, the "table was served with
three courses, at the first of which Earl Talbot, as
Steward of his Majesty's Household,[1] rode up from
the hall gate to the steps leading to where their
Majesties sate." This, doubtless, was a survival of
the original, but forgotten service, and it brings
the High Stewardship into line with the office of
dapifer as exercised, we have seen, in early days and
in other realms and places.

Indeed, it seems a natural inference that the
dapifer set the meat before the king as the 'butler'
set the drink. If so, the two offices would be
much on the same level.[2]

But on no account must the steward's functions
be confused with those of the chamberlain. In
dealing with the "famous" (p. 191) record of
Queen Eleanor's coronation (1236) Mr. Vernon
Harcourt wrote

Simon de Montfort served that day as steward without
let or hindrance,...... As soon as Henry had seated himself at the banqueting table, Simon, arrayed in robe of
office, gave him water in a basin to wash his hands.[3]

The error is quite inexplicable, for this was the
chamberlain's function, and, indeed, the record
expressly states that the chamberlain performed the
service.[4]

[1] Rather in his capacity as Lord High Steward for the day.
[2] There are indications (see, for instance, p. 23 above), that the
steward controlled the kitchen as the butler did the butlery.
[3] *His Grace the Steward*, p. 83.
[4] "Servivit autem ea die de Aqua tam ante prandium quam post,
major Camerarius, videlicet Hugo de Ver" (*Lib. Rub.* p. 759). By

We are not here concerned with the Steward's later duty of presiding over the trial of peers, with which Mr. Vernon Harcourt has dealt so fully, but on two other later developments something must be said.   It was still alleged in the latest edition of Blount's *Tenures* [1] that, under a special commission, " he holds his court (of claims) some convenient time before the coronation. "   But his presidency of that court, which appears to have begun in 1377, certainly came to an end before the reign of Henry VIII. [2]   The other of these functions is that of carrying St. Edward's Crown immediately before the Sovereign in the Coronation procession. This function is still discharged by the noble who is appointed 'Lord High Steward' for the purpose.

How the office became hereditary and descended with the earldom of Leicester has been very fully explained by Mr. Vernon Harcourt.   After Simon de Montfort's fall, it was held by the earls and dukes of Lancaster till it merged in the Crown. The question here is, as was observed above, [3] whether the office was ever held by serjeanty, that is, in virtue of the tenure of certain lands.   There were, as Mr. Vernon Harcourt has shown, four distinct grants of it in less than twenty years (1141-1155), namely those to the Earl of Essex, to Humfrey de Bohun, to the Earl of Leicester, and to the

another error the writer alleged that the *Constitutio* assigned the same pay to the Dispensers as to the *dapiferi* (p. 24), which, we have seen, was not the case (see p. 62 above).

[1] Ed. Hazlitt (1874), p. 296.
[2] *His Grace the Steward*, p. 191 ; Wollaston, *Court of Claims*, pp. 11-12.
[3] See p. 45.

Earl of Norfolk. The terms of these grants are known, and, as I read them, they are all grants of an office in gross. It is true that Mr. Vernon Harcourt definitely claimed that

> Humphrey de Bohun was granted his dapifership.......
> to hold to himself and his heirs as a serjeanty appertaining to certain lands...... there seems not the smallest reason to doubt that the intention was to exact the active duties attaching to the post of dapifer from Humphrey de Bohun and his heirs, as the service to be rendered for the possession of particular properties (p. 34).

But I do not hesitate to say that the charter, which he printed in full,[1] contains nothing of the kind.

In 1232 Amauri de Montfort made over his rights in the lands and the Stewardship to his younger brother Simon,[2] but not as a serjeanty. In 1239, however, he made a fresh grant of them, in which he definitely named the Stewardship as part of the service due from the Montfort share of the Honour of Leicester.[3] But the royal charter confirming that grant does not mention the Stewardship, and, in any case, Amauri's statement could not alter the fact that the Stewardship had not, originally, been connected with these lands. As to the later story that the Stewardship was appurtenant, " not to the earldom of Leicester, but to the honour of Hinckley, " it was shewn by Mr.

---

[1] It was printed by me from the original in *Ancient Charters* (Pipe Roll Society, 1888), pp. 45-6.

[2] *His Grace the Steward*, pp. 81, 112.

[3] " totam partem *(sic)* honoris Leycestrie ...... faciendo inde eis debitum servitium ad illam partem *(sic)* pertinens tam in *senescalcia* domini Regis Henrici predicti quam in aliis servitiis " (*Ibid.* pp. 86, 112).

Vernon Harcourt that, in spite of its persistent repetition, it was based on forgery alone.

THE CONSTABLE

The Constable was, throughout, essentially a military officer ; he is found with the garrison in the castle or with the army in the field.   In the *constabularia* of ten knights we detect the unit of the feudal host, [1] which shows the close association of the constable's office with war. [2]   With him, in his military functions, the marshal was regularly connected, though whether in a different capacity or as his recognised lieutenant appears to be considered doubtful.

The constable ...... and the marshal, whose functions are scarcely distinguishable from those of the constable, reached at a comparatively early date the position of hereditary dignities.   Their military functions, however, preserved them from falling into the class of mere grand serjeanties, and at a later period they had very great importance in the management of the army. [3]

One of the most familiar scenes in English medieval history is that at Salisbury, in the gathering of the barons (1297), when the constable and the marshal together withstood King Edward to his face.   Of Bohun and Bigod, Stubbs has written, " each now held with his earldom a great office of

[1] See my *Feudal England*.
[2] On the Close Roll of 4 Edward II (3 Sept. 1310) is an imperative order from the king to the earl of Hereford and Essex, as Constable of England, to come to Scotland and do his service as Constable of the Army (" ad faciendum ibidem servicium vestrum de Constabular' exercitus nostri, ut tenemini sicut scitis ").
[3] Stubbs, *Const. Hist.* (1874), I, 354.

state. " Called upon to lead the English host, without the king, in Gascony, the earls refused ; " as belongs to me, by hereditary right, " the marshal proudly exclaimed, " I will go in the front of the host before your face : without you, Oh King, I am not bound to go, and go I will not. " " By God, earl, " the king replied, " you shall either go or hang. " The two earls broke away and, at the head of armed horse, defied the King's commands.[1]

As in the army, so also in the famous ' Court of Chivalry ' we find the Constable and the Marshal presiding jointly ; but I would note the fact that in the records relating to this court the Constable has precedence. " A military court, nominally, at all events, under the control of the constable and the marshal of England, is in existence at least as early as the reign of Edward the First. " So wrote Mr. Vernon Harcourt,[2] to whose learned and most valuable chapter on the early history of this court I may refer the reader. Originally a court martial (*curia militaris*), its jurisdiction developed, through cases of honour and of arms — quaintly styled " heroical causes " in the sixteenth century,—till its encroachments had to be checked by law.[3] Even when the Constable had disappeared, the court lingered on as that of the Earl Marshal, the recog-

[1] Stubbs, *Const. Hist.* (1875), II, 132-3.
[2] *His Grace the Steward*, p. 362.
[3] According to the statute 13 Ric. II, cap. 2, " To the constable it pertaineth to have cognisance of contracts touching deeds of arms and war ...... which the constables have heretofore duly and reasonably used in their time. " Stubbs wrote, in indignant language, that an " abuse which had the result of condemning its agents to perpetual infamy was the extension of the jurisdiction of the High Constable of England to cases of high treason. " (*Const. Hist.* III, 282).

nised *forum* for questions concerning coat-armour and titles of honour. [1]

It appears to me probable that the Duke of Buckingham's claim, under Henry VIII, to hold this great and ancient office, not by royal appointment, but by grand serjeanty as of right, [2] was one of the causes contributing to his fall ; for Henry looked upon it as " very hault et dangerous. "[3] Another was his royal descent, as heir of Thomas of Woodstock, whose arms he was entitled to bear "alone", [4] and yet another was his high position, as an ancient noble, in an upstart age. For Henry, like Abdul Aziz, was quick to scent conspiracy and danger to his royal person. And so " the finest buck in England " was pulled down by " a butcher's dog. "

' The Lord High Constable ' is now effectually tamed ; he is appointed by the Crown, and only for the day of coronation, and when he has delivered the regalia to the Lord Great Chamberlain, he has only to walk in the procession on the right of the sword of state. But until the Champion's service was dispensed with, he rode into the banquet on the champion's right, with his ancient partner, the Earl Marshal, on the Champion's left, [5] a sur-

[1] See ' Peerage Cases in the Court of Chivalry ' in my *Peerage and Pedigree*.

[2] See pp. 43, 45 above.

[3] Dyer's *Reports*, 285b. I think this must refer to the doctrine that the ' hereditary ' steward, constable, and marshal, ' or two of them, ' had power jointly to coerce the king (See my *Commune of London*, pp. 317-8, and compare *His Grace the Steward*, pp. 144-152.)

[4] See *Peerage and Pedigree*, II, 358.

[5] The Constable, one notes, here also, occupies the place of honour, as he does in the coronation procession. *Cf.* p. 82.

vival of their old association on the field of battle.

We return to the origin of his office. It is pleasant to be able to pay tribute to the memory of that great antiquary, Madox, who, although writing no less than two centuries ago, knew already, virtually, all that records can tell us.[1] If anything, he was too cautious in the use he made of his materials. It seems to be fairly well established that Walter son of Roger (de Pîtres), who appears in Domesday Book as a tenant-in-chief, was constable (or a constable) under Henry I.[2] A Llanthony writer speaks of him as "Constabularius, princeps militiæ domus regiæ," and though it has been suggested that he was only constable of Gloucester castle, it is certain that his son and successor, Miles, was an actual constable. Dugdale asserts that Henry I gave him "all his father's lands held *in capite*, with the office of Constable of his Court," and he is named as a Constable at Stephen's Easter Court in 1136.[3] When he deserted the king in 1139 he is styled by Gervase of Canterbury "princeps militiæ regis" and "summum regis constabularium," but Gervase was not a contemporary writer and he seems to have here developed the statements of the Continuator of Florence, who styles him "constabularius."[4] From Miles the office descended, with his earldom,

---

[1] *History of the Exchequer* (1711), pp. 28-9.
[2] See the authorities cited by Dugdale (*Baronage*, I, 537), and Mr. A. S. Ellis (*Landholders of Gloucestershire*, 1086) ; also Charter Roll 14 Edw. III, m. 13, No. 26, where he is styled "Walterus Constabularius" in a charter of John (1199) to Llanthony.
[3] *Geoffrey de Mandeville*, pp. 262-3.
[4] *Ibid*, pp. 284-5.

through his daughter, to the Bohuns [1], of whom the Duke of Buckingham was heir.

The Duke, however, claimed, we saw, not as such heir in blood, but as the holder of two manors out of the three alleged to be held by this service. But the only one of the three which the family had held as long as the office was that of Haresfield, Glos., and this was held by knight-service. [2]   There was, however, another manor, which has been similarly mentioned, namely that of Caldicot, which, indeed, had been held even in 1086 by 'Durand the sheriff' [3], from whom it passed to his nephew Walter, father of Miles.   Caldicot lay at that time in the very teeth of the Welsh, an outpost of Norman rule.   Its castle, low on the northern shore of the Severn estuary, and slightly in advance of Harold's Portskewet, is of much later date, but the moated mound of its present keep may well have been thrown up by its first Norman lord. [4] Owing to this advanced position, there is a lack of evidence as to its early tenure, so that, perhaps, one cannot actually disprove the statement that it was held by serjeanty : it is alleged to have been held, with Oaksey (Wilts), by the serjeanty of being Constable of England in an *Inq.p.m.* of 3 Edw. I on Humphrey (de Bohun), earl of Hereford. [5]

---

[1] Doubt is thrown on this accepted view in the learned Clarendon Press edition of the *Diologus* (1902), p. 25, but the argument there from the " honor constabulariæ " is wrong, for the Bohuns had nothing to do with it.

[2] *Peerage and Pedigree*, I, 155.

[3] Domesday Book.

[4] See my paper on 'The Castles of the Conquest' in *Archaeologia*.

[5] *Cal. of Inq.* II, No. 131.   In Hazlitt's '*Blount's Tenures*' (p. 56) it is identified as 'Caldecote, co. of Norfolk' and the date wrongly given !

But no other evidence is vouchsafed. The alleged tenure, therefore, seems to be as baseless as was certainly that of the three Gloucestershire manors.

We must now turn to another constableship, which has been somewhat obscured. This is that which was held in succession by Robert de Ver under Henry I and Stephen and by Henry de Essex under Stephen and Henry II until his fall and forfeiture early in the latter reign. I have else-where shewn that this office was brought to Robert de Ver by his wife Adeline (sister of Robert and) daughter of Hugh de Montfort.[1] She brought him, with the office, the great " Honour of Hage-net " (i.e. Haughley, co. Suffolk), held at the time of Domesday by Hugh de Montfort, who was also of note in Kent. After the forfeiture of Henry of Essex, it was also known, in the hands of the Crown, as " Honor Constabulariæ."[2] In this con-nexion I have pointed out that Robert de Montfort, general to William Rufus is styled " strator Nor-mannici exercitus hereditario jure. "

Under Henry II we meet with yet another constableship, that of the D'Oilly family,[3] of which there are traces also at Stephen's accession.[4]

---

[1] *Geoffrey de Mandeville*, pp. 148, 326-7.
[2] See, for instance, the Pipe Rolls of 15 Henry II and 1 Richard I. *Cf.* p. 80 above.
[3] See Eyton's *Court of Henry II* and Salter's *Cartulary of Eynsham* (Oxford Hist. Soc.) I, 75, 77, 78 ; also *Charters in the British Museum*, I, No. 44,
[4] *Geoffrey de Mandeville*, p. 263 ; *Lib. Rub.*, p. 812.

THE MARSHAL

The present high position of this officer of state is due, it appears to me, to several distinct causes. Of these the first is the early disappearance, for all practical purposes, of his original colleague, or, rather, superior officer, [1] the constable.   Another is the survival, to our own times, of some of the functions of his office, such as the marshalling of state ceremonies and the superintendence of the officers of arms, while the functions of his ancient colleagues have become honorary or obsolete. And yet another is its long association with the great house of Howard, standing at the head of the nobility.

Something has been said in the previous section of his function, with the constable, in time of war. It was, however, his special duty to keep the rolls of the Marshalsea recording the performance of service due with the king's host.[2]   Here again we observe the constable's precedence : the ' Marshal's Rolls' of 5 Edw. I and 4 Edw. II name both officers, and the constable comes first.[3]

"The marshal," Stubbs wrote, "is more distinctly an officer of the court, the constable one of the castle or army." [4]   It is with court and coronation service that we are here chiefly concerned.   The

---

[1] See p. 63 above.   It should have been there added that the subordination of the marshal to the constable is asserted by the editors of the Clarendon Press *Dialogus de Scáccario* (1902), p. 24.

[2] See Mr. S. R. Bird's "The Scutage and Marshal's Rolls" in *Genealogist* (N.S.) I, 65-76.

[3] *Cf.* p. 77 above.

[4] *Const. Hist.* I, 354.

one great precedent for the marshal's state service
was the record of Queen Eleanor's coronation in
1236. That service is there stated to consist of (1)
suppressing tumult in the king's 'house'; (2) acting
as quarter-master or billeting officer ; (3) keeping
the gates of the king's hall.[1] The last of these
functions deserves special attention, because it connects the marshal with the 'hall' as apart from the
'chamber'[2] and also because it distinctly constitu-
tes 'usher' service.[3] It was not the marshal, but
the chamberlain,[4] who kept the door of the 'chamber,' although there has been some confusion on
the point. To this day the (earl) marshal and
(lord great) chamberlain have their distinct pro-
vinces—at Westminster, for instance, the Abbey
and the Palace—and there was counter-claiming
between them at the coronation of James II.

Apart from this state service, the marshal had
important functions as a permanent household
officer. To quote from the valuable introduction
to the *Dialogus de Scaccario* :[5]

The marshal has the special duty of witnessing all
expenditure by the king's officials, and keeps accounts by
means of tallies *(dicas)* both of payments out of the
Treasury and Chamber and of other expenditure. This
right of general supervision may be the 'Magisterium in
Curia Regis de Liberatione Prebende' for which John the
Marshal owed forty marks of silver in 31 Henry I.

[1] " cujus est officium tumultus sedare in domo Regis, liberationes
hospitiorum facere, hostia aulæ Regis custodire " (*Lib. Rub.*, p. 757).
[2] See p. 66 above.
[3] See the sections on " Usher of the King's Hall ' (pp. 108-112).
[4] Whose service is entered in the record immediately before the
marshal's. See also ' the Catteshill serjeanty ' below.
[5] Ed. Hughes, Crump, and Johnson (Clarendon Press, 1902), pp. 24-5.

In the Exchequer the staff of this department consists of the constable, his clerk, and the marshal...... The marshal in the Exchequer has the custody of the vouchers...... he keeps the prison of the Exchequer, administers oaths, and delivers the writs of summons to the usher to be served. Originally the marshal of England performed these duties in person, but afterwards they fell into the hands of a clerk......

The marshal had his deputies both in the Exchequer and in the King's Bench; but the marshal of the Common Bench was a deputy of the Marshal of the Exchequer.[1]

I must here differ from the authors of that scholarly work, for I attach a very different and most interesting meaning to the above word 'Prebende'. Apart from its more usual and ecclesiastical meaning, it denoted, in the words of Ducange, " quod ad victum equo praeberi solet. "[2] Now, on the Close Rolls of Edward II we find " hay, oats, and litter " regularly in the charge of the clerk of the marshalsea.[3] The great interest of the connexion I suggest between the marshal and the horses' oats is that, at the coronation of the Emperor,—

Before the palace gate there used to stand a heap of oats to the breast of a horse ; then comes the Duke of Saxony (as Arch-Marshal) mounted, having in his hand a silver wand, and a silver measure stood by, which was to weigh two hundred marks ; he fills the measure, sticking his wand afterwards in the remainder, and so goes to attend the Emperor.[4]

[1] Judges, it will be remembered, still have marshals.

[2] There are cited, as English instances, " Præbendam quotidianam ad duos equos de granario nostro " and " ad præbendandos equos suos et hospitum suorum. "

[3] *e.g.* order to deliver 500 quarters of oats to him (12 Nov. 1307) ; £220 paid by him for hay, oats, and litter " for the maintenance of the King's horses " (April 1312).

[4] Taylor's *Glory of Regality*, pp. 102-3.

The further back we go, the closer seems to be the marshal's connexion with the horse, though it came to be forgotten. I shall have occasion to insist on it when dealing with 'The great spurs'.

Madox, it appears to me, was right in holding that the marshal also appointed "a deputy or clerk to act for him in the Court holden before the king........ called *Marescallus Marescalcie Curiæ Regis.*" [1] This deputy was the marshal " of the household" (*hospicii*), who is named at least as early as the middle of the 13th century. It may be well to explain, as the fact seems little known, that this deputy regularly sat with the steward " of the household " (who was similarly the deputy of the steward of England) in that household court of the king which had jurisdiction over matters within the 'verge' and which became the court of the Lord Steward. Its pleas were known as pleas of the Hall (*Aule*).[2] It is this deputy who appears to have been known eventually as the 'knight marshal'. In the king's 'ordinances' of 31 Hen. VIII (1539-1540) we read " that the Knight Marshall, or his sufficient Deputie, shall give continuall attendance upon the Court, as well to expell all Boyes, Vagabonds, and Rascalls, being

---

[1] *Exchequer* (1711), p. 33. This would be a parallel development to that by which the jurisdiction at Court of the (lord high) steward devolved on his deputy, the 'lord steward.'

[2] See, for instance, the " letters close " " to the steward and marshal of the king's household " in 1318 and their joint mention in 1322 (*Cal. of Close Rolls*, 1318-1323, pp. 16, 471, 590 ; also *City of London Letter Books*, E. pp. 206-7, for " Pleas of the Hall " held at the Tower, 20 July 1325, and *His Grace the Steward*, p. 424 *note*, for " Placita Aule Hospicii Domini Regis... coram seneschallo et marescallo hospicii sui " in Oxford castle early in 1400).

expulsed out of the Court-gates, as all others resorting thither from time to time as occasion shall require."[1]   Here we have the marshal's police functions, described in 1236 as "sedare tumultus."[2] The earlier ' ordinance ' of 17 Hen. VIII (1525- 1526)[3] expressly assigns to " the Knight Marshall and his officers and deputyes...... execution of all such things as shall concerne the office of the marshalshy within the precinct of the verge."

And among others, the same knight marshall shall have speciall respect to the exclusion of boyes and vile persons, and punishment of vagabonds and mighty beggars,...... and semblably he shall take good regard that all such unthrifty and common women as follow the court[4] may be likewise, from time to time, openly punished, banished and excluded, and none of them to be suffered neere thereunto.[5]

The same ' ordinances ' provide, under " marshalls and ushers of the hall," that " the marshalls of the hall shall give their dayly attendance,"[6] and in ' Queen Elizabeth's household book ' (43 Eliz.) we find, among the " officers of the hall, four marshalls, " with the old-world wage of $7\frac{1}{2}$d. a day.

Their place is, under the white staves, to marshall the hall, when her Majestie shall come thither, or when any embassador...... their place in ancient time was, when the hall was kept, to see the Lord Steward, the Treasurer,

---

[1] *Household Ordinances* (Society of Antiquaries), p. 240.
[2] See p. 83 above.
[3] *Ibid.*, p. 150.
[4] See the next section.
[5] *Household Ordinances*, p. 150.
[6] *Ibid.*, p. 143.

etc...... rightly placed in their degrees, and to see good order kept in the hall. [1]

These must be the 'marshal(s)men' who still, of course, remain. In 1689 the 'knight marshall,' Sir Edward Villiers, had £26 a year, and the five "Marshallsmen" £100 a year between them,[2] and he was directed to "suffer no masterless men, or vagrants, or persons that have no dependence upon us or Our family, to shelter themselves in or about Our house."[3] At the coronation of James II it was the Knight Marshall who "proclaimed the Champion's challenge" in Westminster Hall; at that of George III he cleared the way for the champion; and at that of Queen Victoria he rode at the head of the Marshalmen in the procession to the Abbey.[4]

It is evident that the 'harbingers' also had developed out of the marshal's department. Going back to the *Constitutio*,[5] we read

Quatuor Marscalli qui serviunt familiæ Regis, tam clericis quam militibus, quam (etiam) ministris, die qua *faciunt herbergeriam*, vel extra Curiam morantur, etc. etc.[6]

A century later this function was "liberationes hospitiorum facere,"[7] but in 1377 this is rendered "faire liveree des *herbergages*" in the 'marshal'

---

[1] *Ibid.*, p. 293. The knight marshal was then receiving £66. 13.4d. a year (*Ibid.* p. 250).

[2] *Household Ordinances* (Soc. of Ant.), p. 401.

[3] *Ibid.*, p. 420.

[4] He was Sir C. Montolieu Lamb, Bart. (d. 1860), whose father Sir J. Bland Burgess had been granted the office for life with reversion to his son in 1795.

[5] See p. 54 above.

[6] *Lib. Rub.*, p. 812.

[7] See p. 83 above.

petition to the Court of Claims. [1]   As an excellent
illustration of this function, we read that Henry III,
in 1251, " sent forward his marshals to York
to deliver divers inns to divers magnates against
the solemnization of Christmas." [2]   The privilege
of exemption from this billeting was eagerly
sought, and in 1325, when the " serjeant-herber-
geour of the king's household " billeted the King's
secretary on the house of a sheriff of London,
the sheriff removed the chalk mark, and the
City authorities made good their claim that by
charter of Henry III (1268) no one was to take a
hostel within the City " by delivery of the Marshal." [3]
Under Henry VIII this duty was discharged by
the ' Knight Herbinger ' with his staff of ' gentlemen ' and ' yeomen, ' who had always to be " ready
to make lodging and herbigage " by billeting those
entitled to " Lodging " on private houses. [4]   Under
Queen Elizabeth the ' gentleman herbinger ' had
an extra daily allowance, exactly as under Henry I,
" while he is making herbigage, " and finding for
" lordes, ladyes, and chiefe officers, needful men,
necessary lodgeing. [5] "   Finally, under William and
Mary the two " gentlemen harbingers " were still
paid the ancient wage of $7\frac{1}{2}$d. a day. [6]

From the marshal's functions we pass to the
origin and descent of his office.   Into this I have

---

[1] See my *Commune of London*, p. 303.
[2] *Cal. of Pat. Rolls*, 1247-1258, p. 124. *Cf.* pp. 181, 476, 482.
[3] *Letter Book E*, pp. 206-7.   The original charter is preserved at the
Guildhall, and the text is printed in *Liber Custumarum*, I. 259-260 :—
" Nemo capiat hospitium per vim vel per liberationem Marescalli. "
[4] *Household Ordinances.*
[5] *Ibid.*, p. 293.
[6] *Ibid.*, p. 400.

gone so fully in my paper on 'The marshalship of
England'[1] that I need not here repeat what I have
there written. The main point to be kept in
mind is that I have traced to its source, in the
'marshal' petition to the Court of Claims in 1377,
the persistent error that Gilbert 'Mareschall', Earl
of 'Strogoil' (*i. e.* Pembroke) officiated at the
coronation of Henry II (1154). This led to the
mistaken view that the marshalship 'of England'
was derived from one source, and the marshalship
'of the household' from another. I have shown
that by substituting the coronation of Queen Eleanor in 1236 for that of Henry II (1154) all
this error disappears and everything falls into place.

The really governing record is John's charter
(27 April 1200) which proves that a certain Gilbert and John his son made good their claim, in
the court of Henry I, to the chief marshalship
("magistratum maresc' curie nostre")[2] as against
Robert de Venoiz and William de Hastings who
claimed the same office (*ipsum magistratum*). John
had succeeded his father by 1130[3] and duly appears,
as holding the office, in the *Constitutio*.[4] From his
elder son William (Marshal) descended the marshals
of England, and from a younger son the marshals
of Ireland.

Robert de 'Venoiz', though his claim failed,
held a true 'marshal' serjeanty. The family took
its name from Venoix, just to the south-west of

[1] In *The Commune of England and other studies* (1899), pp. 302-318.
[2] *Ibid.*, p. 306.
[3] *Pipe Roll*, 31 Hen. I.
[4] See p. 61 above for this document.

Caen, and was founded in England by Geoffrey
' Marescal ', who is found in Domesday holding at
Eàst Worldham, Hants, and who, as ' Geoffrey ',
also held at Draycot, Wilts.   The above Robert is
duly entered on the Pipe Roll of 1130; and a later
Robert is found holding part of East Worldham
('Verildham') " by service in the king's household
(*hospicio*), that is, by marshalsey (*per mariscaciam*),"
the record adding that " King William gave it to
Geoffrey Marshal (*Mariscallo*)." [1]   It is interesting
to note that a Caen charter of Henry II (1156-
1157) mentions " the marshal of Venoix," as if he
held an office over there. [2]

That the *chief* marshalship was held by serjeanty,
in connexion with Hampstead Marshal, I do not
believe.   Mr. Vernon Harcourt has cited evidence
that it was, [3] and there is earlier evidence to the
same effect. [4]   Indeed, the entry in the *Testa* itself
(1241-1245) is quite compatible with serjeanty. [5]
On the other hand, the manor is not found among
the recognised Berkshire serjeanties; [6] there is no
proof that the marshals held it so early as the days

---

[1] *Testa*, p. 235.   There are several variants of the service, *e.g.* " per
serjant' quod antecessores sui fuerunt marescalli de hospicio domini
Regis " (p. 233), " pro qua debuit portare unam virgam marescalcie per
totum annum in hospicio domini Regis " (p. 239).

[2] See my *Cal. of Documents*, France, p. 157.

[3] " Rogerus Bygot comes Norfolk et marescallus Anglie tenet xx
libratas terre per serjanciam mareschallie in Hamstede " (Assize Rolls,
Berks, 12 Edward I, No. 48).

[4] *Inq. p. m.* on Roger Bigod, earl of Norfolk in 1270 (54 Hen. III) :
" Hamstede......... held of the king in chief by service of the marshal's
wand " (*Cal. of Inq.* I, No. 744).

[5] " Walterus Mar' com. Pembr[oc] manerium de Hamsted ' in dominico suo de marescaugia, et non facit scutagium " (p. 125).

[6] *Lib. Rub.*, p. 451 and *Testa passim*.

of Henry I; and, finally, the *Inq. p. m.* on the last of the Bigod earls (21 December 1306) expressly states that the manor was held by knight service.[1] It was by this earl's surrender that the office, at his death, came to the Crown.

Mr. Legg, in *English Coronation Records*, seems to be much at sea on the descent of the Marshal's office. We find him writing :—

In 1385 Thomas Mowbray, Earl of Nottingham, was made Marshal of England, with the right to call himself Earl Marshal, which led to his descendant claiming the Earl Marshalship at Henry V's coronation. But since then the claim of the Mowbrays has not met with much approval, and in the *Forma et modus* the Earl of Norfolk is certainly said to be Earl Marshal (p. lxx).

And on p. 172 we read, of the *Forma et modus*, that " the marshalship, however, has already passed into the family of the earls of Norfolk ". It was, on the contrary, solely due to the claim of their Mowbray ancestors that the office of earl marshal was obtained by the Howards (1483 and 1510) and Berkeleys (1486), their co-heirs ; nor could it pass " into the family of the earls of Norfolk, " for the excellent reason that there were no such earls when the *Forma et modus* was composed [2] and that there were not any, afterwards, till 1644 !

Although the marshalship was first associated at so early a date with the family of Howard, the existing Earl Marshalship held by the Dukes of Norfolk is no older than 1672. The important

---

[1] " tenuit manerium de Hampstede Mareschal....... per servicium feodi unius militis " (35 Edw. I, No. 46 A).

[2] According to Mr. Legg's date.

functions of the Earl Marshal, especially in connexion with a coronation, are matters of common
knowledge.

A MARSHALSHIP AT COURT

Between the King's marshals it is not easy to
distinguish. Even in the days of the *Constitutio*
the marshal's department (*Mareschaucia*) [1] had four
marshals as well as the master marshal ; but as the
latter only is mentioned by name [2] we do not know
if these included the office dealt with in this
section. It obviously falls, however, within the
marshal's province. [3]

About the middle of the 12th century, if not
indeed rather earlier, Robert Doisnel was holding
at least five manors by the service of performing
its duties. Later evidence enables us to make this
statement. His daughter Juliane, inheriting his
office and his land, was given in marriage by
Henry II to one of his trusted stewards (*dapiferi*),
William Fitz Audelin. This we learn from William's *Carta* in 1166. [4] Styling himself the King's
Marshal [5] (*Marescallus*), he claimed that he held all
the land of Robert Doisnel which had not been
subinfeudated " per servitium suum sine aliquo [6]
servitio nominato [7] sicut Marscaucia [8] Regis." His

---

[1] The word still exists, as *Maréchaussée*, in French.
[2] *Liber Rubeus*, p. 812 and p. 89 above.
[3] See p. 86 above.
[4] *Lib. Rub.*, p. 209.
[5] This must have been in right of his wife.
[6] ' alio ' in Black Book.
[7] This I take to mean that no part of it was charged with a quota of
service.
[8] " de Marescalcia " in Black Book.

wife, having no children by him, gave her estate at Little Maplestead [1] to the Hospitallers by a charter addressed " omnibus hominibus et amicis suis Francis et Anglis. " [2]   Of her gift there is still a tangible memorial in the round church erected at Little Maplestead by the brethren.

By her death the succession opened to her collateral heirs, William de Warberton (*i.e.* Warblington) and Enguerrand de Munceaus (*i.e.* Monceaux). In 1199 they undertake to give the king no less than 500 marcs for the heirship. [3]   By a fresh arrangement in 1204 William pays for obtaining possession of his land of " Shirefield, Cumpton, Tieuresham, and Angr'. " [4]   But in 1205 there is an important payment of 100 marcs by Waleram " de Munceaus " for his reasonable share of the inheritance of Juliane as against William de Warberton, saving to the said William his rights as the elder coheir. [5]   And the sheriff is thereupon directed to apportion the inheritance accordingly. [6]

These details may appear wearisome, but they bear on a point of some importance. [7]   It would seem from the case before us that there was a third alternative to partition and impartibility. [8]   " A tenement held by serjeanty " has been insufficiently

---

[1] " totam villam meam de Mapletrestede. "

[2] The text is printed in a note to Morant's *History of Essex*.

[3] *Rot. de Obl. et Fin.*, p. 19.

[4] *Ibid.*, p. 217.

[5] " quod una medietas illius hereditatis remanet predicto Willelmo *cum esnetia.*" *(Ibid.*, p. 310.) For 'esnetia' see p. 38.

[6] " Faciat partitionem de terra que fuit ipsius Juliane in Sirefeld' et in Cumtone secundum formam prescriptam" *(Ibid.).*

[7] See p. 38 above.

[8] See p. 42.

distinguished from the actual performance of the
office by which the land was held. For the land
itself, as in this case, might be, and was, partitioned,
although the *esnetia* was retained by the elder co-
heir [1] and might possibly carry with it the actual
performance of the office.

The clue to the identity of the lands belonging
to this serjeanty is afforded by William's payment
in 1204.[2] The four manors there named are
Sherfield upon Loddon and Compton in King's
Somborne, Hants, Teversham, Cambs., and Little
(or High) Ongar, Essex. All these can be duly
connected with the marshal's service by records.
In the *Red Book* (p. 460) the serjeanty appears as if
divided :—

Willelmus de Warblintone per marescauciam in domo
regis. Waleram de Muncellis tenet per idem servitium.

In the *Testa* we have fuller information. On
p. 232 the serjeanty is said to be " of the old feoffment, " [3] that is, created previous to the death of
Henry I. Similar to the *Red Book* entries are those
on p. 235 :—

Willelmus de Warblinton tenet Scirefeld per serjant'
marescalcie in domo Regis.
Waler[am] de Munceus tenet cum (*sic*) Cumpton per
serjant' Marescaucie.

[1] " Willelmo plenam saisinam habere faciat (vicecomes) de medietate
predictarum terrarum cum esnetia, et de alia medietate predicto Waleram', et qualiter illam particionem fecerit, et quis eorum quam porcionem habuerit domino Regi scire faciat per litteras suas. " (*Rot. de Obl.*,
p. 310.)
[2] See above.
[3] "Thomas de Warblington tenet Syrfeld per serjant' marescall' de
domino R. de veteri feoffamento, sed nescitur per quem."

Here we see the result of the partition. Again we have another version on p. 237 :—

Willemus de Warbelington tenet Silefeld (*sic*) de domino R. per serjant' marescaucie domini R. et valet x *li.*, et ipse eam tenet hereditarie.

Terra Willelmi de Montellis (*sic*) in villa de Cumpton pertinet ad marescauciam domini Regis et respondet Willelmo de Warblinton de x libris.

Finally, the *Inq. p.m.* on William de Monceaux (*Muncellis*), in 27 Henry III, states that —

Compton Manor was held by the said William of Thomas de Warblington by service of $\frac{1}{3}$ knight's fee ; the manor pertains to Sirefeld manor, which the said Thomas holds of the king in chief by serjeanty. [1]

Here we have the senior co-heir holding of the king by serjeanty, and the junior alleged to hold of him by knight-service.

So far we have been dealing with the two Hampshire manors, but there were others, we have seen, in another part of England. The Teversham manor is found among the Cambridgeshire serjeanties in the *Testa* (p. 358) :—

xx libratæ terre quas Willelmus filius Adelin tenuit in villa de Tevresham per serjant' marescalcie sunt escaete domini R. in custodia S[tephani] de Turnham.

But the *Red Book* entry takes us further :—

Willelmus de Warbintone x libratas in Teveresham, quæ fuit Willelmi filii Audelini, per serjanteriam (p. 530).

So also, the *Testa* enters the Essex manor :—

Willelmus de Munceus tenet Parvam Ang' de domino R. de Mareschaucie, que fuit de baronia Gilberti de Tani (p. 269).

---

[1] *Cal. of Inq., Hen. III*, No. 12.

Here again we have the manors, though alleged to belong to the serjeanty, divided between the co-heirs.   To these manors must be added, as part of Juliane's inheritance, that of Little Maplestead.[1] It is a notable fact that all three were held by John son of Waleram in 1086,[2] for there are indications that Juliane may have been among his representatives.[3]

In that case there has been confusion of these manors in the east of England with those in Hampshire, which had not been John's, and which had probably been given to be held by this serjeanty.

It is only from later evidence that we learn the actual nature of that marshalship in the King's household which constituted this serjeanty.   As an illustration of court life and of those police functions which were part of a marshal's duty,[4] it is too curious to be omitted.   Madox, who placed it at the head of his " Grand Serjeanties *in capite*, " showed, by the record he[5] cited, that the details must have been given when the serjeanty was arrented in 1250[6], although we do not find it among

---

[1] See p. 93 above.

[2] There is reason to believe that the knight's fee " in Essex" which was held of William Fitz Audelin *(jure uxoris)* in 1166 by Baldwin Wiscard *(Lib. Rub.*, p. 209) was yet another, *viz.* Old Saling, which was held of John Fitz Waleram by Turstin (Wiscard), his tenant at Greenstead by Colchester, in 1086.

[3] She may have inherited her name from that " Juliana uxor Willelmi de Hastings" who appears under Essex on the Pipe Roll of 1130 as owing £7 " de veteri auxilio militum Waler[anni] avi sui" (p. 58).

[4] " Cujus est officium tumultus sedare in domo Regis...... hostia aulæ Regis custodire." A.D. 1236 *(Lib. Rub.*, p. 759).

[5] *Baronia Anglica*, p. 242.

[6] " Sicut continetur inter serjantias arrentatas per Robertum Passelewe anno xxxiiii Regis H."

the Hampshire arrentations in the *Testa*. But the
earliest published record is that of Blount from a
plea of 8 Edw. I (1279-1280) :—

> Johannes de Windreshull tenet manerium de Shyre-
> feud...... per serjantiam inveniendi unum serjantum ad
> custodiendum meretrices in exercitu domini Regis. [1]

Madox, who did not mince matters, cited in full
the record from the Fine Roll for Easter 1 Edw. III,
from which Blount had made an extract. From
this it appears that John de Warblinton, who then
made a fine of ten marcs for his relief, had succeeded in 10 Edw. II (1316-7) his father Thomas, [2]
who held

> per serjantiam essendi marescallus de meretricibus in
> hospitio Regis, et dismembrare (*sic*) malefactores adjudi-
> catos, et mensurare (*sic*) galones et bussellos in hospitio
> Regis.

It has indeed been contended by Blount and
others after him that *meretricum* here merely meant
laundresses (*lotricum*). The two terms, however,
would not be mutually exclusive, [3] and when one
finds, in the case of the companion serjeanty, that
Catteshill was alleged to be held " per serjantiam
marescalli duodecim puellarum quæ sequuntur
curiam domini Regis, " all doubt is removed on

[1] He was in charge of the manor at this date, but handed it over to
Thomas de Warblington in 1281.
[2] See also *Cal. of Inq.*, VI, No. 42, where John acknowledges
14 March, 10 Edw. II, that he holds "by serjeanty of Marshalcy,
carrying a wand in the King's guesthouse (*hospicio*) when required."
The rendering " guesthouse " is wrong.
[3] If one may venture to quote Goldsmith,—
    " The chest contrived a double debt to pay,
    A bed by night, a chest of drawers by day."

comparing this entry with the very curious record
cited by Ducange :—

Et si soloit estre que le Marescal devoit avoir douze
damoisellez a la Court le Roy, que devoient faire seire-
ment à son Bacheler que elles ne sauveroient aultres
putains a la court qu'elles mesmes ne ribaudes sans
avowerie de altre ; ne laron ne mesel, qu'elles ne les
monstreront au Marescal.

It was a strange result of the serjeanty system
that Juliane must have held, as lady of the manor,
this office in her own right, and that Edeline de
Broc must have similarly held that which was
associated with Guildford.[1]   The Sherfield service
is duly found in Inquisitions on the death of suc-
cessive holders, actually appearing for the last time
as late as the days of James I (1603-4).   Unlike,
however, the marshalship of the hawks, this service
does not appear to have ever formed the subject of
a coronation claim.

THE CATTESHILL SERJEANTY

This Serjeanty is at once notorious because of
the service occasionally attributed to its tenure and
of some importance as forming the subject of a
coronation claim.   Catteshill adjoins Godalming
in Surrey and the story told by the jurors of
Godalming Hundred in 1212 is this :—

Henricus Rex senior dedit Cateshull Dyvo Porcell
patri Radulfi *(sic)* de Broc et Henricus Rex (II) pater
domini Regis fecit cartam suam Radulfo de Broc tenere

---

[1] See the section on "The Catteshill Serjeanty."

de eo *per serjanciam hostiarum de camera domini Regis* ut de R[ege ?] et post mortem ejusdem Randulfi Stephanus de Turneham habuit predictam villam cum filia ipsius Randulfi per predictum servicium (*Testa*, p. 225).

It is in the first place difficult to imagine what name is represented by "Dyvo," and, in the second, difficult to believe that this Porcell was father of Ralf (*sic*) de Broc. An entry however, on the Pipe Roll of 1130 gives us a sure starting-point. On p.50 we read :—

Gaufridus porcell(us) redd. comp. de xx marc. arg. pro terra patris sui de Gateshela.

Clearly then, in 1130, Geoffrey Porcel had succeeded his father in possession of Catteshill, which, therefore, had been severed from the royal manor of Godalming. This Geoffrey appears to have given a hide of land at Windsor to Reading Abbey, the great foundation of Henry I, and to have there taken the cowl. His gift was confirmed by the Empress and then by Henry II. [1]

I suspect that, in the *Testa* entry above, we should read, "patri Radulfi *Purcel*," for in a Charter assigned by Eyton to 1155, Henry II granted to Ralf Purcel, his usher, the office of Robert Burnel, his uncle. [2]   A Ralf Purcel had remission of Dane-

---

[1] *Testa*, p. 128.
[2] *Cart. Ant.*, F. 19.   Robert Burnel duly appears on the Pipe Roll of 1130 as excused payment of his Danegeld under Oxfordshire, Stafford-hire, Northants, and Bucks, which accords with his being the holder of some office or serjeanty. It should be added that in 1210 Ralf Purcel is entered, under Buckinghamshire, as giving the King £10 "pro habendo officio suo in hospicio domino Regis secundum cartam Henrici Regis et confirmacionem domini Regis super hoc" (*Rot. de Obl.*, p. 83).

geld on five hides in Surrey in 1156.[1]   It seems
to have been another Ralf Purcel who had such
remission on five hides in Staffs,[2] and who was
holding two thirds of a fee of Robert de Stafford
in 1166,[3] for this holding was in Shareshull and is
found in the hands of the Porcels, his heirs.

Very possibly Randulf de Broc, who was in
favour with Henry II,[4] secured Catteshill, as he
did other lands in the neighbourhood, by grant of
Henry II and not by inheritance.   He left four
or five daughters, of whom Edelina, the eldest[5] was
married to Stephen de Turnham, a Kentish land-
owner.[6]   In 1206 this Stephen bought from the
King (1) his confirmation of £15 of rent in
" Ertendune " with the Hundred etc., which Henry
II had given him to hold in fee farm at £15 a year,
a tenure which Richard I had changed to half a
knight's fee, and (2) his confirmation for himself
and his wife Edeline, daughter of Randulf de Broc,
of the grant and confirmation by Henry II to the
said Randulf his usher and marshal (" hostiario et
marescallo suo ")[7] of the whole land and office of
his (Randulf's) father of whomsoever held and of
all the land held in Guildford which belonged to

[1] *Pipe Roll, 2 Hen. II*, p. 12.

[2] *Ibid.*, p. 29.

[3] *Liber Rubeus*, p. 267.

[4] He came into prominence in the Becket quarrel by being put in
charge of the possessions of the See of Canterbury.

[5] *Cal. of Inq. Henry III*, Nos. 317, 365.

[6] Son of the founder of Combwell Abbey. Dugdale (*Baronage*, I, 663)
confused him with Stephen " de Turonis, " which misled Foss (*Judges*,
II, 120) and Stubbs.   A valuable note on Stephen de Marçai (*Turo-
nensis* or *de Turonibus*) will be found in Meyer, *Guillaume le Maréchal*,
III, 95.

[7] This double office will be dealt with below.

Reginald de Resting', his kinsman,[1] etc. This
important record helps us to clear up much confusion between the Catteshill serjeanty, which was
that (we shall find) of usher,[2] and the Guildford
serjeanty, which was that of marshal. The Catteshill serjeanty had, we find, an important outlying
portion at (New) Windsor itself. In 1212 its
constable made return that :—

Stephanus de Turnham tenet Walenton scilicet duas
partes unius carucate terre et xxvij solid' terre de redditu
assise, per uxorem suam filiam Randulfi de Broc, per
serjantiam custodiendi ostium camere. [3]

A later entry shows us Adam de Stawell holding
one hide in " Waleton[4] per serjant' custodiendi
hostium domini Regis. "[5]

Early in the reign of Henry III Edelina " del
Brok, " duly appears as holding Cateshill by the
serjeanty "servandi hostium camer' domini Regis. "[6]
She was then a widow, Stephen having died about
the end of John's reign. [7] She left by Stephen five
daughters and co-heirs,[8] but the Cateshill serjeanty
again passed to the eldest of these, Mabel, who
married first, Robert de Gatton, and then Thomas

---

[1] *Rot. de Obl. et Fin.*, p. 193.
[2] *i. e.* of the 'chamber', not of the 'hall'.
[3] *Testa*, p. 129.
[4] A marginal note adds " in villa de Wyndelsor. "
[5] *Ibid.* p. 108, *Cf.* p. 124, where it appears as " in Nova Wyndeles...
unam hidam per serjant' de baronia Randulfi de Broc. " The index,
as so often, is here sadly deficient.
[6] *Testa*, p. 227.
[7] *Rot. Pip.*, 16 John.
[8] Dugdale, *Baronage*, I, 663.

de Bavelingham. [1] By Robert she had a son and heir, Hamo de Gatton. [2]

Meanwhile the tenure had been complicated by accretion of inheritance. In the winter of 1170-1171, Master David of London was despatched to Rome, on the Becket business, as an envoy of the King and the Bishop of London. He was rewarded by a grant of land in Artington in the royal manor of Godalming, with £15 a year. [3] This land was secured from him by Randulf de Broc in fee-farm for that sum [4] and thenceforth descended with Catteshill.

Randulf also secured from Henry II the wardship of Roger Testard's heir, who held some land in Guildford, and afterwards obtained the land, which descended with his eldest daughter to Stephen de Turnham, held " per servicium marescauciæ. " [5] This holding was quite correctly entered, in her widowhood, as held by her separately " per mariscallem in curia domini regis. " For Catteshill she owed service as usher ; for her Guildford lands service as " marshal. " This is further proved by the arrentation in 1250 of "Richard Testard's Serjeanty in Guildford" as it is expressly termed. [6] It is very important to observe that the duties of

---

[1] See *Bracton's Note Book*, Cases 1171, 1410, 1765.

[2] *Ibid.*, Case 1171.

[3] *Pipe Roll*, 17 *Henry II*, and *Testa*, p. 225.

[4] *Testa*, p. 225.

[5] *Ibid.* She was impleaded for this land by William Testard in 1217 (*Bracton's Note Book*, Case 1347).

[6] " Serjantia Ricardi Testard in Geldeford pro qua debuit esse marescall' in hospicio domini Regis, et dismembrare malefactores in hospicio domini Regis adjudicatos, et mensurare gallones et bussellos in hospicio domini Regis " (*Testa*, p. 228).

this office, as there recorded, are precisely similar to those of the marshalship connected with Sherfield upon Loddon, as we have seen in the section "A Marshalship at Court." As for this Guildford Serjeanty, the result of its arrentation was that the service was changed to that of a knight's fee.[1]

Here I break off for a moment to glance at yet another holding, which had come in through Randulf's wife Damietta in 1204-5.[2] This was 'Frollebury' in Hampshire. We find Stephen de Turnham entered as holding it in right of his wife (Edelina) " per serjantiam custodiendi hostium domini Regis, "[3] and she herself subsequently held it as " Edelina de Frolebir'," by a service recorded in the same words.[4] As this land came to her from her mother, and not from her father, who held Catteshill by that service, one is tempted to suggest that these entries were due to a very possible confusion with her Catteshill serjeanty.

To such confusion, clearly, is due the substitution of the " marshal " service, due for the Guildford holding, for the " usher " service due for Catteshill, the former being further defined in terms which made it notorious.[5] There would seem to have

---

[1] Et dictus Ricardus faciat servicium feodi unius militis pro parte sua quam tenet. " *Cf.* pp. 17, 28 above.

[2] Close Roll, 6 John.

[3] *Testa*, p. 235.

[4] *Ibid.*, p. 236.

[5] Blount cited entries from Plea Rolls that Robert de Gatton held Catteshill "per serjantiam Marescalli duodecim puellarum quæ sequuntur curiam domini Regis, " and that Hamo de Gatton held it " per serjantiam ut erit Marescallus meretricum cum dominus Rex venerit in partibus illus. " Hamo is also said to be described as " mareschallus de communibus fœminibus, sequentibus hospitium domini Regis. " (' Esch.

been similar confusion in the case of another usher
serjeanty, that of the Delameres, for Henry de la
Mara (or " de Mara ") is returned as holding in
Oxfordshire " eodem modo (*i. e.* " ut sit hostiarius
Regis ") et quod servet meretrices " (*Lib. Rub.*,
p. 456), or simply " per sergentiam custodiendi
meretrices sequentes curiam Domini Regis " [1]
(*Testa*, p. 107).   Another and a curious instance
of confusion is found in the *Red Book* version of
the 1212 returns, where we read, under Surrey
serjeanties, of Edelina's husband :—

> Stephanus de Turneham tenet in Cateshull per servi-
> tium mappariœ *(sic)* et iiij libratas in Gudeford per servi-
> tium mareskalsiæ. [2]

How Catteshill came to be returned as held by
napery service it is impossible to say.

The Catteshill serjeanty figured in a claim to
prerogative wardship by the Crown[3] of which there
is a record in the *Red Book*, the editor dating it
for reasons only known to himself '*Circ.* 1275.' [4]
Earl Gilbert (de Clare) claimed the wardship of the
heirs of Geoffrey de Lucy " recently deceased, "
then in the King's hands, on the ground that
Geoffrey had held of him by knight-service[5] and

---

29 Edw. n. 58') See, for further discussion of the point, Blount's *Tenures*,
Ed. 1815, p. 210-214 ; Ed. 1874, pp. 126-8.

[1] This will be dealt with in the section on " The usher of the King's
Hall "(p. 110).

[2] *Liber Rubeus*, p. 561.

[3] See p. 35 above.

[4] It is obviously subsequent to the death of Geoffrey de Lucy in 1284.

[5] Richard de Lucy had held one knight's fee of the Honour of Clare
in 1166 (*Lib. Rub.*, p. 403), but the holding by a former Geoffrey of
four knight's fees, in Bucks, of the Honour of Gloucester (*Ib.* p. 536),
more probably accounts for the claim.

held nothing *in capite* of the Crown. Thereupon the Treasurer and Barons of the Exchequer were ordered to examine its rolls and see if and what Geoffrey or his predecessors had held in chief. They made the extraordinary report that, according to the rolls, Ranulf de " Broke " had held the Catteshill serjeanty and had left two daughters and co-heirs, Edeliva (*sic*) and Juliana, who succeeded on his death to all his possessions, and did homage for them to the Crown. They added that on the (Pipe) Roll of 9 John (1207) they found Geoffrey de Lucy, grandfather of the late Geoffrey, paying 3000 marcs (£2000) for marrying Juliana de " Broke, " then the childless widow of Peter de Stoke, with all her inheritance.[1]

The whole of this alleged connexion with the Catteshill serjeanty, on which was based the claim to prerogative wardship, was sheer fiction. Edelina had no younger sister named Juliana, but she had several younger sisters whom this report ignores.[2]

The Pipe Roll of 9 John and the Fine Roll of that year do prove the payment of £2000 by Geoffrey for Juliana, widow of Peter de Stokes, and a suit of 1217 shows Geoffrey and his wife Juliana bringing an action for the advowson of Wigginton (Herts) as her right.[3] She claimed as, maternally, granddaughter and heir of Eva " del

---

[1] " Ranulphus de Broke tenuit de rege in capite manerium de Catteshulle in com. Surr. per serjantiam custodiendi hostium Cameræ Regis : qui quidem Ranulphus habuit duas filias, Edelivam scilicet et Julianam, quæ, mortuo eodem Ranulpho, successerunt eidem tanquam filiæ et hæredes, " etc. etc.

[2] See the *Inq. p.m.* on her sister Sibyl, in 1254 and 1256 cited above.

[3] *Bracton's Note Book*, Case 1336.

Broc " by her husband Walter " de Chesneto."
This was clearly that Walter ' de Caisneio, ' who
was holding five fees of the Earl of Gloucester in
1166, [1] and who married Eva, daughter of Eustace
" del Broc. " [2]

The earl, however, did not challenge this un-
founded statement. He contented himself with
stating that the late Geoffrey de Lucy had held
none of the lands which Juliana had held *in capite*,
either at Catteshill or anywhere else. And he
added the strange assertion that Robert de Vere,
earl of Oxford, was " in seisin of doing the service
of the aforesaid serjeanty and had been seised thereof
at the King's coronation, [3] where he, and not
Geoffrey, performed the said service. " After a
full hearing it was decided that, as Geoffrey himself
had been in the King's wardship, by virtue of the
homage done to Henry III by his father, and had
died a homager of the King, the wardship belonged
to the King, by reason of the said homage, " even
though Geoffrey held nothing of the aforesaid
serjeanty or of the other holdings which his grand-
mother (*avia*) Juliana or his other predecessors had
held of the King *in capite*. " [4]

One fact at least here emerges definitely. We
are dealing with three Geoffreys in succession, not,
as was assumed by Dugdale (followed by Blaaw [5]

---

[1] *Lib. Rub.*, p. 289.

[2] *Eynsham Cartulary* (Oxford Hist. Soc.) I, 79, 80.

[3] *i.e.* in 1274. This is a noteworthy assertion in view of the fact
that we know so little of that coronation, and that the earl who made it
would have been present. But the earl of Oxford did not hold Catteshill and cannot have claimed this serjeanty.

[4] *Lib. Rub.*, p. 1014.

[5] *Barons' War* (1871), p. 112.

and others), with two only.[1] The Geoffrey de
Lucy who supported John in the great struggle
for the Charter, was the grandfather, not the father
of the Geoffrey who joined the barons' party against
Henry III and whom Simon de Montfort included
among those whom he could safely summon to
Parliament in 1264. As these Lucys were important people, with lands in eight counties, and played,
we have seen, a part in history, the correction is
worth making.

It was the coronation of Richard II, for which
we have our first great record of a court of claims,
which raised the question whether the " usher "
service due from the Catteshill serjeanty concerned
a coronation. Nicholas Hering, steward of the
King's lands in Kent and holder of Catteshill in
right of his wife, a descendant of the Gattons,
claimed to act as usher of the King's Chamber.
His claim was unsuccessful, and rightly so, no
doubt, on the ground that this ushership was not
a coronation service.[2] As a matter of fact, at the
Queen's Coronation in 1236 which formed the great
precedent, the ushership of the King's Hall appears
as the Marshal's,[3] and that of the King's Chamber
as the Chamberlain's.[4] It was this office which
must have been discharged by the earl of Oxford,
as Great Chamberlain, at the Coronation of Edward
I, when the Earl of Gloucester had supposed him

---

[1] *Baronage*, I, 566-7.
[2] In the *Const. dom. Reg.* there is an usher of the Chamber (*hostiarius
cameræ*) who received fourpence a day " ad lectum regis " when the
King was travelling (*Lib. Rub.*, 813).
[3] " hostia aulæ regis custodire " (*Lib. Rub.*, p. 759).
[4] " custodia cameræ et hostii " *(Ibid.).*

to be acting as holder of the Catteshill serjeanty. This, therefore, is a good example of an office which was discharged on ordinary occasions by a mere tenant in serjeanty, but which, on Coronation day, fell to an officer of State.   In spite, however, of the failure of the claim, it was revived by Sir George Moore, as owner of Catteshill manor, more than two centuries later, at the coronation of James I.   No decision was then given.

THE USHER OF THE KING'S HALL (1) [1]

This was a fairly important serjeanty, for its lands lay in three counties.   Its holders were a family of De la Mere (or De La Mare), a name which was not rare and which does not imply the common origin of all those who bore it.   In addition, for instance, to this family, which held by serjeanty its lands in Oxfordshire, Gloucestershire and Wiltshire, there was another family of the same name, lords of Fisherton Delamere, which held lands by knight-service in the same three counties.

The former's lands were at Alvescote and Middle Aston, Oxon, Winterbourne Gunnor and Laverstoke, Wilts, and Windrush, Glos.   The last of these was held in Domesday by an English thegn, Chetel ; the rest by another English thegn, " Saricus. "   The service due is variously stated, but " the serjeanty of being usher (or chief usher) of the door of the king's hall " appears to have

[1] See p. 83 above.

formed its main feature.[1]   The same version is
given in the record of " arrentation " under Windrush,[2] and under Alvescote.[3]   Gunnor, however, is
said, in a return for Bampton Hundred, to hold
Alvescote by the service of keeping (by deputy)
the door of the king's bedchamber.[4]   Nevertheless
Henry de la Mare holds at Alvescote as usher of
the hall[5] and, in another place, as usher simply.[6]
The word " usher " has changed its meaning and
we no longer associate it with the keeper of the
door (*huis-huissier*).   The Scottish " door-ward,"[7]
being formed from the English, not the French, is
more explicit.

The arrentation, however, of Winterbourne records Gunnor's service as that of keeping the
King's brushwood and litter[8] and changes it to that
of half a knight's fee for the lands in the three
counties which had not been alienated.[9]   Henry de

---

[1] See the Inquisitions on Gunnor de la Mare—the lady from whom
Winterbourne Gunnor derives its name—in 1249 and 1250 (*Cal. of
Inq.*, vol. 1).

[2] " Debuit esse hostiar[ius] de aula domini Regis " (*Testa*, p. 78).

[3] " Debuit esse hostiaria *(sic)* in aula (or de aula) domini Regis."
(*Ibid.*, pp. 114 & 115).

[4] " Per serjentiam inveniendi unum militem ad custod' hostium
thalami Regis." (*Ibid.*, p. 108) or " hostiarium ad hostium thalami, "
etc. (*Ibid.*).

[5] " Per serjentiam custodiendi ostium aule domini Regis. " (*Ibid.*,
p. 106).

[6] He is entered as holding Alvescote and Middle Aston " per serjant'
de esse hostiar' domini Regis "... " per servicium custodiendi hostium
domini Regis. " (Ibid., p. 118).

[7] More familiar in the surname " Durward. "

[8] " pro qua debuit custodire buscam et literam domini Regis" (*Testa*,
pp. 146, 147).

[9] " Et ipsa Gunnora faciat servicium dimidii feodi unius militis pro
parte sua quam tenet, tam in com. Oxon' et Glouc' quam in com' predicto, que non est alienata. "   *Cf.* p. 28 above.

la Mare also is in one place entered as holding Winterbourne by the service of being " marshal of the
litter " [1] although in another the record makes him
hold " ut sit hostiarius Regis. " [2]   Under Oxfordshire, again, in one entry he is shown as holding at
(Middle) Aston " per sergentiam custodiendi meretrices sequentes curiam domini Regis," [3] although in
another he holds there by usher service. [4]   All this
is a further warning of the caution needed in
accepting such statements as these.

THE USHER OF THE KING'S HALL (2)

The special feature of this serjeanty is that we
can trace it clearly back to Domesday Book itself
(1086).   Among the King's serjeants (*servientes
regis*) of Somerset entered in that record, we find
John the Usher (*hostiarius*) holding " Pegens, "
" Peri, " " Wincheberie, " and " Hustille, " while
" Newetune " and " Candetone " are held of him
by under-tenants. [5]   Four out of these six places
we recognise among the lands named as held by
his representative, Richard of Wigborough, in
1250, by usher service.

When the great inquest into tenures was made
in 1212, this serjeanty was held by a lady, Ellen
the (female) usher (*hostiaria*).   She was returned
as holding Wigborough [6] and her other lands in

---

[1] " Marescallus domini Regis de litera " (p. 143).
[2] *Ibid.*, p. 143.
[3] *Testa*, p. 107.   Cf. p. 104 above.
[4] *Ibid.*, p. 118.
[5] D. B., I. 98b.
[6] In South Petherton.

Somerset by usher service. [1]   A few years earlier
she had, as Helen " Hostiaria " daughter of William
the usher (*Hostiarius*), made an agreement with the
prior of Bruton concerning the oratory at Wigborough. [2]   Her father, whose name is thus given us,
appears as a benefactor of Montacute Priory in a
charter of John as Count of Mortain (1189-1199),
which records his gift, as William "Hostiarius," of
messuages in Hunstile (in Goathurst), [3] one of John
the usher's Domesday holdings.   This is entered in
the *Testa* (p. 172) as an alienation from the serjeanty.

Early in the reign of Henry III, William's
daughter is entered as Ellen " de Wikeberg, " who
is married to Eustace de Doveliz and holds her
lands at Wigborough and " Peggenesse " [4] by serjeanty of being usher of the King's door. [5]   A plea
roll of 1243 records Eustace as holding in both
places *jure uxoris* by serjeanty that he should be
usher in the hall of our lord the king. [6]   The son
and heir of Ellen was Richard the usher ('Arussir'), [7]
otherwise Richard de Wigborough, in whose time
the serjeanty was " arrented, " being then (1250)
described as that of " usher of the great hall. " [8]
Only the alienations were " arrented ; " the service
remained. [9]   Richard died in 1270, holding " by

[1] " Per hostiaritatem " (*Testa*, p. 162).
[2] *Bruton Cartulary* (Som. Rec. Soc.), No. 165.
[3] *Montacute Cartulary* (Som. Rec. Soc.), No. 13.
[4] Horsey Pignes in Bridgwater.
[5] " Per serjantiam ussar' ostii domini Regis " (*Ibid.*, p. 167).
[6] *Somerset Pleas* (Som. Rec. Soc.), Nos. 1127, 1128.
[7] *Cal. of Inq.*, I, No. 885.
[8] "pro qua debuit esse hostiar' domini Regis de Magna Aula per
totum annum " (*Testa*, pp. 171, 173).
[9] " Et faciet servicium consuetum predictum " (*Ibid.*, p. 171).

service of being usher of the king's hall," [1] and was succeeded by his son William.   In 1284-5 William is recorded as holding Wigborough by serjeanty of being usher in the king's hall and " Pegenesse " by an arrented payment of 40s. [2]

In 1324 a William de Wigborough died and was found to have held the same lands by the same service.   He was succeeded by his brother Richard. [3]

THE CHAMBERLAIN

It would have excited considerable surprise, had it been generally known that in 1901 the late Lord Ancaster formally petitioned the Court of Claims that, as Lord Great Chamberlain, he might

have livery and lodging in the King's court at all times, and bring to His Majesty on the day of His Majesty's Royal Coronation His Majesty's shirt, [4] stockings, and drawers : that your Petitioner, together with the Lord Chamberlain of the Household [5] for the time being may dress His Majesty in all his apparel on that day : and that your Petitioner may have all profits and fees thereunto belonging, viz. forty yards of crimson velvet for his robes against the day of His Majesty's Coronation, together with the bed wherein the King lays (sic) the night previous to the Coronation, with all the vallances and curtains thereof, [6] and all the cushions and clothes within the chamber, together with the furniture of the same, and also the night robe of the King wherein his

---

[1] Cal. of Inq., Hen. III, No. 754.

[2] Feudal Aids., IV, 277.

[3] Cal. of Inq., VI, No. 596.

[4] It was similarly the privilege of the Grand Chambellan, in France, to bring the King his shirt at his Levée.

[5] i.e. his permanent deputy at court (see pp. 7, 85 above).

[6] A ' four-poster ' is here assumed.

Majesty rested the night previous to the Coronation, and likewise to serve His Majesty with water on the said day of His Royal Coronation and to have the basins and towels and the cup of assay for his fee.

And yet the form of this petition was in strict accordance with precedent and with the almost Chinese conservatism which regulates these matters.

Had not the Earl of Lindsey, Lord Ancaster's predecessor, solemnly petitioned the Court of Claims, two centuries before, that he might enter the chamber of his " Tresredoubte seigneuresse " Queen Anne, before she rose, on coronation day, and bring her " sa chemise et ses base et privie draps " and dress her, and receive all the fees, including " le nuite Robe de la Reyne "? [1] But, grotesque as these survivals may, at first sight, appear, it is one of the objects of this work to explain the light they throw on the ways of a remote past. It has been suggested above [2] that the king's 'chamber' may have been at first his bedchamber, and that the fees of the 'chamberlain' preserve the memory of the fact. To make their meaning clear, we must glance at other chamberlains and at the fees which they received. The queen consort's chamberlain, we shall find, received her bed and basins " and the other things that belong to the chamberlain ; " and the archbishop of Canterbury's chamberlain received, at his enthronization, the bed, the ewer and the basin. [3]

[1] His father had acutely claimed " les nuyte Robes le Roy et la Reigne " at the previous coronation, William and Mary being joint sovereigns.

[2] See pp. 67-8.

[3] Bartholomew de Badlesmere, a local baron, held Hothfield of him

The point that I wish to press is that the chamberlain's fees, although evidently representing the whole contents of the bedchamber, came to be divided into two portions, received in respect of distinct services. Of these, one was the ewer and basins, with the towels, for "serving the King with water"; the other was the bed and nightshirt, with all the furniture of the bedchamber. The first mention, in England, of these fees is at the coronation of Queen Eleanor in 1236, when the Great Chamberlain received the basins and towels as his fee, for the former service : [1] the ewer is not mentioned. Thenceforward, we shall find, this service, with its fees, was claimed as a separate "office," and even as an office distinct from that of Great Chamberlain. The hereditary Great Chamberlains made it the subject of separate petitions at each coronation, to the Court of Claims, and did not even claim it *as* Great Chamberlains.

I desire, therefore, to show why it came to be distinguished from that office of chamberlain to which it essentially belonged. I say "essentially," because, we shall see, it was performed, in this country, by the Deputy Chamberlain, the Queen's Chamberlain, and the Archbishop of Canterbury's

"by serjeanty, viz :— by service of attending upon him with water to wash his hands on the day of his enthronement at Canterbury ; and he shall have the ewer and basin, and shall also be the chamberlain of the aforesaid Archbishop for the night, and shall have the Archbishop's couch for his fee" (*Cal. of Inq.* VII, No. 104, p. 91). The date is 1328. Ten years later, his son Giles was found to have held Hothfield by the same service (*Cal. of Close Rolls*, 1337-9, p. 555).

[1] " Servivit autem ea die de Aqua, tam ante prandium quam post, major camerarius... Recepit etiam, tanquam jus suum, bascinos et manutergia unde servivit. " (*Lib. Rub.*, p. 759.)

chamberlain, while, abroad, it was similarly performed by the hereditary chamberlains in Normandy. So essential a feature, indeed, was it of
the office that, at the coronation of the Emperor,
the Margrave of Brandenburg, as Arch-Chamberlain, came " on horseback with a sylver basin of
water of the value of twelve marks, and a clean
towell, which being alighted, he holds to the
Emperour." [1]

It is necessary to prove my statement as to the
chamberlains of Normandy, who were known, from
their lordship, as the chamberlains of Tancarville.[2]
In 1182 William de Tancarville was, in Normandy,
chief chamberlain in fee.[3] King Henry was keeping his Christmas court at Caen, with his sons
and his son-in-law. Water was brought to him, to
wash his hands, on the great day of the feast, by
his acting chamberlain (*cubicularius*),[4] when William, bursting through the throng, with a great
following of his knights, flung aside his mantle, as
was the way with ' ministers ',[5] snatched the silver
basins and roughly took possession.[6] The other
officer resisted, but the king ordered him to let
them be, and William, after " giving water " to the

[1] Taylor's *Glory of Regality*, p. 103.
[2] The ruins of their castle are still visible on a cliff above the mouth
of the Seine.
[3] "summus ex feudo regis camerarius, vir nobilis genere" (Walter Map).
[4] This word directly connects the chamberlain with the bedchamber.
So does Jordan Fantosme's story of " li chamberlens " in the bedchamber,
where the weary King was being lulled to sleep by the massaging of his
feet, parleying with the impatient messenger who brought the great
news from the North on that summer's night in 1174.
[5] " sicut mos est ministrorum " (*Ibid*).
[6] " arripuit traxitque fortiter ad se " (*Ibid*).

king and the princes, handed the basins to a fol-
lower of his own.   The other officer asked in vain
for their return, the king refusing to interfere.

Charged on the morrow, in public audience, by
the steward of Normandy, with appropriating the
basins, William retorted that they were his due, of
which his underling had wrongfully endeavoured
to deprive him.[1]   It is the proof of his right that
he offered which is here so important.   His father,
he said, when he founded the abbey of St. George
at Tancarville, placed therein the basins which he
had duly received, without question, from the hands
of King Henry the First, and which were there, as
witnesses, to that day.   Witnesses also were those
in the Priory of Ste Barbe.[2]   If this testimony was
not sufficient, he was ready to assert his right in
his own person in whatever way the court desired.[3]
We have here a definite statement that the chief
chamberlain of Normandy was receiving the basins
in right of his office at least as early as the days of
Henry I.

If, then, the " giving of water " to the sover-

[1] " justa vi jureque traxi pelves, summus domini regis camerarius,
quas ille subditus meus extorquere conatus est injusta violentia " (Ibid.).

[2] " Pater meus, cum abbatiam fecisset in Tankervilla beato Georgio,
posuit in ea pelves quas a manibus regis Henrici primi jure suo sine lite
tulerat, quod adhuc ibi testantur, similiter et idem aliæ testificant in
monasterio beatæ Barbaræ. "   The latter was the Priory of Ste. Barbe-
en-Auge in Écajeul-sur-Dives, of which these chamberlains were patrons.
The former seems to be an error for the abbey of St. Georges de
Boscherville much higher up the Seine and founded by the family a
good deal earlier (See my Cal. of Docs., France).

[3] " si vero tantis non adhibetur fides instrumentis, si quis se juri meo
præsumpserit adversarium opponere, praesto sum illud asserere quacunque
vi vel virtute sanxerit haec curia, nemine pro me nominato, sed in
persona propria " (See, for all this, Map, De Nugis [Camden Soc.]
pp. 232-4).

eign and the right to receive the basins as fee were
the chamberlain's recognised due, how was it that
in England it was treated as a separate office ? The
answer I suggest is that, though the basins were
part of the furniture of the bedchamber, yet the
actual service, being performed, not in the ' chamber ', but in the ' hall ',[1] was treated as outside the
chamberlain's special province.   It is the only service which is named as performed by the chamberlain at Queen Eleanor's coronation (1236), though
it is explained by the record that he had to act,
further, as chamberlain when the *King* was crowned.[2]   As the record restricts the duties of the
Queen's chamberlain to her own quarters,[3] I infer
that the basins included in his fee were those
in her " chamber," while those received by the
great chamberlain (" major camerarius ") were, as
stated, in respect of his service at the banquet in
the hall.

Ten years ago, the point was of some importance, and I drew up a special memorandum on
the subject for the use of the Crown.   Its object
was to rebut the allegation in Lord Ancaster's
Printed ' Case ' that " At the coronation of King
Edward (VI) the claim of the Earl of Oxford (to
the office of Great Chamberlain) was admitted."
If this statement had been correct, it would have
seriously affected the case for the Crown.   But I
was able to show that, on the contrary, the office

---

[1] See pp. 66-7 above.

[2] " Ad quem spectat Cameraria in *Regis* coronatione et custodia
camerae et hostii. " (*Lib. Rub.*, p. 759).

[3] " sibi jus vendicavit in domo Reginæ " (*Ibid.*).

of Great Chamberlain was exercised, on that occasion, by the Crown nominee ; that it was not even claimed by the earl of Oxford ; and that what he did claim was only " to serve the King the day of his Coronation of water, as well before dynner as after," and to have " the basons and towells " for his fee. Of the office of Great Chamberlain he made no mention. And he appealed to the record of the Court of Claims in 1377 when the earl of Oxford had successfully claimed, by a separate petition,[1] in similar terms, to perform this service.[2] His claim was allowed " forasmuch noe other man claymeth the said office, " and the fact that it was not claimed by the Crown's nominee, the Great Chamberlain in possession, proves that the original connexion between the two ' offices ' had then long been forgotten.

The other portion of the chamberlain's fees, namely the bed and furniture of the bedchamber, raises no question. As an illustration of his claim to the bed occurring similarly abroad we may take that of the Vicomte d'Aunay, as Chamberlain of Poitou, in 1410.

Quand mondit seigneur viendra premierement a Poitiers que je dois de mon droit avoir son lit garni de tous les paremens qui seront, esquels il couchera la premiere nuit. [3]

That the Great Chamberlain claimed the whole contents of the bedchamber is clear from the record

---

[1] " quandam aliam petitionem. "
[2] to serve " de eaue si bien devant maingier comme apres le jour de leur coronement. "
[3] See Ducange's *Glossarium*.

of the Court of Claims for James I's coronation, when " the costly chairs, seats, cushions, hangings and other ornaments " were included, the whole contents being compounded for at £200. This redemption for cash became the recognised practice, even as the King to this day redeems, at his coronation, for a hundred shillings the sword he offers in the Abbey. At Anne's coronation the Great Chamberlain received £300 " as a Composition for yᵉ furniture of her Maties Bedchamber and for 2 pieces of Arras hangings of the story of Caesar and Pompey, and the Green Velvet embroidered state set up in Westminster Hall." At that of George I he obtained £350, the perquisites to which he was entitled including " two rich pieces of Arras hangings of a Sett called Tobias " and " one piece of Tapestry hangings of a suit called the Seasons."

The fee, however, for the other service, namely the ewer and basins—a ' cup of assay ' in addition was regularly claimed and refused—was always received in kind, and it is significant that the earl of Oxford leaves by will to his son Robert in 1371 two silver basins.[1] At the coronation of James I, when, as at the present time, the banquet was dispensed with, this service was not performed, and the fee for it was withheld.

Apart from the forty yards of crimson velvet, which were always petitioned for and received, the Great Chamberlain was entitled by custom, in addition to his fee, to be assigned a ' box ' in the Abbey as if in return for his services at the actual coronation. This, which was a very valuable per-

[1] Dugdale's *Baronage*, I, 193.

quisite, was petitioned for in 1901, but "disallowed," as not "provided of right."[1] The services in the Abbey were not claimed in the normal petitions,[2] but at the Restoration the earl of Oxford (an unsuccessful claimant) named them thus :—

que le dit Comte d'Oxford, come cheife et principall Chamberlan d'Angleterre puit, le jour de Coronacion du nostre Seigneur le Roy, attender le Roy et porter avec lui al dit Coronacion le Coeffe et Gaunts et draps de lynnen de user a l'unction du Roy, cy pour ses mains come pour son teste, et aussi porter l'Espee du Roy avec le scabare que sont destre offrees et aussi les autres Offerings et Oblations du dit Roy, cest a dire dix livres sterling d'or et un marque d'or, et apporter avec lui une Robe Royall avec une Couronne pour le Roy apres service divine avec autre Royall array et vestuments pour le Roy, aussi qu'il puit a le Coronacion du Roy devestir et disrober le Roy jusques a son cotte et sa chemise quand le Roy sera vestu et Appareille avec sa regalite, et puis estre proche al Roy jusques a ceo que le dite Coronacion sera pleinemente finiee et accomplis, et apres le Coronacion finiee desvestir les Regalities du Roy.

This recital is of interest for comparison with present usage.

In England the association of the Chamberlain with the King's treasure is lost sight of so early that it is practically non-existent, unless indeed it lingers, as seems to me possible, in his charge, as described in the above recital, of the king's " Offerings et Oblations." On the Continent, however, it was well established[3], and in English municipal

---

[1] Wollaston's *Court of Claims*, pp. 131-3. The claim to the velvet also was disallowed, somewhat strangely (*Ibid.*, pp. 23-4).

[2] Possibly because they carried no specified fee.

[3] *i.e.* at medieval courts.

life, of course, the chamberlain was often a financial officer: [1] to this, doubtless, refers the key, the chamberlain's badge of office. Edward the Confessor, as the story goes, kept his silver in his bedchamber itself.

> Now arrived Hugelin
> The chamberlain, who takes some money,
> Carries off as much as he wished
> To pay to his seneschals,
> To his caterers and marshals,
> But in his haste he forgets
> That he shuts not the chest.[2]

Hugh the Chamberlain was a real man, and so was Herbert who, in the next reign, is styled in the Abingdon History (II, 43) " regis cubicularius et thesaurarius, " a style which again connects the king's treasure with his bedchamber. Of Herbert the Chamberlain and the *camera curie* (roughly equivalent to the Privy Purse) we shall hear again below.[3]

With his usual sound judgment, Madox, in his *Baronia Anglica* (p. 158), selected the Great Chamberlainship as an instance of ' Offices in heritage. '[4] For we have the actual text of Henry I's charter bestowing that office—which had been held by Robert Malet, a great man in Domesday—on

[1] *e.g.* in the City of London. The same practice is found in Germany.
[2] Luard's *Lives of Edward the Confessor* (Rolls Series), p. 207. The word for ' caterers ' is ' achaturs ' (*Cf.* ' The King's larderer ' below).
[3] The chamberlains of the Exchequer were, of course, distinct from the Great Chamberlain, as was the Exchequer itself from the *camera*. They both appear to have held by serjeanty. See, for Mauduit, my paper on " Mauduit of Hartley Mauduit " (*Ancestor*, V, 207), and, for Fitz Gerold, *Testa*, p. 153, and *Red Book*, p. 486.
[4] See also his *Exchequer* (1711), p. 40.

Aubrey de Vere and his heirs.   In this case, therefore, at least, there is no question of serjeanty.   No
land whatever was held in connexion with the office.

I need not labour anew the troublous problem
of its descent.   It had always been a puzzle to
antiquaries why this office in fee should have first
passed to an heir-male to the exclusion of heirs-
general, and then, on the contrary, to an heir-gene-
ral (of the whole blood), to the exclusion of the
heir-male.   In 1901-2 we cleared it up at last.
The one point to bear in mind is that, as I then
proved, the Earl of Oxford who had held the office
from 1526 to 1540 had done so, not by hereditary
right, but under a grant from the Crown for his
life.   Consequently, his son's allegation, made to
the Court of Claims for Queen Elizabeth's coronation, that his father was seised of the office " as of
fee " was directly contrary to fact. [1]

Owing to the absence of a counterclaim, the
falsehood was not exposed, [2] and the allowance of
his claim, in error, has been the root of title of
every Great Chamberlain from that day to this.
In spite, however, of this exposure, the House of
Lords decided not to re-open the question.   For
" Nullum tempus occurit regi " we must now substitute the principle " Quieta non movere. "

By the " Act for placing the Lords " (31 Hen.
VIII c. 10) the great officers are ranked thus : —
"the Great Chamberlain first, the Constable next, the

---

[1] See my papers, " The Great Chamberlain " in *Monthly Review*
(June, 1902, pp. 54-5), and " Notes on the Great Chamberlainship
Case " in *Ancestor* (IV, 19).

[2] See, the section on ' the Queen's Chamberlain ' for other false
allegations by the earls.

Marshal third, the Lord Admiral the fourth, the
Grand Master or Lord Steward the fifth, and the
king's Chamberlain the sixth." This, however,
is obviously a merely arbitrary arrangement, which
is based on no historical principle, which confuses
the great officers and their deputies, and which
interpolates the Admiral in their midst.

THE DEPUTY CHAMBERLAIN

Winfrith-Newburgh, in the county of Dorset,
derived its name from a family of Newburgh (*i. e.*
Neufbourg) which held it from the days of Henry I
by 'chamberlain' service. The 1212 return states
that Robert ' de Novo Burgo ' then held it with
(the lordship of) the Hundred of Winfrith and
part of that of Hasler, together with lands in
Lulworth (to the south) and Burton (to the north)
by 'chamberlain' service,[1] and that his ancestors had
done so since the days of Henry I, who must have
carved out this holding from the Winfrith group
of Royal demesne. Hard by were Ower Moigne
with its ' larderer ' serjeanty and Wool with its
' baker ' serjeanty. A few years later the service is
defined ; Robert holds Winfrith " by the service of
giving water to our lord the King at Christmas,
Easter, and Whitsuntide."[2] Here again we find
the chamberlain connected with the basin, and we
have also a welcome reference to the three great
Crown-wearing days of the Norman kings.

In 1250 this serjeanty was " arrented ; " its alien-

---

[1] " per servicium camerarii " (*Testa,* p. 164).
[2] *Testa,* p. 166.

ations were compounded for. On this occasion
the service was recorded in the same terms, with
the addition that the basins and towels were to be
received as fee, *unless* the earl of Oxford should be
present.[1]   As the earl of Oxford was Great Chamberlain, I term this serjeanty that of the 'Deputy'
Chamberlain, although it was, clearly, restricted to
"basin and towel" service, and did not extend to
the "chamber." In 1285 John 'de Novo Burgo'
was returned as holding Winfrith by performing
this service at Christmas, for which he received
the silver basins.[2] Two generations later, Robert
de Newburgh was found, at his death, to have
held the manor by the service of giving the King
water on his Coronation day, receiving the basin
and ewer as his fee.[3] So late, even, as the year
1486 a Newburgh was still holding Winfrith-
Newburgh "with the Hundred...... by service of
giving water for the King's hands on Christmas
day, and he shall have the silver basins from which
he gave the water."[4]

That a serjeanty of such ancient date, with its
service so well defined, a serjeanty, moreover, of
such long continuance in the family of its first
holder, should have failed to obtain recognition
would seem most unlikely. But when the lord of
the manor claimed, as against the lord of the manor

[1] "debuit dare aquam ad manus domini Regis die natalis, die pasch'
et pent', et habere pelves et manutergia nisi comes Oxon' presens esset"
(*Testa*, pp. 171, 174).

[2] "habebit bacinos argenteos de quibus dederit aquam" (*Feudal Aids*,
II, 9).

[3] "habebit pelvem cum lavatorio pro servitio predicto." (*Inq. p. m.*
12 Edw. III).

[4] *Cal. of Inq., Henry VII*, I, p. 18.

of Heydon, [1] to perform the old service at the coronation of James II, and again at that of George IV, his claim was unsuccessful. For the Court of Claims is the slave of precedent ; it has always enquired if a service has been ' allowed ' by the Court before : the historical right to perform it goes for nothing in its sight. *Beati possidentes !*

BASIN AND TOWEL SERJEANTIES

The privilege of holding the basin and towel, when the King washed his hands on coronation day, appears to have been highly valued. In addition to the claims of the Great Chamberlain and the Deputy Chamberlain, there were various minor claims, of which the Heydon serjeanty is the most notable, as having formed the subject of successful claims from the coronation of Richard II to that of George IV.

Heydon, which was formerly in Essex, in the North-Western corner of the county, was transferred to Cambridgeshire by Act of Parliament in 1895. It formed in Domesday (1086) the solitary holding of Robert son of Roscelin in that county, and though the Domesday arrangement for Essex does not enable us to distinguish the manors held by serjeanty, its position in the survey is such that it may have been so held.

The other Domesday holding *in capite* of Robert Fitz Roscelin was in Stepney. This is, perhaps, worth noting, for, if the Domesday " Stepney "

---

[1] See ' Basin and towel serjeanties. '

included Bromley (which is not named in the survey), it would have included the land which Ida Triket subsequently held by the service of holding a towel for the King's hands on his coronation day.[1]   The record proceeds to say that it had been divided by her heirs between the (Benedictine) nuns of Stratford (at Bow) and the canons of Holy Trinity (Priory).[2]   The tenure of these two houses is mentioned in another entry[3] and it explains the statement cited by Blount from a plea-roll of 22 Edward I (1293-4) that the Prioress of St. Leonard's of Stratford held fifty acres in Bromley " per servicium inveniendi domino Regi unum hominem ad tenendum manutergium ipsius Regis in coronatione sua. "   If the above conjecture, which is nothing more, should be correct, it would carry back the serjeanty to the days when Robert's Domesday holdings were still one.

I think it probable that in this serjeanty we have the explanation of a plea advanced by Ida Triket in 7 John (1205-6) relating to Sharnbrook, Beds.[4]   The Trikets had inherited the two hides which Robert Fitz Roscelin had there held as an under-tenant of Count Eustace (of Boulogne).[5]   Ida pleaded that her husband Roger had alienated this land to Ailward the Chamberlain (*temp.* Hen. II.), who gave it to Newnham Priory,

---

[1] " Ida Triket tenuit quandam terram in Brembeleg' per serjant' tenendi unum manutergium ad manus domini Regis ad coronacionem suam." *Testa*, p. 360.

[2] *Ibid.*

[3] *Ibid.*, p. 362.   For Ida Triket's relations with these two houses, and for Bromley, see *Ancient Deeds*, A. 1827-1835.

[4] See *Plac. Abbrev.*, p. 48.   Cf. *Hist. of Eng. Law*, I, 270.

[5] Domesday, I, 211.

" et dicit quod de sergantia Domini Regis est terra illa, et non potuit nec debuit aliquis sergantiam dilacere nec aliquo modo alienare." She must have claimed that it formed part of the lands held by the towel serjeanty, though it was really held by knight-service of the Honour of Boulogne. It was afterwards agreed " quod terra illa non est de sergantia Regis," but her plea shows that the serjeanty was already of such old standing that its true origin was uncertain.

When we first meet with mention of this serjeanty, it is curiously involved with another. For in the early days of Henry III we read, under Essex, that Thomas Pikot ' of Radeclive' holds the moiety of Heydon by the serjeanty of holding the basin at the King's Coronation.[1] It is added that Thomas Pikot holds the other moiety "per serjantiam tenendi manutergium ad coronacionem domini Regis," while, under Nottinghamshire, we read that Thomas of " Hedon " holds " Radeclive " by goshawk service.[2] Another Essex entry[3] tells us that Thomas ' de Heyden' held one moiety of Heyden by towel service[4] and Peter son of Robert Picot the other moiety by basin service, both at the King's coronation. There is, therefore, abundant evidence that the Picots who held the goshawk serjeanty at Ratcliffe-on-Soar were the same family as those who held this serjeanty at Heydon.

[1] *Testa*, p. 266.
[2] " Villa de Radeclive est serjantia domini Regis de ostricer[ia]. Thomas de Hedon tenet per dominum Regem." *Testa*, p. 19.
[3] *Testa*, p. 276 ; *Lib. Rub.*, p. 457.
[4] " Serjanteriam tualliæ."

Thomas " de Heyden," however, was a person apart. I find him acting as vice-chancellor to Richard I in Normandy in 1198.[1] In 1203, as a clerk (*clericus noster*) of John, he was holding lands, with a female ward (Constance dau. of Robert Furree), in Heydon,[2] and in 9 Henry III (1224-5) he paid 50 marcs for the custody of the heir and land of Peter Picot his brother-in-law. In 11 Henry III a plea roll cited by Morant shows him as holding the wardship of Thomas son of Peter Picot.   Finally in 1235 his nephew Thomas Picot gave a palfrey for confirmation of all his lands in Heydon.[3]

The upshot was that the manor descended in two moieties in the Picot family, the one moiety held by basin, the other by towel service.   This certainly indicates the division of an original basin and towel serjeanty.   In 1286 Peter Picot, at his death, held " by service of holding a basin before the King at his coronation. "[4]   In 1324 Nicholas de Segrave was found to hold Heydon by the double service, *viz* : " by the serjeanty of holding a basin and towel in the king's hall on the day of the king's coronation." [5]   There continued to be much confusion as to the apportionment of the service : under Edward III, Richard de Kelsall was found at his death to have held by towel service (*tenendi*

---

[1] See my *Calendar of docs. France*, pp. 91, 384, and *Cal. of Charter Rolls*, II, 306.

[2] *Rot. Litt. Pat.*, I, 27b.

[3] *Excerpt e Rot. Fin.*, I, 124, 276 :—" tota terre que pert' pred. T. de Heydon in Heydon quam idem T. de Heydon dedit predicto T. Picot."

[4] *Cal. of Inq.*, II, No. 602.

[5] *Ibid.*, VI, p. 187.

unum manutergium), but his son, in 1367, by basin and ewer service. [1]

Yet, only ten years later, John Wiltshire, citizen of London, who had acquired Kelsall's moiety, petitioned the Court of Claims, successfully, for the towel service.

Come le dit Johan tient certains tenements en Heyden queles fount le moytee del Manoir de Heyden de nostre sieur le Roy par sergeantie, cestassavoir de tenir un towaile quaunt nostre dit sieur le Roy lavera ses mains devant manger le jour de son coronement...... qil puisse estre accepte le dit office de sergeantie faire en la forme susdicte.

The petitioner made the usual appeal to " le record de leschequer, " as proving that John, son of John Picot had held by this service, and on this ground his claim was granted.   But as the service was performed by a deputy,—the king's uncle, the Earl of Cambridge,—and as no fee was claimed, one does not see that John gained much.

From the Wiltshires the manor of ' Heydonbury ' [2] passed to the Asplands, and finally, shortly before the death of Queen Elizabeth, it was acquired by the typical London citizen who is met with so often as the founder of an Essex family.   Grocer and Alderman, Sheriff and Lord Mayor, Sir Stephen Soame hastened to signalise his new position by claiming the service at the coronation of James I. The claim was allowed to his descendants at and from the coronation of Charles II, but when Sir

---

[1] " Per serjantiam tenendi j pelvem et lautarium ad coronacionem domini Regis."

[2] The termination 'bury' is found on the Hertfordshire side of Essex.

Peter Soame petitioned, for the coronation of James II, to hold the basin and ewer for one moiety of the manor, as well as the towel for the other, this further claim was rejected, nor was he even allowed to hold the towel, save by deputy (the Earl of Kent).

It is, however, noteworthy that, at the last coronation banquet, that of George IV, the Lord of the Manor of Heydon, though only an esquire, was (according to Sir George Nayler's report) allowed to act as towel-horse ("holding the towel") in his own person.   Mr. Legg, taking his name from that report, speaks of him as " Peter Soame John Everard Buckworth Herne Soame Esq., in whose family the manor had been at least since 1685 " (p. lxxix).   It had only, however, been devised to them by Sir Peter Soame, a stranger in blood, in 1798.   As to the above amazing name— which reminds one of the line in *Rejected addresses*, " Long may Long Tilney Wellesley Long Pole live "—the works of reference on the baronetage describe this gentleman as Peter, son and heir of Buckworth Buckworth-Herne, who added " Soame " to Buckworth-Herne in 1806, making it a triple surname.   His three intervening Christian names remain unaccounted for.

This serjeanty well illustrates the stereotyped character of decisions by the Court of Claims. When the towel service, in respect of a moiety of the manor, had been successfully claimed under Richard II, this formed the standing precedent, and it is even probable that the long insistence on a deputy was due to the fact that the claimant in 1377 was a mere London citizen.

It is an illustration of the honour of " basin and towel " service that, under Edward IV, it was the business of the King's Chamberlain to assign " knyghts or other worshypful astate for the towell and for the basyn, " and that " to serve the King of his bason " was part of the regular duty of the " knyghts of (the) household. " [1]

There was also a " towel " serjeanty connected with Steepleton, Dorset. In 1212 Geoffrey de St. Clair was returned as holding " Stapelton " by serjeanty, namely by bearing a towel before the Queen at Easter, Whitsuntide, and Christmas and the King's coronation. [2] This entry is of double interest as a very early reference to a coronation service, and as containing also a distinct allusion to the three crown-wearing days of the Norman kings. An entry of a few years later records this towel service. [3]

It is a mere guess, and perhaps not a likely one, that this " towel " developed into the " cloth of pleasaunce " held before the Queen. [4] At the coronation banquet of Richard III, the Queen sat at table, and " on every side of her stoode a countesse holding a cloth of pleasance when she listed for to drinke. " This is clearly the " fine cloth before the Queen's face whenever she listed to spit or do otherwise at her pleasure," which was held at Anne

---

[1] *Household Ordinances* (1790), pp. 32, 33.

[2] " per serjantiam, scilicet per unam tualliam ferendam coram domina Regina ad festum pasch' et pentecost' et ad nativitatem domini, et ad domini Regis coronacionem " *(Testa, p. 162).*

[3] per serjantiam manutergii." *Ibid.,* p. 167.

[4] In the *Red Book* (p. 547), the service is given as " debet tenere die Paschæ coram domina Regina unum manutergium."

Boleyn's coronation by the countess of Oxford, standing on her right, and the countess of Worcester, standing on her left. The mention of countesses on both occasions, as discharging this office, is decisive on the point.

Lastly, we have the evidence—probably worthless—of the " Inquest after death " on Margery " de Ripariis," Countess of the Isle (of Wight), that is, of Devon, in 1292, that she held Nuneham Courtney (" Newnham "), Oxon, by service of giving the King water to wash his hands on Christmas Day and carrying off the basins and towel (as fee).[1] The *Testa*, however, enters the manor as held, in her own right, by a previous Countess Margaret as one knight's fee (p. 100). I have shown in another place[2] how it descended to her from the Courcys, who had held it from the Conquest.

THE QUEEN'S CHAMBERLAIN

This serjeanty is of special interest because the coronation service rendered in respect of it is duly recorded in that precious account of Queen Eleanor's Coronation (1236) which was the great precedent in these matters. We there read that no one claimed any right in the Queen's house save

[1] " Ita quod ipse qui tenet manerium dabit domino Regi aquam ad lavandas manus suas die Natalis Domini, et asportabit et habebit pelves et manutergium" (See Hutchins' *Dorset*, I, 436). Can this strange allegation have originated in her (Wiltshire) serjeanty of " Chamberlain of the Exchequer," on the supposition that every " Chamberlain " owed the king ' basin and towel ' service?

[2] *Ancestor*, No. 1, pp. 244-245.

G(ilbert) de Sanford, who said that, of ancient right from his predecessors, he ought to be the Queen's Chamberlain and to have the custody that day of her chamber and her door, which right he obtained. And (it is important to be observed) he received, as his right, the whole of the Queen's bed and the basins and the other things which belong to the Chamberlain.[1] This fee exactly corresponds with that of the King's Chamberlain,[2] who similarly claimed (and claims) the basins and the bed.

The lands held by this service were the two Hertfordshire manors of Great Hormead and Nuthampstead (in Barkway) and the three Essex ones of Fingrith (in Blackmore), Margaretting ('Ginge') and Woolverston (in Chigwell).[3] The Hertfordshire estate enjoyed the distinction of appearing in Domesday as the holding of Edgar Ætheling himself, the only holding left to him. The three Essex manors appear together in a group among the King's lands.[4] An important entry in the *Testa* (p. 270) shows us the Hertfordshire manors held " de veteri feoffamento," which carries back the serjeanty to the days of Henry I.

One seeks, therefore, to trace it on the roll of 1130. In that record we have mention of an

[1] " De prædictis autem officiis nullus sibi jus vendicavit in domo Reginæ, excepto G[ileberto] de Sanford, qui a veteri jure prædecessorum suorum dixit se debere esse camerarius Reginæ, cameram et hostium ea die custodire, quod ibidem obtinuit. Habuit autem tanquam jus suum totum lectum Reginæ et bascinos et alia quæ spectant ad camerarium *(sic)*." *Liber Rubeus*, p. 759.

[2] And with that of the Archbishop of Canterbury's Chamberlain.

[3] *Liber Rubeus*, p. 507 ; *Testa*, p. 266.

[4] D. B., II, 5.

Adam "camerarius," to whom is remitted for Danegeld sixteen shillings under Hertfordshire and twenty four under Essex. This would represent a holding of eight hides in the former county and twelve in the latter. The Domesday assessment for the former is 8¼ hides, which is probably near enough, but that of Fingrith, unfortunately, is wanting for the Essex portion, so that one cannot speak positively. Moreover, Adam "camerarius" is also excused twenty shillings Danegeld under Hampshire, and no Hampshire land belonged to this serjeanty. [1]

In the 1212 returns for the Essex lands of the serjeanty, they are entered as held by John de Sanford "per serjant' camer' domine Regine.... per serjant' t(h)alam' Regine," and the Hertfordshire tenure is "per serjant' Regine." [2] At an early date the separate existence of this serjeanty was lost through the marriage of its heiress, Alice de Sanford to Robert (de Vere), Earl of Oxford (1263-1296). She died in 5 Edward II (1311-1312), seised of this serjeanty, which was thenceforth, by a singular coincidence, combined with the office of Great Chamberlain, which was held by the De Veres with similar duties to the King.

But now comes the difficulty. The lands of her inheritance were divided between her sons and

---

[1] There is, further, an entry on the roll (p. 150), under Middlesex, that "Adam et Samson filii Aldwini Camerarii redd. comp. de xxviii li. pro terra patris eorum." We cannot trace them under Middlesex, but eighteen years later in the second Winchester survey (*Liber Winton,* p. 545) we find the land "que fuit Alwini camerarii" held by a man who is paying the large rent of £2.9.4 to Samson *(Sansoni)*, evidently Aldwin's son.

[2] *Testa,* pp. 269-270.

her daughter, and the serjeanty thus dismembered.
Two of the estates, Fingrith in Essex and Great
Hormead in Hertfordshire, passed to her sons, the
Earl of Oxford and his younger brother, Alphonso,
respectively; three of them, Woolverston, Margaretting, and Nuthampstead, formed part of the
marriage portion which her daughter Joan brought
to her husband, Earl Warrenne.[1]   There arises
here an important question as to the law of serjeanty.   When the lands had been dismembered,
who was entitled to perform the service?[2]   It seems
clear that in such cases the right remained appurtenant to all the manors, and further, though the
two manors retained had passed, in this case, to
two brothers, each of them, we shall find, was
returned as entitled to the office in respect of his
manor.   It seems, therefore, perfectly clear that
the earls could not claim exclusive right to the
office when they only held two of the manors.[3]

Nevertheless, they seem to have considered that
the right was theirs alone, and indeed they went
further; they spoke of their Sandford lands as part
of the ' barony ' of Sandford, although they were
held by serjeanty, and they even assumed the title
of Baron Sandford, and to such good purpose that,
under Charles I, the judges held that the barony of
Sandford was among those which had been held by
the earl of Oxford *temp.* Henry VIII, and which

[1] Dugdale's *Baronage*, I, 80, 192 (the names are there unrecogni-
sable).
[2] See p. 43 above for this point.
[3] Fingrith and Hormead were re-united on the death of Earl Robert
in 1331, when he was succeeded by Alphonso's son, John.

had descended to his heirs general.[1]   The later earls, however, continued to assume it as theirs, and the last earl of all hoped, to my own knowledge, that it might descend to his heirs.

Their claim appears in the Inquisitions taken after their deaths.   On the death of Alphonso de Vere, he was returned (1328) as holding Great Hormead " by service of guarding the Queen's Chamber on the night following the day of her coronation.[2] His elder brother Robert, Earl of Oxford, died shortly after him, and was returned, in 1331, as having held Fingrith "in chief by serjeanty, *viz* :— serving in the Queen's Chamber, as chamberlain, on the day of her Coronation, receiving for his fee as is fitting *(pro feodo suo percipiendo sicut decet)*. "[3]

The escheator was ordered, 17 May 1331,[4] to give seisin to John de Vere, the earl's nephew and heir, and Fingrith is again named among the lands as held by this serjeanty.[5]   A year before the earl's death a most important writ was issued for the earl, which proves that he actually received his fees for officiating at the coronation of Queen Philippa.   The King informs his officers of the Exchequer, 2 April 1330, that the Earl had petitioned,—as he and his ancestors, the Earls of Oxford, had been, by hereditary right, cham-

---

[1] Collins' *Precedents*, p. 175.

[2] *Cal. of Inq.*, VII, No. 116.

[3] *Ibid.*, No. 379.

[4] This document was printed among the ' proofs ' in the Great Chamberlain Case (and wrongly dated ' 1332 ').   It was evidently supposed to relate to the *Great* Chamberlainship, which is not even mentioned in it.

[5] " per serjanciam, videlicet, serviendi in camera Regine loco camerarii die coronacionis sue " (Originalia Roll, 5 Edward III).

berlains to the queens of England at their coronations, time out of mind, and had received certain fees — that he might receive them, as having officiated ; and he adds that, of the fees claimed, he has given the earl the queen's shoes (*calciamenta*) [1] and three silver basins, from one of which the queen washed her head (*pro locione capitis sui*) and from the others her hands, and has compounded with him for the queen's bed at a hundred marcs (£66.13.4), which they are to pay him. [2]

Although the record states that the earl had produced proofs to the king, [3] his allegations were impudent. He must have known perfectly well that the office had not been exercised by his ancestors, the earls of Oxford, [4] but had come into his family through his mother, and that it was *not* held " by hereditary right ", but in virtue of the tenure of certain manors, of which only one was in his hands. This is one of the three statements made by the earls of Oxford with regard to their ' chamberlain ' offices which I denounce as fraudulent.

For some reason or other we seem to have no record of early petitions by the Earls to the Courts of Claims for this office. At the coronations of Richard II and of Henry IV, with which begin the records of Courts of Claims, there was no Queen

---

[1] This is the word used for the King's coronation ' buskins. '

[2] Liberate Roll, 4 Edward III, m. 7. *Cf.* p. 119 above.

[3] " per diversas evidencias nobis per prefatum comitem exhibitas plenius apparebat quod idem comes et antecessores sui officium illud diebus coronacionum reginarum predictarum habere et hujusmodi feodum percipere consueverunt. "

[4] " et ipse et antecessores sui comites Oxon' officium camerarie diebus coronacionum reginarum Anglie..... a tempore cujus contrarii memoria non existit facere et exercere..... consueverunt. "

Consort, so that there was no office for which to petition. For the coronation however of Elizabeth, consort of Henry VII (Nov. 1487), a court of claims was appointed,—

That all maner of men, what(ever) Estate or degree they were of, that held any lands by service Royall, that is to say to doe any service at the Coronation of the Queene shold come in and shew theyr clayme, etc.

Thereupon the Earl of Oxford put in his claim " to be chamberleyn "

in regard that he holds the manors of Fringrith in the County of Essex and Hormede in the County of Hertford for the service of Chamberlein of England. [1]

He therefore claimed " to perform the said his service " at the Queen's coronation. This claim, of course, was entirely erroneous in form ; for the office of Queen's Chamberlain was wholly distinct from that of " Chamberlain of England, " though he happened to hold them both. It ought to be observed that the claim is made in respect of the two manors which, we have seen, had descended to the earls. [2]

Before the Court of Claims which sat (July 1603) for the coronation of James I, Edward, Earl of Oxford, the spendthrift earl, who dissipated the great estates of his house and who " was the first that brought perfumed gloves and such fineries out of Italy into this kingdom, " claimed not only the great Chamberlainship (" grand Chamberlaine

[1] This document is taken from the State Papers (Domestic).
[2] See p. 135 above.

d'Angleterre "), but also, by a separate petition, " to be Chamberlain of the Queen, the King's wife. " In its curious " Norman " French, his claim ran thus :—

> que come il tient sicome ses auncestors ont tenuz le mannor de Fingry ovesque les mannors de Hormeade, Ginges, et part del Ulsamston in lez counties de Essex et Hertford per serjantie, cestascavoir per le service destre chamberlaine de Roignee feme le Roy et de guarder chamber le Roigne et le huis de ceo al jour de coronement le Roigne et daver tout le lite del dit Roignee et les bassines et les auters choses quex apperteigne a le chamberlaine, etc.

This claim, purporting to be made in respect of four out of the five manors which originally formed the serjeanty, was a most impudent proceeding. Two out of these four manors had never even descended to the earls ; Fingrith he had himself parted with many years before, and Hormead was the subject of a counter-petition on behalf of its real owner, Daniel Cage, gentleman ! [1] The latter claimed the office as being " seised in his demesne as of fee" of that manor. Both claimants further petitioned to have a clerk in the Exchequer to receive the Queen's gold and take from it sixpence a day for its receipt. This was the further claim which was made by Gilbert de Sandford at Queen Eleanor's coronation (1236), the consideration of which was deferred.[2] It is clear from the silence of the record that neither claim was successful.

---

[1] The Earl had licence to alienate the manor of Great Hormead to Anthony Cage so far back as 1 May 1579 (*ex inform.* General Editor, Victoria County History).

[2] " Vendicavit etiam se debere habere clericum in scaccario ad exigen-

It is not, therefore, surprising that, when again advanced, it was again unsuccessful, especially as it was made in respect of the manor of Fingrith alone. Such claim was made by the Cory family for the coronations of James II, William and Mary, and Anne ; by Mr. William Fytche for that of George II and his Queen (1727), and finally in 1911, by Mr. Adolphus G. Maskell, for the coronation of George V.

THE CHIEF BUTLER

The holder of this office was, by general admission, one of the great officers of state in this country and abroad.[1] Even before the Conquest a Waltham Abbey charter is witnessed by Wigod " regis pincerna," as if to remind us that Edward was adopting continental fashions in the names of his court officers. [2]

In Normandy Duke William had, on the eve of the Conquest, a butler, Hugh ' Pincerna ' (or ' Buticularius '), whom one charter enables us to identify as Hugh d'Ivry. [3] After the conquest he

---

dum aurum Regine qui percipiet, ut dicit, de prædicto auro qualibet die sex denarios pro liberatione ; sed fuit dilatum usque ad prædictum terminum. " (*Lib. Rub.*, p. 760). This is followed by a statement that the rightful amount of the Queen's gold was ten per cent on the amount of all fines. Compare *Dialogus de scaccario* (1902), p. 157: " adest clericus regine ad hæc constitutus," etc.

[1] In the Empire the Arch-Butler carried, as his symbol of office, the covered cup that figures on some Butler coats of arms.

[2] See my paper on the officers of Edward the Confessor in *Eng. Hist. Rev.*, XIX, 91.

[3] See my *Calendar of documents preserved in France*, Nos. 73, 81, 1167. Roger d'Ivry also (his contemporary and probably his brother) is found attesting as ' Pincerna. '

is found again attesting as Hugh ' Pincerna, ' and
he was certainly the Hugh d'Ivry who held Ambrosden (Oxon) in 1086, and probably the Hugh
' Pincerna' who then held some lands in Beds.[1]

By about the middle of the reign of Henry I
the butlership is found held by another family.
High in his favour were two brothers, William and
' Nigel '[2] d'Aubigny (de Albini), who took their
names from Aubigny in that Norman province of
the Cotentin which had been, in earlier days, his
portion.   On William he bestowed the office of
chief butler (of England), an appointment to which
all claimants have traced, ever since, their root of
title.   In order to distinguish him from his namesake, William ' de Albini' of Belvoir—who was
known as William ' de Albini' the Breton (Brito)
—he was regularly styled William ' de Albini
Pincerna. '   To provide him with a territorial
endowment, Henry constructed for him a substantial fief in Norfolk,[3] where he established at
Buckenham his castle, and founded at Wymondham
an abbey.   The whole controversy as to the right
to this great and ancient office turns upon his
tenure of these lands.   Did he hold his office in
virtue of his tenure of this fief or of some portion
thereof?   Or was it held in gross?   And, if the
latter, ought it to descend to his heirs in blood, or
to those who held that earldom of Arundel which
his son subsequently obtained?

---

[1] *Domesday*, I, 216.   He is mentioned as " pincerna regis. "
[2] Not to be confused with the Domesday lord of Cainhoe, Beds.
[3] See *Lib. Rub.*, p. 397 : " Hoc est tenementum Willelmi Pincernæ
Domini Regis, de dono Regis Henrici. "

But we must not anticipate the history. William d'Aubigny (or his son and heir of the same name) was doubtless the " Magister Pincerna " of the *Constitutio Domus Regis*,[1] and in 1136 he attended Stephen's Easter Court as Butler (*Pincerna*) with the other officers of state.[2] In 1137 he crossed with Stephen from Portsmouth and was with him at Rouen, again as ' Pincerna.'[3]

The younger William, as is well known, married about this time the relict of Henry I, Queen Adeliza, obtaining with her the splendid dower of the castle and ' honour' of Arundel, and Waltham in Essex also. That he did not become thereby earl of Arundel I was able, for the first time, to prove.[4] The chronicle of Waltham Holy Cross, explaining in a notable passage that his marriage had turned his head,[5] pointedly speaks of " Willelmus ille, pincerna, nondum comes, "[6] thus proving that, although not yet an earl, he had succeeded to his father's office of butler.

We now pass to a strange incident, which I am disposed to place some twenty years later, and which illumines for a moment the office of chief butler. The story is told us by no other than King Henry the Second, through the mouth of Walter Map.[7]

---

[1] *Lib. Rub.*, p. 811.
[2] See my *Geoffrey de Mandeville*, pp. 262-3.
[3] *Cal. of Charter Rolls*, III, pp. 338, 375.
[4] *Geoffrey de Mandeville*, pp. 322-4.
[5] " Quem post discessum Regis Henrici conjugio Reginæ Adelidis contigit honorari, unde et superbire et supra se extolli cœpit ultra modum ut (non) possit sibi pati parem, et vilesceret in oculis suis quicquid præcipuum præter regem in se habebat noster mundus " (*Ibid.*).
[6] *Ibid.*
[7] *De Nugis curialium* (Ed. Camden Soc.), pp. 234-5.

The place was Paris, and the year, I make it, 1158.[1]
The Kings of England and of France were seated
at meat together, when there suddenly burst upon
them, fresh from pilgrimage to the east, the haughty
Earl of Arundel, on whom no one had set eyes for
the space of three years. Flinging off his rough
cloak, the great, strong noble caught sight of the
vessels of wine, and, on the officiating butler refusing to give them up, hurled him to the ground.
Then, falling on his knees before the King of the
French, he explained that he was by hereditary
right, as his own king knew, chief (*princeps et primus*) of the butlers, and that the man he had over-
thrown had insolently refused him his right. That
his violent action was accepted as a jest, not as an
insult, was a precedent Henry urged, for the similar
action of William de Tancarville[2] being pardoned.[3]

---

[1] This was the only year in which Henry, as King, can have been
in Paris with Louis. And the Earl is here made to speak of him as
King. Otherwise one would guess that he had joined the second
crusade (1147) and returned after three years, to find Henry, as Duke,
in Paris.

[2] See the section on the Great Chamberlain.

[3] Rex autem ait :...... "Memores autem in hoc casu vos oro fieri
quod cum Parisius in hospitio meo dominus meus Ludovicus rex et ego
consedissemus, astante nobis pincerna meo, subito domum ingressus
Willielmus comes Hyrundella, recens a reditu Jerusalem, quem nemo
nostrum videret triennio preterito, nobis breviter salutatis, pallam villo-
sam quam sclavinam nominant velox abjecit et vasa vini rapidus inhœ-
sit, pincernamque renitentem, ut erat magnus et fortis, impulsu dejecit,
flectensque genua coram domino rege Francorum subintulit : 'Domine mi
rex, quod hic agitur non est excessus aut reverentiæ vestræ contemptus ;
scit dominus meus rex quod de jure decessorum meorum pincernarum
princeps sum et primus ; hic autem quem dejeci præsumpsit arroganter
sibi jus meum cum detinuit quod obtulisse debuerat non petenti.' Sic
et hæc ille Willielmus et a tanta curia nomen facetiæ retulit, non arro-
gantiæ. Vobis autem hoc ideo recordor, et ex aliis actis instruamini, ne
cujusquam amore sit huic Willielmo censura nostra curiæ remissior, vel

Next in order of date is a notable passage in the chronicle of ' Benedictus Abbas' describing the King's Christmas feast, in 1186, at Guildford. [1] On that occasion the Earl of 'Arundel' [2] performed, we read, the service due from him at the coronations and solemn feasts of the Kings of England. [3] That is to say, he was chief butler. We must now skip a longer space, namely half a century.

The great precedent for the services due on coronation days was the record of those rendered at Queen Eleanor's crowning in 1236 ; and on the butler's office its details are exceptionally full. [4] We first read that, on this occasion, Earl Warenne served in the place of Hugh d'Aubigny, Earl of Arundel, to whom the office of butler belongs, because he was under excommunication. [5] We then learn that, under him and by his side, there

odio alicujus districtior; æqua lance libretur quod audistis, quatinus licet hæc illa curia videatur interior, non judicetur interior *(sic)*." Quoniam igitur nemo juri suo est factus obviam *(sic)* omnium judicio Willielmus obtinuit.

[1] Eyton, p. 275.

[2] This earl was normally styled Earl of Sussex.

[3] " In illo vero festo predicti comites de Leicestria et de Harundel et Rogerus Bigot servierunt ad mensam Regis de servitio quod ad illos pertinebat in coronationibus et solemnibus festis regum Angliæ" (Vol. II., p. 3).

[4] " De officio Pincernarie " *(Lib. Rub.*, pp. 758-759).

[5] " Servivit ea die comes Warennæ vice Hugonis de Albiniaco, Comitis de Arundel, ad quem tunc *(sic)* illud officium spectat. Fuit autem [eodem] tempore [idem] sententia excommunicationis [innodatus] a Cantuariensi [Archiepiscopo] eo quod cum fugare fecisset Archiepiscopus in foresta dicti Hugonis in Suthsexa, idem Hugo canes suos cepit." Mathew Paris, however, gives as the reason Earl Hugh's youth :—"loco Comitis Arundeliæ ; eo quod adolescens erat idem comes Arundeliæ, nec adhuc gladio cinctus militari." He was still a minor 28 June 1234, but was of age, 10 May 1235, when—though only as Hugh 'de Albiniaco'—he was given possession of all his castles by the Crown.

served Master Michael Belet, who had a secondary right to the office, in virtue of which he held the cup filled with wine, ready to be handed, when the King required it, to the Earl of Arundel, that the Earl might hand it to the King. For he held, it is added, butler's office (*pincernariam*) in the King's household of ancient right. [1] Master Michael's right to " stand before the King " was challenged, it appears, for himself by the Mayor of London, but he was told by the King that no one but Master Michael ought to serve there. [2]

After the banquet the Earl Butler (*comes Pincerna*)[3] received the King's cup, with which he had served him, as his right, and Master Michael received that earl's robe as his right. His own robe he gave to Henry 'de Capella', his kinsman, who was wont to serve the King with his cup on the other days of the year. But this was a voluntary gift.[4]

We may recognise in this formal ceremonial three grades of office, the butler, assistant butler, and deputy assistant butler. This phraseology I borrow from the cumbrous, but familiar form

---

[1] " Servivit autem sub eodem in latere suo Magister Michael Belet, cujus est illud officium secundario, ut teneat cuppam porrigendam Comiti Arundelliæ vino refectam cum Rex exegerit, ut comes eandem Regi porrigat. Habet etiam Magister Michael Pincernariam in domo Regis, sub Comite, de jure veteri." See the section below on 'The assistant butler.'

[2] " Major civitatis Londoniæ...... vendicavit locum Magistri Michaelis astandi coram Rege ; sed repulsus fuit præcepto Regis, dicentis quod nullus de jure ibi deberet servire nisi Magister Michael." The Mayor's coronation service will be dealt with separately under 'The assistant butler.'

[3] Compare the expression 'Earl Marshal' for one who was both Earl and Marshal.

[4] " Non tamen tenebatur dare nisi vellet."

"Deputy Assistant Quartermaster General," preserved, characteristically enough, by the British War Office.   As for Michael Belet, he held an ancient serjeanty with which we shall deal below.   His kinsman was no tenant by serjeanty, but can be identified as holding in fee-farm of the abbot of Westminster at Denham, Bucks.[1]

The male line of the earls of Arundel, whose right was thus unquestioned, came to an end within a few years of the coronation of Queen Eleanor, namely in 1243.   What became, in these circumstances, of the office of chief butler ?   The question turned, as in other cases, on the right by which the office was held.   Did the last earl hold as heir in blood to William d'Aubigny, butler to Henry I, or as tenant in chief of certain lands, or as earl of Arundel ?   To those who have followed its early history, the last alternative must seem a very strange suggestion.   As a matter of fact, however, the second and third hypotheses were those respectively adopted by the subsequent claimants of the office ; and it is specially to be noted that no appeal is found to *æsnecia*—the position of the eldest daughter —as conferring a right to the office.[2]

No fewer than fifty pages of Mr. Wollaston's *Court of Claims* are required for the petitions and counter-petitions of those who in 1901 claimed to be recognised as chief butler at the coronation of King Edward VII.   " It is unfortunate, " he observes, "that the Court held itself bound by the terms of the Proclamation to exclude those petit-

[1] *Testa,* p. 246.
[2] See p. 38.

ions from its notice, as referring to the banquet, thereby postponing the settlement of a very interesting question. " (p. 16). As the question is thus left open, one may venture to offer some attempt to state the facts.

The three claimants were :—

(1) the Duke of Norfolk, the right of whose predecessors, as earls of Arundel, had been repeatedly allowed.

(2) Mr. F. O. Taylor, as lord of the Norfolk manor of Kenninghall.

(3) Lord Mowbray, Segrave and Stourton, as senior representative of the *second* sister of Hugh, earl of Arundel (d. 1243), through the Howards, his claim being that the office was hereditary in the blood. This was practically the first occasion on which that claim was advanced.

The several petitions are strange examples of what lawyers can make of history when they take it in hand. In that, for instance, of the Duke of Norfolk it was formally alleged " that at the Coronation of Edward III, the said Edmund, earl of Arundel served the said office," [1] though " the said Edmund " had been actually beheaded under Edward II, while the family had lost the earldom, castle, and honour of Arundel, when Edward III was crowned. On the other hand the two remaining claimants, in their eagerness to expose the weak point in the claim of the earls of Arundel,—namely that the D'Aubignys had held the office before

---

[1] *Court of Claims*, p. 229.

they were earls of Arundel,—were both committed to the statement that William d'Aubigny ' Pincerna' had received his office and his lands from the Conqueror himself, a statement which, we have seen, is wholly opposed to fact.

Lord Mowbray alleged " that the office of Butler was, under the Conqueror, held by William de Albini, *Pincerna*," and that " the office of Butler to the King of England was throughout this period " (*i.e.* down to 1102) " held by the De Albini family " and urged

that the Castle and Manor of Bokenham, or Buckenham, in Norfolk were found by an Inquisition taken in the third year of the reign of Edward I to have been granted by King William the Bastard to William the Butler, who was William de Albini. [1]

As this evidence is at once disposed of by the contemporary evidence of Domesday, one does not see why " an Inquisition " of some two centuries later should be here invoked. It is the more strange as on the next page good use has been, evidently, made of my own *Geoffrey de Mandeville* [2] including its citation from the *Chronicle of the Holy Cross*— or as Lord Mowbray is made to term it, " the Holy Ghost "—*of Waltham*. [3]

Mr. Taylor, we read, similarly alleged that

the Manor of Kenninghall and the lordships or Manors of Bokenham (otherwise Buckenham) and Wymondham, all in the County of Norfolk, together also with the Manors of Rising and Snettisham in the same county,

---

[1] *Ibid.*, p. 252. See below for this Inquisition.
[2] See p. 142 above.
[3] *Ibid.*, p. 253.

were granted in the time of William the Conqueror by
the Crown to William d'Albini, to be held in grand
serjeanty by the service of being chief Butler to the Kings
of England on the day of their Coronation, upon which
account he was called *Pincerna Regis*.[1]

This curious petition further states that the
second William was created earl " in or about the
year 1151 (but [*sic*] prior to which year, he is
described as *Pincerna Regis*), " although, as I have
shewn, he was created earl not later than 1141.[2]
Neither petitioner appears to have seen anything
incongruous in making this first earl, who died in
1176, the son of a man who reccived his fief in the
days of William the Conqueror.

This would seem to be the best place at which to
introduce the inquisition which appears to be referred to more or less inaccurately in the petitions
of lord Mowbray and of Mr. Taylor.   It is on the
Hundred Rolls (1274-5) that we find it.

dominus Robertus de Tateshale tenet manerium de
Bickenham (*sic*) in hundredo de Shropham, et dominus
Rex Willelmus Bastard dedit illud cum Kenynghal et
Wymondham *Hug*[*oni*] Butelar[io], et te[netu]r per ser-
vicium quod ille qui tenet dictum manerium (*sic*) debet
esse botel[arius] domini Regis.[3]

Here is the very information we want, but di-
vorced, by the lapse of two centuries, from what
we have seen to be the facts.   It is, however,
excellent evidence for the belief then prevailing,
especially as the return to the *Inq. p. m.* on Robert's

---

[1] *Ibid.*, p. 267.
[2] *Geoffrey de Mandeville*, p. 322.
[3] *Rot. Hund.*, I. 467 b.   The italics are mine.

father, shortly before (1273), states that he held Buckenham by butler service.[1]   For the return of 1274-5 undoubtedly implies the belief that the holder of Buckenham was the King's butler.

That return is thus referred to in the allegations made in Lord Mowbray's petition :—

That the castle and manor of Bokenham, or Buckenham, in Norfolk were found by an Inquisition taken in the third year of the reign of Edward I to have been granted by King William the Bastard to *William* the butler *who was William de Albini.*

That the Castle and Manor of Bokenham included also the Manors or reputed Manors and lands of Kyninghall, Wymondham, *Castle Rising, and Snettisham, and possibly other lands,* the whole being known as the '*Butelaria*' held of the King in chief by the service of Butler to the Kings of England. [2]

One would really like to know who the expert was to whom we owe this paraphrase.

Mr. Taylor's petition retorts thus :—

The Manor of Kenninghall and the Lordships or Manors of Bokenham (otherwise Buckenham) and Wymondham... *together also with the Manors of Rising and Snettisham.....* were granted in the time of William the Conqueror to *William d'Albini,* to be held in grand serjeanty by the service of being Chief Butler to the Kings of England on the day of their coronation......   The Manor of Kenninghall was not included in the Manor of Bokenham as alleged by Lord Mowbray's petition, but was an independent Manor.   On the division of the D'Albini estates, the Manor of Kenninghall became the *caput serjeantiæ,* etc. [3]

[1] See below.
[2] *Court of Claims,* p. 252.   The italics are mine.
[3] *Ibid.,* p. 266.   The italics (in English words) are mine.   It will be seen that the original grantee, who is given simply as *Hugh* on the

But in this triangular duel, this great Battle of the Butlers, Mr. Taylor had himself to submit to being told, in the Duke of Norfolk's petition, of an "alleged decision" on which he relied, that there does not "exist any such decision" and that Blomefield's statement about it "is wholly untrue".[1]   Mr. Taylor countered with an effective record, but his argument that Blomefield "was the rector of Fersfield, the adjoining parish to Kenninghall," and must therefore have known the facts about the coronation of Edward III,[2] will hardly convince historians of to-day.

Leaving for the present these petitions, let us see if the known facts, from an historical standpoint, enable us to decide the question.

We must first set aside the claim of the earls of Arundel, of which, for an historian at least, they effectually dispose.   Legally—so far as the matter can be said to be one of law—their claim could hardly be disputed.   For at every coronation of which the facts are known it has been allowed if made, with the sole exception of that of Edward III, when the family was, for the time, disinherited. Historically it 'has not a leg to stand on,' for the fact that the d'Aubignys held the office *before* they acquired the earldom is, as the opposing claimants urged in 1901, absolutely decisive against the claim that it was held in right of the earldom.   Nor was any attempt made in the Duke's petition to reply

Hundred Rolls, is transformed in these petitions into "William d'Albini." One wonders whether "Hugh" was derived from the "Hugo Pincerna" of Domesday.   (see p. 141 above).
[1] *Court of Claims*, p. 237.
[2] *Ibid.*, p. 269.

to this argument.   Even so late, indeed, as 1168,
the office was still distinguished so carefully from the
earldom that, a separate return having been made
for the Norfolk fief of the earl as of " William
d'Aubigny the butler " (1166), he was similarly
charged for the aid due from it, not as earl of
Arundel, but as "Willelmus de Albeneio Pincerna."[1]

If one is asked to account for the origin of the
erroneous belief that the earldom carried the office,
the answer is simple.   Courts of claims have always
adopted a rule of thumb method ; they looked only
at precedents and did not go behind them.   A
Fitzalan earl of Arundel would claim, in the usual
form, to serve the office of butler as it was served
by his predecessor Hugh, earl of Arundel, in 1236.
The fact of such service could not be disputed, and
it was not in accordance with the practice of the
court to investigate the title of earl Hugh.   That
the office was held in right of the earldom was a
view which would naturally follow.   Of such
confusion other cases will be found in this volume.

We have now disposed of the accepted view,
but there still remain two others.   That the office,
as was contended in Lord Mowbray's petition, was
unconnected with land and was vested in William
d'Aubigny and his heirs in blood is the view that
I should prefer to take, on the ground that this
was certainly the case with the office of Great
Chamberlain and was so also, probably, with the
other offices of state.   The Butlership of Ireland
also appears to have been unconnected with land.
And this view is further confirmed, at first sight,

---

[1] *Pipe Roll,* 14 *Hen. II*, p. 21.

by the fact that the Norfolk fief was undoubtedly admitted, in 1166-8, to be held by knight-service.

On the other hand, it is but fair to say that, looking at the question independently and not from the standpoint of counsel urging the claim of his client, one can find, at least, certain evidence that the manors in respect of which the butlership was alleged to be held were distinct from that portion of the fief which was held by knight-service. This is, I think, a new view and it requires explanation. The *carta* of 1166 [1] enumerates seventy-seven knight's fees as held by William d'Aubigny 'pincerna,' but the great demesne manors of Buckenham, Kenninghall, etc., which 'the butler' retained in his own demesne, are found in 1086 in the hands of the King himself. [2] They were not part of the fiefs named as given him by Henry I. Moreover the great Norfolk inquest of 1212 returns the earl of Arundel as holding Buckenham, Kenninghall, Wymondham, Rising and Snettisham, and adds in each case that " by what service is unknown. " [3]

There is here, certainly, no mention of tenure in serjeanty by butler-service, but there is, at least, no statement of tenure by knight-service. [4]

It must always be remembered that, unfortunately, the findings of juries in 'inquests after death' cannot be accepted as proof; but the great test of tenure remains in liability to scutage. And we

[1] *Lib. Rub.*, pp. 397-9.
[2] *Domesday* II, 126 b., 127.
[3] " Nescitur per quod servitium " (*Testa*, pp. 293-5).
[4] Perhaps, however, it might be argued that the jurors meant that they could not apportion on each manor its quota of knight-service.

cannot find that Buckenham or Kenninghall—the two manors in respect of which claims have been made to the office—were ever liable to scutage.[1] We have, moreover, for what it is worth, the finding of the jurors in 1273 that Robert de Tateshale (senior co-heir of the D'Aubignys) held Buckenham with the Hundred of Shropham, and the Hundred of Freebridge also, "by serjeanty of butlery,"[2] and further a finding in 1335 that Joan de Tateshale had held in Buckenham "a moiety of the manor..... held in dower of the King in chief, by service of being the King's butler."[3] The office was claimed in virtue of the lordship of this manor at the coronation of Charles II and at that of George IV.

Kenninghall, the other manor in respect of which it has been claimed, fell to a junior co-heir of the D'Aubigny earls. The evidence as to the manors which passed to this co-heir is confused and contradictory. On the death of Isabel, widow of the last D'Aubigny earl, she was found (Aug. 1283) to have held (as dower) Snettisham and the Hundred of Smithdon " by service of butlery " and Kenninghall " by 3s. 4d. blanch farm."[4] The manors then passed to Mohaut, a junior co-heir, who already held Castle Rising (as his capital messuage of the D'Aubigny inheritance), by knight-service, as it was alleged.[5]

---

[1] This, however, is not conclusive, for the records of 1166-8 appear to show that the whole liability of the Norfolk fief was more than covered by the portions of it which had been enfeoffed.

[2] Cal. of Inq., II, No. 4. Compare the return in the Hundred Rolls, two or three years later, given above.

[3] Ibid., VII, 684. Cf. No. 590.

[4] Cal. of Inq., II. No. 540.

[5] Ibid., No. 128.

Nevertheless, on the death of Roger de Mohaut, it was found (1296) that he had held all three manors " per servitium pincerne. " [1]

From the whole tangle of evidence there emerges the general idea that Buckenham and Wymondham, Kenninghall, Rising, and Snettisham were all held by the D'Aubignys as the King's butlers ; and as the two first passed to the Tateshales and the three last to the Mohauts, there was naturally much question as to who was entitled to the office, if, as was alleged, it was held by serjeanty.

Unluckily, there was no claim in 1901 either as heir of Tateshale or as lord of Buckenham, so that there was no one to uphold the rights of either.   Lord Mowbray could only claim as " *one of* the heirs of William de Albini, *Pincerna*. " [2] Mr. Taylor claimed that " on the division of the D'Albini estates, the Manor of Kenninghall became the *caput serjeantiæ*," [3] although, if any manor could claim this distinction, it would, we shall see, be Buckenham, and, even of the above portion of the manors, Castle Rising, not Kenninghall, was expressly assigned as the *caput* " on the division of the ..... estates. " [4]

This division is of some interest to students of the feudal system, as illustrating a principle of descent prevailing under the Normans.   Its most notable example is in the case of the Conqueror himself, who bequeathed to his eldest son his

---

[1] *Court of Claims*, p. 255.
[2] *Ibid.*, p. 262.
[3] *Ibid.*, p. 266.
[4] *Cal. of Pat. Rolls*, 1232-47, p. 408.   Compare p. 154 above.

ancestral duchy of Normandy, while leaving his
' conquest,' the English throne, to his second son
William. So also, the greatest of his followers,
Roger de Montgomery, " literally the foremost
among the conquerors of England," [1] was succeeded in his English ' conquest,' the ' earldoms' of
Arundel and of Shrewsbury, not by his eldest, but
by his second son. There are other instances in
point. [2]

It appears to me that this principle, if broadly
applied, would explain the assignment, on the death
of Hugh, Earl of Arundel (1243), to Fitz-Alan, the
heir of his *second* sister, of the castle and " honour "
of Arundel with the " honour " of Petworth, [3] that
great domain which the first Earl had added to
his own inheritance. In any case the eldest co-heir
(as he is expressly styled), Robert de Tateshale,
was assigned the *caput* of the old inheritance,
as Buckenham must have been, together with
Wymondham, [4] where the D'Aubigny earls lay

---

[1] Freeman's *Norman Conquest.*

[2] Touching upon this early principle, the authors of the *History of
English Law* (1895) speak of Glanvill's distinction between *hereditas* and
quæstus and of his view that a man's " power over his conquest is greater
than his power over his heritage, " so far as alienation from his son and
heir is concerned (II, 306). They add that " in borrowing from beyond
the Tweed the words *heritage* and *conquest* we show that in England the
distinction soon became unimportant. " The principle, however, of
which I am speaking has to be carefully distinguished from the Scottish
" Law of Conquest, " by which on the contrary " Landis Conquest "
would descend to the heir of the acquirer's *elder* brother, though his
" heritage " would pass to the heir of his next *younger* brother. See
Riddell (*Peerage and Consistorial Law*, II, 838-840), though he does, no
doubt, speak of " the law of conquest" as " familiar to the feudal law
and Normandy. "

[3] See his *Inq. p. m.* in 1272 (*Cal. of Inq.*, II, No. 812).

[4] Some miles north of Buckenham.

buried in the abbey of their own foundation.   But as the Norfolk fief was divided between him and the youngest co-heir, they can, neither of them, have had so rich a share as Fitz-Alan.

It was urged on behalf of the Duke of Norfolk, in 1901, that—

In 30 Edward I, A.D. 1302, Robert de Tateshale petitioned the King and claimed to have the service, alleging that his grandfather, Robert de Tateshale, was received three times in the reign of King Henry III to do the office, and did it.   Whereas (*sic*) it appears by the *Red Book of the Exchequer* that the Earl of Arundel and not Robert de Tateshale, served the office by his deputy.[1]

But between these statements there is no contradiction.   No one could have claimed to serve the office before the earl's death (1243).   But there remained a space of some 30 years (1243-1272) within which Robert's grandfather, then senior co-heir of the earls, may well have been ' received ' as alleged.   It was further urged for the Duke that Robert's claim was " not successful, for at the coronation of King Edward the Second the earl of Arundel served the office. "[2]   But this omits the important fact that Robert died the year after making the above claim (31 Edward I), leaving a son who died a minor, the last of his line,[3] before

---

[1] *Court of Claims*, p. 235.

[2] *Ibid.*, p. 236.

[3] His inheritance was split up between three co-heirs, the eldest, Thomas de Cailly, obtaining the castle of Buckenham and one fourth of the manor.   On the death of this Thomas, some ten years later (10 Edward II), the jurors found that half the manor of Buckenham was held by his predecessor's widow, the rest being apparently divided between the three co-parceners, and that the " manor is held of the King by service of being the King's butler. "   (*Cal. of Inq.*, VI, No. 48). This subdivision must have greatly weakened the claim.

the accession of Edward II.   At the coronation of
Edward I (August 1274) some one must have
officiated, for it was solemnised with due splendour.
But unfortunately we do not know who it was.   It
cannot have been John FitzAlan, then lord of
Arundel,[1] for he was only 7½ years old at the
time.

We read, indeed, in the latest product of historical scholarship on the subject that—

> At the coronation of Edward I, in 1276 (*sic*), it was
> found that the chief butlership was held by the tenure of
> the manors of Kenninghall, Buckenham and Wymondham.[2]

But, as the coronation of Edward I was in 1274,
there is evidently something wrong, and one can
only surmise that the author was thinking of the
Hundred Rolls return to that effect, or of some
other Inquisition.   To continue the above quotation :—

> In 1327 the earl of Arundel claimed the office..... The
> Montealt family is now merged in that of the Duke of
> Norfolk, who is therefore (*sic*) chief butler as well as
> Earl Marshal.[3]

As in 1327 there was no earl of Arundel, the
office could not well be claimed by him.   And the
' Montealt ' family is not " merged in that of the
Duke, " who does not even hold their manor of
Kenninghall, in right of which they claimed.   Indeed, the Duke's petition presented in the same year
(1901), argued vigorously *against* the claim of the

---

[1] The *earldom* of Arundel was not revived till later.
[2] *English Coronation Records* (1901), p. lxxii.
[3] *Ibid.*

Montealt family and in favour of his Grace's own claim, not by descent from them, but as Earl of Arundel ! There would seem, therefore, to be still room for such an attempt as I am making to state the facts of the case.

At the coronation of Edward II (1308), Edmund (Fitz Alan) earl of Arundel undoubtedly served, though Mohaut, youngest of the co-heirs, had claimed the office, a claim which he made successfully at the next coronation (1327), as was shown by Mr. Taylor in 1901.[1] But this, as I observed above, was doubtless owing to the disinherison, at the time, of the earls of Arundel. The next coronation (1377) is the first for which we possess the record of a court of claims, from which we learn that the earl of Arundel, claiming in right of his earldom, was unsuccessfully opposed by the lord of the manor of (Nether) Bilsington in Kent. The Bilsington serjeanty, the claim of which to serve at the coronation banquet was eventually recognised in another form, is dealt with elsewhere in these pages. In 1377 the above claim was rejected on the ground that, after parting with the manor, the earls of Arundel had continued to serve as chief butlers, and that the lord of Bilsington could show no precedent for the exercise of the office by his predecessors.

The earls, however, were not allowed to retain the coveted honour without challenge. Only a few years later (1381) the lord of Buckenham and Wymondham claimed restitution of the office, a claim which was revived in fresh circumstances for

[1] *Court of Claims*, p. 269.

the coronation feast of Queen Katherine (1420/21). The claims made upon that occasion have not received, I think, sufficient attention.   That of the earls of Arundel was rent, as it were, in twain; for on the death of Earl Thomas in 1415, his heirship in blood had passed to his three sisters, but the castle and honour of Arundel passed to his heir male under a family entail.   Both parties claimed the office in 1420/21, the three sisters as representing the earls of Arundel in whom it had been vested,[1] and the heir male, John Fitz Alan, *not* as earl of Arundel (for his right to the earldom was in dispute), but *as seised of the castle and honour of Arundel.*[2]

This claim is most important, for it differs wholly from that of his predecessors and his successors, namely that they were entitled *as earls of Arundel.* Probably the Court of claims, groping as usual for precedent, thought that John FitzAlan had at least one point in common with his predecessors, namely his tenure of Arundel, while the three

[1] Their petition is epitomised in the Duke of Norfolk's petition of 1901 (*Court of Claims*, pp. 240-241).   They claimed that their ancestors had been seised " in right of the earldom of Arundel...... and they prayed to be received at the Coronation of Queen Katherine by Richard *(sic)* Lenthall their deputy. "   The youngest sister had married Sir *Rowland* Lenthall, wrongly given as " *Robert* Lenthall" (p. 240).   Their position should be compared with that of the three sisters and co-heirs of the Earl of Oxford in 1526.

[2] " Setting out his title to the Castle and honour of Arundel, and claiming that those who were seized of the said Castle and honour from the time whereof memory is not, had served the office of Chief Butler at the Coronations of the Kings and Queens of England " (*Ibid.*, p. 241). The falsity of this claim is obvious from the fact that at the Coronation of Edward III, less than a century before, the earl of Kent (the King's uncle), though seised of the castle and honour, had neither claimed nor served the office.

co-heirs had neither the earldom [1] nor the tenure.

After this the earls of Arundel continued to be allowed the office, except that there seems to be no evidence as to the coronation of Edward IV. It may be pointed out, however, that just before it, Sir John (afterwards Lord) Wenlock, a great supporter of the King, was granted, " with the advice of the council...... the office of chief butler of England" for life, " in the same manner as Ralph Boteler, knight, lord of Sudeley, held it." [2]   In spite, however, of the identity of style, it is possible that the *honorary* office remained with the earls of Arundel, while that in which Wenlock succeeded Lord Sudeley was the actual headship of the butler's department, of which we read in the *Liber Niger* of King Edward's household :—

Office of Butler of England capital, unto whome the Styward and Thesaurer of Household make yerely warraunt...... this sergeaunt capitall Buttler...... taketh wages of houshold vij *d*.ob. [3] and clothing xlvj *s*. viij *d*. with the serjeauntes......   It hath lyked the Kinge now, [4] by the avyse of his full sadde and noble counsayle, to discharge this greate Butler of all the pourveyances of wynes for the King and his houshold, and to exempte him from this courte, lyke as is nowe the office of Privey Seale, the office of Marschalsey... Taylour, armourer, pavyllioner, and other moe that sumetyme were here incorporate...... which littelyth this courte to no small blemysshe, but to greete profit shall prove and worship for the Kinge. [5]

---

[1] It was claimed by the (Mowbray) Duke of Norfolk, representing the eldest.

[2] *Cal. of Pat. Rolls,* 1461-7, p. 8.

[3] 7½ *d*. a day was the wage of several household officers (see pp. 86, 88).

[4] *i. e. Temp.* Edward IV.

[5] *Household Ordinances* (Society of Antiquaries), pp. 73-4.

This duplication of the office of Chief Butler would roughly resemble the existence to-day of a Great Chamberlain and a Lord Chamberlain ; but a period in which the office of Privy Seal was spoken of with those of tailor and armourer was obviously far removed from our own.

The earls of Arundel appear to have duly exercised the office from the coronation of Richard III till that of Edward VI, when it was again unsuccessfully claimed by the Lord of Buckenham. Once more—at the coronation of Charles II (1661) —was their claim unsuccessfully opposed from the same quarter. But the singular thing is that on this occasion the earl (or rather his trustees for him), while, as usual, claiming " that the said office is appendant to his county or earldom of Arundel," added to it the further and clearly contradictory claim [1] that he held the manor of Kenninghall, " which is and anciently of long time heretofore was held in grand serjeanty, that is to say, to be the principal and Chief Butler of England on the days of the Coronations of the Kings of England." [2] This was a tactical blunder as amazing as it was wanton, for the whole question was at once re-

---

[1] The Duke of Norfolk's petition in 1901, after speaking rightly of " the trustees of Thomas (sic) Duke of Norfolk, Earl of Arundel, who claimed the office, " proceeds, if correctly copied, to quote the further claim as that " of the said Henry (!) Earl of Arundel " (Court of Claims, p. 244).   Either this is a mere blunder or it is taken from the petition of his nephew Duke Henry, at the coronation of James II.

[2] " Plutot que mesme le Duc tienne en son droit et en son demesne le mannor de Kenninghall ove les appurtenances en le county de Norfolke qui et auncientment et de long temps par devant fuit tenus en grand serjeantie c'est ascavoir destre le principal et chief botelier d'Angleterre. " Compare the Earl of Arundel's phrase in 1158, " pincernarum princeps sum et primus " (p. 153).

opened by this fatal admission.   If Kenninghall
was held in serjeanty by the service of acting as
chief butler, it is obvious that the office was not
held in right of the earldom of Arundel.[1]   The
two claims are contradictory.

Moreover if the serjeanty be thus admitted, it
is not the manor of Kenninghall alone that is
concerned.   Buckenham has at least as good a
claim, and in my opinion, a better ; for it
clearly formed the *caput* of the alleged *butelaria*.
Nevertheless the Dukes (as Earls) thenceforth
regularly continued to add at coronations this
second claim "up to and inclusive of that of
George IV,"[2] the last occasion on which a chief
butler was required.   It was, therefore, natural
enough that when they claimed anew in 1901,
after parting with the manor, their claim was
opposed by Mr. Taylor, whose father had bought it
from them.[3]   As there is no longer a coronation
banquet, the claims could not be decided.

I have endeavoured to state, without partiality,
the evidence bearing on the origin of this most

[1] Kenninghall had been acquired by the family long after they had
made their claim as earls.   It is obviously to Kenninghall that the
"Lords' Committee on the Dignity of a Peer" refer in their third
Report (1822) where they observe that "at this day the Duke of
Norfolk, as inheriting the property of the Arundel family *(sic)*, enjoys
part of the ancient Barony of Albini in Norfolk, and has been allowed
to perform the Service of Butler as incident to the tenure of that
property" (p. 82).   Apart from the interest of the latter part of this
statement as evidence of the authors' belief, its earlier portion is
erroneous, for Kenninghall did not come to the Dukes of Norfolk by
inheritance from the D'Aubignys.

[2] *Court of Claims*, p. 274.

[3] *Ibid.*, p. 275.

ancient office. To sum up, we have seen, at least, that it cannot have been originally held in right of the earldom of Arundel, and that it must have been granted either as a territorial serjeanty or as an office in gross. For both views there is something to be said. The presumption afforded by the other great offices of state is in favour of the latter view. Especially is this the case with the office of Great Chamberlain, which had its root of title in the same reign. On the other hand, so far as we know, there has never been a grant of the Chief Butlership by charter. If the whole of the Norfolk fief was held by knight-service, there is no room for serjeanty. If, however, three or more of its great demesne manors were held by a separate tenure, that tenure may, as alleged, have been butler-service. But it is, at least, highly significant that in no official list of Norfolk serjeanties is this service found. And this is further emphasised by the fact that the Kentish manor of Bilsington does appear as a serjeanty and was arrented as such.[1] It was, indeed, on this fact that its holder wisely rested his case when he claimed the butler's office in 1377.

There is, as we have seen, abundant proof that Norfolk jurors returned certain Norfolk manors, of which Buckenham was clearly the head, as held by the service of acting as chief butler. But the evidence in the case of the Great Chamberlain demonstrates the utter worthlessness of such returns. The decisive test of scutage cannot, in their case, be applied, and as I said, it is not possible to prove

[1] *Testa*, (See below).

definitely whether they were held, as was the rest
of the fief, by knight-service or not.[1] That they
were held by serjeanty I hold " not proven. " But,
whatever view historians may take of the origin of
this office, one can hardly doubt that a Court of
Claims would award it to the earls of Arundel with
its right, at the banquet of the crowned King, to
a golden cup and cover and its disputable claim to
such further perquisites as the wine that was left
over from the feast and " the vessels that lay under
the bar. "

THE ASSISTANT BUTLER

At the coronation of Queen Eleanor in 1236
there was a dispute as to this office between the
Mayor of London and " Master " Michael Belet.
Mr. Wickham Legg writes, in the " Introduction "
to his book :—

In 1236 the manor of Sheen was held by Michael Belet
as King's butler ; and he had to find two white cups for
the king. The office that Michael Belet held on that
occasion appears to have been due to a gross piece of
favouritism on the part of Henry III.[2]

With this view I cannot agree. What the record
states is this :—

servivit autem sub eodem [comite] in latere suo Magister
Michael Belet, cujus est illud officium secundario......
Habet etiam Magister Michael pincernariam in domo
regis sub comite *de jure veteri* (p. 60).[3]

[1] Because there seems to have been no part of the total quota due that
remained chargeable on the "demesne."

[2] *English Coronation Records*, (p. lxxix).

[3] See *Lib. Rub.*, p. 758.

The allegation of "ancient right" is entirely confirmed by the Pipe Roll of 1130 (31 Hen. I), in which we read, under Surrey, that John Belet accounts for £67. 3. 3. " pro rehabenda terra sua de Sceanes " (p. 49). Sheen, now Richmond, was the manor held by this service, as we learn from the *Testa*. Its abstract of the 1212 Inquest (p. 226) states that Sheen, which had been in the King's demesne, had been given by Henry I to the predecessors of Michael Belet, then in possession, (to hold) by butler service. [1] Six years earlier (1206) this Michael had given £100 for his succession to the butlership. [2]

The pedigree becomes difficult to follow owing to collateral successions, but we know that in 1218-1219 Wimund de Raleigh gave a hundred marcs for the wardship of Michael Belet's daughter and heir,[3] and that, very shortly afterwards, he was holding the Sheen serjeanty as her guardian.[4] The industry of Blount has preserved an entry on a Surrey plea roll which he dates 19 Henry III,— but which must be later,[5] for it refers to the arrentation,—giving a different version of the service, namely the presentation of cups at the Coronation

---

[1] " Syenes, quod fuit dominicum domini Regis H. vet' dedit manerium de Syenes antecessoribus Mich[aelis] Belet qui nunc tenet, per serjantiam pincerne " (The text is corrupt).

[2] Magister Michael Belet dat centum libras pro habenda pincernaria domini Regis sicut jus suum " (*Rot de obl. et fin.* [6 *John*], *p.* 358).

[3] Pipe Roll, 3 Hen. III.

[4] " Wimundus de Raleg habet custodiam filie et heredis Nichis (*sic*) Belet cum hereditate sua in Senes ; et debet esse in custodia domini Regis ; et valet per annum x li. praeter duas dotes ; et idem Wimundus habet custodiam predictam per Willelmum Briwere ; et (est) serjantia domini Regis de buteleria sua " (*Testa*, p. 227).

[5] See *Testa*, p. 228.

banquet. [1] When the serjeanty was " arrented "
(in 1250) it was in the hands of Emma Oliver and
Alice de Valletort, the daughters and co-heirs of
John Belet,[2] and it seems to have been a clear case
of a serjeanty being held jointly, and not being
deemed " impartible. " Apart from the fines
imposed for alienation, the two sisters arranged
that each of them should hold as half a knight's
fee that portion of her property which she had not
alienated.[3]

At about the same time, Emma ' Belet ' (who
was apparently a widow) sued John de Valletort and
Alice his wife for land in West Sheen. The plea
contains much information on the pedigree.[4] Sheen
was thenceforth held by knight-service: the butler-
service was at an end.

We now return to the allegation that Michael
Belet was allowed to usurp the place of the Mayor
of London at Queen Eleanor's Coronation (1236).
His office, we have seen, was no new one, and, as
I read the records, the Mayor's claim to take his
place in 1236 was rightly rejected by the King.
Mr. Legg asserts that " the City of London, which

---

[1] " Othonus (sic) de Grandison et Johannnes de Valletorta et Alicia
uxor ejus tenent villam de Chenes (sic) de serjantia inveniendi, die
Coronationis Regis, duos albos ciphos ad prandium ; et modo arrentata
est. " The form " Chenes " disguises the identity of the place.

[2] " Serjantia Emme Oliver et Alicie sororis ejus in Schenes, que fuit
Johannis Belet patris earum, pro qua debuit esse pincerna domini Regis "
(*Testa*, p. 228).

[3] " Johannes de Valletorta, qui duxit in uxorem Aliciam predictam,
alteram heredem dicte serjantie,........ faciat servicium dimidii feodi
unius militis de parte sua quam tenet que non est alienata...... Et
predicta Emma faciat servicium dimidii feodi unius militis de parte sua
quam tenet que non est alienata " (*Testa*, p. 229). *Cf.* pp. 28-9 above.

[4] Wrottesley's *Pedigrees from the Plea Rolls*, p. 495.

had served in butlery at the Coronation of Richard I, is set aside in favour of Master Michael Belet " (p. 57). But what we read of the former occasion is : " Cives vero Lundonie servierunt de pincernaria, et cives Wintonie de coquina " (p. 50). There is no mention here of the Mayor, nor, indeed was there a Mayor at the time.[1] In 1236 a novel claim was advanced by the Mayor, namely to take Michael's place at the King's table.[2] I do not gather that the right of the *citizens* to serve in the butlery was denied, and indeed the record admits that the City is bound to render that service. The personal claim of the Mayor was compromised by his serving the two bishops on the King's right.[3]

When we come to the Court of Claims for the Coronation of Richard II, we find the Mayor and citizens claiming (through the Recorder): (1) that the Mayor in virtue of his Mayoralty should personally serve the King, both in hall at dinner and in his chamber afterwards, with the King's gold cup, and should receive the gold cup and ewer as his fee ; (2) that " the other citizens," chosen by the City for the purpose, should serve in the butler's office as assistants to the chief butler, both in hall and in the great chamber. It entirely confirms my own view that, while no objection was raised to the citizens' claim, the Court reported to the King

[1] See my researches on the subject.

[2] " Andreas autem, Major civitatis Lundoniæ qui ibidem venerat ad serviendum de pincernaria cum ccc et lx cupis, eo quod civitas Lundonie servire tenetur in auxilium majoris pincernæ, sicuti et civitas Wintonie de coquina in auxilium senescalli, vendicavit locum magistri Michaelis astandi coram Rege, sed repulsus fuit precepto Regis dicentis quod nullus de jure ibi deberet servire nisi magister Michael. "

[3] " et ita concessit Major et servivit duobus episcopis a dextris Regis. "

that the Exchequer records proved the service now claimed for the Mayor to have been formerly discharged by the chief butler and the fee received by him. [1] The King, thereupon, to gratify the Londoners and encourage them to loyal devotion, compromised the matter by allowing the Mayor to serve him in his chamber, [2] receiving the golden cup and ewer as his fee. The chief butler—on this occasion the Earl of Arundel—would serve him, however, in hall, at the coronation banquet, and would receive the gold cup there used as his fee. [3] The Crown, therefore, had to find two gold cups, one for the chief butler and one for the Mayor as his assistant. [4]

The Mayor's fee, however, must have been of older date, for a notable petition on the Rolls of Parliament from Richard Bettoyne of London states that he, being Mayor, had discharged the office of butler at the Coronation of Edward III, [5]

---

[1] " pro eo quod per recorda et evidencias in scaccario Regis residencia est compertum quod capitalis Pincerna domini Regis pro tempore existens....... dictum servicium quod pro predicto Majore est vendicatum facere et hujusmodi feodum optinere solebat temporibus retroactis " etc., etc.

[2] " cum idem dominus noster Rex, post prandium, cameram suam ingressus vinum pecierit (*sic*), dictus Major predicto Regi de cipho aureo serviret. "

[3] The partial success, on this occasion, of the Mayor of London was perhaps due to the fact that the butler serjeanty of the Belets had long come to an end.

[4] We read accordingly, of the coronation of Edward VI, that eighty ounces of " *demi* souveraine gold " were "employed upon making of three cuppes of gold gevin the day of the Coronacion to therle of Arundel, Sir Edward Dymmocke and the Mayour of London for their claymes. " (*Acts of the Privy Council*, 1547, p. 65.) After the banquet the Mayor of London, " bearyng his cuppe in his hande, with his brethren went through the hal to their barge. "

[5] We know hardly anything of this Coronation.

with 360 'valets,' all in one livery, each of them carrying a silver cup, as at the previous coronations,[1] and had received the accustomed fee, namely a gold cup and cover, with an enamelled gold ewer,[2] but that the Exchequer had ordered the Sheriffs to distrain upon his property to the amount of £89. 12. 6. in payment for his fee! He said they would gladly pay the fee if they were discharged from the service.[3]

Eventually the Mayor's persistence was rewarded to some extent, for he was allowed to perform his service at the banquet itself when James II was crowned.

The Lord Mayor of London, attended by twelve principal citizens, came from the cupboard and presented on his knee a bowl of wine to the King in a gold cup which he received as his fee;[4] and with his attendants repaired to dinner at the lower end of the hall.

But indeed, two centuries earlier, at the coronation of Richard III, this was already the practice.

At the end of dinner the Mayor of London served the King and Queene with Sweete wine and had of ech of them a cup of gold and a ewer of gold.[5]

This was before "the King returned to his chamber." Mr. Legg observes that :—

[1] This is extremely important as confirming the almost incredible statement that a previous mayor had so served, with 360 ' cups, ' at the coronation of Queen Eleanor in 1236 (see p. 168 above).

[2] " le fee q'appendoit a cel jorne, c'est assavoir un coupe d'or ove la covercle et un ewer d'or enamaille. "

[3] *Rot. Parl.*, II, 96 (quoted in *His Grace the Steward*, p. 183).

[4] " one Cup of Gold for the Lord Mayor of London " is named, in the Lord Chamberlain's Records, vol. 429, fo. 9, as provided.

[5] Legg, *op. cit.* p. 197.

While the King and Queen are eating the wafers,[1] the Lord Mayor of London who assists the Chief Butler in "botelry," brings a bowl of wine in a golden cup, which he retains as his fee (p. lxvi)...... The Lord Mayor of London claims to serve in botelry and to assist the Chief Butler in his duties. The citizens of Winchester also claimed this service ; but after 1236, when they were put aside by Henry III [see below Doc. VIII p. 60], they do not appear to have attempted a claim again (p. lxxx).

This is one of the strangest errors in Mr. Legg's 'introduction,' for, on referring to the passage he cites from his own pages, we find that the citizens of Winchester did not claim to serve in the botelry, but in the kitchen, and were not " put aside " by the King.

Moreover, his own statement on p. 57 (see above) is that it was "the City of London" which was "set aside" by the King in 1236. It was, as a matter of fact, at the re-coronation of Richard in 1194, which he has so strangely overlooked, that "the citizens of Winchester also claimed this service,"[2] and were " put aside " by the venal King (for 200 marcs!) and relegated, as before, to the kitchen.[3] Held in the monks' refectory, it was a glorious banquet (*epulabantur splendide*).

Lastly, the Mayor and citizens of Oxford claimed to serve in the butlery with the citizens of London. Mr. Wollaston's book is only concerned with actual Courts of Claims, so that his first mention of this service is at the coronation of Charles II.

---

[1] See the section on " the waferer serjeanty."

[2] Possibly because this ceremony took place at Winchester.

[3] " Cives autem Lundoniarium, data regi mercede ducentarum marcarum, servierunt de pincernaria contra calumniam civium Wintonie. Cives vero Wintonie servierunt de coquina " (*Hoveden*, III, 247).

But we get a glimpse of it much earlier, for at the coronation of Anne Boleyn, where twelve citizens of London assisted the chief butler by waiting on him " at the cupboard," the Mayor of Oxford kept the buttery bar. At the coronation of Edward VI he again made good his right " to ayde the chief butler in his service of ale at the barr." [1]

As a matter of fact the Oxford privilege appears to be the oldest of all so far as records are concerned. Although known to us only by a late *inspeximus*, there is a charter of Henry II granting to the citizens of Oxford as an additional privilege, " et quod ad festum (*sic*) meum [2] mihi serviant cum illis de Butteillaria mea." [3] This charter was not known to Eyton, but it seems to belong to the opening day of 1156, when the King was on his way to Dover. [4] The importance of this date is that the words " cum illis " carry back the service of the citizens of London even further.

THE BILSINGTON SERJEANTY

This is a most difficult serjeanty to deal with. Bilsington was a manor in Kent, which was alleged

[1] Taylor's *Glory of Regality*, p. 141.

[2] This is a somewhat ambiguous phrase. It does not specify the coronation and yet, being in the singular, it cannot cover the crown-wearing days. Possibly the *inspeximus* text is corrupt.

[3] Ogle's *Royal letters to Oxford*, p. 4. " Illi " are the citizens of London.

[4] Eyton's *Court and Itinerary*, p. 15. Its witnesses are Thomas the Chancellor, Reginald, Earl of Cornwall, Hugh (wrongly given as Henry) Earl of Norfolk, Richard de Humez the Constable (of Normandy), Warin Fitz Gerold the chamberlain, Manasser Biset the Steward (*dapifero*) and Jocelin de Balliol.

to have been held by the earls of Arundel by the service of being king's butler.[1]   The question that was raised, and that had to be solved, was the nature of the service due from the manor after it had passed out of their hands.

One cannot here trace the whole history of the manor, but it is important to correct Mr. Legg's erroneous statement that " it was originally in the possession of the Albini family, Earls of Arundel, but was alienated in the time of Edward III [2] " (*sic*). It was alienated, on the contrary, in the time of Henry III, when the male line of the " Albini " family came to an end.   The statements in the *Testa* (which are confined to the " arrentation " of the serjeanty in 1250) are fully confirmed by the charter rolls and patent rolls.

The manor had undoubtedly been held by Hugh earl of Arundel (who died in 1243), and the *Testa* states that John Maunsel held, of the gift of his heirs, a moiety " of the said serjeanty by sufficient confirmation of the King specifying the said ser- jeanty "[3] (p. 216).   Now the patent rolls shew that as early as July 15th, 1243, John Maunsel had a grant, during pleasure, of the manor, which the King had impounded as " land of the Normans, " and that he had licence, 28th May, 1244, to receive the earl's lands there from his heirs.   Two years later (22 April 1246) the king confirmed to him all the earl's inheritance in Bilsington, which the

---

[1] " pro qua debuit esse pincerna domini regis " (*Testa*, p. 216 *bis*).

[2] *English Coronation Records*, p. lxxviii.

[3] Hasted holds that there were two manors, of which Nether Bilsing- ton was the chief, and that only one of them was alienated to Maunsel ; but the records, we shall see, speak of his obtaining all the earl's lands there.

earl's heirs had given him, as it was found to be not "land of the Normans," and on Oct. 7, 1248 the king granted him "all fines for alienations of lands pertaining to the serjeanty of Bilsington, which the said John has of the gift of the heirs of Hugh, sometime earl of Arundel, and which the king has confirmed to him by charter." [1] This brings us to the "arrentation," when the "butler" service was recognised.

Was it wrongly recognised? Stapleton asserts that the earls of Arundel had no connexion with Bilsington till it was granted, as escheat of the Normans, to William, earl of Arundel, during pleasure, in 1207, [2] and complains that Hasted falsely ascribes its acquisition to William de Albini in the reign of Henry I. [3] Stapleton's authority is very great, but Hasted seems to be right. For the tithes of Bilsington were given to Rochester by William "de Albengneyo" [4] (i. e. the original "Butler"), whose daughter seems to have brought Bilsington to her husband. [5] This, however, does not prove that he was butler in right of Bilsington ; the alleged tenure may have had its rise, on the contrary, in his office. [6]

---

[1] *Cal. of Charter Rolls*, I, 292, 338. John then founded Bilsington Priory, endowing it with part of his lands there. He was, of course, the famous royal chaplain and official of Henry III, who became so wealthy a pluralist.

[2] Stapleton's point that it had previously been held by Robert de Courcy is confirmed by the *Testa* (p. 216), where we have to recognise Bilsington under the disguise of "Kulsintone," which had escheated to the King.

[3] *Liber de Antiquis Legibus*, p. xl. (note).

[4] *Lib. Rub.*, p. 751.

[5] Dugdale's *Baronage*, I, 118.

[6] See the section on "The chief butler."

The very slight evidence in the *Testa* is supplemented by two records which were noted for us by Blount. The first is an entry on the Hundred Rolls (1275) that the Prior of Bilsington holds part of the serjeanty there by the tenure of serving the King with his cup on Whitsunday. [1] The other is a Kent plea roll of 21 Edw. I (1292-3), on which we read that the earl of Arundel's "ancestors" used to hold Bilsington by the serjeanty of being king's butler on Whitsunday. [2] The concurrence of these two documents as to a "Whitsunday" service is very curious ; one can only suggest that it refers to the annual court at Westminster, the nearest of the three to Kent, being held at Whitsuntide.

At the first and famous Court of Claims, in 1377, the earl of Arundel's claim to serve as chief butler was opposed by Edmund Staplegate, who claimed that, as he held the manor of Bilsington

par les services destre Botiller de nostre sieur le Roi a sa coronement, come pleinement appiert en le livre des fees de serjanties en exchequer nostre sieur le Roi...... profre de faire le dit office de Botiller et prie quil a ce soit receu.

He added the very interesting fact that his wardship and marriage had been given to Geoffrey Chaucer ('Chausyer'), from whom he had purchased them. Edmund was well advised in appealing to the Exchequer record, as all claimants endeavoured to do, for the *Testa*, as we have seen, did recognise the service, though it did not, as he alleged, refer to the coronation.

[1] " ad serviendum dominum Regem, die Pentecostes, de coupa sua. "
[2] " per serjantiam essendi pincerna domini Regis in die Pentecostes. "

The earl had tersely claimed the office, without vouching any record, for in his case there was nothing in the *Testa* to which he could appeal. But Edmund Staplegate was a small man, and the earl a very great one, nor could the former cite an actual precedent, which is what the Court has always required. [1] So, after long discussion and hearing of evidence, [2] it was decided that there was not then time to settle the matter finally, and that, as the earls could show [3] possession of the office, after their alienation of the manor, the earl should serve at that coronation, with a *salvo jure* to Edmund.

At a very much later time, the coronation of Charles II, Edmund's claim was revived. The lord of the manor of (Nether) Bilsington was allowed, as his service, to present three maple cups (which he did by deputy), and this strange substitute for the original claim was thenceforth regularly allowed down to the last banquet, that of George IV, when a deputy presented the cups. By a curious—and economical—custom the King presented to the Mayor of Oxford, as his fee for helping at the banquet, the three cups he had just received from the lord of the manor of Bilsington. [4] I can, however, prove that he was less shabbily treated in the 17th century. For the coronation of James II, as for that of Charles II, there was

[1] See p. 152 above.

[2] " auditis quampluribus recordis, racionibus, et evidenciis... curie monstratis. "

[3] " per recordum de scaccario est compertum. "   It is not easy to say what this " recordum " can have been.

[4] Taylor's *Glory of Regality*, p. 225 ; Legg's *English Coronation Records*, pp. lxvi, lxxx.

provided " One guilt Bowle for the Mayor of Oxford, " as for the King's Champion. [1]

SERJEANTY OF "THE HOSE"

Nothing, perhaps, in this work has caused me greater difficulty than the meaning of that " hose " or " huse " which we find associated with wine. In the *Constitutio domus regis* we meet, not, indeed, with *hosa*, but with *hosarii* as on the staff of the butler's department,[2] and Robert "Hosarius" occurs as a considerable holder of land on the Pipe Roll of 1130 (p. 72) under Sussex. But so completely did the term baffle the *Red Book* editor that he had to leave *Hosarii* untranslated.[3] He does, indeed, observe that " Probably the confusion between the offices of hosiers of the Wardrobe and Buttery respectively is of old standing "[4], but neither in old English nor in old French can we find " Hosier " used for a buttery officer. Ducange, we find, takes (under *Osa*) these *Hosarii* to be wardrobe officers in charge of the King's hose.

When we turn to serjeanties, we find, under Berkshire, in the *Red Book* (p. 451), Roger de St. Philibert holding land " per serjanteriam serviendi in Husa. " In the *Testa* we read, further, that Hugh de St. Philibert held the land " *in Bray* per serjantiam serviendi de Husa " (p. 128), and

---

[1] Lord Chamberlain's Records, Vol. 429, fo. 9.
[2] "Hosarii in domo commedent ; et hominibus suis unicuique iij den." (*Red Book*, p. 810).
[3] p. ccxci. *Cf.* p. 60 above.
[4] p. ccxcix.

finally that he held " in dominico suo Treswell (*sic*) infra limites manerii de Bray de domino rege in capite per serjantiam de la Hurse " (*sic*). [1] This would not tell us much if it were not for a welcome entry for which we are indebted to Blount :—

" Hugo de Sancto Philiberto tenet manerium de Creswell, in com. Berks., per serjantiam ducendi butellos *(sic)* vini ad jentaculum Domini Regis—et vocatur illa *Serjantia de la Huse*,—per regnum Angliae. " [2]

We thus know that the estate was the manor of Cresswell in Bray, on the Thames, the manor house of which (associated with traditions of Nell Gwyn) is known from its early possessors as Philberts (or Filberts), and that the serjeanty was alleged to be connected with the carriage of wine. The *Inq. p. m.* on the elder Hugh records him as holding Creswell, " whence his ancestors sometime served de la Huse. " [3] The Record office editors were evidently baffled by the phrase " de la Huse " and even seem to have strangely imagined that the service was done to a " family of de la Huse " (p. 368).

We turn in vain to Ducange for light on " Huse " as a term connected with wine, but under " Hosa " we have one entry which is of great importance, though he seems to have deemed it suspect as a

---

[1] *Testa*, p. 124.

[2] From " Plac. Coron. apud Windesore, 12 Edw. I, Rot. 40 in dors." Blount's later editors give separately, under Bray, the *ocreæ* entry mentioned below, from the *Testa*, and render it—" The Serjeanty of serving our lord the King with his boots " !

[3] *Inq. p. m.* of 1249 in *Calendar of Inq.* (1904), I, No. 137. ' Creswelle ' is there identified as Carswell, I do not know why.

mere emendation. [1]   This quotation, from a Charter of 1034, speaks " Ricardi de Lillabona qui
hosam vini Comitis ferebat. "   By itself it might
be suspect, but the Pipe Rolls of Henry II's reign
afford decisive evidence that there is no mistake.
In that of the 4th year (1158) we have a charge
" pro barilz ferratis et non ferratis et buttis et
bucellis et summis et sumariis et *hosis* magnis et
parvis. "   In that of the 6th year (1160) we have
a charge (among things for carrying wine) of
" ij *hosis* ad vinum ad opus Reginæ " (p. 13), and
in that of the 11th year (1165) a charge of £9
" pro *hosis* ad vinum et pro Buttis Bucellis et
Barhuz et quatuor carrettis " (p. 31).   Again in
the 17th year (1171) we have 32 sh. charged " pro
Buscellis et *hosis*" (p. 147).

We are still, however, in the dark as to what
the *hosa* was.   There is mention on the rolls of
tuns and butts, of hooped casks, and barrels and
wineskins [2] (*utribus*), but the *hosa* baffles us.   My
own impression is that, in the first place, the term
became obsolete early, and that, in the second, the
vessel must in some way have suggested a boot.
As to obsolescence, the gloss in the entry cited by
Blount and the mention of the service as a former
one, support my view, as does the fact that the
term occurs so rarely and only in early days, and
disappears from the Royal Household.   As to the
latter, the phrase "hosis *ad vinum*" suggests that there

---

[1] " Mendum esse suspicor."
[2] *Pipe Roll*, 16 Henry II, p. 15.   Mr. Freeman speaks of " Waggons
loaded... with casks of wine " as shown on the Bayeux Tapestry, but it
also shows wineskins among the things brought over by William at the
Conquest.

were other " hosæ " from which these had to be distinguished. And this, we know, was the case, for the old French *housse* and medieval *hosa* meant a boot, or rather covering for the lower leg which might also cover the foot. It might thus mean leggings or greaves, but also a complete covering which included the foot, thus giving us our word ' hose. ' Strictly speaking, greaves were " Caligæ ferreæ " [1] or " *ocreæ*, " [2] and is is significant that the *hosa* of Ducange's entry is equated in another version of the text by " ocrea, " [3] while the Cresswell serjeanty is in one place entered as serving " de ocreis domini Regis. " [4] This looks to me like an entry by some scribe who did not understand what *hosa* meant.

We have, however, yet another gloss upon this word ' hose, ' which enables us to check Blount's reading. On the Hundred Rolls there is an entry of about the same date which runs thus :—

Hugo de Sancto Philiberto tenet duas hidas terræ in predicto manerio per serjantiam ad portandum cum domino rege unum Buscellum *(sic)* vini. [5]

The meaning of " buscellum " is known : it is the old French *boucel*, defined as a " petit tonneau " (little barrel). It would seem probable that Blount's ' butellos ' is but one of his misreadings, though the " buscellis " of the early Pipe Rolls are, we have seen, entered as distinct from the " hosis. "

---

[1] *Pipe Roll*, 17 Hen. II, p. 147.
[2] " Caligis et ocreis " *(Ib.* 16 Hen. II, p. 15); " pro ocreis Regis, xl sol. " *(Ib.* 5 Hen. II, p. 3).
[3] See above.
[4] *Testa de Nevill*, p. 108. *Cf.* p. 178 above.
[5] *Rot. Hund.*, I, 12.

There remains the interesting question whether the office of this serjeant can be traced in the household of later times.   We find that in Queen Elizabeth's reign there was in the Department of the Cellar ('Sellar') a "Yeoman of the Bottles," whose function it was "to carry wine and drinke for the King, when his Majestie rideth abroade," and that in 1610 Prince Henry had "a Groome of the bottles for the field," and that a "bottle groome" was included in the households of Charles II and of William III.[1] His office must apparently have resembled that assigned to Richard de Lillebone in 1034.[2]

It would seem to be at least likely that the surname "de la Hose" (or "Huse") was derived from service "de la Huse."   Bartholomew de la Hose held a fee of Adam de Port in 1166,[3] and was clearly therefore, the successor of that Geoffrey "de Hosa" who is entered under Berkshire on the Pipe Roll of 1130 (p. 123) as paying "ut resaisatur de terra sua quam tenet de Adam de Port." Indeed, under John, this fee is entered as held "de honore de Kyntone."[4]   Finally, this fee is identified, under Henry III, as held by Bartholomew "de la Huse" *in Denford* of the Honour of "Kynton."[5]

---

[1] *Household Ordinances* (Society of Antiquaries).
[2] See p. 179 above.
[3] *Red Book*, p. 279.
[4] *Red Book*, p. 143.   See *Genealogist* (N.S.) XVI, 6-13, where I have shown who Adam de Port really was, and have identified 'Kyntone' as Kington, Heref., Mr. Hall the editor of the *Red Book* having made it a "Kington, co. Dorset" in one place and an unknown Wiltshire manor in another !
[5] *Testa*, p. 109.

A further entry shows us this Bartholomew " de la Huse " holding two hides in Great Farringdon of the King " per serjeantiam ostur', " [1] and a suit of 1231 proves that this land was in " Inglesham " and that Bartholomew was charged with witholding suit for it at the Abbot of Beaulieu's court at Farringdon. [2]   He pleaded that he held his land of the king " per unum austurcum custodiendum. " Inglesham lay on the border of Berks and Wilts and we find an entry under Wilts that Bartholomew " de Husa " held it in chief of the king " per servicium mutandi quoddam ostorium de veteri feofamento, " [3] a statement which carries back the serjeanty to the days of Henry I.   This enables us to identify the holding with that which Geoffrey de la Huse held in 1212. [4]

Although the family has been here dealt with for the interest of its name [5] and for the early date to which that name can be traced, one may note that it affords an excellent instance of a family holding by knight-service as under-tenants [6] and also by serjeanty as tenants in chief.   Their position

---

[1] *Ibid.*, p. 126.

[2] *Bracton's Note Book*, Case 655.   He is there Bartholomew " de la Hose."

[3] *Testa*, p. 154.   See the section on " Goshawk serjeanties " for an explanation of this service.

[4] " Galfridus de la Huse tenet in F[er]enden et Inglesham L solidatas terre per serjantiam custodiendi unum accipitrem " *(Testa*, p. 128 ; *Cf. Red Book*, p. 486).

[5] We have also on the Pipe Roll of 1130 a William " de Hosa " under Berkshire, and men of the name under Middlesex and Cornwall.

[6] A Geoffrey " Hosatus " returned his holding (under Wilts) in 1166 as one fee held in chief, but although the editor of the *Red Book* has combined the families, we have seen that the representative of ours in 1166 was Bartholomew " de la Hose."

is well illustrated by an entry on the Pipe Roll of
3 John (1201) which Madox cites thus :—

De finibus militum et scutagiis. Idem Vicecomes redd.
comp. de iij marcis de Galfrido de la Hose, ne transfretet
et *(sic)* pro feodo j militis de honore de Kinton ; et de
dimidia marca de Simone Puncard qui tenet per serjanteriam.

The true meaning of this entry is that Geoffrey
" fined " for his serjeanty *and* paid two marcs
(scutage) for his knight's fee held of the honour of
Kington.   The two holdings were in the same
hands, but the tenures were kept distinct. [1]

A BUTLERY SERJEANTY

An obscure little serjeanty in the Butler's department is that of the Kivilly family, which must
have taken its name from Quévilly near Rouen.
We read on the Pipe Roll of 1130, under Essex,—

Robertus filius Siwardi r.c. de xv marc. argenti pro
ministerio et uxore Hugonis Chivilli (p. 53).

To this Robert a large sum is remitted for Danegeld, but evidently not in respect of ' Chivilli '
lands.   For the *Testa* records, under Essex, the
verdict of the Writtle jurors in 1212 that.

Quedam terra in Borham quam Willemus de Kiveli
tenuit,—et dimisit illam episcopo Lond' Willelmo de

---

[1] See p. 27 for Madox' misunderstanding of these lists.

Sancte Marie ecclesia ;[1] et predictus episcopus dimisit eam
Rogero filio Alani,—pertinet ad manerium de Writel', et
quod solet reddere per annum ad curiam de Writel xx *s.*
(p. 270).

They further alleged that Godebold of Writtle,
having been captured by the notorious Geoffrey de
Mandeville under Stephen, mortgaged the land,
for his ' redemption, ' to William's predecessors.
But on p. 269 we read that

> Willelmus de Kiveli tenuit in Borham dim' car' terrae
> quam rex H. dedit Hugoni de Kiveli, sed nescitur per
> quod servicium etc.

Although we cannot definitely connect the land
with the office, it is clear that this William, and
Hugh before him, held office under the Butler, for
the Pipe Roll of 1199 records that—

> Willelmus de Chevill' redd. comp. de xl marcis pro
> habendo officio suo in Domo Regis quod pater suus
> habuit, scilicet ostium Pincernae, et servire in Domo ut
> pincerna, et wardam, jus *(sic)* quadrigae portantis utensilia
> Pincernae, et prisas vini cum pertinentibus ad officium
> illud. [2]

This record is curiously illustrated by two entries
on the rolls of Henry II. On that of 1179 we
read

> Et in custamento ducendi vina per domos Regis per

---

[1] 1198-1224.

[2] Rot. 1 John (Essex) as cited by Madox *(Exchequer)*. The Oblate
Roll of 1 John (1199) also records, under Essex, this payment by
William de Chiveli for his office in the butlery " sicut antecessores sui "
(p. 17).

Angliam £18.16.11, per breve Regis et per visum Hugonis de Kivilli et Roberti fratris sui (p. 108)

while on that of 1177 the brother only is mentioned :—

Et pro vino ad opus regis £14.3.4 per breve Regis per Robertum de Kivilli (p. 166).

The office of the Kivillis was that of usher of the Butlery—which is mentioned in the *Constitutio* [1]— but, it must be repeated, there is no actual proof that it was connected with land and was, as such, a serjeanty.

THE BEER-BUYER'S SERJEANTY

At West Hendred, Berks, was a small serjeanty belonging to the Butler's department. On the Oblate Roll of 3 John (1201) we read, under Berkshire, " Willelmus de Henrede...... tenet per sergent' pinc[ern']. " In the *Red Book* (p. 451) Richard de Henrede holds " per serjanteriam custodiendi cervisiam, " an entry which expands in the *Testa* into

Ricardus de Hanred tenet de domino Rege in villa de Westhanred c solidatas terre per servicium serviendi de cervis ' in Butellaria domini Regis (p. 108).

In the 1212 survey, however, the *Testa* (p. 128)

---

[1] " Hostiarius Butellariæ consuetudinarium cibum, et iij ob. homini suo " *(Lib. Rub.*, p. 810).

makes the service that of keeping *(custodiendi)* the beer, as in the *Red Book*.

In the Hundred Rolls William de Spersholt is given as holding one third of West Hendred of the king by the service " quod debet emere cervis ' in hospicio domini Regis. "   And this version of the service is found also in a plea of 12 Edward I (1283-4) cited by Blount, where William ' de Insula ' is given as holding a carucate there " per serjantiam emendi cervisiam ad opus domini Regis."

THE KING'S DISPENSERS

The history of this race of ' Dispensers ' will be dealt with here somewhat fully, because, in spite of their tenure of this court office for some two centuries, they seem to have been somewhat overlooked.   Their history, so far as I know, has never been worked out, and their pedigree, remarkable for its antiquity, has served merely as a quarry for the pedigree-mongers who constructed for the noble house of Spencer a descent that carried back their line to medieval times.   Deserving as it does a better fate, I have here rescued it from oblivion and set it forth, I believe, for the first time.

The real clue to the history of these hereditary Dispensers is found in their tenure by serjeanty of Great Rollright, Oxon.   And the source on which we are dependent for tracing the pedigree of the family is the cartulary of Abingdon Abbey.

This is a serjeanty that, without question, can be carried back to Domesday. In that record (106b) we read under " Terra..... ministrorum regis "— the right heading for serjeants—that Robert the son

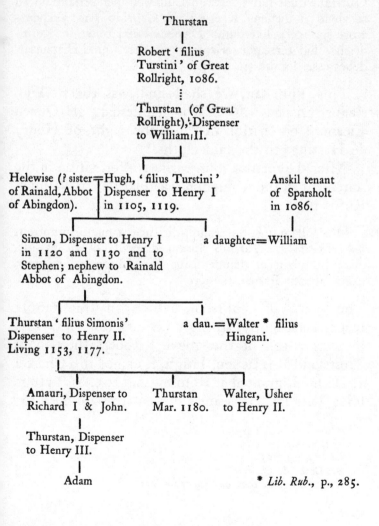

Thurstan
|
Robert ' filius Turstini ' of Great Rollright, 1086.
⋮
Thurstan (of Great Rollright), Dispenser to William II.

Helewise (? sister of Rainald, Abbot of Abingdon). = Hugh, ' filius Turstini ' Dispenser to Henry I in 1105, 1119.

Anskil tenant of Sparsholt in 1086.

Simon, Dispenser to Henry I in 1120 and 1130 and to Stephen; nephew to Rainald Abbot of Abingdon.

a daughter = William

Thurstan ' filius Simonis ' Dispenser to Henry II. Living 1153, 1177.

a dau. = Walter * filius Hingani.

Amauri, Dispenser to Richard I & John.

Thurstan Mar. 1180.

Walter, Usher to Henry II.

Thurstan, Dispenser to Henry III.
|
Adam

* *Lib. Rub.*, p., 285.

of Thurstan[1] holds 5¼ hides in ' Rolendri ' and
that Osmund holds of him two hides in ' Lude-
welle. '   In the *Testa* we have these relative
entries :—

> Thurstanus Dispensator tenet in Magna Rolendr' v
> hidas terre per serjantiam de dispensator' Regis (p. 108).
> Galfridus duas hidas terre in Ludewell' per serjantiam ad
> serviend' in dispens' R[egis] sub Galfrido[2] *(sic)* Dispens-
> atore (p. 108). Turstanus Dispens[ator] tenet in Rolin-
> drich v hid' terre per serjantiam, videlicet quod Dispensar'
> debet esse domini (p. 118).

This Thurstan, we shall find, was that " Turstanus Dispensarius " who contested, at Queen
Eleanor's coronation in 1236, the right of Henry
de Hastings to the tablecloths.[3]

After Domesday our earliest information is the
statement in the Abingdon Cartulary as to William
Rufus that

> Mox villam quæ Speresholt dicitur rex manu immittens
> *suo dispensatori Turstino* ipsam donavit, quam et ille,
> quamdiu vixit, et deinde filius ejus Hugo, ad regimen
> usque abbatis Faricii, tenuere.[4]

The name of Thurstan, which in this family
recurs persistently, strongly favours the view that
he was a son of the above ' Robert the son of
Thurstan.'[5]   His son, Hugh, is named in a Charter
of Henry I, granted at Romsey in 1105, as " Hugo
filius Turstini, curiæ meæ dispensator " and as the

---

[1] " Robertus filius Turstini."
[2] This appears to be an error.
[3] *Lib. Rub.*, p. 757.
[4] *Ab. Cart.*, II, 37.
[5] But he may have been brother or nephew.

holder of ten hides at Sparsholt, for which he is directed to do homage to the Abbot. [1] There is also a writ of Henry I, addressed " Hugoni filio Turstini" [2], relating to that friction with the Abbey to which we owe our knowledge of the pedigree, and, two years after the death of Abbot Faricius, —that is, in or about 1119—we have him, as ' Hugo dispensator,' giving the tithes of Sparsholt and naming Helewis his wife. [3]

That Hugh was followed immediately by Simon in the possession of this land and office is clear. But whether Simon was his son or his brother is not at present certain. We read of this Simon that, being with the King in Normandy, [4] during the four years interregnum at the Abbey (1117-1121), after the death of Abbot Faricius, he got possession, through him, of Markham church, the more easily because, as nephew to Abbot Rainald, [5] he was heir to William, Rainald's son. [6]   He occurs, as ' Symon Dispensator, ' on the Pipe Roll of 1130 (31 Hen. 1), which shows him as excused, under Oxfordshire, 30 sh. for Danegeld, while it also records, under Gloucestershire, a payment for the pleas of his sister's son, Odard of Carlisle. [7]

[1] *Ibid.*, II, 126.
[2] *Ibid.*, II, 91.
[3] *Ibid.*, II, 159.
[4] From which Henry returned in 1120.
[5] This proves that Simon's mother was a sister of that Abbot.
[6] *Ibid.*, II, 66.
[7] " " Symon dispensator debet xl m. argenti pro placitis quod rex habebat versus Odardum de Chaerleolio sororium suum" (p. 79). See, for Odard, my paper on " Odard of Carlisle " (*Geneal.*, [N.S.] VIII, 200-204), where it is shown that he and Hildred " of Carlisle, " his father, were both living in 1130, and my earlier paper on " Odard the sheriff" (*Ibid.*, V, 25-8) where I have proved that he was quite distinct

Another of his sisters is proved by the Abingdon cartulary to have married the dispossessed William son of Anskill of Sparsholt, a marriage through which some of the lands were regained by him. Finally, he is mentioned under Stephen as giving Tadmarton with his daughter to Walter " filius Hingani, " [1] who was living in 1166. [2]

With Thurstan, Simon's son and successor, we emerge into the light of day. He had already succeeded his father in 1153 [3] and in the early days of Henry II's reign the King caused the usual dispute between him and Abingdon Abbey to be heard at Woodstock before himself and three of his justices, Gregory of London, William Fitz John, and Nigel de Broc. [4] In 1158 Thurstan was excused from certain payments due from his lands in Oxfordshire and elsewhere [5] and in 1159, under Yorkshire, from his quota to the *donum* of the Archbishop of York. [6] How he came to appear

from Odard " of Carlisle " with whom Mr. Hodgson Hinde identified him. See also Canon Prescott's learned notes in *Register of Wetherhal* (pp. 143-147).

[1] *Ab. Cart.*, II, 183.

[2] *Lib. Rub.*, p. 285.

[3] *Ab. Cart.*, II, 184.

[4] *Ibid.*, II, 186. The mention of Gregory is of interest because he figures, also as Gregory of London, in another Woodstock document (see my *Calendar of docs. France*, p. 533) and is clearly identical with that " Gregory " whom the lost Pipe Roll of 1155 shows us as sheriff of London in the early days of Henry II, *i. e.* till Michaelmas of that year (*Lib. Rub.*, p. 658). This is a notable instance of the practice (which I have elsewhere explained) of sheriffs (and their families) assuming a surname from the county town of which they were sheriffs. "Gregory" also appears on the Roll of the next year (1156) as a justice in Bucks and Surrey, and accounts, as " Gregory," on that of 1159 (p. 3) " de placitis de tempore suo."

[5] *Pipe Roll*, 4 Hen. II, pp. 144, 150.

[6] *Ibid.*, 5 Hen. II, p. 31. *Cf. Lib. Rub.*, p. 697 (1162).

under Yorkshire will be explained below. He was similarly exempted from his quota to that of the abbot of Abingdon. [1]

In these entries Thurstan is styled merely " filius Simonis ; " but in 1165 we have him, under Gloucestershire, entered further as Dispenser. [2] The entries concerning him in the returns of 1166 are of special interest for his name being therein entered under three different forms. As Thurstan " filius Simonis " he held half a fee of Abingdon Abbey and half a fee of Walter de Bolebec ; [3] as Thurstan " Dispensator " he held a fee of Robert " de Scrupa ; " [4] and under the unique and unexpected form of Thurstan " de Lechantone " he held half a fee of the Archbishop of York. [5] This, though entered under Yorkshire, was at Compton Abdale in Gloucestershire, where his heir Adam le Despenser held of the Archbishop in 1284-5. [6] And, as for his style ' de Lechantone, ' it is derived from Leckhampton in the same county, which was alleged to form part of his serjeanty. [7] It is of interest to note that the half fee held of Walter de Bolebec was an Ewelme (Oxon) ; for it was held there by the later Thurstan of the Countess of Oxford (née de Bolebec) who held of the earl marshal, [8] as her ancestor Hugh (de Bolebec) had

[1] *Ibid.*, p. 37.
[2] " Et pro 849 summis frumenti £35. 7. 6 liberat' Turst' fil' Sim' dispens' " *(Pipe Roll*, 11 Hen. II, p. 12).
[3] *Lib. Rub.*, pp. 306, 317.
[4] *Ibid.*, p. 295.
[5] *Ibid.*, p. 415.
[6] *Feudal Aids*, II, 238.
[7] *Testa de Nevill*, p. 81.
[8] *Testa*, pp. 100, 106.

held of his predecessor, Walter Giffard, in Domesday.

It was some time before 1166 that he is found, as Thurstan " filius Simonis " at Rhuddlan among the witnesses to a charter of Henry de Oilli, the King's constable, to which are also witnesses Manasser Biset, the King's steward (*dapifer*), Michael Belet, and some administrative officers. [1]

We may now approach the quaint anecdote told by Walter Map, in which Thurstan figures as the King's dispenser (*dispensator regis*) and as discharging his office at court. The object of the story is to illustrate the courtesy enjoined by Henry II. Adam ' a Gernemeu, ' whose office it was to seal the writs at court, declined to seal an official document for Thurstan, free of charge, as he should have done, and, when accused of this by Thurstan, retorted that the latter had declined his request to send him two of the King's cakes, when he was entertaining friends. The King decreed that Thurstan—the words "abjecto pallio genibus flexis" should be noted [2]—must present the two cakes (*gastella*), decently enveloped in a white napkin, to Adam, who would then seal and hand him the writ as required. The story is worth quoting in the original Latin : I have supplied the word " Simonis, " which has, clearly, been omitted. [3]

[1] *Charters in the Brit. Mus.*, I, No. 44.
[2] *Cf.* pp. 115, 143 above.
[3] " Mos curiæ nostræ fuit ut gratis fierent et redderentur brevia sigillata ministris curiæ quæ nomina sua vel negotia continerent. Detulit autem dispensator regius reum sigillatorem, quod breve nomen suum et negotium continens ei negasset sine pretio reddere. Turstinus filius [Simonis] dispensator erat, Adam a Gernemue sigillator. Auditis igitur his, hæsitante curia, regem advocant ; qui cum Turstinum audivisset,

Apart from the glimpse we thus obtain of the King's court and its ways, it is of interest to note that the two officers engaged in this squabble were among those justices in eyre who played so large a part in Henry's administration. Adam of Yarmouth ("a Gernemue") so acted in 1169 and 1173, while Thurstan, who was similarly employed in the latter year, actually had for a colleague on his eyre Walter Map himself![1] This gives life to the story. Thurstan, indeed, was not only so acting again in 1176-7, but was entrusted, after Becket's murder, with the administration of the revenues of his see. Such was the man who had the keeping of the King's cakes and was ordered to present, on bended knee, two of them to his fellow " minister."

Thurstan left three sons, Amauri, who succeeded him as King's dispenser, Thurstan, and Walter the

audivit Adam dicentem, 'Susceperam hospites et misi qui precaretur dominum Turstinum quod mihi duo liba de vestris dominicis daret. Qui respondit, "Nolo." Cum autem postea vellet breve suum, memor illius "Nolo," similiter dixi "Nolo."' Rex vero condemnavit eum qui dixerat primum 'Nolo.' Sedere fecit Adam ad stannum (*rectius* scannum) coram posito sigillo brevique Turstini ; coegit autem Turstinum, abjecto pallio genibus flexis, Adæ præsentare duo gastella regis, mantili candido decenter involuta, susceptoque xenio, jussit ut Adam ipsi breve redderet, fecitque concordes, et adjecit ut non tantum sibi deberent invicem ministri subvenire de suo propio vel de fisco, sed etiam domesticis, et quos necessitas urgeret alienis " (*De nugis* [Ed. Camden Soc.] pp. 231-232). The custom *(mos)* here alleged by Map seems to be thus referred to in the 'Household Ordinances of Edw. IV' (p. 29). The chancellor, we read, receives a fee of wine that he may favour the King's household and servants. "Wherefore all the lordes aforetyme which have byn chauncellers allwey graunted and continued this privylege to every estate and degree, high and lowe, of the felyship of the King's householde...... to have all suche writtes as he shall nedefully shewe for hymself by his proper name...... seale free." The chancellor, it must be remembered, was originally, a member of the Household (see p. 54).

[1] Pipe Roll, 19 Hen. II.

King's usher.   On the Pipe Roll of 1180 there is
an important entry, which proves not only that
Amauri had succeeded his father as Dispenser, [1]
but that he had a younger brother, Thurstan, a fact
which was not known.   To this Thurstan was
given as wife the daughter of Richard Butler of
Cropwell Butler, Notts. [2]

In January 1184/5 two of them jointly attested,
as Amauri the Dispenser and Walter son of
Thurstan Fitz Simon, [3] a Royal charter, and on
July 15th, 1186, a fine was levied before the King,
at Feckenham, between the Prior of Dunstable and
Amauri, King's Dispenser and Amabel his wife. [4]
This Amabel was the daughter of Walter de
Chesnei (by Eva de Broc), [5] and she clearly brought
to her husband the five knight's fees which her
father had held of the earl of Gloucester in 1166, [6]
for Amauri " Dispensator " was holding them in
1187. [7]

[1] Foss and Eyton made the father live to a later date, but another
Thurstan Fitz Simon must have been here confused with him.

[2] " Et in terris datis Turstino fratri Amaurici dispensatoris cum filia
Ricardi Pinc[erne]...... de Crophulla " (Rot. Pip. 26 Hen. II, p. 137).
This was the Richard who acquired the important Warrington fief by
marriage with Beatrice dau. and heir of Mathew de Vilers.   I suspect,
therefore, that this marriage, previously unknown, identifies for us " a
certain youth " who is thus referred to in the 1212 survey of Lancashire :—" Et dum Willelmus [Pincerna] erat in custodia Radulfi filii
Bernardi...... idem Radulfus dedit villam de Croppil cum pert' cuidam
Juveni cum sorore ejusdem Willelmi " (Testa, p. 402a).

[3] Eyton, Henry II, p. 261.

[4] Harl. MS. 1885, fo. 22.

[5] See, for the charters proving this, the Eynsham Cartulary, in its
valuable and scholarly edition by Mr. Salter (Oxford Hist. Soc.) Vol. I,
p. 80, where Amauri (Almaricus) styles himself " Dispensator domini
regis. "

[6] Lib. Rub., p. 289.

[7] Ibid., p. 67.

Amauri is duly found holding the lands of his ancestors in the *Testa* (p. 119) :—

Almaricus Dispensator ij car' in dominico, et in vill' ij caruc' in Ewelm', et valent c sol.

Idem in dominico ij car', et in vill' ij car' in Magna Rollend', et valent per annum ciiij sol., per servicium Dispensar', et dicit quod fecit servicium illud, et modo facit pro eo gener suus, et offert iij marcas.

He was also sheriff of Rutland at the accession of Richard I, and from that King he obtained the lands at (Kings) Worthy, co. Hants and Stanley (Regis), co. Glouc., which had been granted to his brother Walter, the usher, by Henry II, he being then Walter's heir. [1]   These lands were again confirmed to him by King John. [2]

Amauri's widow, whose name was Ada, was living in the early days of Henry III. [3]   His own name has had a curious fate, for, owing to his incorporation by heralds into the fabulous pedigree constructed for the modern Spencers, it was revived, in the senseless form " Almeric, " for the first of the Spencers, Lords Churchill, [4] and has been given to several of his descendants.

[1] Cart. Ant., DD. 8, 11.

[2] *Rot. Cart.* 5 John.   In this document his brother is styled Walter Despencer, from the family office.   It has been assumed that Amauri was *younger* brother to Walter, but it is clear that he succeeded his father Thurstan as Dispenser.   The grant of the Worthy lands to Walter " the usher " is assigned by Mr. Eyton to 1181.   They had formerly been held by Hugh Tirel, who, according to the Pipe Rolls, had lost them some fifteen years before.   One of the later entries in the *Liber Rubeus* (p. 210) is concerned with these two estates, but the editor identified " Wordi " as " Worthy " merely, and leaves " Stanle " unidentified as in " co. Hants " !

[3] *Testa*, p. 107.

[4] This was in 1779, early in the tide of these revivals.   The French

Amauri's son and successor, Thurstan, is he who figures in the *Testa*[1] and of whom we read that, at the Queen's coronation in 1236, he unsuccessfully claimed against Henry de Hastings to serve " de naperia. "[2]   He died in 1249, holding lands in five counties, and left a widow, Lucy.

He was succeeded by Adam le Despenser, who is found holding the ancestral lands in the returns of 1284-5[3] and who died in 1295, leaving a widow Joan and a son and successor, Amauri, who is similarly entered as holding them in those of 1303.[4] But the family, as entries on the rolls prove, were now alienating these lands,[5] and Great Rollright itself, the *caput* of their serjeanty, was acquired by Robert Burnell, Bishop of Bath and Wells (d. 1292), whose ambition to found a family led him, as is well known, to purchase estates on a vast scale, as well as to have a pedigree from the Conquest invented for him by the monks of Buildwas.[6]   An interesting record of May 28, 1317, informs us that the King had enquired into the descent of the manor, and that the rolls of the Exchequer proved that

Thurstan le Despencer held 100*sh.* of land in Great

name Amauri—whence our surname Amory—was Latinised by scribes as *Amalricus* or *Almaricus*. " Almeric " is neither Latin, French, nor English.

[1] See p. 188 above.
[2] *Lib. Rub.*, p. 757.   See the section on ' Napery Service. '
[3] *Feudal Aids.*
[4] *Ibid.*
[5] It is, perhaps, significant that, in 1276, Adam Dispenser owed £25 to a London tailor *(Close Rolls).*
[6] *Dictionary of National Biography*, where it is observed that " on his death he was in possession of estates in nineteen counties."

Rolandrith yearly of the late King by the serjeanty of being his despencer..... and as it appears by the inquisitions concerning the late bishop's lands returned into the late King's chancery that the bishop was seised of the manor at his death in his demesne as of fee, and that he held it of the late king by the serjeanty of serving him in his spence *(dispensa),* [1] etc. etc.

In the following century we are surprised to find the collectors of the aid *pur fille marier* in 1401-2 ignoring all that had passed since the days of Henry III. They record the payment thus :—

Et de v*s.* receptis de herede Turstini le Despensare, pro centum solidatis terre in Boulondrych Magna tentis de domino rege sine medio per parvam serjantiam. [2]

Even a century later still the ancient tenure was in force. For in 17 Hen. VII (1501-2) Sir John Hungerford admitted that he held—as his father, Sir Thomas, had held before him—the manor of (Great) Rollright by grand serjeanty, namely that of serving the King in his " dispensary " (or " spence "), when directed to do so. [3]

THE KING'S PANTLER [4]

" He was a fellow of some birth ; his father had been king's pantler. " So writes Robert Louis

---

[1] *Cal. of Close Rolls,* 1313-1318, p. 411.

[2] *Feudal Aids,* IV, 172. The collectors were only to collect from (1) knights' fees, (2) socage tenures *in capite.* This was a serjeanty tenure, not socage. But the facts illustrate the lapse of petty serjeanty into socage, though it is not easy to understand how the King's dispensership could be deemed *petty* serjeanty.

[3] " per magnam *(sic)* serjantiam ; viz, serviendi domino Regi in dispens' sua quando precipiatur " (record cited by Blount's editors).

[4] Re-printed, with alterations and additions from *The Archæological Journal,* Vol. lx.

Stevenson in his *François Villon*. To the modern reader the phrase could hardly convey a meaning; and yet it is one that is singularly rich, not merely in etymological, but in antiquarian interest. Ducange, indeed, in his learned disquisition, refers to Pharaoh's chief baker; but, without taking the king's pantler so far back as this, we may claim him as the holder of a feudal office, the officer of the bread. We may take as parallel two officers and their offices, in order that these may illustrate one another by the changes of name and meaning. The " butler " derived his name from the bottle, the " panneter " from the bread (*pain*). The office of the butler was the " butlery, " now corrupted to " buttery ; " the office of the " panneter " was the " pannetry, " now corrupted to " pantry. " Here I use the word " office " in the double sense it still retains, namely, the function discharged by the officer and the place in which he discharged it.

It is possible to trace and account for the corruption and changes of meaning which these words have undergone. In the *Babees Book*, as in feudal records, the " l " of " pantler " is still absent ; " if thou be admitted, " we there read, " in any office, as butler or panter. " But a false analogy, it is thought, with " butler " produced the corruption " pantler. " The fate of the words has been widely different ; for while " butler " survives in daily life, unchanged and familiar, " pantler " has long been obsolete. With their offices, however, it is just the contrary ; for while the " butlery " lingers only in the " buttery hatch " of our college days, the " pantry " is a term of daily use ; it denotes, however, to modern ears the one place where, certainly, we should not find the bread, but where, most paradoxically, we should probably find the butler.

And now we will return to early days when the Norman dukes possessed their *pannetier* in imitation of their suzerain lords, whose officer of that name was destined to become the " grand pannetier de de France. " [1] The evidence for the existence of the Norman *pannetrie* will be found in my " Calendar of documents preserved in France, " where is printed the abstract of a royal charter to Odoin ' de Mala Palude. ' The date of this charter is of very great importance, but is a question of extreme difficulty. I have discussed it at some length in a paper on 'The chronology of Henry II's charters. ' [2] Here one can only say, briefly, that the text is late and corrupt, and that, although the king's style is that of Henry II, the witnesses' names distinctly point to the closing years of Henry I's reign. Explaining this difficulty in the above work, I gave the tentative date 1156-7, but have now decided, as stated in that paper, to reject the style and assign the charter to the days of Henry I. The late M. Léopold Delisle, greatest of Norman antiquaries, originally assigned the charter to " vers 1170, " but, applying his supposed discovery on the charters of Henry II to this one, placed it, a few years ago, " after 1173 " and even much nearer to the end [1189] than the beginning [1154] of the reign. [3] But although he arrived at this conclusion

[1] This officer is dealt with at the end of this section.

[2] In *Archæological Journal*, LXIV (1907), pp. 63-79.

[3] " la date est beaucoup plus voisine de la fin que du commencement du règne. "

on what had been his special subject, I hold him to be wholly wrong. If I am right, and the charter belongs to the time of the 'Constitutio', it becomes of great interest in connexion with that document.

Addressed to the Archbishop of Rouen and granted at Montfort, this charter confirms to Odoin

the whole ministry of his *Panetaria*, with livery in his court, every day that he is at Rouen, namely four penny-worth of bread from the *depensa*,[1] and one *sextaria* of knight's wine from the cellar, and four portions from the kitchen, one of them a large one, two of the size for knights, and one *dispensabile*. And Odoin is to find the king bread in his court, and to reckon by tallies with his dispensers *(dispensariis)* and with all his bakers, and he shall receive the money and give quittances to the bakers. And when he sends to Rouen for bread, Odoin is to bring it at the king's cost, and every pack horse shall have twelve pence, and every pannier-bearing one six pence, and every basket carrier a pennyworth of bread ; if the bread is brought by water, the boatman shall have six-pence a journey ; and Odoin is to have all that is left of the bread of the *panetaria*, when the king makes a journey, and to have the charge of, and jurisdiction over, the king's bakers at Rouen and within the purlieus of Rouen, and all their forfeitures, and the weighing of bread, and all fines and forfeited bread, etc. . . . nor is anyone but Odo and his heirs to execute the jurisdiction of the *panetaria* or over the king's bakers, under penalty of ten pounds (p. 465).

I have quoted at this length from the charter in order to show that the *panetaria* at this early

---

[1] This word is still preserved in some French institutions as *dépense*. See p. 62 above.

period was concerned, indeed exclusively concerned, with that bread from the name of which the
word itself was formed. When we turn to the
document known as the *Constitutio domus regis*, or
organisation of our royal household,[1] we cannot, I
think, identify a *panetarius* therein, but we do find
an accountant of the bread, a *computator panis*, who
must have reckoned by tallies with the bakers, as
Odoin was appointed to do in the above charter,
and as pantlers always did in later days. And his
mention is immediately followed by that of the
" four bakers, " two of whom are allowed forty
pence for purchasing a Rouen bushel (*modium Rothomagensem*) from which they have to turn out a
certain number of loaves, according to the kind.
Apart from the accountant and the bakers, a master
dispenser of the bread (*dispensator panis*) is mentioned ; but I can find no mention of an actual
" panneter " or " pantler. "

For what may be termed the ' master ' pantler
we must turn to the coronation rolls of later days ;
but before we do this, it may be well to mention a
fact hitherto, perhaps, unknown. An inquisition
after the death of William Mauduit, Earl of Warwick, taken in 1268, shows us Richard ' de Bosco '
holding in Chedworth, Gloucestershire, " by serjeanty of being the king's pantler for three feasts
yearly. " I cannot find this serjeanty mentioned
in the *Liber Rubeus* or the *Testa de Nevill*, and my
reason for attaching importance to it is that the
" three feasts " are clearly the great annual courts
at which the Norman Kings wore their crowns.

[1] See p. 54 above.

On these solemn feastdays the services of a " panneter " or " pantler " would, we shall find, be
required,and I lay stress on this serjeanty's association
with the " three feasts, " because it is thereby
taken back to very early days.   Henry the Second,
it is true, revived in his first three years the holding
of these solemn feasts ; but " after 1158, " in Dr.
Stubbs' words, " he gave up the custom altogether. " [1]

The early existence of this serjeanty seems, therefore, clearly proved.

It is, as I have said, to coronation records that
we have to turn for the office of the great
" panneter " or " pantler, " of which the first
mention is more than thirty years earlier than that
of the above inquisition.   At the coronation of
Queen Eleanor, in 1236, the first great precedent
for the coronation services, we read that Walter de
Beauchamp, of " Haumlega, " who holds from of
old the office of panetry (*panetaria*), brought on
the salt-cellar and knives, and did the pantry
service that day, and after dinner received the
knives and salt-cellar as his fee.[2]   We observe that,
though *panetaria* is the word used for the office
here as in the charter of Henry I., there is nothing
here about bread, with which that charter was
exclusively concerned.   Indeed, Mr. Wickham
Legg writes " that the office of the Panneter was
to carry the salt-cellar and carving knives to the

---

[1] *Constitutional History*, I, 562.

[2] " Salarium (*sic*) et cultellos apposuit Walterus de Bello Campo de
Haumlega cujus officium a veteri panetaria. Servivit autem eodem die de
panetaria et sui sub se prandioque peracto cultellos et salsarium tanquam
de jure suo sibi competencia recepit " (*Red Book of the Exchequer*).

king's table ; these, with the spoons, he receives as
his fee." [1]   Of the bread Mr. Legg says nothing,
doubtless because our coronation records make no
mention of it in connexion with the panneter's
office.   But this I shall discuss below.

Meanwhile I may note that Mr. Legg tells us
"that the office is filled by the Lord of the Manor
of Kibworth-Beauchamp ; this manor was held by
the Beauchamps of Dumleye, and later by the
Earls of Warwick." [2]   The corrupt and unmeaning
name of " Dumleye " seems to come from the
Liber Regalis, where it appears as " Dumelye, " [3]
while in the *Forma et Modus* it degenerates into
" Duneleus." [4]   But in the original record, we
have seen, it is " Haumlega, " which represents
Elmley Castle, the hereditary seat of that house of
Beauchamp which inherited the Earldom of Warwick in 1268, on the death of William Mauduit. [5]
Elmley, as I have elsewhere shown, [6] had descended
to them, like Kibworth, from the Domesday holder,
Robert Despenser.

Robert's name suggests an interesting speculation.
At the coronation of Richard II Thomas Beauchamp, Earl of Warwick claimed the office successfully, in right of Kibworth-Beauchamp, [7] but

---

[1] *English Coronation Records*, p. lxxvi.
[2] *Ibid.*
[3] *Ibid.* p. 108.
[4] *Ibid.* p. 181.
[5] See p. 201 above.   In another part of the *Red Book* (p. 567)
" Aumlega, " Worcestershire, is named ; this was Elmley Lovett.   The
official editor, Mr. Hubert Hall, identifies it as Ombersley.
[6] *Feudal England*, 176.
[7] " ratione manerii de Kibworth, com. Leicestr " (Taylor's *Glory of
Regality*)

the Harcourts had held the manor by knight-service
of the earls,[1] and there is no trace of its having
been previously held by serjeanty.   Is it possible
that the pantlership held by the Beauchamps of
Elmley in 1236 was originally the dispensership of
the bread ? We have seen that, in the case of the
Hastings family, the two offices were strangely
confused, and there certainly was a dispensership
in the Beauchamp family.   For the Empress Maud
had " given and restored " to William de Beauchamp the dispensership which his father Walter
had held under Henry I,[2] and which was doubtless inherited from Robert ' Dispensator. '   On this
hypothesis the office was held, by inheritance, in
gross, and its holder's tenant at Kibworth-Beauchamp may have merely acted as his deputy when
he was not himself present.   But, in any case, it is
always well to remember that any assertions of a
connection between the right to a given office and
the tenure of a certain manor require to be received
with great caution.

Full information on the subject is found in
Nichols's great work on Leicestershire, under Kibworth-Beauchamp.[3]

At the coronation of George II. the then holder
of the manor, Sir William Halford, petitioned the
Court of Claims (1727)[4] " to be admitted to per-

---

[1] *Testa*, p. 92.

[2] " dedi ei et reddidi..... dispensam ita hereditarie sicut Walterus
pater ejus eam de patre meo H. rege tenuit (*Geoffrey de Mandeville*, p.
314). We have seen above (p. 200) that the Norman ' depensa' was
that of the bread alone.

[3] Vol. II. part 2 (Gartree Hundred), 635, 636, 645-647.

[4] A previous unsuccessful claim seems to have been made at the

form the office of great panneter on the day of the
coronation of the king and queen, as being seised
in fee of the manor of Kibworth-Beauchamp, in
the county of Leicester ; and to have allowance of
the salt-cellars, knives, spoons, clothes and coverpane, together with the other fees and accustomed
perquisites of that office." Nichols prints his
counsel's arguments, and tells us that the Commis-
sioners "disallowed the claim upon a presumption
that if it had been just it would not have been so
long continued," which last word is clearly an
error for "discontinued." But he points out that
the claimant suppressed, as being fatal to his claim,
the grant of the manor by Queen Elizabeth in
1559, to Ambrose Dudley, to be held by the
service of being pantler (*panetarius*) after the coronations of kings and queens. [1] For the manor, which
had previously lapsed to the Crown by the attainder
of John Duke of Northumberland, was now granted
with a special limitation in tail male, and on the
extinction of male issue " it reverted to the
Crown . . . and consequently the service of
pannetry was thereby extinct."

The claimant's main object was to prove that
the ownership of the manor carried the service ;
but his evidence for this was weak. It appears to
me to have consisted, virtually, of findings in
inquests after death, which, as I had occasion to
note in the Lord Great Chamberlain case, were not
unfrequently erroneous. Thus, in 1341, Thomas

---

coronation of William and Mary (1689) by the then holder of the
manor, William Boveridge.

[1] This grant is printed in full by Nichols.

de Beauchamp, Earl of Warwick, is recorded as holding the manor " by the service of being the King's *panetarius* on his coronation day. "[1]   In 1304 Philippa, wife of Guy de Beauchamp, is returned to have died seised of the manor held of the king *in capite*, by the service of laying the king's cloth (*ponendi unam mappam super mensam*) on Christmas Day.[2]   This is a notable variant of the service, and the mention of laying the cloth is, we shall find, important.   In 1400 Thomas de Beauchamp dies seised of the manor "by grand serjeanty, namely, by the service of being the chief panteler on the day of his coronation,"[3] and in 1406 his widow, Margaret, is returned at her death as holding the manor by the same service.[4]   There is not in this, I think, any absolute proof that the pantlership was held in the right of the manor till Queen Elizabeth joined the two, artificially, by her grant to Ambrose Dudley.

We may now return to the records of the Coronation service.   The two great mediæval precedents were the coronations of Queen Eleanor in 1236 and of Richard II. in 1377, and the records of both, which are well known, will be found in Mr. Wickham Legg's *English Coronation Records*. From it (p. 135) I take the actual petition of Thomas Beauchamp, Earl of Warwick, in 1377. After claiming the privilege of carrying the third sword, the earl continues :

---

[1] Nichols cites " Fines in Scaccario, Mich., 17 Edw. III. "
[2] Nichols cites " Esch. 43 Edw. III. pars. 1, No. 20.
[3] Nichols cites " Esch. 2 Hen. IV. No. 58, Leic. "
[4] Nichols cites " Esch. 8 Hen. IV. No. 68, Leic. "

Et ensement ses ditz Auncestres ont ewes l'office de
Panetrie et mesmes l'office serviz par eux et lour deputes
et Ministres enlours propres persones des salers coteaux
et coillers et mesmes les salers coteaux et coillers ont ewes
et reicus pour leur feodz ensi come ses ditz Auncestres
ont faitz et auant ces heures.

On this claim the Court gravely decided that
the earl had made out his right to the office, and
to the salt-cellar and knives as his fee,[1] but that as
there was no evidence of his right to make off with
the spoons (*cocliaria*), that point must be referred
to the king.   And the king, we read, subsequently
decided, on the ground of certain evidence (*pretextu
quarundam evidenciarum*), that the earl should have
the spoons.   But, for us, this is the earliest evidence
of a claim to the spoons being recognised.

At the coronation of Henry IV (1399), according to Sir William Halford's counsel, the same
Earl Thomas petitioned to serve the office with
" saliers, cotels, et coters, " and had his claim
allowed.   Here one may add the interesting fact
that the earl, by his will in the following year,
1st April, 1400, bequeathed as heirlooms his cup
of the swan and the knives and salt-cellars for the
coronation of a king.[2]   Accordingly we read, in an
MS. account of the coronation of Henry V., that

---

[1] Baker renders this decision as " to bear the third sword before the
king and also to exercise the office of Pantler " (*Chronicles.*)

[2] Nicolas's *Testamenta Vetusta*.   The great prize, probably, was the
" salte, " such, for instance, as that which Henry the Seventh acknow-
ledged receiving, 1 Nov. 1485, from Richard Gardiner, merchant of
London : " a salte of golde with a cover stondyng upon a moren' gar-
nyshed with perles and precious stones, the which salte was sumtyme
belonging to Richard late in dede and not in right Kyng of England,
and delyvered to the said Richard Gardyner by one William Dabeney,
late Clerke of the Jewells of the said late pretended kyng. " (*Report on*

the then Earl of Warwick had " les drapes, les
selers, les coclers, que furent mult riche, et tout les
autres fees de l'office. "   Here, we note, the cloths
(*drapes*) appear among the fees for the first time.
According to another Cottonian MS., at the coronation of Henry VII.'s queen, in the third year of
his reign, " the office of the pannetry, " with its
fees, viz. " coteux tranchanz et la sala et le coverpayne, " were petitioned for by three persons in
right of the earldom of Warwick, as guardians,
Nichols suggests, of the infant earl.   It is doubtful,
however, who was then the actual holder of the earldom.   Lastly, at Edward VI.'s coronation, John Viscount Lisle claimed " to be panterer the day of the
king's coronation and the queen's ; and to bear the
salt and the carving-knives from the pantry to the
king's table ; and to serve by himself, his ministers
and deputies, to the office of pantry during dinner-
time, and he claimeth to have thereby the same
salt and knives, and also the spoons, served to the
king's table that day. "   He claimed that his step-
father, Viscount Lisle had executed the office at
Queen Anne Boleyn's coronation in right of his
wife, through whom he himself was " right heir
from Richard, Earl of Warwick ; " and his claim
was allowed. [1]   No evidence was produced as to

Historical Manuscripts in various collections, II. 296.)
    At the actual date referred to in the text (1400) we read of six white
silver salt-cellars, gilt on the " swages, " without covers, weighing 8
pound 15s., four others, and a cover of a silver-gilt and polished salt-
cellar, all late the property of Richard II., and then in the custody of
Richard de la Panetrie (*sic*).— *Calendar of Patent Roll.* p.293.
    [1] See, for all this, Nichols, *ut supra*, p. 646 ; and compare for Lord Lisle's
heirship of the eldest daughter of Richard Beauchamp, Earl of Warwick,
my article on " The Great Chamberlain Case " in *The Ancestor*, IV. 11.

Anne Boleyn's coronation beyond the allegation in
Lord Lisle's claim ; but in an account of that coronation I find the entry, which refers to his step-
father, " Lord Lisle, panter. " [1]   An interesting
description of Anne's coronation tells us that
" around her was an enclosure into which none but
those appointed to serve, who were the greatest
personnages of the realm, and chiefly those who
served ' de sommeliers d'eschançonnerie et de panetrie, ' " [2] were admitted.

It was confessed by Sir William Halford's counsel
that after, at any rate, Elizabeth's reign, there was
no trace of the office being exercised or even
claimed at coronations ; although, as we have just
seen, " it was classed with no less a dignity than
the butlership (eschançonnerie). [3]   And, as I observed
above, this was the actual ground on which the
claim was rejected.   But he also failed to adduce
proof that the office had ever been claimed in right
of the tenure of Kibworth-Beauchamp.   Indeed,
his own evidence showed that at Edward VI.'s
coronation John Dudley, Viscount Lisle, had claimed the office as " right heir from Richard, Earl of
Warwick. "   And here it is not irrelevant to
observe that he was heir only of the eldest of the
earl's three daughters, and that if the nature and
admission of his claim had been known to Lord
Ancaster's counsel, in the Great Chamberlain case,
they would possibly have made a strong point of

[1] *Letters and Papers*, Henry VIII. 1533, p. 278.   A contemporary
account published in *Tudor Tracts* (Archibald Constable & Co.) names
him as " panterer. "
[2] *Ibid.* 265.
[3] Unless this word here denotes cupbearers.

it, as the claim of Lord Ancaster rested mainly on the ground that such offices as these should descend entire to the heir of the eldest daughter ; but the instances adduced in proof were all of remote date.

As yet we have found nothing in the coronation records to connect the office of the pantler (or the " panneter ") with bread. Sir William Halford's counsel, it is true, stated that " his chief business, if one may guess from the name of his office, was to provide bread ; and upon that account, I presume, the coverpane has been always allowed at former coronations to those who have executed this office."[1] But this is a false etymology, though a not unnatural guess, if we may trust the *New English Dictionary*, which states that, as with the " counterpane," the " pane " represents not bread, but cloth. There seems, however, to be reason for doubting this derivation.

The absence of any mention of the bread itself is obviously due to the fact that it was not among the fees claimed for discharge of the office. But there is evidence from other sources which directly connects the bread with the knives and the great salt as belonging to the pantler's office. If we go back, so far as France is concerned, to the close of the thirteenth century, we find a bishop of Angers writing as follows :—" When we were seated there came a noble, Sir Guy de Camilliaco, in a tunic, bearing a cloth (*mappam*) upon his shoulder, which he set on the table before us, his officers assisting him ; and when this was done, he set two rolls (*panes*) before us with his own hands, and other

[1] Nichols, *ut supra*.

rolls on the said table at which we were sitting, which office was incumbent on him by reason of the fief of Camilliacum which he holds of us. Wherefore he was bound to undertake the office of *Panistarius* that day . . . . After dinner he had all the cloths (*mappas*) of the said places, because it was his right. " [1] Here we see the *panistarius* placing the lord's bread on the table, and also laying the cloth (*mappa*). This laying of the *mappa* we have already heard of as the tenure by which a Countess of Warwick held Kibworth, and we also found an Earl of Warwick alleged to have received, as *panetarius*, the *drapes* at Henry V.'s coronation. But so far as actual claims are concerned " le coverpayne " alone appears. Moreover, there was, from the earlist times, another and recognised claimant to the table-cloths, the *mappas* : this was the napier, the officer of the napery. [2] It is clear then that, in this country, the pantler had no claim to the table-cloth, and this is further confirmed by the fact, to which we shall come, that the table-cloths, in household economy, were not in the pantler's department.

From this it follows that the " *coverpane*," which was what the pantler claimed, was, as I have already said, something distinct from the table-cloth (*mappa*).

For the details of the pantler's function at the coronation feast we must turn to the instructive directions for another, but a strictly parallel solemnity, *viz.* the enthronization banquet of the Archbishop of York in 1465. At this great feudal

---

[1] See, for the Latin text, Ducange (1886), VI, 128.
[2] See the section on ' Napery service.'

ceremony, when George Nevill sat in state, Sir John " Malyvery " (Mauleverer) officiated as " Panter, " a fact sufficient to demonstrate that the post was, as at coronations, honorary. I only regret that the narrative, which I found with some difficulty,[1] is too lengthy for quotation at such length as it deserves.

Hereafter followeth the service to the Baron-bishop within the close of Yorke :—

Item, the Yeoman of the Ewrie must cover the hygh Table, with all other Boordes and Cubbordes.[2] . . .

Then the Panter must bring foorth Salt, Bread and Trenchers, with one brode and one narrow knyfe, and one spoone, and set the salt right under the middest of the cloth of estate, the Trenchers before the Salt, and the bread before the Trenchers towardes the Reward, properly wrapped in a Napkyn,[2] the brode knyfe poynt under the Bread, and the backe towardes the Salt, and the lesse knyfe beneath it towardes the rewarde, and the Spoone beneath that towards the rewarde, and all to be covered with a Coverpane of Diaper of fyne Sylke. The surnappe must be properly layde towardes the salt endlong the brode edge, by the handes of the forenamed Yeoman of the Ewrie ; and all other Boordes and Cubberdes must be made redy by the Yeoman of the Pantry with Salt, Trenchers, and Bread.

Also at the Cubborde in lyke manner must the Panter make redy with Salt, Bread, Trenchers, Napkyns, and Spoones, with one brode knyfe for the rewarde . . . and the Carver must go to the table, and there kneele on his knee, and then aryse with a good countenance, and properly take off the coverpane of the Salt, and geve it to the Panter, which must stand still. . . . .

[Dinner being over] Then the Panter must make his obeysaunce before the Table, kneeling upon his knee

[1] In Leland's *Collectanea*, VII. 7, *et seq.*
[2] *Cf.* p. 192 above.

with a Towell about his neck, the one ende in his ryght hande, the other in his left hande, and with his left hande to take up the spoones and knyves properlye, and with his ryght hande to take up the Salt bowyng his knockels neare together, with his obeysaunce, and so return to the Pantry.

The order that the Panter must " make his obeysaunce before the Table kneeling upon his knee " should be compared with Lord Montagu's order, in Elizabeth's days, that his pantler should make " two curteseyes " even to his empty dining table and " a small obeysance " when placing the bread, etc. thereon ;[1] for it illustrates the Laudian canon of 1640, advocating " reverence and obeysance " on entering church and chapel, " not with any intention to exhibit religious worship to the Communion Table, the east, or church, " etc. It also helps to illustrate " the Black Rubric. "

I now pass to a document of the period, the *Liber Niger* of the King's House *temp*. Edward IV. Here we read that

the office of Panetry hath a sergeaunt, which is called chief Pantrer of the King's mouth and mastyr of this office . . . . . . he receivythe the brede of the serjeaunt of the bake-house by entayle[2] . . . . . . other 3 yoman in this office panters . . . . . . these yomen by assent . . . . . . sette the saltes in the halle and take them up last.

We also read of the " clippinges " of bread which are afterwards found as the recognised fees of pantry servants, and that the countrollers " oftyn-tymes see that they be not pared too nigh the

[1] See p. 218, below.
[2] *i.e.* by tally.

crumbe. " [1]   Among the multitude of other departments we may note " the office of Ewary and
Napery. " [2]

In the ordinances of King Henry VII. we read
that " the karver must see the paintre (*sic*) take
assay of the bread, salt, and trenchers. " [3]

Those of King Henry VIII., in his seventeenth
year, speak of such servants as " buttler, pantler
and ewer " being present at the king's dinner ; [4] and
in later ordinances of the same king we read of
" the Sergeant of the pantry . . . . dayly
tallying with the sergeant of the bakehouse the
number of bread that he doth receive of him. " [5]
Under Queen Elizabeth, in 1602, we find " the
Pantrey " entered, as usual, immediately after " the
bakehouse, " while " the Seller, " " the Buttery, "
and " the Ewery " appear as other departments. [6]
And we read of its fees : " The sergeant hath for
his fee all the coverpannes, drinking towells, and
other linen clothe of the king's side that are darned " (*sic*) ; while " the gentlemen have the like fee
of the queene's side, " and the yeomen " all the
chippings of breade spent within the said office,
for the which they find chipping knives, " [7] Here
we are at once reminded of Shakespeare's contem-

[1] *Household Ordinances* (Society of Antiquaries [1790]), 70 and 71.
[2] *Ibid.* 83.
[3] *Ibid.* 118.
[4] *Household Ordinances,* 153.
[5] *Ibid.* 232.
[6] *Ibid.* 283.
[7] *Ibid.* 294. For the Ewry (*Aquar'*) the fees consisted of the " diaper "
and " plaine clothes " that were " dampned " (p. 296), and this last
word is used in other departments, which throws grave doubt on the
" darned " of the Pantry.

porary phrase :—" A good shallow young fellow ;
a' would have made a good pantler, a' would ha'
chipped bread well." [1]   As we might expect from
the conservatism that distinguished the royal household, the connexion of the pantry with the bake-
house and the bread continued close throughout ;
when the Gentleman Usher under Charles II. went,
as the phrase ran, " for to fetch All-Night for the
king, " he made his way first " to the pantry, there
to receive the king's bread, and well and truly to
give the officer of the mouth the saie thereof ; "
next to the buttery and the pitcherhouse, and then
to the ewry, " there to receive the king's towell,
bason, and water. " [2]   And even under William
and Mary, when the Court was on its " removes, "
the bakehouse and pantry occupied jointly one of
the train of vehicles in the lumbering caravan. [3]
Moreover, the " gentleman and yeoman " who was
at the head of the pantry was still receiving wages,
I have reckoned, at the rate of 7 $\frac{1}{2}$ d. a day, the
same rate, apparently, as under our Norman kings. [4]

We must turn, however, from the royal household to those of the great nobles if we would obtain

---

[1]   2 Henry IV. II, sc. 4, l. 258.
[2]   *Household Ordinances*, 374.
[3]   *Ibid.* 414.
[4]   *Ibid.* 395.   The heads of the Buttery, Chaundry, Accatry, Queen's
Privy Kitchen, etc., the Gentlemen Harbingers and the two heads of
the cellar, were all similarly receiving, in 1689, £11 8s. 1$\frac{1}{2}$d. as yearly
wages, which odd sum works out at 7$\frac{1}{2}$d. a day.   Payment of wages at
the rate of so many pence (or halfpence) a day was the rule in Norman
times.   In the *Constitutio Domus Regis* the Harbingers and the chamberlain of the chaundry are found receiving 8d. a day under Henry I.
The sum of 7$\frac{1}{2}$d. is a quarter of the dispenser's pay under Henry I., and
an eighth of that of the Chancellor and *Dapiferi*, which seems to have
been the unit. (See also pp. 83, 86).

full details of the pantler's office and functions.
The closing years of the sixteenth and the early
ones of the seventeenth century are rich in rules
and ordinances for the great households of the
time.   We will take first the pattern orders suggested for the household of an earl, with its " seller,
buttry, pantry, and ewry, " the four departments
which are regularly found in these elaborate households. [1]

Herein we read of the " yeoman and groome of
the pantry " :

The Yeoman should be a man of seemely stature,
wearing his apparell clenly and handsome, in regard he
commeth dayly to the Earles table.   He is to receive the
manchet, cheate, and sippet breade, from the bakers by
tale ;.....   He and the groome are to keepe the saltes,
spoones and knives very faire and cleane.....   He is every
night to accompt to the clarke of the kitchin what breade
of all sortes is received, how much spent, and what
remaineth.....   He and the groome are to chipp the
breade, but they are not to chopp of(f) great peeces of
the bottomes of the loaves to make the chippings the
better, which are their fees ; but to this the cheefe officers
and clarke of the kitchin are often to look (p. 29). [2]

Of the Yeoman of the Ewry, who here again
receives the cloths and napkins from the keeper of
the Napery, we read that " albeit he be not so
personable a man as the Pantler, yet should goe
neate and handsome in his apparell " (p. 30).

[1] In the *Northumberland Household Book*, for instance, we have the
"yoman of the Sellar, " "yoman o' th' Pantry," "yoman of the Buttry"
"yoman o' th' Ewry" (p. 41), the second being also styled the " pantler "
(p. 88) or "pauntler " (p. 305).

[2] R. Brathwait's *Some Rules and Orders for the Government of the House
of an Earl* (1821).

Our next authority is " A breviate touching the Order and Government of a Nobleman's house, " in which we read (1605) of " The yeoman of the Pantrie " that

Hee is to receave all breade from the baker, and to tallie with him for the same, and to enter the dailie chardge what is spennte..... and to carrie the salte with the carvinge knife, clensing knife, and forke, and them to place upon the table in dewe order, with the breade at the salte, and then to cover the breade, with a fynne square clouth of cambrick called a coverpaine (which is to bee taken of, the meate being placede on the table and the lorde sett) by the carver and delivered to the pantler.[1]

This is the passage on which I rely for the meaning of the word "couvrepain." The removal, we see, here takes place precisely as at George Nevill's enthronization feast.

The last of my three selected documents is the most important of all, the finest thing I know on the English ritual of the table. It is buried away in the seventh volume of *Sussex Archaeological Collections* (pp. 174-212), and is styled the " Booke of orders and rules of Anthony Viscount Montague in 1595. " In it the noble author writes as follows on the pantler :

THE YEOMAN OF MY PANTRYE AND HIS OFFICE.

I will that the Yeoman of my Pantrye doe receave of the Yeoman of my Seller by Inventorye or billes indented interchangeably betweene them all such plate as shall apperteyne to his office, viz., saltes, plate, trenchers, spoones, and knives hefted with silver, and be answerable

---

[1] *Archaeologia*, XIII. 333-4.

to him for the same.   I will that he receave the breade
of the Baker, by tale, and keepe a true reckonninge of
the receipts of the same and doe weekely make accompte
thereof to the Clarke of my Kitchen ;.....   I will that
being warned by the Yeoman Usher to prepare for my
dyett, he doe arme himselfe, and have all thinges in a
redynes for my service, and beinge come for by him shall
followe him through the Hall to my dyninge chamber
dore, and from thence go even with him on his right
hande unto my table makeinge eche of them two curteseyes thereto, the one about the middest of the chamber,
the other at the boorde ; which done, he shall place the
salte, and laye downe the knyves, and then lay myne own
trencher with a manchet thereon, and a knife and spoone
on either side ; and my wife's in like manner ; at every
which service ended, he shall make a small obeysance :
and having fully done, and together with the Yeoman
Usher made a solempne courtesye, he shall departe so
conducted oute, as he came in.

I will that everye meale, after the first course, he
followe my service uppe havinge a purpyn [1] with breade
on his arme and a case of knyves in his hande, to supplye
their wantes that shall neede : and after that I am sett
that he come upp some tymes to see that there be noe
wante of breade or any other thinge that belongeth to his
office ; and after everye meale ended and the voyder
taken awaye, that he come and orderly take off the salte
and knyves, and with due reverence return, soe bearinge
them downe as he brought them uppe (p. 204).

In this invaluable description we see the " salte "
and knives ceremoniously brought to the table and
removed therefrom by the pantler precisely as they
had been by the Great Pantler at the coronation
feast, and as they had been at the York feast a
hundred and thirty years before.   The spoons are

---

[1] A bread basket (*pour pain*).

added, as they had been since Richard II.'s coronation, while the placing of the manchet and service with the " purpyn " directly connect the pantler with the bread from which his name was derived.

Moreover, in another part of this document we read of the " Baker and his office ":

I will that my Baker receave all his wheate of my Granator by talle, and deliver his breade by the like talle to my pantrye, and that att everye monethes ende he doe make accompte to the Clarke of my Kitchin of all the wheate that moneth by him received, and howe many cake of breade he hath delivered the same moneth to my Pantler (p. 209).

It will be remembered that the pantler's duty of accounting by tally with the baker, which occurs in all these documents, was expressly named in Henry I.'s grant of his *panetaria*, in which Odoin is charged to keep account by tally with the king's bakers ; also that the *computator panis* is named in the *Constitutio domus regis*. From this we may, I think, infer that, under Henry I, the bread, when baked, was delivered by tally to the pantler (*computator panis*), who, in turn, delivered it by tally to the spence, whence it was "dispensed " to the household by the " Dispensator panis." [1]

It is clear, however, that the laying of the cloth,

---

[1] It may be interesting to note that in that early document he is immediately followed by the bakers, who had, like Lord Montague's baker, to produce so many loaves from each hushel of wheat.

"modium Rothomagensem, de quo debent reddere xl siminellos dominicos, et cl sal', et cclx panes de pistrino." *Liber Niger* and *Liber Rubeus.*

" the rate that is appoynted him to make of every hushelle (viz). of full and plumme wheat, every loafe to weighe sixteene ownces from the oven, and of barren and hungrye wheate fifteen ounces and an halfe or thereabouts, and that there be made of that size, thirtye caste of bread of everye bushell " (p. 209).

as apart from the placing of the " salt," etc. was in England the function of the yeoman of the Ewry,[1] and that the Great Pantler, therefore, at the coronation feast cannot have been entitled to the cloth (*mappa*) as his fee.   But of far greater importance, as distinguishing the English *panetaria*, is the fact that, in England, the king's pantler never enjoyed, so far as we can find, that jurisdiction over all bakers which was vested in the *grand panetier de France*, and which, as we have seen, was expressly conferred in the grant by Henry I. of the Norman *panetaria*.

Of the *grand panetier* we read :

On désignait autrefois en France sous le nom de grand panetier un grand officier de la couronne, chargé de servir le roi à table, concurremment avec le grand échanson[2], dans les jours de ceremonie, et sous l'autorité duquel se trouvaient tous les boulangers demeurant à Paris et hors des portes. . . . .

L'office de grand panetier était toujours posséde par un homme de la plus haute noblesse.   En 1332 Bouchard

---

[1] Even in the Royal Household the Ewry included the Napery, but in the coronation services the two were differentiated and the offices of Napier and of Ewer were vested in different persons. But at the enthronization feast of the archbishop of York, the cloth (" surnappe "), we have seen, was laid by the serjeant of the Ewry, and this was also tbe procedure in Lord Montague's household.   His Lordship's directions were that the yeoman of his Ewry should " laye the table cloth fayre uppon both his armes, and goe together with the Yeoman Usher with due reverence to the table of my dyett, makeinge two curtesys thereto, the one about the middest of the chamber, the other when he cometh to ytt, and there, kissinge ytt, shall laye ytt on the same place where the sayd Yeoman Usher with his hande appoynteth casteinge the one ende the one waye, the other ende the other waye ; the sayd Usher helpeinge him to spreade ytt, which beinge spredde and reverence done, " the yeoman of the Pantry is to place the " salte, " etc.   The whole ceremonial deserves to be compared with that of the York feast in 1465.

[2] *Cf.* pp. 61, 209 above.

de Montmorency était *Panetarius Françiæ*, et en cette qualité il eut un procès avec le prévôt des marchands et des échevins de la ville qui, soutenant les intérêts des boulangers, l'entravaient dans l'exércise de sa jurisdiction ...... Louis XIV., par un édit du mois d'août 1711, supprima la jurisdiction de ce grand officier, qui plaçait au bas de l'écu de ses armes la nef d'or et le cadenas qu'on paraît autrefois à côté du couvert du roi.[1]

In the eighth volume of his *Histoire généalogique de la maison de France*, 1733, Père Anselme devotes eighty pages to his history of the " Grands pannetiers de France " (pp. 603-682), at the head of which the *cadenas* and the *nef* are rudely shown in woodcuts. But a better description shows us the richly wrought *nef*, which was replaced in the sixteenth century by the *cadenas*, a square plate two inches high, with a cover, which held the knife, fork, and spoon, salt, pepper and sugar. A still more close connection with the mediæval custom is seen in Montaigne's account of the *cadenas* used by the Cardinal de Sens even in Italy:

" devant ceux à qui on veut faire un honneur particulier . . . on sert de grands quarres d'argent qui portent leur *salière*, de même façon que ceux qu'on sert en France aux grands. Aux dessus de cela, il y a une serviette pliée en quartre ; sur cette serviette le *pain*, le *couteau*, la fourchette, et le *culier*."[2]

Here we have the salt, the bread, the knife and the spoon, which formed, as we have seen, the pantler's province, with the addition of the fork that marked an advance in civilisation.

---

[1] *Grand Dictionnaire Universel*, XII. 113.
[2] *Ibid*. III. 43. The italics are mine.

NAPERY SERVICE

The officer who had charge of the royal table-
linen is named ' Maparius' or ' Napparius ' in the
Constitutio domus regis.[1] The equivalent of this
term in coronation documents is " the naperer, "
but the true English form appears to be Napper,
or Napier, both of which have become surnames.
I have avoided the difficulty by speaking of "napery
service. "

There appears to have been always some confusion between the position of this officer and that of
the pantler, or even the dispenser, on the one hand,
and the serjeant of the ewry on the other.[2] In the
Liber Niger domus of Edward IV " the office of
Ewary and Napery " was served by a serjeant " in
covering of the bourde with wholesome, cleane,
and untouched clothes of straungers."[3] He received
" the charge of alle napery by measure, for the
Kinge and his chambre and halle."[4] He was entitled to " one sompter-man and horse for the
Kinge's stuffe, founden by the Thesaurer his charge
of housholde. "[5]

For his fee he had the " perused clothes, so that
with honestye they will noe longer serve, ...

---

[1] *Lib. Rub.* p. 808, see p. 54 above. The survey of Winchester,
temp. Henry I, shows "Audoenus napparius " holding a good house
(p. 531), and his widow (" uxor Oini naparii ") is named on the Pipe
Roll of 1130 (p. 143).

[2] See pp. 211, 220 above and pp. 223-4 below.

[3] *i.e.* cloths untouched by strangers.

[4] See p. 66 above.

[5] *Household Ordinances* (Society of Antiquaries), p. 83. Under Henry
I this officer had, similarly, "Homini suo iij *ob.* in die ; et j *d* ad sum-
marium " (*Lib. Rub.* p. 808).

clothes surnape, footeclothe, and such others . . . . .
to be fee to the serjeaunt, *except at any coronation.* "
The right to the napery used at the coronation banquet was a contested matter.

From an early date we detect the existence
of an honorary napery service. At the head of his
pedigree of Hastings Dugdale places " William de
Hastings, Steward to King Henry the First, which
office he held by serjeantie, in respect of his tenure
of the mannor of Ashele in com. Norf. *viz.* by the
service of taking charge of the Naperie (*id est*, the
table-clothes and linen) at the solemn coronations
of the Kings of this Realm. "[1] This statement is
badly confused. The office of the Hastings family
was not that of ' steward,' and the tenure of the
manor is not recorded till a good deal later.[2] It is
the manor of Ashill, Norfolk, though identified as
" Ashley " in Hazlitt's edition of *Blount's Tenures*,
and, worse still, as " Ashley in Essex " in Legg's
English Coronation Records (p. lxxv).

Blount has noted for us evidence of its ' pantler '
tenure so early as 1204-5.[3] In the *Testa* it is
variously entered, the tenure being given as ' dispenser ' service in 1212[4] and again in two later
entries,[5] though two other entries record it as

---

[1] *Baronage*, I, 574.
[2] Dugdale vouched the *Testa de Nevill*, which relates, of course to a
later date.
[3] " Johannes de Hastings tenet manerium quod vocatur le Uppe
Hall in Ashele, in capite de domino Rege, per serjantiam essendi panetarius domini Regis. " *Rot. Fin.* 6 John, m. 28 dors.
[4] " Willelmus de Hasting' tenet x libratas terre in Asle per serjantiam
scilicet existendi despensarius in Despensa Domini Regis" (p. 294).
[5] " De serjant' dicunt quod Henricus de Hasting tenet c solidatas
terre in vill' de Aselelegh per serjant' dispense " (p. 299) ; " Henricus

'pantler' service.[1] It will be observed that in
none of these entries is the tenure given as napery
service, and yet in the very period covered by these
returns, *viz.* in 1236, Henry de Hastings claimed
successfully, as against Thurstan the Dispenser,[2]
the right to render Napery service at the coronation
of Queen Eleanor, and to receive the table-cloths,
when removed, as his fee.[3] It is difficult to see
what right a 'dispenser' could allege to the office,
though a 'pantler,' possibly, had some.

The right, however, had now been established,
and at the coronation of Richard II,[4] Ashill, then
still in the hands of the Hastings family, was again
allowed to confer the right to this service, as it also
was at that of Henry IV, when Lord Grey de Ruthyn,
who had then inherited the manor, claimed it as
against John de Drayton. In the interval between
1236 and these later dates, John de Hastings had
been returned in 1325 as holding, at his death, this
manor "by serjeanty of napery."[5] When, however, the old service was claimed in right of

de Hasting tenet quandam terram in villa de Asseles per servicium
dispensar'" (p. 283). This latter entry is of 1236 (see p. 30 above).
[1] "Henricus de Hastinges tenet Aschele de domino Rege per serjantiam Panetrie" (p. 290) ; "Henricus de Hastinges tenet quandam
serjantiam de Panetr' domini R. in Essele, et valet per annum c solidos"
(p. 296).
[2] See p. 196 above.
[3] "De Naperia—servivit ea die Henricus de Hastinges, cujus est
officium serviendi de nappis a veteri. Vendicavit tamen illud officium
Turstanus Dispensarius ea die, asserens suum esse debere a veteri. Sed
Rex repulit eum et admisit Henricum ea die assignans eisdem diem de
contentione...... Extractas vero post prandium nappas, tanquam suas et ad
officium suum spectantes, recepit" (*Lib. Rub.* p. 757).
[4] The fee, on this occasion was "les napes quand ils soient suistretz."
[5] *Cal. of Inq.* VI, p. 386.

Ashill [1] at the coronations of James II, George II, and George IV, the claim was not allowed.

Apart from this manor of Ashill, there were at least two other estates which were held by napery service. One of these was at Little Missenden, Bucks, [2] and the other in Chadwell and West Thurrock, in the southernmost part of Essex. [3] It is possible to carry back both these services a good deal further than has hitherto been known, namely to the reign of Henry I. For on the Pipe Roll of 1130 we find Danegeld, under Bucks, remitted to Michael " Naparius " [4] (p. 102), while under Essex we find a remission of a " murdrum " payment to " Torellus Naparius " (p. 56) and also the entry of a considerable sum tendered by " Torellus Naparius " that he may hold in peace his land of

---

[1] The manor had been alienated by Richard (Grey), earl of Kent, in 1512, and the tenure was subsequently changed to Knight-service (Taylor's *Glory of Regality*, p. 132).

[2] "Serjantia Walteri Mauntel in Parva Messenden, pro qua debuit esse Naparius domini Regis" (*Testa*, pp. 256-257). See also *Cal. of Inq. Hen. III*, No. 162.

This serjeanty reappears as at Chesham (adjacent to Little Missenden) in Michaelmas Term, 13 Edward III, when Richard de Wedon gave 12sh. 6d. for his relief on two messuages etc. in Chesham held "de Rege per serjantiam essendi napirus Domini Regis."

[3] "Will' filius Will'i Tarel *(sic)* tenet in Parva Turrak et in Chaundewell per serjant' essendi custus *(sic)* napar' domini Regis" (*Testa*, p. 266). "Will's Thorel tenet' in Chaldewell per serjant' Naper'" (*Ib.*, p. 267). "Serjantia Will'i Torel' in Chaudewell' et in Thorrok pro qua debuit custodire nappas in hospicio Regis (*Ib.*, p. 268).

The Pipe Roll of 1207 records 40 marcs as due from William Torel "pro habendo officio Naperiæ Regis," and the Fine Roll of 1207-1208 (9 John) records him as giving the king 60 marcs and a palfrey "pro habendo officio naperie domini Regis." The *Inq. p. m.* on John Thorel in 1282 duly records this tenure by serjeanty.

[4] He has a similar remission on p. 86, which suggests to me that he was then holding at Hartwell, Northants.

the earl's fee in Thurrock."[1]   Clearly "the earl" was the Count of Eu, and the place, therefore, West Thurrock.[2] We thus obtain the origin of that manor in West Thurrock which appears later, for several generations in the hands of the Torel family.[3]

It should be observed that in the cases of both these serjeanties their holders were then known by the name of their office ("Naparius"). We shall meet with further instances of this practice below.

Originally seated at Torell's Hall in Little Thurrock,[4] the holders of this serjeanty subsequently acquired extensive estates in Essex, but their line ended in an heiress under Henry VIII (1544). The tenure was returned in several Inquisitions as that of serjeanty, grand serjeanty, or petty serjeanty as King's Napperer in his household, or on his coronation day, *plus* an annual payment of ten shillings in the Exchequer.[5] It is, however, doubtful if these returns were right, for, when the serjeanty was 'arrented' under Henry III, William Torel exchanged its service for that of the sixth of a knight *plus* ten shillings a year.[6] In spite of this, Sir John Leveson, who had purchased Torrell's Hall a few years before, claimed and was allowed to act as 'naperer' at the coronation of James I

---

[1] " terram suam de feodo Comitis de Turroc" (p. 59).

[2] Not Greys Thurrock, which Morant (erroneously) made to be the Count's holding.

[3] Morant's *Essex*, I, 92.

[4] For a suit of 1219 in which they were concerned see *Bracton's Note Book*, Plea 47. 'Loures,' the place to which it relates, was really Bowers Gifford.

[5] Morant's *Essex*, I. 227.

[6] *Testa*, p. 268.

(1603), and the same claim was made, though not allowed, at that of George IV.[1]

Another Essex instance of napery service affords a very early example of pecuniary commutation. In the Writtle inquest of 1212 we read that Menigar ' le Napier' alleges that Henry I enfeoffed his predecessors by napery service, but that when the earl of Arundel married Queen Adeliza, in the following reign, he changed this service into an annual payment of twenty shillings.[2] This Menigar had been preceded by a Ralf 'Naper' or 'le Napier', who appears as a leading inhabitant of Waltham (Holy Cross) in 1168.[3] Conversely, King John changed the service of one knight due from Pishill, Oxon., into serjeanty, the service being the annual render of a tablecloth (*nappam*) worth three shillings.[4]

THE WAFERER SERJEANTY

This is a particularly good example of a recognised office in the King's Household being dischar-

---

[1] Wollaston, *Court of Claims*, p. 308.

[2] "Menigarus le Napier dicit quod Rex Henricus avus (*sic*) domini Regis feodavit antecessores suos per serjantiam de Naperie et dicit quod quando comes de Arundel duxit Reginam Aliciam in uxorem removit illud servicium et fecit inde reddere xx sol. per annum, et predictus Menigarus tenet illud feodum de abbate de Waltham per idem servicium de xx sol." Writtle Inquest in *Testa*, p. 270.

[3] *Pipe Roll*, 14 *Henry II*, pp. 40, 49.

[4] "Robertus Napparius habet feodum unius militis de hereditate uxoris sue in Pushull, et dominus Rex perdonavit predicto Roberto et hered' ejus per cartam suam predictum servicium militare per unam nappam de precio iij sol. vel per tres solidos reddendos pro precio illius nappe ad scaccarium..... ad compotum constabuli." Inquest of 1212 in *Testa*, p. 115 ; *cf*. p. 107 : "Robertus le Nap' tenet..... per sergentiam inveniendi...." and p. 118 ; also *Red Book of the Exchequer*, p. 145.

ged, on the occasion of his coronation, by the tenant in serjeanty of certain lands.

The "Office of Waferes" is fully described in the Black Book of Edward IV's Household. [1] It hathe one yeoman making wafyrs, and saufely and clenely to kepe them covered and under lock and by assay to be delivered for the King's mouth to the sewar . . . . . . He taketh for the stuffe of this office, after the prices of estates, being present in courte, first for the flower (*sic*) of the sergeaunt of bake-house dayly or wekely as he hathe nede by a tayle [2] betwext them bothe, and suger of the greete spycery; towells of raygnes, towelles of worke, and of playne clothe, fyne coffyrs, small gardevyaundes and bakyng irons. and of the office, if it nede, egges . . . . The statutes of noble Edward the Thirde, for certaine reasons used in thoose dayes, gave this office greete wages, clothing and higher lyverey than he taketh nowe because his busynesse was muche more.

Under the yeoman there was a groom "that can make wafyrs as be used in this courte," and serve in the yeoman's absence, and a page "to lerne the cunnynge service and dewties of this office."

In Elizabeth's days we read that the yeoman of the Wafery and "his fellow groome make wafers at festival times, as they are appointed by the clerke comptroller and clerke of the spicery". Eventually this ancient office seems to have been merged in that of the confectionery; but in early times it was probably of more importance. *The Rotulus Misæ* of 11 John (1210) records a gift by the King to the Emperor Otho's Waferer (*Wafrario*).

The Waferer serjeanty was of ancient date and of very long continuance. The Essex manor of

[1] *Household Ordinances* (Society of Antiquaries), p. 72.
[2] *i.e.* tally. See p. 219 above.

Liston Overhall was already held by this tenure in
1185, when Avicia de Lyston, widow of Godfrey
the Chamberlain, and daughter of Robert de Lyston,
with a son who was of age, was bound, as its holder,
" facere canestellas ad summonicionem ad festum
regis." [1]   We can therefore hardly doubt that her
father had held it before her.   In 1212 John de
Liston held " per serjanteriam faciendi canestellos ",[2]
and, early in the reign of Henry III, his heir held by
the serjeanty of making "canestellos"[3] or "wafres".[4]
Godfrey de Liston is found holding, in 1226, by
the service of making them " ad coronacionem
domini Regis ; "[5] but the *Inq. p. m.* on Godfrey de
Liston in 1267 returns him as holding the manor
" by service of making wafers (*vafras*) when the
King wears the crown, at the King's cost. "[6]   This
variation is of some importance as pointing back to
the three annual crown-wearings of the Norman
Kings.[7]

The service continues to be returned in Inquisitions after death as that of making wafers at the
coronation, to which is added, in 1332, that of
serving them to the King, they being also then
defined as five in number.   In 1367 Joan, widow
of William de Liston, was similarly returned as

[1] *Ret. de dominabus.*
[2] *Lib. Rub.*, p. 506.
[3] *Ibid.*, p. 457,
[4] *Testa*, p. 267.
[5] *Ibid.* and plea roll of 11 Hen. III (Morant).
[6] *Cal. of Inq. Henry III*, p. 203.
[7] Yet another variation is given by Morant from a Chelmsford plea
roll of 39 Hen. III.   He is there said to hold forty shillings' worth of
land in Witham " by the serjeanty of carrying flour to make Wafers on
the King's birthday, wherever his Majesty was in the Kingdom. "

having held the manor by the service of placing five wafers before the King at his coronation, but her son sold his reversion to a London wine merchant, Richard Lyons, who succeeded at her death, and made good his claim, in 1377, to act as waferer at the coronation of Richard II.[1] " He had, " Morant observes, " the misfortune of being beheaded in 1381 by that insolent rebel Wat Tiler, whose master he had been. "[2] The King then made a fresh grant of the manor (12 April 1382) to be held as before by Waferer service,[3] but it subsequently passed by fine to William Venour, whose claim to act as Waferer was allowed at the coronation of Henry IV.

It was apparently by trustees that, in 1413, the claim was made at the coronation of Henry V. On that occasion the materials required were set forth in the claim and are of interest for comparison with those employed in the " wafery " of Edward IV.[4]

En primes un pipe de flour.   Item xxx loves de sugre. Item xx lb. dalmonds puriple....,.   Item un dimid lb. de saffron pur bastrons......   Item j. dozen de towailles de Paris.   Item ij. Paris bulteres.   Item xl aulnes de streignours.   Item xx aulnes de canvas pur celours,[5] etc.

---

[1] " Come il soit tenant du Manoir de Liston, par cause de quel Johan de Lyston et ses Auncestres de temps dont memorie ne court ont fait les Wafres dont les nobles progenitours nostre sieur le Roi quore est ont estee servy le jour de lour coronement. "

[2] He had also been, as Stubbs writes, Lord Latimer's " partner in some gigantic financial frauds. "

[3] *Cal. Pat.*, 1381-5, p. 120 :—" by the service of making wafres and serving the King at his coronation."

[4] See p. 228.

[5] Legg's *English Coronation Records*, p. lxxviii, and Taylor's *Glory or Regality*, p. 146.

A certain portion of these materials, including the baking irons, were retained as the fee.

The service continued to be returned in inquisitions, and occasionally claimed at coronations, till at that of Charles II it was allowed to Thomas Clopton of Liston Hall. His son William claimed to make and serve the wafers at the coronation of James II (1685) and " to have all the instruments of silver and other metal used about the same, with the linen, and certain proportions of ingredients, and other necessaries, and liveries for himself and two men ; which claim was allowed " and the perquisites compounded for at £30. [1] The service was again successfully claimed by the Clopton family at the following coronations, but the manor was alienated, under George II, to a brother of the Duke of Argyll, whose son performed the service for him at the Coronation of George III. Together with others connected with the banquet, it figured for the last time at that of George IV, when Mr. John Campbell of Liston Hall performed it. [2]

The " wafers " linger on in France under the form of ' gaufres ' (etymologically the same), and are still, made in the ancient way, the delight of Paris children.

---

[1] Sandford's History of the Coronation of James II.

[2] It was petitioned for, of course unsuccessfully, at the Coronation of Edward VII, by an officer who, though not himself the owner of the manor, explained that he was " decorated with the Burmese medal and D.S.O." (Wollaston's *Court of claims*, p. 283.)

THE KING'S BAKER

In the Dorset Hundred of Winfrith, rich in serjeanties, we find Robert ' de Welles ' entered in 1212 as holding two hides in Wool (' Welles ') and one in Galton [1] (' Galdon '), which had been held of the king and his ancestors, from the conquest of England, " per servicium pistoris. " [2] Another entry shows us William ' de Welles ' holding forty shillings' worth of land there " by the service of making the King's bread. " [3]   On William's death an inquisition records him as holding the same amount of land there by the service " of being the king's baker. " [4]   Here again the invaluable Pipe Roll of 1130 comes to our help and shows us Hugh " filius Ber " as " pistor Regis " in Winfrith Hundred (p. 15), while as " pistor " he is further excused the payment of three shillings Danegeld (p. 16). [5]   This would be the payment on a hide and a half, and on turning to Domesday we find ' Alward, ' a king's thegn, holding a hide and a half in Wool (' Welle '), which he had similarly held before the Conquest.

We might, therefore, be tempted to say that as early as 1130 Wool was held by the service of acting as king's baker.   But the other portion of the serjeanty is really the older ; for Domesday

[1] in Owermoigne.

[2] *Testa*, p. 164 ; *cf. Red Book*, p. 547.

[3] " per serjantiam faciendi panem domini Regis in hundredo de Winfrod " (*Testa*, p. 166).

[4] *Cal. of Inq. Henry III*, No. 920.

[5] The entry in both cases is " Hugo filius Ber pistor(is ?) ".

shows us Osmund the baker (*pistor*) holding a hide and an eighth in ' Galtone. '

The other Domesday baker, Erchenger, appears under Cambridgeshire, where he held five-sixths of a hide at Comberton. This land is found held, in later days, by serjeanty of the bakehouse,[1] and when it was arrented in 1250, the service due was recorded as that of bringing to the King every day a hot simnel for his dinner.[2] The land had then passed into the hands of Barnwell Priory, and the writ issued in its favour on this occasion[3] is of special value, because it is dated 28 April 1250 and addressed to Robert Passelewc and his fellows, then actually engaged in arrenting the serjeanties.[4] The Priory was to hold the land (121 acres) for a payment of 6s. 8d. a year.

THE KING'S LARDERER

To the office of Larderer (or Lardener) at the Coronation of the Sovereign there have, from an early date, been two rival claimants. The one was the lord of Sculton (now Scoulton), Norfolk, known from its early holders as Sculton Burdeleys; the other was the lord of the Essex Manor of

---

[1] " per serjant' pistrini " (*Testa*, p. 358).

[2] " pro qua debuit ferre domino Regi unum siminellum calidum singulis diebus ad prandium suum. Et pro hoc servicio debet idem Robertus habere qualibet septimana unum quarterium frumenti et totum furfur de pane dominico Regis " (*Ibid.*, p. 357).

[3] It is printed both in the *Testa* (p. 358) and in the Barnwell Cartulary.

[4] " dilecto et fideli suo Roberto Passelewe et sociis suis justic' ad, fines serjant' capiend' assignatis. " (*Liber mem. Ecclesie de Bernewelle*, p. 93).

Great Easton and of other scattered manors, all of which were originally held by the family of Moyne. Sometimes one and sometimes both of these claims were successful : and so persistent was their rivalry that one of them was represented by petition for the Coronation of Queen Victoria, and the other for that of Edward VII.

In the *Constitutio Domus Regis* the larder was a recognised department of the household, staffed on the same principle as the others, with a Chief (*Magister*) Dispenser of the larder, Dispensers under him, who served in turn, larderers, and an usher.[1] How soon it came to be represented among the serjeanties one cannot say precisely. If we take the Great Easton serjeanty, we find, under Essex, in 1130, a remission of 10 sh. danegeld to William ' Monachus,'[2] which would represent a holding of five hides. This was precisely the assessment of Great Easton, as given by Domesday, and it would appear that this manor was the chief one of the Moyne serjeanty.[3]

On the other hand, it is possible, I find, to identify the whole group of four manors,—Ower Moigne, Dorset, Shipton Moyne, Glouc., Mad-

---

[1] *Lib. Rub.*, p. 809.

[2] *Rot. Pip.* 31 Hen. I, p. 59.

[3] " Essex. Henricus le Moigne filius et heres Willelmi le Moigne finem fecit cum Rege de xviij *l.* pro relevio terræ suæ de Eystan quam de Rege tenet in Capite per serjantiam Lardineriæ Regis ; quam quidem terram Radulfus Monachus antecessor ipsius Henrici tenuit per eandem Serjantiam, et valet terra illa per annum xviij *l.* sicut continetur in rotulo Testæ de Nevill sub titulo Hundredi de Dunmawe" (Pasch. Comm. 26 Edw. I. Rot. 80 a in bund. 25 and 26 Edw. I). — Madox' *Exchequer*. The reference in the record is to the *Testa*, p. 268, where (early in the reign of Hen. III) Ralf ' Monachus ' is said to hold his land of Eyston, worth £18 a year, "per serjant' lardenariæ."

dington, Wilts, and (Great) Easton, Essex,—in respect of which Sir John Moigne claimed to serve at the coronation of Henry V, as having been held in Domesday by Mathew de Mortagne ('Maci de Moretania'). [1] This is an interesting, but a puzzling fact ; for the same roll records, under Essex, that Mathew was succeeded by his nephew, Robert (not by William ' Monachus '). A further complication is introduced by an entry on the Pipe Roll of 5 Richard I (1193), which shows us, indeed, Great Easton as already held by larderer service at that date, but which gives, apparently, a William de Clinton as its holder. [2] It is true that the Dorset jurors of 1212 definitely assert that the serjeanty dated from the days of Henry I, [3] but assertions of this kind on their part need to be received with caution.

From quite another quarter we get some suggestive hints. In 1223 Ralf ' le Moynne ' was impleaded by the Abbot of Cirencester for setting up a gallows and pillory in Shipton (Moyne) to the injury of the Abbot's franchises and for cutting off, in his court, a woman's ear for theft. Ralf produced, in reply, a Charter of " King Henry, " which seems to have granted Shipton with all the

---

[1] His Wiltshire Manor is given as Winterbourne, but must be Maddington, which is not named and which is tucked away on Salisbury Plain in the folds of the Winterbourne valley.

[2] " Willelmus de Clinton red. comp. de x marcis pro habenda seisina de terra sua de Eston, que est serjantia Lardar' Domini Regis " (Madox' *Exchequer*).

[3] " Radulfus Monachus tenet manerium de Oweres cum pert' a domino Rege per servitium serjantie de coquina *(sic)*. Antecessores ejus tenuerunt ista tenementa a tempore Regis H. primi per predictum servicium " *(Testa*, p. 164).

liberties with which Richard " de Daunfrunt " had held it, and asserted that his predecessor Geoffrey had set up a gallows accordingly.[1]   Now it is a singular fact that a Charter of Henry II, in or about 1175, is witnessed by a Robert ' Monacus, ' son of Henry de ' Damfront.'[2]   Another plea takes us further.   In 1230 Ralf ' le Moynge ' brought an action for some land in Maddington (which was appurtenant to Shipton) against Walter son of Hugh, who pleaded that his father had been enfeoffed, fifty years before, by Geoffrey ' le Moynne', uncle (*avunculi*) of Ralf's Father.[3]   The Geoffrey to whom we are thus referred is found, not indeed as Larderer, but as holding office in the Exchequer in the early years of Henry II.[4]   It is, however, certain that he held the lands of the serjeanty, for the Pipe Roll of 1162 records remission to him (as an official) of his Danegeld on Shipton Moyne (21 hides), Maddington (4 hides), and Great Easton with Mathew de Mortagne's other Essex manor (10 hides).   The roll of 1163 proves further that he must have held Mathew's Berkshire manor of Lambourne, for it records remission to him of Danegeld on (its) four hides. The same test shows him holding in 1156 the two

---

[1] *Bracton's Note Book*, Case 1651.   The pillory he could only justify on the ground that he had one at " his Essex manor " (Great Easton) !

[2] Eyton, *Antiquities of Shropshire*, VIII, 154.   A Henry ' de Domnofronte ' witnesses a charter of Henry II at Domfront in 1157 (see my *Cal. of Docs., France*, p. 299).

[3] *Bracton's Note Book*, Case 402.

[4] He is Marshal of the Exchequer in 1165, and acted in some financial capacity in the Household.

Essex manors, Owermoigne, Shipton Moyne, and Maddington. [1]

Having thus carried back the history of these lands, we are confronted with a fresh difficulty when we turn to the nature of the service. Under Shipton Moyne and (its appendant) Maddington, the service is that of being buyer for the King's Kitchen ; [2] under Owermoigne it is serjeanty of the Kitchen or serjeanty of buying things for the Kitchen ; [3] in Essex it is lardener serjeanty or keepership of the King's larder [4] or even of being buyer for the King's cauldron. [5] The serjeanty, evidently, was that of the ' accatry ' as well as that of the larder.

But although the departments of the larder and the ' accatry ' were in later days quite distinct, there was, of necessity, between them a very close connexion. For it was the buyer's function to furnish the larder with provisions. [6] At the close, for instance, of Elizabeth's reign we read that the Serjeant of the Accatry

is to govern the office of the Accatry, and to see that there be beeves and muttons in the Queene's pastures, for the daily expence of her Majesties house, and that there be in store ling, codde, stockfish, herrings, salmon, salte-eeles, white salte and grey salte ; that with these provisions

---

[1] *Rot. Pip.* 2 Hen. II, (Record Commission).

[2] " debuit esse emptor coquine domini Regis " *(Testa*, pp. 78, 147).

[3] " servicium serjantie de coquina...... serjantia emendi quæ spectant ad coquinam domini Regis " *(Ibid.*, pp. 164, 166).

[4] " per serjantiam lardenarnie " .... " per s' custod' lardar' Regis " *(Testa*, pp. 268, 276).

[5] " per serjantiam ut sit emptor ad cauderam domini Regis " *(Ibid.*, p. 266).

[6] See p. 121 above for the King's ' achaturs. '

he may furnish the Larder with such provisions as shall be weekely made unto him by the officers of the boarde, the clerk of the kitchen, or the serjeant of the Larder.[1]

An Essex plea-roll of 11 Henry III (1226-7), cited by Blount, records the service as that of accatry,[2] and a Hampshire one of 8 Edward I (1279-1280) gives the two hides at 'Lyndeshull,' Hants, as held by the ushership of the larder;[3] but simple lardener service is returned for Owermoigne in 1285,[4] and the same return was made[5] at that date for Shipton Moyne.[5] The Essex service was similarly given not long afterwards as " per serjantiam lardineriæ Regis."[6]

Thenceforth, the service continued to be that of ' Lardener' only, and, after the manor of Great Easton had passed by marriage from the Moynes to the Stourtons, John, 1st Lord Stourton was found, at his death (1462), to have held it by the service of being the King's lardener on the day of his Coronation. The Stourtons alienated the manor, which, under Henry VIII, was held by Sir Ralph Warren, Lord Mayor of London, who, at his death (1553), was returned as having held it by the serjeanty of being the King's lardener and pur- veyor of his Kitchen on his Coronation day. The heiress of the Warrens brought the manor to Sir Henry Cromwell of Hinchinbrooke[7] but his spend-

---

[1] *Household Ordinances* (Soc. Ant.), p. 289.
[2] " ut sit emptor domini Regis in coquina sua."
[3] " per serjantiam custodiendi hostium lardarii domini Regis."
[4] " pro qua erit lardinarius domini Regis percipiendo feodum inde pertinens " *(Feudal Aids*, II, 9. *Cf.* p. 16).
[5] " per serjantiam essendi lardinarius regis *(Ibid.*, p. 244).
[6] See p. 234 above.
[7] Grandfather of the Lord Protector.

thrift son, Sir Oliver, sold it, in 1597, to Henry
Maynard, secretary to the famous Burghley, who
claimed within a few years its coronation service,
and who founded, in Little Easton adjoining, the
afterwards ennobled family of which Lady Warwick
is the heir.

We will now trace the early history of the rival
serjeanty of the larder. The earliest entry in the
Testa is that in the 1212 survey (p. 294), which
runs :— " Domina Laurette tenet in Sculeton [1] C
solidatas terre per serjant' existendi lardarius (*sic*)
in lardario domini Regis. " The lady who was
thus bound to service in the King's larder occurs
in another list of serjeanties (p. 286), which may
be of even earlier date, as " Laureta Picot "
holding lands in Sculton worth £6 a year " per
servicium serviendi larder' Regis. " After this
the manor is returned as held by members of the
Burdeleys family, who owe the same lardener
service in general terms. [2] Hugh de Burdeleys
died in 1251, [3] and was succeeded by his son
Geoffrey, who died in 1264 holding by serjeanty
of being larderer [4] and leaving a son John, who
died in 1283, holding " of the King in chief by
serjeanty of the king's larder. " [5] In 1329 a later
John, son of Geoffrey Burdeleys, held Sculton " of
the king in chief by service of being the King's

---

[1] now Scoulton.
[2] *Testa*, pp. 283, 290, 296. They also held Burdelys manor in
Stagsden, Beds., and at Oakington and Maddingley in Cambridgeshire
by knight-service as under-tenants.
[3] The Norfolk *Inq. p. m.* is missing.
[4] *Cal. of Inq.*, I., No. 589.
[5] *Ibid.*, II., No. 465.

larderer (*lardenarius*) at his Coronation "[1] and, some years subsequently, Margaret, relict of John, held by service of coming to the King's Coronation with a knife and axe to perform the office of Larderer."[2]

Scoulton had been entailed on this John and Margaret and their heirs by John's father, Geoffrey, in 14 Edward II (by licence), and they were jointly seised thereof from 1322 till 30 July 1329, when John died.[3]   Nevertheless, it was alleged before Richard II's Court of claims that Geoffrey Burdeleys had performed the service at the coronation of Edward III[4] (1327/8).   As we have no records for that coronation, the statement cannot be tested.

John FitzJohn, who claimed, in right of his wife, " destre chief lardener al coronement nostre dit sieur le Roi" (Richard II), further relied on an Inquisition of 21 Edward III, when it was found " que le dit Manoir estoit tenuz par mesme le service. "   This Inquisition was taken on the death of the last of the Burdeleys family, John, son of the John and Margaret mentioned above.   His lands were divided between his two sisters, of whom the younger married Gilbert " atte Chamber, " and in 1399 Edmund " de la Chambre " claimed and was

---

[1] *Ibid.*, VII. No. 261.

[2] *Ibid.*, No. 589.

[3] See, for all this, the entry of 24 April 1330 on the Close rolls, where the manor is expressly said to be " held of the King by the service of being the King's Lardener at his Coronation." At that date Margaret, the widow, was remarried to Nicolas de Thony and had brought him the Manor.

[4] " le quel service monsieur Geffroy Burdeleye fist au coronement sire Edward aiel a nostre dit sieur le Roi quore est pur lez services de mesme le Manoir."

allowed the service, at Henry IV's Coronation, as Lord of Sculton.   It was at the next Coronation, that of Henry V, that the lord of Sculton's claim disappears for the time, possibly owing to a minority, and is replaced by that of Sir John Moigne, as Lord (as explained above) of four manors jointly. At the Coronation of James I the contest settles down to a conflict between the lords of Sculton and of (Great) Easton, the latter manor having been purchased a few years before by Sir Henry Maynard.   Both claims were allowed, selection being left to the King, and this result was repeated at the Coronations of Charles II, James II, William and Mary, and Anne.   At those of George I and George II Lord Abergavenny alone, as lord of Sculton, claimed and had his claim allowed.   At that of George IV, when many claims were revived, the lord of Sculton had to contend against the counter-claims of the lords of no fewer than three Moigne Manors, Great Easton, Shipton Moyne and Maddington.   All four claims were allowed. Lord Maynard petitioned for the office in respect of the Manor of Great Easton at the Coronation of Queen Victoria, [1] and Mr. G. J. T. Sotheron-Estcourt at that of Edward VII in respect of the manor of Shipton Moyne. [2]

It is necessary to explain that Lardener service was by no means connected only with the larder of the King's Court.   Venison had to play, in early

---

[1] Mr. Wollaston found the petition in the Crown Office although it does not figure on the Coronation Roll.

[2] The Estcourts had been seated there from the 13th century, holding originally under the Moignes.

days, a large part at the King's table, and the
dependence, at that time, on salted meat in winter
made it necessary to salt and store, in certain forests,
the flesh of the deer there killed.   For this purpose local larders with local larderers were established.   A good instance of this is afforded by a
serjeanty which, I propose to show, can be clearly
carried back to the days of Henry I.

An early charter of King Stephen, addressed to
the magnates of Yorkshire, runs thus:—

> Sciatis me reddidisse et concessisse [1] Johanni larderario
> meo de Eboraco et David filio suo terram suam totam
> quam tenet de me in capite cum ministerio suo de
> larderio et liberacione sua... sicut tenuit die qua rex Hen-
> ricus fuit vivus et mortuus. [2]

A charter of Henry II confirmed to David his
' larderer of York ' his right to pasture at Cortburn
(in Bulmer), as held in the time of Henry I, with
pasture for his mares and she-goats in the Royal
Forest.[3] As "David Lardarius" (or "Lardinarius")
he made in 1166 the return for Bertram de Bulmer's fief, on which, he said, he held a fifth of a
fee himself. [4]   In the early days of Henry III a
namesake held the serjeanty:—

> David Lardinarius tenet I serjantiam et est custos
> gaiolæ forestæ et venditor averiorum pro debito Regis. [5]

In 1250 we find it styled " serjantia domini

---

[1] These are the terms for a re-grant.
[2] Inspeximus by Richard II in *Cal. Pat. Rolls*, 1385-1389, p. 19.
[3] *Ibid.*
[4] *Lib. Rub.*, pp. 428-429.   This David appears on the Pipe Rolls,
from 1165, as receiving, under Yorkshire, a regular allowance of five-
pence a day.
[5] *Ibid.*, p. 467 ; *Testa*, pp. 365, 375, 376, 378.

Regis faciendi lardarium domini Regis apud Ebo-
racum." [1] The Inquest after death (1260) of David
" le Lardiner " is more precise in detail. His messuage in York and land in ' Bustardthorp ' and
Cortburn are

all held of the King in chief for keeping the King's gaol
of the forest, [2] making and keeping the King's larder, and
finding salt at his own cost ; and for this he shall have
" crura superiora et loynes, " and shall make sales for the
King's debt, [3] etc.

In letters close of Edward II the Sheriffs are
usually directed to provide the huntsmen with salt
for the venison ; in those of July 22nd, 1316, a
"lardener " is expressly mentioned as accompanying
the huntsmen and hounds to the Wiltshire forests,
and the venison is directed to be sent up to
Windsor. [4]

THE 'MAUPYGERNOUN' SERJEANTY

This is probably the most familiar of the serjeanties connected with the kitchen. It is notable
not only as having formed the subject of a series
of coronation claims, but also as being, practically,
traceable back to Domesday Book. Among the
king's serjeants (*servientes regis*) of Surrey in 1086
we find Tezelin the cook holding Addington

---

[1] *Testa,* p, 377.

[2] The great Yorkshire forest of Galtres, reaching to the walls of York.

[3] *Cal. of Inq. Hen. III,* No. 753. He also held at Skelton of Robert
de Nevill (heir of the Bulmers).

[4] The receipt of venison in the King's larder is seen even in the *Constitutio,* under 'The great kitchen' (*Magna Coquina*) :—" Caretarius
lardarii similiter. Serviens qui recipit venationem intus commedet "
(*Lib. Rub.,* p. 810).

('Edintone'), a substantial manor, of the king.
Although his name is suggestive of foreign, rather
than of native origin, the group of entries in which
he occurs is headed 'Terræ Oswoldi et aliorum
tainorum,' and the other names found in it are
those of English thegns, [1] with the possible exception of 'Teodricus aurifaber,' who, however, is
expressly stated to have held the same land under
Edward the Confessor. It is proved by later
manorial history that it was the same Tezelin who
held of William de Warenne a manor in Perching
and Fulking, at the foot of the South Downs, near
Poynings. There also he occurs in connection
with English tenants, two of whom precede him.
He gave his son, however, the Norman name of
William. This we learn from one of the Lewes
Priory charters cited by Mr. Stapleton in his
learned introduction to the *Liber de Antiquis Legibus*.[2]

But, in spite of his wealth of erudition and of
record references, he does not appear to have
classified or dated the returns in " that invaluable
record, the *Testa de Nevill* " (p. x). It is a task
of much labour, but the value of the *Testa* depends
on its accurate performance. The earliest and
most important entry of this serjeanty in the *Testa*
is that on p. 225, where I have identified the
returns as belonging to the great Inquest of 1212.
We there read that Bartholomew 'del Chennay'
held part of Addington by kitchen serjeanty, and

---

[1] It is in the Schedule prefixed to Surrey that this same group is
headed "Oswold', Teodricus, et alii servientes regis." This is contrary
to the practice of Domesday, which normally first deals with the foreign
'servientes,' and then with the English 'taini.'

[2] Camden Society, 1846.

that King Richard gave that part, with Barthol-
omew's daughter, to Peter, son of the Mayor of
London ; that King John afterwards gave it with
Peter's daughter to Ralf, the merchant-taylor
(*Parmentario*), and that at the time of the Inquest
(*nunc*) it was in the King's hand.[1]

This statement is of much interest, as confirming
the date of the return as given above. For the
evidence collected by Mr. Stapleton proves that
Joan, Peter's daughter, was the widow of Ralf le
Parmentier in 1212, and was given to William
Aguillun on October 5th of that year, with her land,
which had been in the King's hand (*in manu nostra*).[2]
This is why Addington was returned in June 1212
as " in manu domini Regis. "

Peter was the eldest son of the first Mayor of
London, Henry Fitz Ailwin, and appears to have
died in his father's lifetime, for seisin of his land
was given to his son-in-law Ralf le Parmentier,
30th October 1207.[3] According, however, to
Mr. Stapleton, he is said in another *Testa* entry
" to hold the moiety of Addington by the service
of the Kitchen. "[4] If so, that entry, we have seen,
must be older than 1207. Now the *Liber Rubeus*,
in that list of serjeanties which its editor[5] dates,
from "internal evidence," as of 1212-1217 (p. 456),

---

[1] " Bartholomæus del Chennay tenuit quandam partem in Edintun in
capite de domino Rege per serjantiam coquine, et nescitur ex cujus dono,
et Ricardus Rex dedit eandem partem Petro filio majoris Lond' cum filia
predicti Bartholomæi, etc...... et nunc est in manu domini Regis. "

[2] *Op. cit*, pp. ix-x.

[3] The mayor did not die till 1212 (24 July-5 Oct.). See my papers
on him in *The Antiquary* for 1887 and the *Dict. Nat. Biog.*

[4] No page is cited.

[5] Mr. Hubert Hall of the Public Record Office.

has the entry ; " Petrus filius Majoris Londoniæ medietatem de Adintone per serjanteriam coquine," and yet in that other list which he dates as 1210-11 (or 1210-1212) makes his son-in-law and *successor*, Ralf le Parmentier the holder (p. 561) ! What is the explanation ? We turn to what the Editor gives, on p. 456, as the parallel returns in the *Testa*, only to find that neither of them corresponds with the list on that page. And then we discover for ourselves that the really corresponding list is on p. 417 of the *Testa* (II, 878), where the seven Surrey entries are identical word for word.[1] Such is the lamentable editing of the ' *Red Book of the Exchequer.* '

Joan, daughter of Peter, brought to William Aguillun not only the Addington serjeanty, inherited through her mother, but the Watton-at-Stone (Herts) serjeanty, derived from Peter's father, Henry, Mayor of London. The Mayor was still holding it in June 1212, when it is entered as that of finding a foot archer for the Welsh wars.[2] He was dead before 5th Oct. 1212, and on the 17th Nov. the Sheriffs were directed to allow Margaret, his relict, her reasonable dower.[3]

Early in the reign of Henry III, William Aguillun (in right of his wife) was holding this land by the

[1] The explanation, therefore, is that in both these lists the Addington entry is cut down from the earlier return, which spoke of Peter as a former holder.

[2] " Henricus Major Lond' tenet Watton per serjant' inveniendi unum hominem peditem ad exercitum domini Regis in Wallia cum arcu et sagittis, et antecessores sui tenuerunt per idem servicium de antecessoribus domini Regis " (*Testa*, p. 270).

[3] *Rot. Litt. Claus.* This, again, confirms the date I assign to this return.

same service[1] and, of course, the Addington serjeanty, which is now entered as held

per serjantiam faciendi hastias in Coquina domini Regis die
coronacionis sue vel aliquis pro se debet facere ferculum
quoddam quod vocatur ' Girunt,' et, si apponatur sagina,
tunc vocatur ' Malpigernoun.'[2]

Here we have an early and direct reference to
the Coronation, and a statement, which apparently
is only made here, that the service included making
spits (*hastias*) in the King's kitchen.[3] Thenceforth
the two serjeanties descended together.

In a record of 39 Hen. III (1254-5), cited by
Blount from a plea-roll, the mess (*ferculum*) is similarly described.[4] The common earthenware pot
in which it was made is again mentioned in 1304,
when an Inquest was held at Addington, October
14th, after the death of Hugh Bardolf, to whom
the land had descended in right of his wife.[5] His
relict, Isabel, held the two serjeanties at her death
(1323), that of Addington " by service of making
a dish called ' maupigernoun ' at the King's Coronation, "[6] and was succeeded by Thomas Bardolf,

---

[1] *Testa*, p. 266.

[2] *Testa*, p. 229. Later in the reign (1234) we have the service described as " inveniendi unum cocum in coronatione Regis ad faciendum
cibum, qualem Senescallus præceperit, in coquina Regis " (See p. 24).

[3] The word *Sagina* (*seym* below) is said to mean fat or lard.

[4] " per serjantiam faciendi unum ferculum in olla lutea, in coquina
domini Regis, die coronationis sue, et vocatur mess de Gyron ; et si sit
Seym in illo ferculo, vocatur Maupigyrnun. "

[5] " per servicium ad inveniendum unum cocum ad coronamentum *(sic)*
domini Regis ad faciendum unum ferculum, quod vocatur Mees de
Geroun, sumptibus Domini Regis, in una olla lutea. "—*Lib. de Ant.
Leg.*, p. lxxxviii. Stapleton thought these the " fullest and most correct
details as to its tenure, " not knowing, apparently, Blount's record.

[6] *Cal. of Inq.*, VI, No. 454.

who held Addington at his death in 1330.—

" by service of serving before the king, on the day of his Coronation, three dishes of a certain food called ' Maupygernon,' viz. one before the King, the second to the Archbishop of Canterbury and the third to whom the king shall assign it." [1]

We may now pass to the first recorded coronation claim, that of William Bardolf (1377) :—

monstre William Bardolf que come il tient certeines terres en la ville de Adynton come de son heritage tenuz due Roi en chief per sergeantie, cestassavoir de trover le jour del Coronement nostre tresredoute sieur la Roi un homme de faire une messe quest appelle *dilgirunt*, et si apponatur sagimen, adonque il est appelle Malpigeryun, en la Cosyn [2] del Roi etc. etc.

It seems to me that this claim gives us the transition form [3] from the " mess de Gyron " of 1254-5 to the "mess of Dillegrout," which is the form that Mr. Wollaston adopts, following late antiquaries. According to Mr. Wickham Legg, " the Lord of the Manor of Addington has to bring a dish of gruel called Dillegrout or Malepigernout" (*sic*) ; [4] but I think it clear that "Dillegrout " is what is termed a " ghost word. "

It has been ingeniously suggested that this mess of potage (as it is subsequently described) may be represented by the recipe for " Bardolf" in an Arundel MS., *said* to be of early 15th cent. date. It runs thus :

[1] *Ibid.*, VII, No. 243.
[2] *i.e. cuisine.*
[3] *i.e. dil Girunt.*
[4] *Eng. Cor. Records*, p. lxxviii.

Take almonde mylk, and draw hit up thik with vernage, and let hit boyle, and braune of capons braied and put therto ; and cast therto sugre, claves [cloves] maces, pynes, and ginger, mynced ; and take chekyns parboyled and chopped, and pul of the skyn, and boyle al ensemble, and, in the settynge doune from the fire, put thereto a lytel vynegur alaied with pouder of ginger, and a lytel water of everose, and make the potage hanginge, and serve hit forth. " [1]

After the Reign of Richard II this " mess " was presented at coronations, from the reign of Charles II onwards, by the Leigh family, but the " merry monarch, " we are told, carefully abstained from eating it. It was still presented by the lord of the manor at the coronation of George III, and even at the last banquet, that of George IV, the right was claimed and obtained by the Archbishop of Canterbury. [2] Accordingly,

the Deputy appointed by his Grace the Archbishop of Canterbury, as Lord of the Manor of Bardolf, otherwise Addington, presented the mess of Dillegrout, prepared by the King's Master Cook. [3]

This was its last appearance (July 19, 1821).

THE KING'S SAUSER

Among the Cumberland serjeanties, it was reck-oned, was that of Adam " the Queen's cook," who held Salkeld in John's reign by the annual render of a pound of pepper. [4] Whether this was a true serjeanty might be fairly doubted, though it seems

---

[1] *Household Ordinances* (Society of Antiquaries), p. 466.
[2] The Archbishops held Addington from 1807 to 1897.
[3] Sir George Nayler's narrative reprinted by Mr. Legg (p. 358).
[4] *Lib. Rub.*, pp. 462, 494 ; *Testa*, pp. 380, 381.

to be so classed;[1] but the entry on the Oblate
Roll of 3 John (1201), " Tenet in sergent' "
(page 158) must be deemed decisive.   The land,
it appears from the survey, had been held by
' cornage,' that is, by the payment of 27s. 11d.
under that head, but this payment was remitted
when the King granted him the land.

That it was given him by King Richard is not
only asserted in the survey of 1212, but on the
Oblate roll of 3 John (1201), when he had to give
the king £5 for regaining seisin, though he had
been wrongly ousted, as he proved by producing
the charters of King Richard and of John himself
(p. 119).   But this was not the only land that was
given to this favoured cook.   It is from no English
record that we gain our knowledge of the fact, but
from a charter among the archives of that famous
abbey of Fontevraud, where Eleanor, the old queen,
was then expiating the somewhat flighty youth of
half a century before.   Queen of the English,
Duchess of the Normans, Duchess of Aquitaine,
she recites that her dearest son King Richard (there
interred the year before) had given her the land of
Upperby and Farmanby, which used to pay at the
exchequer forty shillings a year, and that she now
gives it to her faithful servant (*servienti*) Adam the
cook and Joan his wife, to be held quit of cornage
etc., by the payment only of a pound of cummin
yearly at Carlisle.[2]

Adam was thus " the queen's cook. "   But both

---

[1] *Red Book*, p. 494 ; *Testa*, p. 380.
[2] Original charter of A.D. 1200, still preserved at Angers (see my
Calendar of documents preserved in France, p. 394).

in the *Testa* and in the Red Book we find him styled "cocus" and "salsarius," while in both the entries on the Oblate Roll (1201) he is "Adam salsarius." King John had his own "salsarius," to whom he made grants,[1] and so had Henry III.[2] In the next reign (1278) the king's steward was ordered "to deliver to Master Ralph the Sauser (*Salsario*), the King's serjeant, a wardship," etc.[3] Now this carries back to a very early date a curious little department in the King's Household. Under Henry VI, the "Saulcery," as it was termed, was of more importance than later, for it had its "sergeant," clerk, and six other officers. By the time of Henry VIII "the pastry and Salsery" (or "Sawcery") had become one department, but we obtain at this date[4] some light on its nature. Of the £54 allowed for it, £50 was for "mustard, vinegar, and verjuice," and £4 for "herbs for sauces." The supply of vinegar was ingeniously increased, it seems, by making a raid upon the cellar, when there had been a bad vintage.

"It hath been oftyntymes, in yeres togydyr, that the Kinge hath had the advauntage of the feeble and dulle wynes, to make thereof venegere, and to delyvur it to the sergeaunts of the saucerye."[5]

Under Queen Elizabeth "the pastery" alone is

---

[1] "Gaufrido Salsario servienti nostro." (*Rot. de Lib.*, 3 John [1201], pp. 20, 49, 108).

[2] Grant to "Master William, the King's sauser, and Hugh de Bradele, king's serjeant" (*Cal. of Pat. Rolls*, 1247-1258, p. 207). "Le Sauser" became a surname; it was that of one of Edward II's huntsmen.

[3] *Cal. of Close Rolls*, 1272-9; p. 441.

[4] Ordinances made at Eltham, 17 Henry VIII (1525-6).

[5] "Office of Sellar *(sic)* within the King's household" in Edward IV's "Liber Niger Domus" (*Household Ordinances*, p. 76).

named, but the two departments were still distinct, for even in the days of William and Mary (1689) " the pastry and salsary " are mentioned together, and the " salsary-man " was drawing £30 a year board wages.

Returning to Adam "salsarius," one cannot but feel that his holding was hardly a true serjeanty, for no service was attached to it. And the render of a pound of pepper or cummin was of the nature of quit-rent. It shows how easily petty serjeanty could pass, in such cases, into socage.

THE SCALDING SERJEANTY

A very curious serjeanty was connected with the manor of Bures in South Essex, now, corruptly, Bowers Gifford. Early in the reign of Henry III, we find Robert de Sutton holding there by serjeanty, by the service of scalding the King's hogs.[1]

But in one entry the service is defined as " per serjant' de *Cauderie*. "[2] Although the meaning is the same, a strange error has been caused. For the word, as with so many others, was misread in Blount's *Tenures*, and connected with the chaundry or department of the wax. Even in the latest edition of his work (1874) the serjeanty figures as that " of the chandelry " (p. 49).[3]

---

[1] " Per serjant' escaldandi porcos Regis." *Lib. Rub.*, pp. 457, 507; *Testa*, p. 276. On p. 507 of the *Red Book* he is said to hold under Roger de Leybourne.

[2] *Testa*, p. 267.

[3] Blount's actual source seems to have been a plea-roll of 11 Henry III, where he read the word " eschanderie," and rendered it " The Chandry, where the candles were kept."

One is tempted to associate this serjeanty with
the office of " the scalding house " in the King's
Household, but only geese and fowls are mentioned
as there dealt with, [1] while " the boiling house "
was only concerned with beef.   An allusion to the
necessary scalding of the hogs is found in an old-
world recipe for " Pygges in sauge " :

Take pygges and scalde hom, and wash hom clene, and
smyte hom on gobettes, and sethe hom in water and salt,
and when thai arne ynough, take hem up, and let hem
kele, then take sauge and parsel and grinde hit, and do
thcrto brede steped in vynegur, and grynde hit smal, and
take the yolkes of harde egges and do therto, and grynde
hit al togedur and tempur it up with vynegur sum dele
thick ; then put thy pygges in a faire vessel, and poure
the sewe above, and serve hit forth colde. [2]

Although Robert de Sutton, we have seen, is
entered as holding the lands under Henry III, he
appears to have alienated them in marriage, with
his daughter Margery, to William Bigod, a cadet
of the earls of Norfolk, in the days of John, with
his serjeanty of the Hundred of Barstaple,[3] etc., the
gift being confirmed by John in his 11th year
(1209-10).   In 1228 Roger de Leybourne passed
by fine to William Bigod and Margery his wife
two carucates and two marshes in " Bures " with
the advowson of the church. [4]   It was this William
Bigod who was entered in 12 Hen. III as holding
with his wife in Bures " by the serjeancy of the

[1] *Household Ordinances* (Society of Antiquaries).
[2] *Ibid.*, p. 432.
[3] *Cart. Ant.*, H. 2.
[4] *Essex Fines* (E.A.S), p. 83.

Eschauderie. " [1]   From them this serjeanty appears
to have passed in marriage with a daughter Gundred [2] to William Giffard from whom (or from
whose heirs) Bowers Gifford derives its distinctive
suffix. A Chelmsford plea of 1255 gives the service of this William for Bures as that of making
the King's lard or bacon wherever he was in
England, [3] but after this, the scalding serjeanty,
thus associated with the names of great baronial
houses, fades from view.

TURNSPIT SERJEANTIES

Of interest in more ways than one was the
tenure of the Ashwell (Hall) estate in Finchingfield,
Essex. It was a kitchen serjeanty which was held
in Domesday by a cook ; it hints at an honorary
service on the old Crown-wearing days ; it had a
recognised *caput* ; and it has led learned men into
the wildest blunders.

The Domesday holding of Walter the cook
(*cocus*) was half a hide in this Ashwell and half a
hide in Shalford adjoining. It is Ashwell that is
referred to when the *Testa* tells us that (early in
the reign of Henry III) Simon de ' Achwell '
holds by serjeanty in Dunmow Hundred and has to
be the King's turnspit. [4] A little later, Roger de
' Eswell ' holds a virgate in ' Eswell ' by serjeanty
of being the King's turnspit. [5] Roger's serjeanty

---

[1] Morant's *History of Essex.*
[2] Gundred was an old Bigod name.
[3] Morant's *History of Essex.*
[4] " debet esse hastelarius domini Regis " (p. 268).
[5] " per serjantiam quod sit hastillarius domini Regis " (*Ibid.*, p. 266).

was 'arrented' (in 1250), and the entry gives us a
fresh variant of the name :—

Serjantia Rogeri de Axswell, in Axswell, pro qua
debuit esse hastillarius in coquina domini Regis in princi-
palibus festis, alienata est in parte *(Testa,* p. 268).

Here we see the honorary character of this
service in the King's kitchen ; it was due on the
principal feast-days, probably the old crown-wearing days of the Norman kings.

The word " hastillarius " presents no difficulty.
In the ' Establishment of the king's Household '[1]
there is mention of the " hastelarius " and of the
" hastalaria, " and Morant, the historian of Essex,
defines the serjeanty as " the service of finding a
broche, or spit, of maple to roast the King's meat
on the day of his coronation ", and cites an inquest
after death (1361) in which the service is given as
that " of turning one broche, or spit, in the King's
kitchen on his coronation day."[2] Nevertheless,
' Blount's Tenures' (Ed. Hazlitt), which gives the
service correctly, following Morant, under ' Ashwell' and under ' Finchingfield, ' records it under
' Hashwell (*sic*), co. of Essex,' as " the serjeanty of
being a spearman[3] (*sic*) of our lord the king " and
repeats a solemn disquisition which informs us that
" the spear or lance is among the oldest weapons
recorded in history " ! There was one other mistake that could be made, and the Public Record
Office has made it. Dealing with the *Inq. p. m.*

---

[1] 'Constitutio domus Regis' *(Lib. Rub.,* p. 810).
[2] A turnspit in the royal kitchens was termed a 'turnbroche.'
[3] Blount's extract, " per serjantiam esse hastilarius domini Regis " is
quite correct.

on Roger 'de Eswell',under whom the serjeanty was arrented, and failing to recognise where in Essex the serjeanty was, the editor, reading "hostiler," produced the "serjeanty of being the usher of the King's guesthouse.[1]"   "Which serjeanty," the record proceeds, "was put into money and he paid ½ mark yearly."

As a matter of fact the half marc was paid in respect of the alienated portions only,[2] and for the rest Roger was charged with the twentieth part of a knight's service;[3] but Morant has shown that the turnspit service was returned in Inquests at least as late as 1444.[4]

At Hungerford there was another turnspit, or at least kitchen, serjeanty. In 1212 Geoffrey 'Ponsard' was returned as holding there a virgate "per serjantiam ad Hardland Carv[5]" (sic), but a few years later Simon 'Punchard' is entered as holding two virgates there "per serjant' hastillar.[6]"

This again is wrongly rendered in Hazlitt's "Blount's tenures" as "the serjeanty of being the king's spearman," though it was clearly turnspit tenure : indeed in the Red Book it is "per serjanteriam hastæ tornandæ...... hastas tornandi" (pp. 451, 514). There is in the *Testa* yet another and very curious variant of this serjeanty, in which the holder's name is mangled out of recognition.   On

---

[1] *Cal. of Inq.*, I, No. 867. *Cf.* p. 97, note 2 above.
[2] *Cf. Testa*, p. 268:—"Et dictus Rogerus fecit inde finem,..... videlicet per annum dim. marc."
[3] *Cf.* p. 28 above.
[4] *Cf.* p. 18 above.
[5] *Testa*, p. 125.
[6] *Ibid.*, p. 107.

p. 127 we read that Richard 'Possat' holds the virgate in Hungerford " per serjant' faciendi Harz in coquina domini Regis." Finally, in 1263, we have the " Inquest after death" on Godfrey ' Punsard' (or 'Puncard') in which the service is returned as that " of finding withies for hanging up pieces of meat in the King's kitchen (*harde ad laquand* "*pecias carnium in coquina*) ".[1] It is at least clear that these " harde " are the " harz " of the *Testa* (p. 127), and I would make the bold suggestion that in the phrase, " *harde* ad *laquand*' pecias *carn*ium " we have the clue to the meaning of that weird " Hardland Carv " in the *Testa*'s nightmare text.

THE KING'S TAILOR

Among the puzzles of that puzzling record the *Constitutio Domus Regis* is the entry " Tallator Regis in Domo sua commedet ; et homini suo iij *ob*. "[2] This entry occurs in the midst of the Chamberlain's department, where the chamberlains are jostled by the man who carried the king's bed and by the man who was responsible for the king's bath. What was the King's ' Tallator ' ? Can it have been his tailor ? That Henry I had a recognised tailor is a fact brought to light by a charter of Henry II (confirmed by Edward II), which gives to Robert de St. Paul, his chamberlain, " totam terram que fuit Eschorsan (*sic*) cissoris Henrici regis, avi mei, cum ministerio ejus. "[3]

[1] *Cal. of Inq.* I, No. 547.
[2] *Lib. Rub.*, p. 811.
[3] *Cal. of Charter Rolls*, III, 417.

The editor of the record, Mr. Hubert Hall, asserts that—

Cissor would certainly have been the title applied to the King's Tailor, and the official here referred to was doubtless the Tally-cutter, in the suite of the Treasurer and Chamberlains (*Red Book*, p. ccxcix).

But is this certain ? He himself, in an earlier work, had contended, on the contrary, that ' tailor ' must be meant, [1] and in a very early contemporary mention of a king's tailor I find him styled ' Tailator. ' We meet with this mention in a fragment of a Winchester survey, of which there is a transcript in the *Testa* (p. 236). We there read that " King John has given to William his tailor a certain house on his demesne called Chapmanneshalle. " [2] This house re-appears in the survey *temp.* Edward I as " a certain large house in which are sold linen cloths in Winchester, " and which " King John gave to William his tailor (*cissori suo*) " for an annual render of a grey (fur) *pelisse*. [3]

---

[1] See p. 60 above.

[2] " Dominus Rex Johannes dedit Willelmo Tailatori suo quendam domum " etc.   In John's actual charter, granting the house to William " Cissori nostro," it is styled " the house which is called the linen shop" *(linea selda)*, an interesting glimpse of the trade of Winchester and its ' chapmen '.

[3] *Archæol. Journ.* VII, 375.   This render is also referred to on the Close Rolls.   In 1276 (Oct. 22), the king having made a grant of the " yearly rent of a fur-cloak *(pellicio)* of grey *(griso)* that William le Tailleur owes to the king for a house in Winchester, and the arrears of the same," he " orders the barons (of the exchequer) to cause the cloaks to be appraised " etc. *(Cal. of Close Rolls,* 1272-1279, p. 313).   In 1312 the house is " held in chief by the service of rendering a pilch *(pellicium)* of greywork *(grisonis)* yearly *(Ibid.,* 1307-1313, p. 416) and again, later in the year, as " by the yearly service of rendering a pilch of greywork " *(Ibid.,* p. 472).   Finally in 12 Edw. II (1318-9) Robert de Dunstaple " tenens terrarum quae fuerunt Willelmi le Taillour," duly render-

This is decisive, but I think we may further identify this house as that from which William ' Le Taylur' was receiving an annual marc of rent under Henry III and in which he was succeeded by his son William in 1250.[1] It is certain that in 1235 two Winchester Jews had to buy out the claim of " William the King's tailor " for lands in that city which had been granted to him by the king after being purchased by themselves.[2]

But there is further evidence of equation. In this same volume of Mr. Hall's edition (p. 1078), we find ' Raynerius Taliator' as one of the York moneyers in 1243. His name, luckily, occurs about this very time, in another record, as Reiner " le Tayllur. "[3] Again, also in the Red Book, we find, among Oxfordshire serjeanties (p. 456), that Emma de Hampton held one carucate by the service "talliandi pannos regis." The Testa in two of its entries (pp. 115, 134) records her service in the same words, which might well suggest a tallying, or checking, of the royal wardrobe ; but in a third we find the important variant :—

Emma de Hamton tenet de domino Rege in villa de Niwenton xl s. terre per servicium scindendi linos (sic) pannos domini Regis et Reginae (p. 107).

---

ed at the Exchequer "Tria pellicia de griseo, quorum quodlibet est de VII fessis, pro iij annis," i. e. 8-10 Edw. II (Madox' Exchequer).

[1] Cal. of Inq. Henry III, No. 183.

[2] Cal. of Pat. Rolls, 1232-1247, p. 122.

[3] Cal. of Pat. Rolls, 1232-1247, p. 355. He was sent to Bordeaux by the chamberlains of the Exchequer in charge of 10,000 marcs for the keeper of the wardrobe. There is nothing strange in the choice of a "Tayllur" as a monetarius; for a Draper, a Dyer, and a Cook are also found in the list, while a ' Taliure' (unindexed) occurs, on the same page, as a warden of the Carlisle mint.

Here then we obtain *scindendi* as the equation of *talliandi*, as *scissor* (or *cissor*) was that, we saw, of *tailator*. The fact is that between the names of the tailor (*tailleur*) who 'cut' clothes and of the talley-cutter, who 'cut' wood,[1] there would always be risk of confusion.

The right form of the surname or name of occupation derived from the tally (*talea*) was apparently *taleator*, and it is significant that we first meet with it in connexion with Winchester. On the Pipe Roll of 1130 (p. 41) we find three shillings of 'aid' remitted there to Godfrey 'Taleator' and in another entry, relating to the New Forest (p. 17) Robert 'Taleator' is excused the payment due for his woodcutter at Eling. Is it too speculative to suggest that the wood was destined for tallies? A Robert 'Taleator' and a Gilbert 'Taleator' are also entered in the second of the early Winchester surveys, that of 1143. It is right, on the other hand, to mention that a John 'contratalliator' (*sic*) —whose name must have been derived from the counter-tally—is found on the Pipe Rolls of Henry II in receipt of a salary of twopence a day from the revenue of Southampton. What his office was is proved by an entry on the Pipe Roll of 1200 (2 John), in which, by the way, the form 'tailliando' is used.[2]

Before passing to the holdings by serjeanty of Roger, tailor to Henry III, something may be said

---

[1] *Cf.* the French name 'Taillebois', which became a surname.

[2] "Ricardus de Leircestria debet x libras pro officio suo habendo in villa de Suthanton quod antecessores sui habuerunt, scilicet de Tailliando contra Prepositos villæ de hoc quod captum fuerit ad opus Regis. Sed recordatum est" etc. (Madox' *Exchequer*).

of William as actual tailor to John. It is, probably, little known that on the *Rotulus Misae* of 1212-1213 we have the detailed tailor's bills sent in by him,[1] not for materials, which were charged for separately, but for making the 'robes' of the king and his friends. William was a ladies' tailor as well ; he made 'robes, ' on the King's account, for the Queen, for the Scottish King's daughters and for Suzanne " domicella, amica domini Regis. " The striking feature of these 'robes, " whether made for men or women, is that each uniformly consisted, like a 'suit' of to-day, of three parts, though these were very different, namely the tunic, the 'over-tunic, ' and the mantle (*pallium*).[2] We can picture to ourselves what these were by studying the vestments of our early kings on the effigy, on the seal, or in records. In John's case they corresponded with the (1) tunic, (2) dalmatic, (3) mantle (*pallium*) of his coronation vestments. In colour also there is a correspondence. Robes were of scarlet, green, or russet, sometimes even of black burnet, but various shades of red[3] were those most in favour, and in the four scarlet 'robes' made for the Mayor of Angoulême and his fellows (1213) we have perhaps the earliest mention of these municipal vestments, which, in that case, are but survivals from a time when kings and nobles,

---

[1] See Cole's *Documents illustrative of English History* (1844), pp. 267, 269. The first extends from Mid-Lent to the summer of 1213, and the other from Christmas Eve 1212 to Mid-Lent 1213. They are entered on the 'dorse' of the Roll.

[2] See, for allusions to this mantle, pp. 115, 143, 192 above.

[3] " escarleta," " escarleta rubea," " escarleta sanguinea." There is one 'robe' of green samite.

knights and mayors walked alike in scarlet.

William was also a military tailor and more. He was paid for furbishing up (*furbiandis*) swords and knives and quarrells ; [1] for cleaning the king's swords of rust, [2] and, as " William our tailor," was paid in 1220, for repairing the young king's crown and *regalia* for the Whitsun coronation at Westminster. [3] The render recorded for his Winchester house [4] gives a special interest to its valuation at 14 sh. when received from him in 1208 [5] and to his purchase at Winchester of grey fur for lining the king's ' over-tunic.' [6] It was at Winchester fair that, in 1233, the Yorkshire and Lincolnshire clothiers, with those of Leicester, had to deliver to " William the King's tailor," the cloth bought for the king's use, [7] but we also hear of his buying oversea, for in 1233 " the king has caused all the merchants of the power of France (to be) arrested in England by his order on account of the taking of William the king's tailor beyond seas. " [8] The last fact I shall record of this favoured tailor is that, in 1227, he had been given by the king that land at Newton Purcell, Oxon., " which Emma de Norhamtona sometime

---

[1] Cole's *Documents*, p. 232.

[2] " pro rubigine gladii domini Regis detergenda " (*Ibid.*, p. 241).

[3] *Cal. rot. claus.* I, 431.

[4] See p. 258 above.

[5] " pro uno pelliceo de griso ad opus nostrum liberato eidem Radulfo per manum Willelmi Cissoris apud Lameheth die Sancti Vincentii (22 Jan.) xiiij sol." (Letters Close, 3 Feb. 1208).

[6] " pro una ferrura de grisio, ad supertunicam domini Regis ad surgendum, emptam apud Wintoniam xxv *s.* ...... per manum Willelmi Scissoris " (Cole, p. 175)

[7] *Cal. of Pat. Rolls*, 1232-1247, p. 23.

[8] *Ibid.*, p. 96.

held of the king,.... to hold on payment of certain shears (*forfices*) at Christmas. "[1] This was the land which Emma de ' Hamtona ' had held by the serjeanty of cutting out the King's linen clothes,[2] and which, after the above grant, was held by William the tailor (*Cissor*) by the service of rendering the said shears.[3]

I pass from tenure by the tailor's shears to tenure by the tailor's needle. Blount has cited and Morant repeated a plea of 1284-5 (13 Edw. I) to the effect that Roger, formerly the King's tailor, held a carucate of land at Hallingbury, Essex, by the serjeanty of paying to the king's Exchequer a silver needle every year on the morrow of Michaelmas.[4] The land was the small manor of Wallbury, and its holder was Roger de Ros, who appears, subsequently to William, as tailor to Henry III.[5] I hasten to add, lest any Taylor, Taylour, Tayleur, or Tailyour should claim this Roger de Ros *alias* Le Tailleur *alias* Le Taluur as his ancestor, and desire to change his name to de Ros, that Roger left no issue, his two sisters being found to be his heirs at his death in 1257.[6] The actual grant to him of the manor of Wallbury was made in 1240 (Dec. 6).[7] When Aymer de

[1] *Cal. of Charter Rolls*, I, 51.

[2] *Testa*, pp. 107, 115, 134. See p. 259 above.

[3] "Willelmus Cissor tenet xl s[olidatas] terre in Neuinton per servicium reddendi quasdam forffices ad warderobam domini Regis" (*Ibid.*, p. 118).

[4] "De serjeanciis dicunt quod...... per serjantiam solvendi... unam acum argenteam."

[5] Morant cites a Plea roll of 1245 recording the render of the silver needle by " Rogerus de Ross, Scissor Domini Regis."

[6] *Cal. of Inq*, I, No. 397.

[7] Gift to Master Roger de Ros, king's tailor,...... of all the land

Valence, Earl of Pembroke, died in 1325, Wallbury figured among his vast possessions, still " held
of the king in chief by service of a silver needle. " [1]

As for Roger de Ros, we find him employed as
tailor in a way that indicates the increase of luxury
and extravagance under Henry III.   He is sent to
the fairs of Provins and of ' Lendit ' to buy, at
great cost, silks and precious stuffs, the king borrowing in all directions and becoming indebted to
the Lucca merchants, in order to provide him with
cash, while at home, in 1256, Henry, having " no
ready money to pay for purchases " which Roger
was to make at Boston fair, wrote urgently to the
justices in eyre on the northern circuit, and the
sheriffs of the northern counties, commanding them
to send up 700 marcs from the proceeds of the
eyre to Roger and his colleague " with all speed
as they would save him from loss and perpetual
scandal. " [2]

THE WYMONDLEY SERJEANTY

This serjeanty, with its well established coronation service, is somewhat difficult to class.   It is

called ' la Walle ' in Hallingebiri, which Gilbert de Hauvill held of the
king's bail, to hold by rendering one silver bodkin (*acum*) or 1d.
yearly " (*Cal. of Charter Rolls*, I, 255).   At the same time, Gilbert de
Hauvill, " out of pity and in compassion for his infirmity," was allowed
to retain the land for life, though he had only held it of the king's
bail, on paying yearly half a marc " to the king's serjeant, Master Roger
de Ros, the king's tailor " (*Cal. of Pat. Rolls*, 1232-1247, p. 240).
This disposes apparently of the puzzling statement, in the *Red Book*
(p. 457, 507) and the *Testa*, that, in 1212-1218, Walter de Hauville
held Wallbury by falconer serjeanty, of the gift of Henry II, or
Richard I, or John.

[1] *Cal. of Inq.* VI, p. 318.
[2] *Cal. of Pat. Rolls*, p. 483.

nowhere spoken of as ' butler ' service or assigned
to the butler's department, although the silver
covered cups on the Argentine coat of arms are
associated with ' Butler ' coats. If we style its
service that of cup-bearer, we shall hardly be mistaken, and this, indeed, is the accepted view. It
has already (p. 61) been pointed out that the cupbearers (*escantiones*) are prominent in the *Constitutio*,
although they are not afterwards officers of the
Household. It is, therefore, significant that this
serjeanty, of which the origin has hitherto been
wrongly stated, can be carried back, as I shall now
show, to the days of Henry I. In 1903 there was
published the calendar of the Patent Rolls for
1399-1401, in which we find an *Inspeximus* (11th
May 1400) for Sir William Argentein of a Charter
of King Stephen granting to John de Argentein
the land and office of his father, Reginald de
Argentein.[1] As no place is mentioned, it would
escape notice that this charter relates to Great
Wymondley, Herts., and to the service attached to
its tenure. Reginald de Argentein, the former
holder, was already dead in 1130, for his widow
Maud then had license to marry again.[2]

The returns of 1212 contain a full record of this
ancient serjeanty :—

Ricardus de Argentein tenet Wilemundeslea de domino
Rege per serjeantiam, scilicet ad serviendum de una cupa
argentea ad coronacionem dicti Regis, et antecessores sui

---

[1] " sciatis me reddidisse et concessisse Johanni de Argentein totam terram que fuit patris sui Reginaldi de Argentein cum ministerio suo "
(p. 293). "Terra et ministerium " was the regular phrase for a serjeanty on the Pipe Roll of 1130.

[2] Pipe Roll, 31 Hen. I.

de antecessoribus domini Regis de veteri feoffamento [1] per idem servicium. [2]

It is, probably, quite unknown that Richard joined the Crusade of 1218, and, after the capture of Damietta (5 Nov. 1219), founded and handsomely endowed a church there in honour of St. Edmund, his patron saint (*advocatus*). In 1220 he wrote in exultation to his kinsman the Prior of (Bury) St Edmunds that St. Edmund had already performed a miracle as soon as the church was opened. A Fleming, who bore a grudge against the saint, abused the nice new statue of him, which Richard had had carved and painted. But the saint had his revenge. As the Fleming, snarling, left the church, he was caught by a saintly booby trap, [3] and was too stunned to walk home without help.

When Richard de Argentein died on his pilgrimage to the Holy Land in 1246, the Inquisition returned similarly that he held Wymondley by service of serving with a cup at the king's chief feasts when directed by the king's steward. [4] His son Giles, a valiant knight, succeeded. [5] At the coronation of Richard II the claim to serve was duly allowed, but at that of Henry IV the claim of Sir William Argentine was unsuccessfully opposed by Sir John [6] Fitz Warren in right of his wife

[1] This again carries back the serjeanty to the days of Henry I.
[2] *Testa*, p. 270. *Cf. Lib. Rub.*, p. 507.
[3] " accidit miraculose quod lignum quoddam supra ostium...... dictæ ecclesiæ de alto corruens grave vulnus...... inflixit " (MS. Bod. 240).
[4] *Cal. of Inq. Henry III*, No. 93.
[5] Mathew Paris.
[6] There seems to be some confusion here. The husband of Maud (the eldest daughter) was Sir *Ivo* Fitz Waryn.

Maud, daughter and heir of Sir John de Argentine. William was not legitimate, but his tenure of the manor gained the day, for this was of the essence of serjeanty.

The manor passed with an heiress from the Argentine family to the Alingtons, and in 1486 William Alington was found to have held it, at his death, " in chief by serjeanty, *viz.* serving the King and Queen on their coronation days with the first silver-gilt cup. "[1]   From the coronation of Charles II to that of George IV, both inclusive, the lords of Great Wymondley had their claims duly allowed, the cup forming the fee.   But with the cessation of the banquet, the service lapsed.

[1] *Cal. of Inq. Henry VII*, I, No. 31.

CHAPTER V

THE KING'S SPORT

We are most of us aware that our Norman kings were consumed with a passion for the chase. The schoolboy learns that the first William " loved the tall deer as though he had been their father, " and that his son and successor met in their pursuit his death. But less familiar is the fact that the last of our English kings [1] was as ardent as themselves in sport. For, in Freeman's words, it is " the pastime which seems least suited to the character of a saint." Never did he fail to attend mass ; but, as soon as mass was over, it was Edward's greatest joy to hear the cry of hounds or to watch his hawks in flight. [2] If one of his Berkshire squires should die, the hawks and hounds he left had to be offered to the king. [3]

Even Harold, his darling hero, " shared, " I fear, the " savage pastime, " in Freeman's words, of the " saintly " king. This I prove from the Bayeux

[1] I ignore, as Domesday does, the upstart Harold.

[2] " Plurimum temporis exigebat circa saltus et silvas in venationum jucunditate...... jocundabatur plurimum coram se allatis accipitribus vel hujus generis avibus, vel certe delectabatur applausibus multorum motuum canibus. His et talibus interdum deducebat diem, et in his tantummodo ex natura videbatur aliquam mundi captare delectationem."

[3] " Tainus vel miles regis dominicus moriens...... si essent ei canes vel, accipitres presentabantur regi ut, si vellet, acciperet." (*Domesday* I, 566).

tapestry, dear to the Professor's heart. After
taking leave of his sovereign, we see him riding to
Bosham, the hawk as ever on his wrist. Before
him go his hounds, deserving more attention than
they have, I think, received. For here again the
famous stitchwork contrives to set before us
minute and accurate detail. As for centuries
after, the hounds are a mixed pack. In front are
a couple of the small hounds (*canes currentes*) duly
giving tongue ; behind them a leash of the great
hounds (*leporarii* or *valtrarii*), distinguished by
their long legs, their powerful hind quarters and
the collars about their necks. [1] We shall meet
with them repeatedly in these pages as forming
part of the mediæval pack, and no one who com-
pares the tapestry, for instance, with that illumin-
ated picture of an early king hunting the deer in
Cott. MS. Claudius D. II. [2] can doubt that the
designer of the stitchwork sought to indicate a
mixed pack. Although for convenience the larger
hounds have to be described as greyhounds
(*leporarii*), they were a more powerful breed, built
on coarser lines, and with a dash of the mastiff. [3]

We are further shown in the 'Tapestry' Harold
going on board, still with his hawk on his hand, a
hound under his arm, while another hound is held

---

[1] " Et Encaynne comme vialtre ou levrer," *(Ogier le Danois)*.

[2] It similarly shows, as typical of the pack, a couple of the smaller
hounds and two of the larger (wearing collars).

[3] Under John we find *valtrarii* as in some way distinct from *leporarii*.
They were, I think, boarhounds, like the French *veaultres*. " L'autre
nature d'alanz veautres sont auques taillez comme laide taille de levrier,
mais il ont grosses testes, grosses levres et granz oreilles et de ceulz s'aide
l'en très bien et a chascier les ours et les porcz."

by the man who follows him. [1]   When captured and brought to William, he has still his hawk.

Although Domesday reveals to us the fact that William retained in his service a number of English huntsmen, the terms used for hawks and hounds were, we shall find, French. [2]   This, as I shall show, enables us to recognise wolf-hounds and fox-hounds in the days of John.   So also the English " fewterer " is derived from the French *veautrier*, the man in charge of greyhounds, [3] while the French original of *braconarius* is represented by the word that now denotes a poacher.

It is impossible to deal with the various serjeant-ies connected with the training and keeping of hounds without some explanation of mediæval hunt-ing.   Those who have had to interpret mediæval records are familiar with the difficulties caused by the varying names of hounds, difficulties which arise partly, no doubt, from actual developments and changes of breed since those far-off days, and partly from the different system of hunting then in vogue.

---

[1] These details are not without historical significance.   Mr. Freeman, who discussed at some length this voyage of Harold, strove to persuade himself that it was merely a "pleasure trip" in the Channel.   William of Malmesbury, he observes, makes him "set out from Bosham purely on a voyage of pleasure and for the purpose of fishing."   But the whole evidence of the tapestry is against this view.   And by its showing us hawk and hound, but no horses, taken with him, it implies that he intended to cross the Channel and would find horses on the other side. In the 12th cent., as the Pipe Rolls show, Henry II used to send his hawks and huntsmen across when he was going to Normandy.

[2] " Osturs, girfaus, e espervers,

Seus e veaultre e levrer."

That is to say, goshawks, gerfalcons, and sparrow-hawks ; (ordinary) hounds and boarhounds and greyhounds.   The French words were latinized, but only, of course, in records.

[3] *Veltrarius* or *Valtrarius* in mediæval Latin.

Broadly speaking, it is possible to trace in the
early part of the twelfth century the same combination in hunting of three distinct hounds that we
meet with in the latter part of the sixteenth. This
may seem a bold statement, but I hope to make
it good. Our starting-point, here again, is that
record of the King's household (*Constitutio domus
regis*) which preserves its constitution as it stood at
the death of Henry I. We there read

Valtrarii, unusquisque .iij. *d.* in die ; et .ij. *d.* hominibus
suis ; et unicuique leporario, obolum in die. Mueta regis
.viij. *d.* in die.... Ductor liemarii .j. *d.* et liemarius,
obolum. Bernarius .iij. *d.* in die ; et magni Harrede
.iiij. debent habere .j. *d.*, et de parvis Harrede VII .j. *d.*
Ad magnos Harrede .ij. homines, et unusquisque .j. *d.* in
die. Braconarii, unusquisque .iij. *d.* in die. Luparii,
.xx. *d.* in die ad equos et ad homines et canes ; et debent
habere .xxiiij. canes currentes et .viij. leporarios. [1]

Employing later evidence to illustrate this passage,
we may clearly distinguish in it :— (1) the velterers with their greyhounds ; (2) the "berner" and
the ordinary hounds ; (3) the "liam hound" (*liemarius*) with the man who kept him in leash (*ductor*).
The Close rolls of the reign of Edward II, early
in the fourteenth century, afford numerous instances
of royal huntsmen sent in detachments to kill deer
for the royal larder. And the normal detachment
contained, in addition to the huntsmen themselves,
(1) velterers with their greyhounds, (2) berners
with their "running hounds", (3) a "berselet" in
charge of a "berseletter." It is also very remarkable that the pack of "running hounds" was nor-

[1] *Lib. Rub.*, p. 813.

mally of twelve couples, the very number named in the *Constitutio*, which were in charge of two berners. The number of greyhounds (*leporarii*) accompanying them varied, but each velterer, normally, had charge of from four to six, the reason being that he would lead a brace or a leash with each hand, or a brace with one and a leash with the other. As for the " berselet ", it must have performed the function of the " Liam-hound," of earlier and later date, namely that of harbouring the quarry by scent.[1]

As an earlier example of the pack of twelve couples and of its combination with greyhounds, we may take the payment by William de Braose, in 1205, for seisin of three famous Monmouthshire castles, viz: 500 marcs, three war-horses, five hunters (*chacuros*), twenty-four hounds (*seusas*), and ten greyhounds.[2] There is also an interesting instance of a pack of six couples, with a "berner", in a fine from the bishop of Ely, in 1202, for a trespass by his huntsman.[3]

Although a good deal has now appeared in print

[1] One may cite, as instances, John Lovel with 24 " running dogs, " six greyhounds, two berners, and a "veutrer " (1311) ; two huntsmen, " whom the king is sending with two berners, six veutrers, twenty-four *haericii* dogs, twenty-two greyhounds, and a bercelet " (1313) ; a huntsman " with two berners, four veutres, twenty-four running *daemericii* dogs, a bercelet, and sixteen greyhounds " (1313) ; a huntsman " with two veutres, two berners, a bercelettar, ten greyhounds, twenty-four running dogs and two bercelets " (1313) ; two huntsmen " with two *haericii* berners, five veutrers, and one bercelletar, and twenty-four *daemericii* running dogs, twenty-four greyhounds, and two bercelets " (1314).

[2] Rot. fin. 7 John, m. 7 (cited by Blount).

[3] " Episcopus Eliensis debet xii. canes de mota et j. limerum " (Pipe Roll, 4 John, rot. 10.) The *mota* was the French *meute*.

on hunting in the 14th and 15th centuries, the only actual drawings of hounds which appear to be known are those in the Phillips MS. of Gaston de Foix, which Sir Henry Dryden gave in his 'Twici' (1844)[1] and which were taken thence by Dr. Cox in his *Royal Forests of England*. It appears to have been overlooked that there is earlier and English evidence in the very remarkable grotesque drawing found in the Rydeware cartulary.[2] Here the victims of the hounds are seen triumphant over them : a hare carries a small slain hound ; a fox leads a brace of greyhounds ; and a big animal bestrides a much larger hound with his nose to the ground, which can hardly be other than the 'liam-hound' (*liemarius*). The same difference in size between this hound and the 'running dogs' is seen in the drawings from Gaston de Foix' work spoken of above.

The serjeanties connected with the "liam-hound" will be duly found below ; but the point I would insist on here is that his use in hunting, and by the same name, connects the two periods I have named. In Turberville's *Book of Hunting* (1576) we have two woodcuts of the huntsman—still called "The Hunte"—holding in his "liam-hound" (pp. 60, 71), in one of which the hound has his nose to the ground picking up a scent.

I am the Hunte, which rathe and earely rise,

. . . .

---

[1] 2nd edition, 1908.
[2] It was reproduced in *Charters and Muniments of the Gresley family* (1895), pp. 118-9, and as a frontispiece to *The Rydeware Cartulary* (William Salt Arch. Soc. 1896).

Then take my Hownde, *in liam* me behinde,
The stately Harte in fryth an fell to finde

. . . .

And when my Hownde doth streyne upon good vent
I must confesse the same doth me content.
But when I have my coverts walkt about
And harbred faste the Harte for comming out
Then I returne, to make a grave reporte.

This system of harbouring the quarry beforehand
with the help of the " liam-hound " is the practice
which unites the two ages, and Turberville's book
describes it in great detail.[1]

Although he speaks of the 'Lyam' by which
the hound was held, the hound itself he terms
throughout, significantly enough, the blood-hound.[2]
The resemblance of the lyam-hound in the Gaston
de Foix MS. to a bloodhound had been observed.

Almost contemporary with the appearance of
Turberville's book [3] (1576)—itself largely a trans-
lation from the French—was that of Fleming's
English translation of Dr. Caius' monograph " of
English dogs " (1576) and Harrison's well-known

---

[1] *e.g.* " in a morning a hounde shall drawe better beeing helde shorte
than if he were lette at length of the Lyam : And yet some Hunters
will give them all the Lyam, but they do not well " (p 76).

[2] pp. 71, 106-7, 115, 129, 130. These passages relate to hunting
the Hart ; but in dealing with the wolf and the bear he terms it the
'lyamehound'.

It is noteworthy that he should write " The best finding of the Beare
is with a lyamhounde," for in the Rydeware cartulary drawing it seems
to be a bear that is bestriding that hound.

He further identifies the two hounds in his directions for hunting the
otter, where he writes that the huntsmen " should first send four
servants or varlets with bloodhounds, or such houndes as will draw in
the lyame...... If any of theyr lyamhounds finde of an Otter let yᵉ
huntesman ...... lodge it even as you would do a Deare or a Bore."

[3] Re-printed (Tudor and Stuart Library) 1908.

description of Elizabethan England. The latter, unfortunately, does but copy from Caius, the Elizabethan parson being, one presumes, no sportsman himself. As for Caius' book, it appears to me to be that of a fantastic pedant and to compare most unfavourably with Turberville's treatise, which is that of a practical huntsman. The learned doctor [1] discourses of " the dog called *Leviner* or *Lyemmer* ; in Latin *lorarius*," and observes [2] that

It is called in Latin lorinarius, "a levitate", of lightness, and therefore may well be called a lighthound. It is also called by this word *Lorarius*, a *Loro* (a thong), wherewith it is led.

It is certain that the ' Lyemmer ' was, on the contrary, a big, heavily-built hound, while of its distinctive use in harbouring the quarry Caius says, and apparently knows, nothing. When, however, we turn to the *Art de Venerie*, [3] attributed to a huntsman of Edward II, William ' Twici ', this work, which takes us back more than half way to the *Constitutio*, shows us the Lyamhound used, precisely as in Turberville's day, for harbouring and unharbouring the quarry. [4] A survival of the practice lingers with the Devon and Somerset, where, the harbourer having communicated to the master, as in mediæval times, the presence of a warrantable stag, two couples of " tufters " are

---

[1] Caius, moreover, treats the Bloodhound (*sanguinarius*) as a wholly distinct breed.
[2] As rendered by his translator.
[3] Edited by Sir Henry Dryden.
[4] " quantez des bestes sunt meuz de lymer ...... Sire, touz ceaus qe sunt enchaces sunt meuz de lymer."

thrown into cover to unharbour him and drive him into the open for the pack.

Turning now to the use of greyhounds, hunting of course by sight, in conjunction with other hounds, hunting by scent, we again find the practice of Turberville's day illustrating the far earlier *Constitutio domus regis*. In that document it seems strange to find eight greyhounds combined with twenty-four ' running dogs ' in the pack that hunted the wolf. But Turberville cites an author who writes :—

Greyhoundes are more afrayde of a Foxe than of a greater beast. For I have seen Greyhounds which would runne hardly at an Hart, yea, would not refuse the wild Bore, nor the Wolfe, and yet they would streyne curtesie at a Foxe (p. 188).

He himself, while explaining that, at that time, wolves were only found in Ireland, observes :—

I have seene a Wolfe (being emptie) out runne four or five brace of the best Greyhoundes that might be founde . . . . . . and unlesse he be coursed with Greyhounds or Mastives, he keepeth the covert . . . . . . A Wolfe will stand up a whole day before a good kennel of houndes unless yᵉ Greyhoundes course him (p. 208).

He also describes in great detail the way in which greyhounds should be set beforehand to intercept the wolf, after which

" lette the Huntsman go with his Lyamehounde and drawe from the carion unto the thickes side where the Wolves have gone in: and there the Huntes shall caste off the thyrde parte of their best houndes . . . The Huntesmen must holde neare in to theyr houndes, blowing harde and encouraging them with the voyce, for many houndes will streyne curtesie at this chace, although they bee lustie and arrant at all other chaces . . . . . . Note that bothe houndes and Greyhoundes will requyre greater fleshing and encouragement to a Wolfe than to any other chace " (pp. 213-5.).

Here the three kinds of hounds are seen working in conjunction. [1]

If greyhounds were used, as we find they were, for hunting the wolf and the wild boar, they must have been fiercer and more akin to the Irish wolf-hound. [2] Here we may learn something from Caius, for he speaks of the greyhound (*leporarius*) as

taking the buck, the hart, the doe, the fox, and other beasts of semblable kind ordained for the game of hunting ; but more or less, each one according to the measure and proportion of their desire ; and as might and hability of their bodies will permit and suffer. For . . . . . some are of a greater sort and some lesser ; some are smooth-skinned, and some are curled. The bigger therefore are appointed to hunt the bigger beasts, and the smaller serve to hunt the smaller accordingly. [3]

Caius, however, has plunged the subject into great confusion by classifying the ' harrier ' as *leverarius*, a hound hunting by scent. For the ' levrer ' was, in old French, the greyhound ; [4] and the Mauleverer family bore greyhounds on its shield. More-

---

[1] Turberville notes that young hounds should never be entered to the hare in conjunction with greyhounds, for, instead of hunting by scent, they would do nothing but "lifte up their heades and looke alwayes to see the Hare before the Greyhoundes, and will never put nose to the grounde, nor beate for it, nor hunte" (p. 170).

[2] See the remarks above on the hounds in the Bayeux Tapestry.

[3] That greyhounds varied a good deal is implied by an entry on the Pipe Roll of 1207 (9 John), where John le Teingre offers 100 marcs " et x leporarios magnos, pulchros, et bonos " (Rot. 14d.)

[4] They are *lefrers* in ' Twici '.

over, their name was already Latinised early in the 12th century as ' Malus leporarius, ' which gives us the French-Latin equation. Further confusion has been caused by Caius' section " of the dog called Gazehound, in Latin Agaseus, " used for hunting " the fox and the hare. " No one seems able to explain what this dog was.

The greyhounds depicted as hunting in conjunction with other hounds are usually shown as white. They are so seen in the illumination of an early king hunting (Cott. MS., Claud. D ii), which is said to be of about the time of Edward III,[1] in that of the death of the boar reproduced in Miss Dryden's *The art of hunting* (1908), and in the illumination prefixed to the same work. In all these cases the contrast with the darker colour of the other hounds is marked. This, probably, explains the service of rendering two white greyhounds for the manor of Sheffield,[2] which has led to much sententious speculation in the later editions of Blount's work as to whether white hares (*lepores*) were meant.

Mention of " a pack of white hounds " is afforded by a Hampshire serjeanty, that of Oakhanger, the holders of which were alleged to have changed a hunting tenure into the service of finding a serjeant in war, without being authorised to do so.[3]

---

[1] But in this case they have black spots.

[2] *Inq. p. m.* on Thomas de Furnival (1333) in *Cal. of Inq.* VII. No. 470.

[3] " Serjantia Jacobi de Hochangre in Ochangre pro qua debuit custodire *unam albam motam canum* domini Regis, et quam serjant[iam] antecess' dicti Jacobi mutaverunt in aliud servicium sine waranto, scilicet inveniendi domino Regi unam servientem in exercitu suo cum uno habergello per quadriginta dies, " etc. (*Testa*, p. 238). In an entry of

THE LIAM-HOUND SERJEANTIES

In the *Constitutio domus Regis* the liam-hound, we saw, figures thus :—

Ductor liemarii j *d.*, et liemarius, obolum.

The editor renders this, " Leader of the limmers " (p. ccxciii),[1] but it is important to observe that only *one* liam-hound (*liemarius*) is entered.   This hound was so named from being held in leash, so that the word *ductor* expressly suggests its character.[2]   It hunted by scent and had " hanging ears something like a bloodhound."   The low pay of the man in charge of it (a penny a day [3]) should be observed. One of the serjeanties connected with this hound was at Aislaby, co. York, where, in 1198,[4] Guy the huntsman (*Wido venator*) held two carucates by the

---

earlier date (p. 235) the tenure is described as " per veneriam ", but in 1317 Oakhanger is returned as held of the king in chief by serjeanty, by service of keeping the king's white pack of hounds when he shall come into the Forest of Woolmer (*Cal. of Inq.* VI. No. 46). For unauthorised change of service see p. 48 above.

[1] *Lib. Rub.*, p. 813.   Even a little earlier, *viz.* on the Pipe Roll of 1130, we have this hound mentioned (p. 3): "j Liemer et iiij seus " (hounds).

[2] Prince Henry, son of James I, had, in 1610, a ' Bowe Bearer and Master of the Lime Hounds.'   This officer appears in the Queen's Household of 1631 as " Master of the Bows and *String* Hounds."   It would seem possible that this office occurs even so early as 1377, when we have an appointment, during pleasure, of John Lovell (a name familiar as that of a huntsman under Edward II, and even under John) " as master of the king's hounds, called *berceletz* " (*Cal. Pat. Rolls*, 1377-1381, p. 71).   But his " licence to expeditate them " (*Ibid.*) is so startling that one turns to the Latin text, where the word is " expediendi. " " Expedire " would seem to have been here mistaken for " expeditare. "

[3] The berners and veutrers had threepence a day each.

[4] I established this to be the date of the return.

service of training one liam-hound. [1] His son
Richard is entered as holding them by the service
of training " the king's limehound." [2] In 1250 this
serjeanty was " arrented," and its service commuted
for the payment of forty shillings a year.[3] Accordingly, in 1262, when Richard de ' Aslakeby '
died, the land was returned as " held of the king in
chief by 40 s. yearly." [4]

But I have been able, with some difficulty, to
trace another serjeanty of the kind, which did not
so come to an end, but continued long enough to
prove the connexion of the ' berselet ' with the
liam-hound.

In the great Norfolk Inquisition of 1212, as
recorded in the *Testa*, we read :—

Willelmus May tenuit in Causton' xx solidatas terre
per veneriam de dono domini Regis Henrici antiqui et
Willelmus May filius Roberti May tenet adhuc per idem
servicium (p. 293).

Willelmus May tenet unam carucatam terre in villa de
Stanhoie de domino Rege per serjantiam venacionis
(p. 295).[5]

In spite of the return that the land in Cawston
was given to William May by Henry I (' Henrici

---

[1] " aptandi unum limer[ium]. " *Testa*, p. 377.

[2] *Lib. Rub.*, p. 467, and *Testa*, pp. 375, 376 : " limerium Regis " and
Testa, p. 378 :— " aptandi unum canem lyemerium. " Blount misread
the word as " liverium, " which puzzled his editors.

[3] It was then described as " servicium affe(c)tandi et custodiendi
unum limerium ad custum suum. " The service was " redeemed " for
the above payment, and the land was to be held as a twentieth of a
knight's fee, " Et ipse et heredes sui quieti erunt imperpetuum de predicto servicio " (*Testa*, p. 376).

[4] *Cal. of Inq. Hen. III*, p. 146.

[5] William May is found acting as one of King John's huntsmen just
before this (*Rôt. de Prest.* 12 John, p. 249).

antiqui '), I cannot trace the tenure further back than Easter 1164, when William May began to draw twenty shillings a year from Cawston, all of which had previously been held by William the King's brother. [1]

In these extracts the serjeanty, we see, is only defined as a hunting tenure; but in later entries we have more detail. On p. 290 the land in Cawston and Stanhoe is said to be held " per serjantiam custodiendi unum Livarium," and on p. 299 the hound becomes "unum lunar[ium]." On p. 285 William May " pascit unum liverium," and on p. 283 (a return which I assign to 1236) the hound is "unum luvarium." Here, the minims being the same in number, I propose to read " limarium," as I also do in the case of " lunarium." As for the forms ' Livarium ' and ' Liverium ', they are but a minim short. This makes perfect sense of unintelligible words. The later history of this land—known as May's manor in Cawston—confirms this reading; for in 1285 (to quote Blomefield) the land is stated to be held " per serjantiam custodiendi unum burtelettum (*i. e.* bercelettum) ad voluntatem sumptibus suis propriis," and in 1309 Joan, relict of Robert de Bedingfield, was found to hold her lands in Cawston and Stanhoe of the king in chief " by the service of keeping a bercelet (*bercellum*) for the king, when he wishes to send a bercelet, there to be kept, receiving for keeping it 14 *d.* weekly. " [2]

But there is a third variant for this same hound.

[1] *Pipe Roll,* 10 Hen. II, p. 34.
[2] *Cal. of Close Rolls,* 1307-1313, p. 163.

In the *Testa* return (p. 299) early in the reign of Henry III the tenure of Cawston by a 'lunar[ium]', *i. e. limarium*, is immediately followed by that of Stanhoe " per servicium custodiendi unum *brachetum*," while in the *Inq. p. m.* on William le May, 1256, the whole of his lands are said to be held " by service of keeping one brachet" (*bragetti*).[1]

Having thus shown that in this serjeanty the liam-hound becomes not only a 'berselet', but a 'brachet', I turn to that of Coton in Lullington, Derbyshire, for further identification of the two latter hounds. In the *Testa de Nevill* Stephen de Beauchamp holds this manor, in 1212, 'per unum brachetum' at the king's coming into Derbyshire (pp. 18, 22);[2] but in 1284-5 Nicholas de Segrave holds it " pro uno berselet cum ligamine ".[3] His father Gilbert held it " rendering yearly one berselet in leash " (*in ligamine*),[4] his father Stephen having bought it of the heirs of Stephen de Beauchamp to hold by the yearly service of a 'brachet'.[5]

Mr. Turner has similarly shown that, in the case of the interesting Whitfield serjeanty, the 'brachet' which had to be trained by the holder of this Northamptonshire manor " ad currendum

---

[1] *Cal. of Inq. Hen. III*, No. 345.

[2] It is a 'brachet' also on p. 20, and in the *Calendar of Charter Rolls*, I, 81.

[3] *Feudal Aids*, I, 248.   I have shown that Mr. Pym Yeatman rendered 'berselet cum ligamine' as 'one bow with a string', and 'brachet', on p. 388 of his 'Feudal History of Derbyshire', as an 'armlet'.

[4] *Cal. of Inq. Henry III*, No. 334, where, by a luckless shot, it becomes Cothes in Prestwold, Leicestershire.

[5] *Close Rolls*, 13 *Hen. III*, m. 20 ; and *Staffs. Collect.*, Vol. V, part i, p. 10.

ad cervum et bissam et damum et damam," [1]
becomes a 'berselet' on the Hundred Rolls. It is
a 'brachet' in an *Inq. p. m.*[2] This serjeanty
appears to have been ended by arrentation in 1250.

If it were not that a 'berselet' is well recognised
to have acted as liam-hound (*viz.* to track and
harbour the game), the phrase " ad *currendum* "
would suggest a " canis currens," hunting in the
pack. The same point arises in a curious little
serjeanty in Woodham Mortimer and Hazeleigh,
Essex. It was alleged in 1284-5 that a certain
Hardekin held 115 acres in Woodham Mortimer
in capite by the serjeanty of bringing up a brachet
of the king, when the king sent it him, and keeping it till it was able to run,[3] which serjeanty had
been " dismembered " for forty years past.

This would take us back to Passelew's arrentation in 1250. But we cannot trace this serjeanty
in the *Testa*, though there is an entry that Hardekin de Hailesl' holds Hailesl' (Hazeleigh), worth
twenty shillings, " sed nescimus quomodo." [4]

Bedfordshire had a ' brachet' serjeanty at Farn-
dish, where the service was that the holder "debuit
custodire domino Regi unum brachetum ad summonicionem Regis." The land was found to be
partly alienated in 1250, and, Ralf Basset exchan-
ging its tenure for that of the thirtieth of a knight's
fee, the serjeanty came to an end.[5]

---

[1] *Testa*, p. 28.   It is also a 'brachet' on pp. 32, 33.

[2] *Cal. of Inq. Henry III*, No. 915.

[3] " nutriendum unum brachettum ...... et custodiendum quousque
habilis fuerit ad currendum."   Pleas at Chelmsford, 13 Edw. I, cited in
Morant's *Essex*.

[4] p. 67.   The entry is of the early days of Henry III.

[5] " sit quietus de servicio dicte serjantie " (*Ibid.*, pp. 256, 257).

The Honour of Lancaster presents, in the survey of 1212, two instances of lands held by the service of finding a 'brachet'.   One is that of Peter de Mundeville, who held three bovates at 'Angortby', in Lincolnshire " per servicium unius bracheti *unius coloris:* " [1] the other is that of William Fitz William, who held a carucate and a half in 'Warebere', Notts, " per j brachetum " and sundry incongruous objects in addition.[2]   One may close this section with the tenure of Grafton, Northants, in 1284, by the service of keeping one white hound (*odorinseci*).[3]   There was a similar serjeanty at Waltham, co. Linc., where land was found, 1325, to be held " as parcel of a serjeanty of keeping a white brachet." [4]

It is significant that in all these serjeanties a single hound is mentioned, while in the case of ordinary hounds (*canes de mota*) a pack (*mota*) seems to have been kept.

'HARRIER' AND WOLF-HOUND SERJEANTIES

Of the royal packs of hounds to which we are now coming, the two that can be traced furthest back are those of the wolf-hounds and the 'harriers.' I hope to show that they both existed in the latter days of Henry I.   But, while the latter were of

---

[1] *Testa*, pp. 407, 409 ; *Lib. Rub.*, p. 571.

[2] *Testa*, pp. 17, 409 ; *Lib. Rub.*, p. 571.

[3] *Feudal Aids*, IV, 12.   The *odorinsecus* was a hound that hunted by scent, and the term is found as an equation of a 'brachet' in the 12th century.

[4] *Cal. of Inq.* VI, No. 706.

long continuance, [1] the former must have ended
very early with the rapid hunting down of the
wolves.

Let us now take in conjunction two hunting serjeanties. They are conveniently brought together
in the *Testa de Nevill* under Wiltshire (p. 143):—

Ricardus de Heyraz tenet dimidiam hidam terræ in
Alwarebir' pro heyrez domini Regis custodiendo.
Willelmus de Loverez tenet unam hidam terræ in
Cuvelesfeld pro loveriz domini Regis custodiendo.

In each case the serjeanty is that of keeping certain hounds for the king ; in each the holder of the
serjeanty takes his name from the hounds. [2]

We will first deal with ' Heyraz '. Among the
Wiltshire serjeanties in the ' Red Book ' we duly
find :—

Ricardus de Hairez per serjanteriam custodiendi canes
Regis (p. 461.)

But we do not find the relative entry in the
Wiltshire serjeanties (pp. 485-8), of the great
Inquest in 1212. Why ? Because the entry there
appears as :

Radulfus de *Baire* [3] j virgatam in Aldwardbiriæ hundredo per serjanteriam (p. 486).

Whether the name has been correctly read by
the editor (Mr. Hubert Hall) or not, he has failed
to detect the identity of the holding, and we consequently find ' Baire ' and ' Hairez ' indexed separa-

---

[1] Christopher ' Tanchard ' (one of the Yorkshire Tancreds) figures in
the national accounts, 1688-1691, as ' Master of the Harriers '.
[2] So also Thomas ' Porcherez ' took his name from the boarhounds.
[3] The italics are mine.

tely, with no cross-reference, although, conversely he insists, as we shall see, on combining in his index, to the student's distraction, names which are wholly distinct as 'variants' of one and the same.

Returning to the *Testa*, in which the returns are very full for Wiltshire, we find this serjeanty on p. 149, [1] p. 147, [2] and pp. 146-7, where we have duplicate entries of the 'arrentation' of this serjeanty by Robert Passelewe (in 1250). In the fuller form it there stands :—

> Serjantia Willelmi de Heyrez in Alwardebur' pro qua debuit custodire in Curia domini Regis canes haeriez domini Regis ad custum Regis.

This 'arrentation' brought the serjeanty to an end, the service being commuted, in the usual fashion, for that of the thirtieth of a knight's fee and two shillings a year. [3] In spite of this, however, we find an *Inq. p. m.* of 1257 on *Richard* Heyraz (alias, de Herez, de Heyrez, de Heraz) recording that he held one virgate in ' Alwarburi' " in chief by service of keeping a pack of harriers at the king's cost... and his pack-horse and groom." [4]

Hitherto we have been dealing with the Wilt-

---

[1] " Ricardus de Hanez (*sic*) per serj. custodiendi canes Regis " ('Hairez' in a duplicate entry).

[2] where the entry in preceding note recurs in the first column.

[3] " dictus Willelmus fecit inde finem... per annum ij*s*.... Et insuper ipse Willelmus faciat servicium tricesime partis feodi unius militis et solvet residuum dicti finis ut sit quietus de dicta serjantia " (p. 146).

[4] *Cal. of Inq. Hen. III*, No 374. One cannot go into minute detail, but I suspect, on comparing this inquest with No. 436, on Richard *or* Ralf de Hayres *or* Hayraz, that there is some confusion. If the former is indeed all one, then its earlier portion must relate to a holding in Clarendon forest ; and, indeed, the writ is directed to the bailiff of Clarendon as well as to the sheriff of Wilts.

shire portion of the serjeanty; but, on crossing the Berkshire border, we promptly come to what may have been another portion, at Bockhampton in Lambourne. In the *Red Book* serjeanties for Berkshire we read (p. 451) : " Willelmus Bachamtone tenet per serjanteriam Heiriz, " and " Willelmus de Bokhamtone, xx solidatas terræ per serjanteriam custodiendi haerez " (p. 513). On turning to the *Testa*, we find the entry, in the return which I assign to 1212,—

Willelmus de Bochampton et Hubertus Hoppesort tenuerunt xl solidatas terræ per serjantiam custodiendi Heyret..... sed pars quæ fuit Huberti Hoppesort est in manu domini Regis post mortem Huberti Hoppesort (p. 128)

On the previous page the entry runs,—

Raerus (*sic*) de Bachampton et Radulfus Hoppeshort tenent tres hidas terræ in Bachampton de domino Rege per serjantiam custodiendi canes hayrar' (p. 127).

The ' three hides ' should be noted. This entry is followed by four others referring to alienations by Humfrey " avus ipsius Raeri. " On p. 125 there is another entry, but it is of no consequence.

Now here we can identify the serjeanty without question on the roll of 1130. For, under Berkshire, we there read (p. 126) that Walter de Hairez was excused payment of six shillings Danegeld, and six shillings represent exactly three hides. With this clue we press back to trace the holding in Domesday. In that record we find ' Edward ', holding of the King at ' Bochentone ' land assessed " pro iij hidis, modo pro dimidia hida " (63 b).

Here then we learn something more. The high
Præ-Domesday assessment, which Domesday shows
us as reduced, had been restored to its original
figures when the roll of 1130 was compiled. I
drew attention, long ago, to other evidence that
this was so.[1]   And even this is not all.   It was an
'Edward' also who held of the king at Alderbury
('Alwarberie') that virgate which we have seen,
in later days, held by 'Haeriz' serjeanty, as it was
an 'Edward' who similarly held the land at Bockhampton ('Bockentone') held afterwards by this
'Haeriz' serjeanty.   The whole thing fits together
like a 'jigsaw' puzzle.

But we must not forget our master document,
the *Constitutio domus regis*.   In the midst of its
hunting section we find this passage :—

Venatores del Harrede, unusquisque iij*d*. in die ; et
magni Harrede, iiij debent habere j *d*. et de parvis Harede,
vij (debent habere) j *d*.   Ad magnos Harrede, ij homines,
et unusquisque j*d*. in die.[2]

It is significant that in the *Liber Niger* version
'Harrede' thrice appears as 'Haired', and once
only as 'Hared'.[3]   The reader will doubtless per-
ceive that we are here dealing with 'Hairez' (as
they were styled above), with hounds, of which four
large ones cost a penny a day to keep, and seven
small ones the same.   And this record is all but
contemporary with the tenure by Walter de 'Hairez'
of the Bockhampton serjeanty.

The entry cited by Blount, as from the Oxford-

[1] *Domesday Studies*, pp. 114-5.
[2] *Lib. Rub.*, p. 813.
[3] *Ibid.*

shire plea-rolls of 13 Edw. I, illustrates this serjeanty at a rather later date. John de Baa there holds two hides at 'Bokhampton' " per serjanciam custodiendi unam meutam caniculorum haerettorum ad custum domini regis." That the pack was kept at the king's cost is a statement confirmed by the Hundred Rolls at a slightly earlier date. We there read (I, 11) that the land is held *in capite* of the King " per serjanciam, scilicet, pro custodiendo viginti et quatuor canes haerett' domini regis," for the keep of which the king paid sixteenpence a day.

In the fifteenth century, and even the fourteenth, the mastership of these hounds, as of other royal packs, was no longer a serjeanty, but an office filled by appointment. In 1388, as the keepership of the 'heriers', it was granted for life to the king's esquire, Adam Ramesey, as it had been held by John Tichemessh and his predecessors, Adam, however, releasing to the king $7\frac{1}{2}$ d. a day payable to him when staying in the household. [1] It was again granted for life, 17 July 1461, to John Wroth, esquire, as that of master of the King's hounds called 'hereres', his pay and that of his assistants being charged on the revenues of certain counties. Richard Strickland, esquire, had been his predecessor. It should be observed that the Bockhampton pack had consisted of twelve couples (the old unit), but John Wroth had a mixed pack, his eighteen couples being supplemented by nine greyhounds, and his three berners, accordingly, by two yeomen 'veauterers'. [2]

[1] *Cal. of Pat. Rolls*, 1385-1389, p. 526.
[2] *Cal. of Pat. Rolls*, 1461-7, p. 22.

Although these hounds are always styled ' harriers ', it is by no means etymologically certain that
their name is derived from ' hare '. The preval-
ence, in early sport, of French terms would rather
lead one to doubt it. Mr. W. H. Stevenson is
inclined, he tells me, to derive the word from a
Norman dialectical form for ' hare ' given by Moisy.
In any case it seems improbable to me that the
' Haired ' or ' Harrede ' of the *Constitutio*—the
' Hairez ' of the Pipe Roll of 1130 [1]—can be derived
from an English word. The official editor of the
Red Book renders ' Harrede ' as ' the Hart ' (p.ccxciii),
and must, therefore, believe that, of these ' harts ',
four large ones, or six (or seven) small ones, were
entitled to a penny a day (p. 813).

Let us turn from the ' Hairez ' to the ' Loverez '.
In the preface to ' The Red Book of the Exchequer '
the editor explains his index system, for personal
names, as follows :—

Personal names have been grouped together wherever
there was a reasonable prospect of identification, and the
numerous variants (*sic*) have been indicated by means of
cross references. The result, though far from complete
or satisfactory, is highly instructive, and not a little
diverting. A glance at the twenty variants (*sic*) of such
a name as De Chaorciis will show the outward dissimilar-
ity of even the best marked forms. It is far different in
the case of a confused personality, the name, for instance,
of Lovel, which, with its variants (*sic*) of Le Lutre,
Lutrel, Luterel, Lupellus, Lupullus, Loverez, Luverez,
Veres, Luvel, Luel, suggests a combination of two bran-
ches of venery in one famous serjeantry. [2]

[1] See p. 287.
[2] *Lib. Rub.*, pp. ccclxxvii-viii.

Now 'De Chaorciis', in its various forms, is the
Latinisation of 'De Chaources', a name derived
from Chaources, the present Sourches (Sarthe), not
far from Le Mans. [1] Mr Hall's index gives us no
fewer than twenty-two 'variants' of the name,
among which one is startled to find 'Jorz'. This
is the perfectly distinct name of a family connected
with a Leicestershire serjeanty, holding, as they
did, by usher service, at Wymeswold and Hough-
ton. [2] They probably derived their name from
Jort (Calvados), for Robert 'de Jorz', who appears
in the returns of 1166 [3] as a holder on the Blyth
fief, is entered, as a Tickhill knight, on the Pipe
Roll of 1162 as Robert 'de Jort'. If 'Jorz' is,
as Mr. Hall imagines, a 'variant' of 'Chaorciis,'
the cross-reference under 'Jorz' should be to
'Chaorciis.' To our amazement, however, we
find that it is to 'Guiz'! Here then is another and
a different name of which 'Jorz' is made a variant.
Needless to say, the family of Gouiz or Guiz had
nothing to do with that of Jorz, but had a substantial holding (five fees) of the Honour of Gloucester,
far away in the South-west.

But let us complete the alleged variants of the
name 'De Chaorciis'. We find that nearly half
of them seem to be varying forms of the well-
known name, Cauz, Chauz, Chaus, etc., which is

---

[1] See Cauvin's 'Historical Geography of Maine' and *Le Château de
Sourches et ses seigneurs*, by A. Ledru (1887).

[2] *Testa*, pp. 88, 93. Members of the family also held by knight-
service on the Eincourt fief and of the Honour of Blyth (Tickhill). The
early Winchester surveys show us Anchetil de Jorz holding houses in that
city under Henry I and Stephen.

[3] *Lib. Rub.*, p. 373. He is indexed by Mr. Hall under Guiz!

duly dealt with, under Cauz, in Dugdale's *Baronage*
(I, 679). The family of this name held a considerable barony, [1] the return for which is duly
found, under Nottinghamshire, in this very work.[2]
Dugdale, of course, knew better than to confuse
this house with that which he dealt with under its
Anglicised name, ' Chaworth '. To treat these
two names as identical, and to throw in also that
of ' Jorz ', is a good example of that absolutely
wanton and uncalled-for confusion, the introduction
of which is one of the chief reasons why I call on
the authorities to cancel this misleading work.

As for the great house of Chaworth (*De Chaorciis*),
its wide estates, acquired through heiresses, eventually passed, with its own heiress, to the royal line
of Lancaster. But from cadets, apparently, there
sprang the Viscounts Chaworth and Byron's Mary
Chaworth,—

> The solitary scion left
> Of a time-honour'd race.

But the point that I would here make is that the
lords of Chaources (Sourches) were lords also of
Mondoubleau (' Mundublel ') [3] of which the ruined
donjon, rent asunder as if by some upheaval of the
earth, is passed by the traveller of to-day on his way
from Chartres to Saumur. The names of either
lordship were consequently borne by the house, as
we see in this very work. [4] This, therefore, is

---

[1] It owed the service of fifteen knights.
[2] *Lib. Rub.*, p. 343.
[3] It lies in the Department of Loir et Cher, N. W. of Vendôme and
E. of Le Mans.
[4] " Dedit Paganus de Mundublel Hugoni de Chaurcis fratri suo...
Patricius de Chaurcis avus Pagani de Mundublel " (*Lib. Rub.*, pp. 297-8).

essentially a case in which cross-references should be given under 'Chaorciis' and 'Monte Dublel'. But, as these would be right and helpful, we here look for them in vain. Instead of them, the editor gives us those tissues of wanton confusion which he is pleased to term "laborious attempts at concentration" (p. ccclxxviii).

Their result—though hardly in the sense he meant—is indeed "highly instructive, and not a little diverting."

Let us pass to the second serjeanty of those in the above entries. What has Mr. Hall to tell us about this "famous serjeantry" (p. 290)? What it was, or why it was "famous", he does not inform his readers. But he does combine, we have seen, as "variants" of the name 'Lovel'—'Le Lutre, Lutrel, Luterel, Lupellus, Lupullus, Loverez, Luverez, Veres, Luvel, Luel.' Surely, even Mr. Hall must know that *Loutre* is French for otter, that 'Le Lutre' is the personal nickname 'Otter', and that 'Lutrel' and 'Luterel' are the diminutives thereof.[1] Surely also he must be aware that Lovel (*Lupellus*) is a personal nickname, meaning merely 'the little wolf', and that with serjeanty or with each other neither of these names had anything in the world to do.[2]

If one has to write vigorously of this wanton confusion, it is because of the intolerable trouble

---

[1] Sir John Luttrell of Dunster (d. 1430) bore upon his signet the device of an otter, with 'Trell' above it (*Dunster and its Lords*, 1882, p. 109).

[2] Loup ('lou'), with its diminutives, Louvet and Louvel (or Louveau), all gave rise to personal names (see Godefroi), and the families of Low and Lovet, in mediæval England, bore wolves upon their shields.

caused thereby to the student. When, for instance, the object of our search is the name 'de Loverez', we have to hunt through more than thirty entries grouped under Lovel (p. 1235) to discover that only two of them relate to the name we want. These are :—

(1) Galfridus de Loverez, j hidam, per serjanteriam venariæ (Wilts). [1]

(2) Willelmus de Veres (Wilts). [2]

As the latter held by knight-service, this reduces the serjeanty entries, under Loverez, here to *one* !

We will first dispose of William, the tenant by knight-service. He is found in the above entry holding of Walter Waleram's fief. Now if we search the *Testa* under *Hampshire*, we find this entry :—

Willelmus de Loverays tenet unam hidam in West-uderlig per quartam partem feodi unius militis de veteri feoff' de Aubr' de Boteraus, et ipsa de Domino Rege in Capite (p. 234).

This represents the holding, in 1166, of William de 'Veres', and proves that form to be an error and the 'Luverez' of the Black Book right. Then, turning to Domesday Book, we duly find under 'Tiderlei' (West Tytherley) this same hide held of 'Waleran' the huntsman by Roger. [3]

The ground is thus clear for tracing the 'Loverez' *serjeanty*. But we soon discover that there were two. For, in addition to the above entry as to Geoffrey's tenure, we read also under Wilts,

---

[1] *Lib. Rub.*, p. 485.
[2] *Ibid.*, p. 242. In the Liber Niger the name is 'Luverez'.
[3] Walter de Luveraz was its under-tenant in 56 Hen. III (*Cal. of Inq.*)

Willelmus Michael, terram in Middeltone per serjanteriam de loverez, et recipit per diem iij *d.* ob. [1]

These entries both come from the 1212 returns ;
and we find the correlatives of both in the later
Testa return on p. 143. The entry there relating
to the ' Cuvelesfeld ' serjeanty has been already
cited : that of William Michael is represented in
the *Testa* by this :—

Ricardus Michel tenet unum cotsetil in Midelton pro
duobus canibus loverez custodiend' ad custum Domini
Regis.

Here, at last, we are on sure ground ; the ' loverez '
were hounds.

But what kind of hounds ? In vain we seek
assistance from Godefroi or Ducange ; the word,
apparently, is not known. Again we turn to our
record. In the *Testa* we find the Middleton serjeanty entered further on as that of keeping
" lepores " (p. 148), " duos canes luverettos "
(pp. 147, 149), " canes luporarios " (p. 147b).
It is clear that we must walk warily. The prev-
alence, however, of French origin in early hunting
terms leads one to guess that ' loverez ' or ' luverez '
were wolf-hounds, as ' leverers ' (or ' levrers') were
hare-hounds. And then we find evidence that this
conjecture is correct. For Blount has copied for
us this record of the days of Henry III :—

Willielmus de Limeres (*sic*) tenuit de Rege in com.
Southampton (*sic*) I car. terr. in Comelessend (*sic*) per
servic. fugandi ad lupum cum canibus regis.

Allowing for his usual misreadings, it is clear that

---

[1] *Lib. Rub.*, p. 487.

William de Lu*v*eres[1] held this carucate by the service of acting as master of the wolf-hounds. Finally, we get from another source absolutely definite evidence on William de Loverez and his serjeanty. We learn from ' Bracton's Note-Book ' that in 1225 William de ' Leueriz ' was impleaded for the hide in ' Cuneleffeldia ' [2] and claimed that he held it of the King " by the service of catching (*capiendi*) wolves in the King's forest, of which service the King is in seisin, as is testified by Hugh de Neville, the chief forester." [3] This, it will be seen, is akin to the ' Pytchley and Laxton ' service.

That, as early as the reign of Henry I, the king did possess a special pack of hounds for hunting the wolf is clear from the *Constitutio domus regis* :— [4]

Luparii xx *d*. in die ad equos et ad homines et canes ; et debent habere xxiiij canes currentes et viij leporarios, etc. etc.

But although this implies the existence of a special pack, it does not necessarily involve that of a special *breed*. Indeed the pack, it will be seen, appears to have been one of the normal mixed character. Even in very recent times we find an instance in point, for the late Duke of Beaufort attempted wolf-hunting in Poitou with hounds from the famous Badminton pack.

The other serjeanty, that at Middleton (Wilts), does not call for special investigation. Its chief value consists of the forms it supplies for the names

---

[1] The number of minims is the same.
[2] This is yet another erroneous form.
[3] *Op. cit.*, p. 1670.
[4] *Lib. Rub.*, p. 813.

of these wolf-hounds,[1] and for the proof it affords
that they actually were wolf-hounds[2] (*canes luparii*).

I have kept to the last, because it appears to be
unconnected with either of these two serjeanties, the
evidence which establishes beyond question the fact
that 'luverez' were wolf-hounds.   On the *Rotulus
Misæ* of 11 John we find a payment at Gillingham
(Dorset) "Odoni et Ricardo duobus Luverez ad se
et canes suos" (p. 118), and another at Christmas, at
Odiham, "Ricardo Luverez et Odoni valtrariis[3]
pro duobus lupis captis apud Clarendone" (p. 144).
These wolves were evidently caught as infesting the
king's forests in Dorset and Wilts.

It is clear that Gillingham Forest (see p. 42 above)
was infested with wolves, for the 1212 survey
shows us a small wolf-hound serjeanty as instituted
by Henry I.[4]

In the summer of 1212 Stephen of Guildford
received 5 sh. reward for capturing, with his master's
hound, a wolf at Freemantle, John's hunting seat
in North Hants,[5] and the same roll records the
payment of 10 sh. to Norman *valtrarius* and Wilekin

---

[1] *i.e.* 'loverez', 'luverettos', 'luvericios', etc.   This last form
resembles closely the form 'lutericios' for ottter hounds (from 'lutre').

[2] See the document of 1320 cited by Blount's editors from *Harl. MS.
34*, p. 80, being the relief of William Michell for his holding "in Middleton Lillebon ten't de Regi in capite per serjantiam custodiendi canes
luparios Regis."   But *cf. Cal. of Inq.* VI, No. 212.

[3] I look upon the term 'valtrarii' as implying the use of large hounds
of the greyhound (*leporarius*) kind.

[4] "Willelmus de Hanton tenet dim' virgatam terre de dono Henrici
regis primi per servicium serjantie de Luverez.   Et idem Willelmus tenet
quartem partem unius virg' terre de dono predicti Regis que solebat
reddere manerio de Gillingham ij *s.* per annum per servicium predicte
serjantie de Luverez" (*Testa*, p. 164).

[5] *Rot. Misæ*, 14 John, p. 233.

Doggett for capturing two wolves in the Herefordshire forest of Trivel. [1]

THE 'OTERHUNTE'.

Otter-hunting, I propose to show, is a sport of
great antiquity ; it can even be carried back to the
days of Henry II. As with other packs of hounds,
the master of the king's otter-hounds appears to
have originally held by serjeanty, but eventually
became an appointed officer.

The otter, of course, was the vermin of the
water, the poacher of the streams and ponds. But
for hunting him there was more reason then than
now: it was, in fact, a necessity. The large number of days of abstinence, combined with the impos-
sibility of obtaining sea-water fish inland, involved
a large consumption of freshwater, that is, coarse
fish, which were kept extensively in fishstews constructed for the purpose. [2] Pike were presented to
a man for stocking his ponds, as bucks would be
given him for his park. The coarse fish, however,
on which King John relied would seem to have
been mainly bream. [3] From Marlborough, for

[1] *Ibid.*, p. 246.

[2] This is well seen in an entry of 13 Nov. 1232, on the Patent Rolls,
giving " protection for Simon Lutrarius (*i.e.* the otter-hunter), retained
in the king's service to keep his stews throughout his manors and to take
otters destroying the said stews " (*Cal. of Pat. Rolls*, p. 2).

[3] Pike and bream appear to have been reckoned the pick of the
coarse fish, for the *Inq. p. m.* on Ralph Wymer in 1273 shows that he
was keeper of the king's fishstew outside the east gate of Stafford on the
terms that " when the king shall be pleased to fish there, the king shall
have all the pike and bream (*lupos aquaticos et breymas*), and Ralph all the
other fish, with the eels. This keepership was numbered among the
Staffordshire serjeanties, and was held earlier in the century by Walter
Wymer (*Testa*, pp. 52, 54).

instance, the sheriff of Gloucester was directed to provide two of the king's servants with bream (*breimes*) from Tewkesbury,[1] and £2.. 7.. 5 was allowed to him for the carriage of "our bream" from "our fishstew" at Hanley to Marlborough.[2] But it was not only as a beast of prey that the otter was hunted ; his pelt also had a certain value.[3]

It is not surprising, therefore, to find that at least as early as the year 1179 Henry II had an otter-hunter, Roger Follus, to whom, as "lutrario suo," he granted a messuage and three virgates in Aylesbury—

by the service of finding straw (*literiam*) for the king's bed, and straw (*stramen*) or grass for decking his chamber (*hospicium*)[4] thrice a year, straw if he should come in winter, and grass if in summer, and of rendering two grey geese (*gantas*) in the latter case, and three eels in the former, that is to say, six geese or nine eels a year, if he came thrice a year, by which service the said Roger and his heirs are to hold the land and the office of otter-hunter (*lutracionem*).[5]

I date this charter in 1179 because of the relative entry on the Pipe Roll of 25 Hen. II (p. 73)—

Et Rogero Follo Lutrario xvjs. in Ailisberia in terra que fuit Ernisii prepositi per cartam regis.

The text is preserved in an 'Inspeximus' of 1378,

[1] Writ of 31 March 1204 (*Rot. de Lib.* 5 John).

[2] A writ of 16 March 1204 orders the sheriff to find carriage for 80 bream to Marlborough (*Rot. de Lib.*).

[3] In Ireland the Prior of Kilmainham gave a " pellem lut[i], " to have letters patent, in 1206 (*Rot. de Fin.*). In England Master Michael the Clerk gave in 1204 five marcs and six " pelles de lutre " to obtain the land he was entitled to in the city of London (*Rot. de Obl.* 6 John, p. 198).

[4] I should prefer to render *hospicium* as " house ". *Cf.* pp. 109-110.

[5] *Cal. Pat. Rolls*, 1377-1381, p. 176.

which also confirms letters patent of John "declaring that Ralph and Geoffrey are the king's otterhunters *(lutrarii)*, and are to be permitted to exercise their office where they can and where they will, without let or hindrance in respect either of their nets or lances." [1]   It is interesting to meet with a gift of ten shillings to Ralf " Lutrarius " and his cousin on the *Rotulus Misæ* of 11 John (1209), and to find it repeated on the same roll (pp. 122, 160) at Scarborough the next year, when the otter-hunters were going to the sheriff's at Nottingham.

The same ' Inspeximus ' gives us the royal charter of 12 June 1235 confirming the transfer, by a charter of the same date, from Ralf the otterhunter of Aylesbury to Robert son of David of all this holding, rendering the service prescribed in the charter of Henry II. [2]   Although it is not found among the lists of serjeanties, this holding must be classed among them, for the Bucks plea of 14 Edw. I (1285-6) cited by Blount enters William son of William of Aylesbury as holding it " per serjantiam," the service being precisely that which the charter of Henry II prescribed. [3]   And this is confirmed by an official record among the *Memoranda* of 18 Edward I, cited on the Fine Roll of 7 Henry VII, [4] which shews that William son of William held it as heir of Master Richard of Aylesbury.

---

[1] *Ibid.*
[2] *Cal. of Charter Rolls*, I, 204.
[3] This service is also found in the *Inq. p. m.* (1278) on the elder William, who was son of the Robert of 1235.
[4] Madox, *Baronia Anglica*, p. 247.

So late as the reign of Henry VII this 'manor,' then called 'Otterarsfee', was held by exactly the same service as in the days of Henry II.[1] But long before this the mastership of the king's otter-hounds had become dissociated from it. So early as 1290 we have a payment to John 'le Oterhunte' for the keep *(putura)* of his eight otter-hounds *(canum lutericiorum)*,[2] and further light is thrown on the history of the pack by an interesting paper on "The Milbournes of Essex and the King's otter hounds" (1385-1439).[3] From it we learn that members of this Dorset family kept the pack throughout that period, its expenses being charged on the issues of Essex and Herts, as were those of the buckhounds on the Counties of Sussex and Surrey. The fees of the master and his deputy were merely those of the hunt servants of the buckhounds, two pence and three halfpence a day, so that they probably represent the two *lutrarii* of John's day, their low wages pointing to a time at least as early as that. For the hounds, however, there was allowed three farthings a day each, instead of a halfpenny as for the buckhounds. Of these hounds there were at first eight (as under Edward I), but a ninth was added in 1418. The total cost of the pack varied from £15.. 11.. 0 to £15.. 11.. 11½.

Edward IV granted for life to Thomas Harde-

---

[1] See it set forth in the *Inq. p. m.* on Richard Baldewyn, its holder, in 1 Hen. VII, and in the record of his brother John's fine for his relief as printed by Madox as above.

[2] Wardrobe account cited by Mr. Turner (*Select Pleas of the Forest*, p. 145).

[3] *Essex Arch. Trans.* (N. S.), V, 87-94.

grove 18 July, 1461, the office called ' Oterhunt ',
with all the same allowances, " from the issues of
the counties of Essex and Hertford, as allowed in
the great roll of 48 Edward III," but the pack
was now reckoned as two greyhounds and ten
ordinary hounds (*canes currentes*). [1] Under Elizabeth the whole allowance was £13.. 6.. 8 (*i. e.*
20 marcs) for the master.[2]

To come to much later times, we find " Symon
Smith, otter-hunter "—successor to the " Rogerus
lutrarius " we met with under Henry II—figuring
in the national accounts under William III (1688-
1691) between the Poet Laureate and the Master
of the Harriers.[3] In addition to his proper pay,
£70.. 2.. 11, he secured in addition as Harbinger,
£524.. 9.. 1!

Of a private pack of otter-hounds the earliest
mention I have noted is in 1227, when the king
confirmed a charter of Geoffrey, bishop of Ely,
confirming one of his predecessor John (d. 1225)
granting to John de Awelton that he " may have
his otter hounds (*canes lutrarios*) and other dogs
free, and that they be not expeditated (*espeautez*)." [4]
This was at March in the fen country. But otter-
hunting is included in mixed sport as early as
1200, when William Fitz Walkelin of Stainsby,
Derbyshire, gave the king £40 for permission to
have his hounds for hunting the hare, the fox,
the (wild) cat (*murilegum*) and the otter in Der-

[1] *Cal. of Pat. Rolls*, 1461-1467, p. 127.
[2] *Household Ordinances* (Soc. of Antiquaries).
[3] House of Lords MSS. 1690-1691 (13th Report Hist. MSS., App.
V), pp. 373-4.
[4] *Cal. of Charter Rolls*, I, 55.

byshire and Notts, and for confirmation of Stainsby.[1]

It may seem improbable to us that the same pack of hounds should be used for all these purposes, but in 1315 the king's pack of *haericii* hounds (with their accompanying greyhounds and bercelets, five in number) " were sent to take foxes, cats, and badgers " in Northamptonshire forests, though their normal prey was deer ! Even in the days of Queen Elizabeth, although Turbeville sometimes speaks of otter-hounds as 'bloodhounds', the breeds appear to have been so imperfectly differentiated that we find him writing:—

for if the Houndes be good Otter hounds and perfectly entred, they will come chaunting and trayling alongst by the rivers side, and will beate every tree roote, every holme, every osier bedde, and tufft of bulrushes ; yea sometimes also they will take the ryver and beate it like a water spaniell...... and thus may you have excellente sport and pastime in hunting of the Otter, if the houndes be good, and that the rivers be not over great...... A good Otter hounde may prove an excellent good buck-hound, if he be not too old before he be entred (pp. 202-3).

THE MARSHAL OF THE HAWKS

This was an important serjeanty in more ways than one. Its lands comprised three manors ; its ' service ' was a very real one and placed it in a prominent position ; and it gave rise in later times to a coronation claim.

In the reign of John, Aubrée de Jarpenville is returned as holding lands in Buckinghamshire and

---

[1] *Rot. de obl. et fin.*, p. 57.

in Kent by a service which is variously described.[1]
As yet we only gather that it had to do with
falcons or with goshawks. Shortly before these
returns, that is in 1211, we find her owing to the
king two palfreys that Ralf her grandson (*nepos*)
and John Fitz Bernard may discharge for her the
serjeanty of goshawk service.[2] But we have to
turn to an earlier document for further light on
her identity and on the family relationship. This
is a charter of 18 March 1204 (5 John), printed
in Lipscomb's ' Buckinghamshire' from Cart. Ant.
I, 30. It is a grant of the marshalship of the
hawks (*avium*).

Sciatis quod ad petitionem et assensum Albride de
Rumenel, que fuit uxor Willelmi de Jarpunvill', qui cum
eadem Albrida ejus hereditatem et marescalciam avium
nostrarum, dedimus et concessimus...... Thome filio
Bernardi, qui habet filiam et heredem predicti Willelmi et
predicte Albride in uxorem, marescalciam avium nostrarum, quam predictus Willelmus habuit....... tenendam et
habendam sibi et heredibus suis ex se et filia predictarum
Willelmi et Albride descendentibus imperpetuum.

This is the grant of an office in gross, not of land
to be held by serjeanty, and the strict limitation is

---

[1] In Kent she holds " per servicium quod sit mariscallus de falconibus
domini Regis.... debet servire Regi de ostriceria sua " (*Testa*, pp. 216,
217, 219 ; *Cf. Lib. Rub.*, p. 468). In Bucks she holds " per serjanteriam
marskalsie avium Regis " (*Lib. Rub.*, p. 557).

[2] " Albreda de Jarpunvill debet ij. palefridos ut Radulfus nepos ejus
et Johannes filius Bernardi possint supplere vices ejus hoc anno de serjanteria Austurcariæ quam Regi debet " (*Pipe Roll*, 13 John, Kent). As
a matter of fact, John Fitz Bernard is duly found acting for her on the
Prestita Roll of 12 John and receiving the ' Prestitum factum austur-
cariis ' at Marlborough, York, etc., through the winter (p. 252). And
on the *Misæ* Roll of 14 John we find mention of letters sent to John
Fitz Bernard and little Ralf (*Rauelinum*) Fitz Bernard at Aylesbury
(Cole's *Documents*, p. 245).

a recognition that the right was in the wife's
blood.[1] In spite of this, however, the office is
subsequently entered, as we have seen, in records
as a serjeanty connected with land.

Aubrée, we shall find, was, in John's days, already
an elderly widow, by no means fitted to take charge
of the King's falconers, and still less to cross the
sea for the purpose. The lands she held by this
service were Ilmer and Aston (Mullins) in Bucks
and 'Essetone,'[2] on which I shall have much to
say, in Kent. When they had descended to her
grandson Ralf—that is, Ralf Fitz Bernard—the
service is again recorded.[3] The alienations from
it were 'arrented' in 1250.

The service, however, continued. Ralf Fitz
Bernard had died in 1238, and in 1251 it was
"John Fitz Bernard, king's yeoman, marshal in
fee of the king's goshawks" who was sent "to buy
and take such birds at the king's market throughout England," with special recommendation to the
wardens of the fairs of Boston, King's Lynn, and
Derby, "where goshawks and sparrowhawks are
for sale."[4] He was despatched on similar quests
in 1253, 1256, and 1258.[5] He died in the
following year, and the jurors found that he held
the Buckinghamshire lands by serjeanty.[6]

[1] See p. 42.
[2] The name is thus given in the *Testa* and the *Lib. Rub.*
[3] "pro qua debuit esse marescallus Austurcorum et avium domini
Regis" (*Testa*, pp. 255, 257).
[4] *Cal. of Pat. Rolls*, 1247-1258, p. 86. Here we have again, in the
mention of Boston and Lynn (to which Yarmouth is added in one entry)
a hint of the trade with Norway in these birds.
[5] *Cal. of Pat. Rolls*, pp. 175, 415, 534.
[6] *Cal. of Inq. p. m.* I, No. 468.

Let us see if we can trace the history of this serjeanty, the lands belonging to which are in two such distant counties as Buckinghamshire and Kent. From a lawsuit of 1220 relating to Aston [1] (Mullins), which is somewhat obscurely reported in ' Bracton's Note-Book,' [2] we learn that Aubrée, whom Alice de Jarpenville vouched to warranty, had claimed Aston as her rightful inheritance in the days of Henry II, and, in conjunction with her husband, William de Jarpenville, had impleaded William de Lisurs and his mother, then in possession, for that land, continuing the suit for six years till it was ended by a fine (*cyrographum*) in the King's court, in his 28th year (1181-2). [3]

The Pipe Rolls prove that at that date William de Jarpenville was actively performing the duties of this serjeanty. That of 1180 shows us £6. 15. 3 spent on the passage across from Dover of king's goshawk-men (*austurcarii*) and falconers " per Willelmum de Gerponvilla " (p. 148). That of 1181 records £43. 17. 5 as spent on the goshawk-men and falconers who crossed with William de ' Gerpunville' and 31*sh.* on ' hutches' for their birds (p. 160). On that of 1182 is the payment of £4 to him for the five goshawk-men who crossed (the channel) to the King (p. 115). So also there is a charge on that of 1185 for the passage, at Dover, of William and the King's ' birds' (*aves*). It is evident that he had charge of this department.

---

[1] It is wrongly identified as Easton, Berks, in the Index.
[2] Ed. Maitland, Case 302.
[3] The land was quitclaimed to them, by this fine, for £107 etc.

But we have not yet traced the history further back than 1180. Can we discover a connexion between the Kent and Bucks manors ? The two latter were held of the Bishop of Bayeux, in 1086, by a certain ' Robert '; but no ' Essetone ' is found in Kent. [1] The *Red Book* editor suggests Ashenden, but this, obviously, will not do. We turn, therefore, to *Feudal Aids* and there find (III, 3) not ' Essetone ', but ' Effetone ' in Langport Hundred, [2] which is duly entered as part of this serjeanty. [3]

' Effeton ' could not be identified by the editor, and the form might well be wrong. But when we turn to Domesday all doubt is dispelled, for we there find ' Afettune ' in Langport Hundred (down in Romney Marsh) and held of the bishop of Bayeux by Robert ' of Romney ' (*de Romenèl*). [4] My suggestion is that this was the ' Robert ' who held Ilmer and Aston of the same bishop in Bucks.

Can we span that dark period of no less than ninety years between 1086 and the year in which Aubrée stated, in 1220, that she had begun her suit ? We first discover a statement in the 1220 plea that a certain (*quidam*) ' David Romenel ' had been seized of Aston ' ut de feodo '. Our task is to connect David with the Kentish lands, and so with ' Robert de Romenel '. With ' Effeton ', however, we cannot connect him. But, in addi-

---

[1] See p. 305 note 2 above.

[2] The ' Essetone ' of the *Testa* is in Langport Hundred.

[3] " partem terre de serjantia, que vocatur Effeton, de Radulfo filio Bernardi, et idem Bernardus (*sic*) tenet.... per servicium custodie unius falconis. "

[4] There is a grant in this ' Effeton ' to Robertsbridge Abbey in Campb. Chart. xxvii, 19.

tion to holding ' Afettune ', with its fifty burgesses
in Romney, of the bishop of Bayeux, Robert of
' Romney ' also held ' Lamport ' with twenty-one
burgesses in Romney, of the archbishop of Canterbury, as one of his knights (*milites*). These two
holdings must be kept quite distinct. Let us try
to trace the second. We have, unfortunately, no
returns of the Archbishop of Canterbury's knights
in 1166, but, luckily for us, we have a flood, and
the flood fills the gap. In 1168 we have an entry
of the payments " de militibus Archiepiscopatus," [1]
and among the remissions we find :—

Et in defectu feodorum *David de Rumenel* et Roberti
de Sancto Leodegario quæ perierunt in marisco de
Rumenel xl*s*

Here then is David ' de Rumenel ' holding of
the Archbishop by knight-service, down in Romney marsh, as ' Robert de Romenel ' had held
before him.[2]

Is this doubted? Then I produce the record of
Aubrée de Jarpenville holding a knight's fee and a
half of the Archbishop in ' Langeport ',[3] which is
where Robert of Romney had held of him by
knight-service. Here, therefore, as at Aston,
David ' de Romenel ' must have been her predecessor.

And now we will go further. Between Robert
(1086) and David (1159) ' of Romney ' I find
the missing link in that Lambert ' de Rumenel '

---

[1] *Pipe Roll*, 14 Hen. II, p. 154.

[2] David appears also, under Kent, on the Pipe Rolls of 5 and 11
Hen. II.

[3] *Lib. Rub.*, pp. 470, 725.

whom we meet with on the Pipe Roll of 1130 under Kent. The entire passage is this:—

Hugo de Albertivilla r.c. de £18. 6. 8 pro recto de terra quam clamat de Archiepiscopatu....... Lambert' de Rumenel r.c. de xl marcis argenti et j dextrario ut teneat in pace terram quam Hugo de Albertivilla clamat, etc. etc. (p. 64)

In other words, Lambert 'de Rumenel' was holding land of the Archbishop (of Canterbury) of which Hugh de Auberville (*Albertivilla*) was seeking to dispossess him. Now Robert and David also, we have seen, so held. With this dispute fresh in our minds we turn back to the Aston suit of 1220[1] and are reminded that Aubrée's opponents in 1176-1182 were William de Lisours and his mother Alice. But who was this Alice? She was a sister of William d'Auberville.[2] Here then are the litigants of 1130 represented half a century later by Aubrée and Alice respectively. In 1221 the co-heirs of David 'de Romenel' quitclaimed their shares to Aubrée, which ended the struggle.

The lands remained in the family of Fitz Bernard till 1315. In 1346 they were confirmed to Sir John de Molyns, Ilmer, and Aston Bernard (now Aston Mullins) being recorded as held by the old service. They then descended, in due course, through Hungerford to Hastings, but were alienated, in the 16th century, to the Dormers. For the coronation of James II the earl of Carnarvon, as lord of the manor of Ilmer, claimed to be " Mar-

---

[1] See p. 306 above.
[2] *Rotulus de Dominabus* : Northants.

shal, Surveyor, and Conservator of the King's hawks in England," but the claim was not allowed.

Three years later, the first Duke of St. Albans, who had been granted in his youth the reversion to the sinecure office of hereditary Master Falconer, succeeded to the post.

THE KEEPER OF THE FALCONS

This was an important serjeanty involving active service, and it figures from an early date in our public records. Unfortunately, our chief source of information on serjeanties, the *Testa de Nevill*, affords us, in this instance, little or no help. As to the nature of the service, the only clue it gives us is that it speaks of the Norfolk portion of the serjeanty as held by "falconer service." It does, however, in one entry, taken from the 1212 Inquest, definitely assign to Henry II the creation of this serjeanty and trace its descent. [1] Happily, however, under Henry III there are several 'Inquisitions after death', the returns to which do throw considerable light on the service. In 1253 we find that the lands consisted of Haconby in Lincolnshire and Dunton with Raynham in Norfolk, that Haconby was held " by serjeanty in augmentation of the serjeanty of Dunton of keeping falcons, " that Dunton was held " by serjeanty of keeping the king's falcons " and that the lastage of Boston was held

[1] " Dunton cum pertinentiis fuit eschaeta domini Regis et fuit dat' Radulfo de Hauvill' primo per manus Henrici Regis patris domini Regis, et postea descendit ad Radulfum filium suum, et de Radulfo ad Henricum filium suum, qui eam tenet per falconariam de domino Rege in capite " (*Testa*, p. 293).

" by service of receiving the king's presents as well
of falcons as of other things. " [1]   In a later Inquisition Haconby is returned as held " by serjeanty
of keeping the king's falcons, " [2] and, finally, when
the serjeanty had been re-united,[3] we find Haconby
returned, in 1271, as " held of the king by serjeanty
of receiving at Boston the gerfalcons sent to the
king, " and Dunton as similarly held " by serjeanty
of keeping the king's falcons. " [4]

Another function of this serjeanty is revealed to
us by the Pipe Rolls of Henry II.   From them
we learn that the Hauvilles were the buyers of the
hawks required for the king.   As early as 1164
ten marcs were expended thus by Ralf de Hauville. [5]
In the year of the crowning of the young king
(1170) it was William de Hauville who was charged with buying hawks (*accipitres*) for him and for
the Scottish king, [6] but Ralf, who (with William
of Yarmouth) was paid £26. 10. 0 for " birds "
sent to Normandy for the King's use. [7]   Later
Rolls show that he was paid £20 in 1179, £28.
6. 8. in 1180, and so forth for buying " birds " for
the king's use. Passing to the reign of John we
find the younger Ralf, in 1200, buying from the
king the daughter of Richard " Masculus " with
her inheritance for his nephew Gilbert at the cost

---

[1] *Cal. of Inq.* I, No. 281.
[2] *Ibid.*, No. 685.
[3] See below.
[4] *Ibid.*, No. 756.
[5] " Radulfo de Hauvilla VI li et XIII s et IIII d. ad emend' accip' "
(*Pipe Roll* 10 *Hen. II*, p. 34).
[6] *Ibid.*, 16 Hen. II, p. 15.
[7] *Ibid.*, p. 2.

of " a good gerfalcon for cranes " (*gruarium*).[1] But
Gilbert had to give the king, in 1205, ten marcs
and a falcon for herons [2] (William of Yarmouth
and Hugh de Hauvill being his pledges) to obtain
seisin of her heritage, Southrop, Hants. Blomefield,
in his History of Norfolk, observes that John in
his sixth year (1204-5) " ordered the bailiffs of
several ports to secure all the hawks and gerfalcons
which should be brought beyond sea till the said
Henry and Hugh should choose what they thought
fit for the king's use ; and no one was allowed to
buy any till this was done." The Hauvilles now
developed into a family of falconers. The *Rotulus
Misæ* of the 14th year (1212-3) is crammed with
Hauville entries. For instance, five of the family
are in one place mentioned together

Henrico de Hautvilla ad iiij[or] girfalcones et j gentilem
falconem et ad i poignatorem suum..... Hugoni de Hautvilla (two and one).... Gaufrido de Hautvilla (4 gerfalcons).... Waltero de Hautvilla (4 gerfalcons).... Gilberto
de Hautvilla (3 gerfalcons). [3]

In another place we have a payment to Walter and
Geoffrey de Hautville and Walter de Merc, [4] going
with the King's falcons to teach (*faciend'*) them to
fly, [5] and in yet another one to Hugh de Hauville
and his fellows, " portitoribus girfalconum, " going
to Aylesbury by the King's command with their
gerfalcons. [6] The actual holder of the serjeanty,

[1] *Rot. de Obl.* 2 John, p. 104. John was devoted to hawking for cranes.
[2] " jactum falconem lanerium " (*Rot. de Fin.* 6 John, pp. 264-5).
[3] Cole's *Documents*, p. 251.
[4] who held the " laner " falcon serjeanty at White Roothing.
[5] *Ibid.*, p. 254.
[6] *Ibid.*, p. 245.

Henry de Hauville, is mentioned with Hugh de Hauville and William ("Wilekin") de Merc as going to Dovercourt to receive four gerfalcons and three "falcones gentiles" and then bringing them to Windsor. [1]

Apart from the actual lands appertaining to their serjeanty, the Hauvilles had a very interesting connexion with the "lastage" dues of certain ports. Henry de Hauville, we have seen, was said to have held those of Boston by the service of receiving the king's falcons, and those of King's Lynn were similarly alleged to have been held by him "*per servicium falconer*," [2] those of Yarmouth by a "service unknown," and those of Ipswich "by serjeanty of falconry" (*falconarum*). [3] Now we have seen that "the marshal of the hawks" frequented specially the fairs of Boston, King's Lynn, and Yarmouth, as those where hawks were sold, [4] and this would seem to be the explanation of the Hauvilles' connexion with the ports named. The Wash, leading up to Boston and to Lynn, appears to have been the main channel by which birds from Norway reached England, and the lands of the Hauville Serjeanty were most conveniently situate ; for Dunton in North Norfolk lay to its east, and Haconby in South Lincolnshire to its west.

Indeed, we have actual evidence that the Hauvilles bought birds at Boston, for, as I observed in my introduction to the Pipe Roll of 1176 : [5]—

---

[1] *Ibid.*, p. 263.
[2] *Cal. of Inq.*, I, No. 361.
[3] *Ibid.*
[4] See p. 305 above.
[5] *Rot. Pip.* 22 Hen. II (1904), p. xxv.

It is to Boston fair that the King's falconer goes to buy the birds that come, probably, from Norway or from Iceland.[1] For under Lincolnshire we meet not only with Norway hawks, but with an Iceland gerfalcon, and in that county the birds appear to have been treated almost as currency.

That is to say that hawks and falcons were offered in payment or part payment of amercements or were offered to the king to secure his favour in lieu of actual coin.[2]

The Inquisitions to which reference has been made were due to a disputed succession. Those who desire to localise in Norfolk the scene of "The babes in the Wood" might keep an eye on Thomas de Hauville, who endeavoured, in 1253, to defraud his infant nephew, the sons of his elder brother. The pedigree was this :—

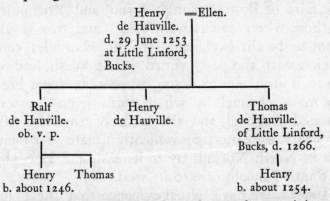

Henry ═ Ellen.
de Hauville.
d. 29 June 1253
at Little Linford,
Bucks.

Ralf
de Hauville.
ob. v. p.

Henry
de Hauville.

Thomas
de Hauville.
of Little Linford,
Bucks, d. 1266.

Henry   Thomas
b. about 1246.

Henry
b. about 1254.

[1] " Radulfo de Hauvill' viij *l.* ad emendas aves ad opus regis in nundinis apud Sanctum Botulfum" (*Ibid.*, p. 77).

[2] A good instance is afforded by the way in which William de "Werbintona" and Enguerrand de "Muntcellis" paid up the large sum of 500 marcs which they had offered for the inheritance of Juliane, wife of William Fitz Audelin whose heirs they claimed to be. See p. 93 above. It is recorded in 1199 that they had then paid in 234½ marcs in cash, a ruby ring, a charger, a palfrey, two goshawks, and two gerfalcons (*Rot. de obl.* 1 John, p. 19).

The Lincoln and the Norfolk juries, though both aware that Ralf the eldest brother had left sons, made return independently that Henry, the father, a week before his death, had enfeoffed Thomas of Haconby and of Dunton and that Thomas was already in full seisin before his father died.[1] But the Lincolnshire jury added that "Henry, son of the said Henry, is believed to be his next heir," that is, to the exclusion of the eldest brother's sons. This statement is of some interest for legal history, as it bears on the *casus regis*, for here, nearly thirty years after the latest case cited by the authors of the *History of English Law*,[2] we find a jury expressing, not a doubt upon the question, but an actual opinion that a surviving son was heir in preference to the sons of his deceased elder brother.[3] But in the case of Thomas, it was not a question of a moot point of law, but of sheer deception and fraud. Early in 1267 a jury returned that "the said Thomas the younger brother, after the death of Henry his father, deceived the King's court so that he recovered seisin of his father's lands."[4] For a time, however, "the wicked uncle" appears to have retained possession. An important entry on the Patent Rolls, 10 June 1256, runs thus :—

Respite from knighthood for Thomas de Hauvyle of Norfolk, who holds of the king by the serjeanty of keeping the king's gerfalcons, and not by knight-service, for

[1] *Cal. of Inq.* I, No. 281.
[2] *Op. cit.* I. 498, from *Bracton's Note Book.*
[3] See my *Peerage and Pedigree,* I, 214.
[4] *Cal. of Inq.* I. No. 657.

a fine of half a mark of gold ; until he will take up the arms of a knight of his own will. [1]

Here we have another distinction between knight-service and serjeanty. Distraint for knighthood was affected by the tenure.

As early as June 1255 it was recognised that the infant son of Ralf was the rightful heir to his grandfather's " lastage " of Boston, and was in the King's wardship. [2] And a similar return followed for the other ports, [3] so that the Lincolnshire jurors' view of heirship [4] was evidently disregarded. Finally the fraud of Thomas was detected and the wardship of his young nephew, with " the lands late of Henry de Hauvyle, " granted by the Crown to William de Renham, " king's yeoman, " 12 March 1257. [5] This suggests the interesting thought that the Crown's right to wardship, oppressive though it has been deemed, may have sometimes caused it, in its own interest, to protect that of the infant heir. The Keepership of the King's falcons continued in the family, and we have an order on the Close Rolls, 3 June 1276, to the Constable of Corfe Castle " to deliver to Thomas de Hauvill, the king's falconer of fee, four laner falcons of the falcons that Elias took in his bailiwick for the King's use, to be kept by Thomas until the king shall cause them to be sent for. " [6]

It is a most interesting fact that the coat blazoned

---

[1] *Cal. of Pat. Rolls*, 1247-1258, p. 479.
[2] *Cal. of Inq.* I, No. 337 ; *Cal. of Pat. Rolls*, 1247-1258, p. 418.
[3] *Ibid.*, I, No. 361.
[4] See p. 315 above.
[5] *Cal. of Pat. Rolls*, 1247-1258, p. 545.
[6] *Cal. of Close Rolls*, 1272-9, p. 293.

for ' Sir Thomas de Hauville ' on the ' Parliamentary Roll ' is " de azure a iij *girfauks* de or e une daunce de or, " [1] that is to say, azure, a dance between three gerfalcons, or. I feel no doubt that this coat was derived from the family's office, as with the covered cups borne by Butlers and the keys in Chamberlain coats.

---

[1] Mr. Oswald Barron, F. S. A., whose knowledge of medieval heraldry is unsurpassed, has kindly given me this blazon and tells me that the word " girfauks " has greatly puzzled the commentators, though it is clear. He considers the arms clearly ' canting, ' *i.e.* haw(k)-vill, in his article on " Heraldry " in the *Enc. Brit.*, but the requisite complete syllable (as in pel-ican for Pel-ham) is wanting.

CHAPTER VI

CORONATION SERVICES

Apart from those serjeanties which were directly associated either with the king's household or with the king's sport, there were many of a miscellaneous character and others of a distinctly military nature, which owed their service, chiefly, in wars against the Welsh. But this chapter deals with services connected only with coronations, services which, with the exception of that of the king's champion and of ' the glove and sceptre, ' cannot be described as serjeanties, but were deemed to be appendant, by prescription, to tenure or to a dignity or to inheritance in blood.

But the word ' coronations ' is here used in a wider sense than that in which it is now employed. There has been frequent mention, in the pages of this work, of the great ' crown-wearing ' days of the Norman kings, to which allusion has been met with in the records of ancient serjeanties. "These were the great annual courts, " as Dr. Stubbs terms them, "held on the great Church festivals, Christmas, Easter, and Whitsuntide ; generally at the great cities of Southern England, London, Winchester, and Gloucester. The king

appeared wearing his crown ; a special peace was
maintained, necessarily, no doubt, in consequence
of the multitude of armed retainers who attended
the barons ; and magnificent hospitality was ac-
corded to all comers. 'Thrice a year,' says the
chronicle, ' King William wore his crown every
year that he was in England ; at Easter he wore
it at Winchester, at Pentecost at Westminster, and
at Christmas at Gloucester. And at these times
all the men of England were with him, archbishops, bishops, and abbots, earls, thegns, and
knights. ' A similar usage was observed by his
sons...... The cessation of the solemn courts under
Stephen was regarded by Henry of Huntingdon as
a fatal mark of national decline. " [1] These ceremonies occupied an intermediate position between
such modern functions as the state opening of
Parliament and the actual coronation at the commencement of a new reign. When William the
Conqueror, in 1070, held his great Easter Court,
in accordance with custom, at Winchester, the
Papal Legates took the opportunity of crowning
him with all solemnity. [2]

It was, normally, on these occasions, the prerogative of the Archbishop of Canterbury to place
the crown upon the King's head. In the year
1109, when the See of Canterbury was vacant, the
Archbishop of York desired, at the great Christmas

---

[1] *Constitutional History* (1874), I. 369 ; so too, I, 268 : " The king
sat crowned three times in the year in the old royal towns of Westminster,
Winchester, and Gloucester. " See also pp. 201-2 above.

[2] " Cardinales Romanæ Ecclesiæ coronam ei sollenniter ei imposue-
runt. " " Eum in paschâ, coronam regni capiti ejus imponentes, in
Regem Anglicum confirmaverunt. "

Court,[1] to exercise this function.   But the Bishop
of London, as Dean of Canterbury, successfully
claimed it for himself, placed the Crown on the
King's head,[2] and sang the solemn mass.[3]

Later in the reign (1121) Archbishop Ralf, who
then held the See, hearing, at the crowning of
Queen ' Adeliza,' the day after her marriage at
Windsor, that the King was seated on his throne,
already wearing the Crown, hastened to him and
angrily enquired who had dared to place it on his
head.   The wretched king, humbly standing, out
of respect for the prelate, feebly murmured, with
downcast looks, that, as he had not taken much
notice, he could not remember.[4]   The primate
refused to proceed with the ceremony until he had
removed with his own hand the crown from the
King's head, the King unfastening the fillet under
his chin, which kept it from wobbling on his head.
The prelate then consented to replace it formally
and proceeded with the mass.

It was observed by Stubbs that, at the three

[1] " Regnum Angliæ ad curiam Regis Lundoniæ pro more convenit et
magna solemnitas habita est atque solemnis " (*Vita Eadmeri*, p. 212).

[2] " Coronam capiti regis imposuit eumque per dextram induxit ecclesiæ " (*Ibid.*).

[3] This also was the Archbishop of Canterbury's prerogative.

[4] " Ad regem accedens, eo sibi suppliciter assurgente, sciscitatus est
quisnam capiti ejus coronam impossuisset.   Ad quod ille, demisso vultu,
se non magnam curam inde accepisse, et iccirco memoriæ id elapsum
modesta voce respondit " (*Ibid.*, p. 292).   So abject was the Sovereign's
position before the church in Præ-Reformation days that the ritual
directed him to lie " grovelling " in the abbey for a part of the Coronation service.

[5] " Pontifex igitur elevatis manibus sustulit coronam de capite regis,
ipso dissolvente ansulam quae sub mente innodata erat ne capite insidens
vacillaret."

[6] *Const. Hist.* (1874) I, 369.

annual courts, "the crown was placed on the King's head, by the archbishop in his own chamber, before he walked in procession." For this he cites Eadmer and the two authorities for Richard's great re-coronation in 1194. But this last event was not an ordinary crown-wearing. At Christmas 1109 [1] the crown, no doubt, was placed on the king's head before he was brought to the church. The record of Queen Eleanor's coronation in 1236 has a curious possible allusion to this practice when describing the 'rayed' cloth over which the King walked in the procession—"incedentis ab aula vel camera [2] sua, *ubi sumit regalia*, usque ad pulpitum in Ecclesia Westmonasterii". As he himself had been crowned before, he here assumes the *regalia* before proceeding to the Abbey. The record goes on to say that the portion of this cloth which lies within the church is its sacrist's fee *in whatever church the king is crowned*. [3] This brings us to the notable document with which we must now deal.

One of the most amazing links between the days of the Conquest and our own has only come to light within the last few months. In his learned monograph on 'Gilbert Crispin, abbot of Westminster', [4] the Dean of Westminster [5] has printed, among his 'selected charters,' one of Henry the First, which he, doubtless rightly, assigns to the year 1100. It is a writ, 'tested' by his chancellor,

---

[1] See p. 320 above.
[2] For the *aula* and *camera*, see p. 66.
[3] " In quacunque fuerit ecclesia coronatus Rex. "
[4] Cambridge University Press.
[5] Now Dean of Wells.

the bishop-elect of Winchester, and addressed to Eudes the steward (*dàpifero*) and Herbert the chamberlain, and it runs thus :—

Precipio quod conventus Westm' et Winton' et Gloecestrie, in omnibus festivitatibus quibus in eisdem ecclesiis coronatus fuero, plenariam de me habeant liberacionem, et earum cantores unciam auri habeant, sicut Mauricius episcopus London' testatus est tempore predecessorum meorum eos habuisse.

The importance of this document is very great. In the first place we have the direct mention of the three annual crown-wearing days of the Norman kings[1] with the strong expression " when I shall be crowned," and the added phrase "in these churches. "[2] Secondly, we have the testimony of Maurice, bishop of London (1085-1107) that, in the Conqueror's days, it was the practice on these occasions for the convent to receive from the king " full livery " with an ounce of gold for the precentor. Here then, clearly, we have the origin of that strange and ancient claim which is made at every coronation by the Dean and Chapter of Westminster, as representing the Abbot and Convent. Its two clauses are:—(1) "The Great Chantor of the Church to have an ounce of gold by the hands of the Treasurer of the King's Chamber " ; (2) " An hundred manchets, the third part of a Tun of Wine, and Fish according to the bounty of his said Royal Majesty for the said Dean and Chapter's Repast on the Coronation Day. " This

[1] See p. 318.

[2] It is of importance to note, in connexion with this document, that Henry I himself was re-crowned (*iterum coronatus*) at Winchester at Easter 1101 (*Annales Monast.*, II, 41).

claim was "referred to the pleasure of his Majesty," King Edward VII. It is a literal translation of the claim in Old French that was made at older coronations. But when we get back to the *Liber Regalis* itself, we have this variant :—

Et providebitur illo die conventui Westmonasterii per regios ministros quod dictus conventus percipiet die eodem de rege centum similas (*sic*) et modium vini ac eciam de piscibus quantum convenit dignacioni regali.

Here we discover that the hundred ' manchets ' represent a hundred of the simnels (*siminella*) that figure so largely in Henry I's ' Establishment of the King's household ' among the ' liberationes ' due to its officers. It seems strange that the *liberacio* to which the convent was entitled on coronation day [1] included only fish, not meat.

There is another charter, which purports to be even earlier, being granted by the Conqueror himself, in which a grant is made to the abbot of Battle and two of his monks of similar ' livery ' at court, on the days of the three crown-wearings, in simnels and wine and messes of food (*fercula*), but these are to be of fish or of something else [2]. Of this charter I made a transcript, many years ago, from a Battle cartulary at Lincoln's Inn, and it has recently been printed in the Calendar of Charter Rolls (III, 196), where it seems to be accepted as genuine. I should, however, reluctantly class it with the other Battle charters there printed as

---

[1] *Cf. Lib. Rub.*, 759, on Queen Eleanor's coronation (1236): " *liberationes* autem assisas predictis a tempore Regis Henrici senioris invenistis alias. "

[2] " Aut de hoc quod erit in curia ".

spurious, if only because it contains the formula " quam fundavi ex voto ob victoriam quam michi Deus ibidem contulit."

The last point of interest in this Westminster document is of more technical character, but of distinct historical importance. This writ is addressed to Eudes the steward (*dapifero*) and Herbert the chamberlain. Why ? Because the former, in virtue of his office, would have charge of the liveries (*liberaciones*), while the chamberlain would be responsible for finding the ounce of gold.[1] The proof of the latter statement is that the claim at the coronation of James I was to receive the ounce of gold " par les mains del Treasurer *du Chambre le Roy.*" This implies that the gold was originally a charge on that *Camera Regis* or *Camera Curie* which figures so prominently on the Pipe Rolls of the 12th century ;[2] and it carries back the system of payment direct into " the Chamber " to the close of the 11th century.

Even when the three Crown-wearing Courts had been finally discontinued, early in the reign of Henry II, the old practice lingered on. John, who had been duly crowned in May 1199, is said to have been crowned again, on his second marriage, late in the year 1200, but the precedent of Henry I's second mariage, in 1121, was evidently followed :

[1] See p. 121 for Herbert the chamberlain ("regis cubicularius *et thesaurarius.* ") The Great Chamberlain formerly carried, as the King's offering in the Abbey, " dix livres sterling d'or et un marque d'or " (p. 120), but now " an Ingot or Wedge of Gold of a pound weight ", which he receives from " the Treasurer of the Household. "

[2] See for instance the Roll of 1165, with its numerous payments to Ralf Fitz Stephen (a chamberlain).

for the king it was a solemn crown-wearing ; for the queen a coronation. [1] The next year, the king and queen kept Easter at Canterbury, and sat crowned in the Cathedral, having received their crowns, as in 1121, from the Archbishop.

Distinct, and intermediate between a coronation and a crown-wearing, were the re-coronations of Stephen and of Richard I, when captivity had dimmed the lustre of their crowns.

Gervase, in whose chronicle alone [2] is recorded the re-coronation of Stephen after his captivity,— an event which I assign to Christmas, 1141, [3]— makes a statement with regard to Richard's re-coronation which, in view of his contemporary authority and of his Canterbury knowledge, has not received, it seems to me, so much attention as it deserves, if, indeed, it has received any. Before describing the actual proceedings, he tells us that, as there had been no precedent for such a re-coronation since that of Stephen [4] (who had been, like Richard, a prisoner), the authorities sent to Canterbury for a record of the ceremonial then employed. He then gives us an abstract of the directions sent in reply, including the headings of the prayers to be used, which appears to have been drawn up like the later *Liber Regalis*. [5] We may say, therefore, with some confidence, that the coronation of

---

[1] " Rex.... coronam gestaturus ;... uxor sua in reginam consecranda." (R. *Coggeshall*, p. 103).

[2] and only in one of its three MSS.

[3] See my *Geoffrey de Mandeville*, pp. 137-9.

[4] More than fifty-two years before.

[5] This is, surely, by far the earliest dated and definite record of the prayers at a coronation service, and it would have added greatly to the interest of Mr. Legg's valuable collection.

Richard I in 1189 is not, as is supposed, the earliest
of which details are known.   The re-coronation of
Stephen may claim that position. Applying this
to one point, difficult and apparently unique, in
the coronation ceremonial of 1189, namely the
mention of four barons carrying four golden can-
dlesticks in the midst of the bishops,[1] we learn from
Gervase that the Canterbury precedent included the
direction " barones cereos ferant, " and that four
barons carried four *lighted* candles before the King,
in the procession, both coming and going.[2] This,
therefore, implies that candles had been so carried
at the re-coronation of Stephen.

In this chapter there is no mention of the
' Hereditary Grand Almoner, ' because his functions, at a coronation, had dwindled down to nothing, even before the abolition of the banquet and
of the procession had put an end to his fees. For
the coronation of Edward VII the Marquess of
Exeter petitioned the Court of Claims for his right
to be ' Almoner ' and

to take from the table of our Lord the King, on the day
of his Coronation, a silver bason to the Almonry accustomed, being before the Lord the King on the day of his
Coronation, and to have the distribution of all the alms
that shall be deposited in the said bason, and one fine
cloth or towel to wrap up the money that shall be given
in alms.... and to have the distribution of all the cloth
that covers the ground,... and likewise to have a tun of
good wine, etc., etc.

---

[1] " in medio illorum ibant quatuor barones portantes quatuor cande-
labra aurea. "   Legg, *op. cit.* pp. xxiv, 48.

[2] " portantibus iiij baronibus iiij cereos accensos ante eum... in eundo
et redeundo portati sunt cerei coram eo. " (I. 526).

But the wine, though always claimed, was never allowed, and the rest of the claim was not argued.

In early days the office was of rather more importance, for in 1236 the almoner had jurisdiction over all quarrels and offences of paupers and lepers, and if one of the latter stabbed another, he ordered the culprit to be *burnt*,—a sound sanitary precaution. Another reason for not discussing this office in detail is that its rightful descent is, historically, very doubtful. It was claimed by Lord Exeter in 1901 as " rightfully possessed of and in the Barony of Bedford in the County of Bedford, and has the present possession of it (which Barony he holds of our said Lord the King in chief to perform and execute the office of Almoner at each Coronation). " But even if the claimant were indeed possessed, as alleged, of that Barony, or even of a portion thereof, it is certain that the said Barony was held of the King ' in chief' *by knight-service*.

Mr. Legg's account, under ' Officers and services', greatly increases the confusion. From him we learn that

The Grand Almoner for the day is the Lord of the Manor (*sic*) of Bedford........ Before Richard II's time the manor (*sic*) of Bedford belonged to the family of Beauchamp. But the manor (*sic*) of Bedford consists of several scattered properties, and consequently since 1377 (*sic*), when this branch of the family of Beauchamp became extinct, there have been several lords of the manor (*sic*) of Bedford. In 1377 it was claimed by John de Latimer and Thomas (*sic*) de Mowbray in virtue of their joint inheritance of the manor (*sic*) of Bedford. It was allowed, but as Thomas (*sic*) de Mowbray was a minor, Sir Thomas Grey was appointed to the office with (*sic*) John (*sic*) de Latimer (p. lxxiv).

Now (1) the office was claimed in respect of the whole *barony* of Bedford, not of the manor; (2) the last Beauchamp of Bedford fell at Evesham, *i.e.* in 1265, *not* 1377; (3) "in 1377" the claimants, as is shown by the record actually printed by Mr. Legg, were *William* 'de Latimer' and *John*, son and heir of John de Mowbray, (pp. 142, 161). As the latter was in the king's wardship, it was found that the king himself would be entitled to perform the service jointly with William! Therefore William de Latimer was admitted to perform it "both for himself and for the aforesaid heir...... and received after dinner the said silver dish for his use and that of the aforesaid heir" (pp. 161-2).

But while, for these reasons, the Almoner's office is omitted, there is, on the other hand, mention of a service which was formally claimed this year, namely, that of carrying "the King's silver harp" at the Coronation. One had not previously associated His Majesty with that instrument.

THE CANOPY BEARERS

The canopy which was borne over the sovereign in the coronation procession is, no doubt, a feature of immemorial antiquity. For the coronation of Edward VII, the barons of the Cinque Ports prayed that, as it had been their privilege to bear this canopy, they might be assigned a place within the Abbey. Their case was ably argued by Mr. Inder-

wick, K.C.;[1] and the Court, of course, admitted
that, if there were a canopy, they were " entitled
to bear it ".   Their counsel went so far as to assert
that " from the Conquest..... every King has used
the Canopy ".   Mr. Legg, however, holds that
the barons of the Cinque Ports are first mentioned
at the coronation of Queen Eleanor (1236), and
that, although the canopy was used at that of
Richard I, it was then " carried by four nobles ".[2]

Undoubtedly, the Cinque Port ' barons ' are not
named by Hoveden in his narrative of Richard's
coronation,[3] but a passage of singular importance
is found in one of the ' Canterbury letters ' of the
time, which throws a flood of light on the subject.[4]
We there read (? 1189) that

pallium etiam quoddam, quod barones Doveriæ et
Quinque Portuum de consuetudine antiqua in coronatione
regis habuerunt, ab ipsis baronibus super altare Christi
oblatum est in memoriam æternam.

That this canopy (*pallium*) should already be described, in 1189, as due " by ancient custom " to
the barons of the Cinque Ports is a very remarkable
fact and carries back, not only their connexion
with the coronation canopy, but also the existence
of their confederation further, perhaps, than any
other real evidence yet discovered.

[1] See Wollaston's *Court of Claims*, pp. 39-46.   See also p. 49 above.
[2] *English Coronation Records*, pp. xxiv, lxxx.
[3] " quatuor barones portaverunt super eos " (the king and two bishops)
" umbraculum sericum super quatuor lanceas proceras. "
[4] *Chronicles and Memorials of the reign of Richard I* (Ed. Stubbs) II, 308:
' Epistolæ Cantuarienses '.   The importance of this passage was duly
mentioned by Mr. Charles Dawson in his paper on the coronation
privilege of the Cinque Ports (*Sussex Arch. Coll.* xliv, 46.)

The fact, however, that a canopy (*pallium*) was carried by 'barons' of some kind at the re-coronation of Stephen in 1141 is proved, in my own opinion, [1] by the fact that it is mentioned in the ceremonial sent as precedent from Canterbury to Winchester in 1194. [2] This was sought for at the re-coronation of Richard I, when, Hoveden tells us, the canopy of silk (*pannus sericus*) was borne by the Earls of Norfolk, Devon ('De Insula Vecta'), Salisbury, and Derby ('de Ferreres'). [3]

At the coronation of Queen Eleanor, in 1236, the Cinque Ports' "claim to this duty was disputed," Mr. Legg tells us, "by the barons of the march of Wales." But careful reading, I think, shows that what the Marchers (*Marchiones*) claimed was, not the right to perform the service, but to carry off the spears on which the canopy was upheld. [4] It is, indeed, with the fees that the record is chiefly concerned. These spears, with the bells at the corners of the canopy, were also persistently claimed

[1] See p. 325.

[2] "portantibus iiij baronibus... pallium in iiijᵒʳ hastis supra caput ejus... In eundo et redeundo portati sunt cerei coram eo et pallium" (*Gervase*, I, 526).

[3] Possibly it was considered that the Cinque Ports privilege did not extend to a *re*-coronation.

[4] The canopies borne by the barons over the king and the queen were of purple silk, "quos quidem *pannos* suos esse de jure vendicant, et illos optinuerunt in Curia, licet Marchiones de Marchis Walliæ.... jus Marchiæ esse dicerent *hastas* inveniendi et *illas* deferendi." Mr. Legg renders this :— "And they claimed the cloths to be theirs by right, and maintained (*sic*) them in the court : *so did the wardens of the march of Wales....* and they said that it was the right of the march to find the lances and carry (*sic*) them " (p. 92). I cannot find the italicised words in his Latin text and the word used by the record for 'carry' is, not *deferre* (which means 'carry *away*'), but *gestare* ("gestabant Barones de v Portibus "). But one must not press this unduly.

by the Dean and Chapter of Westminster,[1] but the Cinque Ports' claim to the *pallium* itself seems to have been undisputed.

The mention of the four (Lord) Marchers is, however, of great interest. They were John FitzAlan, whose Shropshire castles of Clun and Oswestry[2] (' Oswaldestre ') guarded the Shropshire border, and afterwards provided titular baronies for the Earls of Arundel and Dukes of Norfolk ; to the south of him, Ralf de Mortimer, lord of Wigmore, the guardian of north Herefordshire ; in the middle of that county's western border, at its angle salient into Wales, Walter de Clifford of Clifford castle guarding, on its sandstone rock, the pass of the upper Wye ; furthest south, John of Monmouth, whose castle at Monmouth blocked, where three counties meet, the valley of the lower Wye.

Thenceforth, the Lords of the March, as claimants, disappear from view till a real live ' Lord Marcher ' descended from his Welsh fastness on this year's Court of Claims. Sir ' Marteine ' Owen Mowbray Lloyd " is the only Lord Marcher in the kingdom, and still exercises his rights. " [3]

This is a statement of extreme interest : it is, indeed, a revelation. For the authors of the *History of English Law* class " the marcherships on the Welsh border " among " the most splendid instances " of " the lords who had more exalted jurisdic-

---

[1] " les quater hastils ou bastons que supportont le Canope et quater Campanells qui pend al chacun corner du Canope. "

[2] ' Album Monasterium ' in Latin. One would have supposed that it was needless to identify this FitzAlan castle under that name, but the official *Feudal Aids* (1906), IV, 602, 604, renders the name 'Whitchurch'.

[3] *Who's Who.* See also *Burke's Peerage,* etc.

tional powers" (I, 570). Of their powers and their position Dr. Owen writes,—in a valuable paper on *English Law in Wales and the Marches,*—

The powers of the Earls Palatine were so great that the Crown, when it was sufficiently strong, annexed their earldoms, but the powers of the Lords Marcher were greater..... The Lord of Kemes tells us that the Lords Marcher were sworn to perform covenants as full and absolute princes are, whereas Earls Palatine tied themselves by covenants and bonds as subjects do.

... the lords appointed sheriffs, coroners, constables of the castle, chamberlains, chancellors, escheators, and other officers. The writs ran in the name of the Lord, and not of the King ;..... the Lords had the rights of wardship and marriage in respect of their tenants-in-chief, levied scutages..... they had judgment of life and limb, pardoned felons and murderers, " set them to fine or hanged them at their pleasure, "..... They made war and peace with their neighbours at their pleasure..... It will be seen that the Lords Marcher were in theory and in practice sovereign princes. [1]

That of these potentates a solitary survivor " still exercises his rights" in the far west of our island is a strange and thrilling thought. One wonders what would be the fate of Mr. Lloyd George's myrmidons if they tried to penetrate with Form IV to the shores even of that Irish Sea which barred its further progress. Would they be compelled to swallow it, in mediæval fashion, by the vassals of the Lord Marcher ?

The existence of such a phenomenon cannot be too widely known ; it should draw shoals of tourists to this oasis of feudalism in a land which the

[1] *Y Cymmrodor*, Vol. XIV., pp. 17-8, 22.

historian associates with piety, perjury and plunder.[1]

Seriously speaking, however, the reader must turn for information, on this alleged Lord Marchership, to the works of Dr. Henry Owen, who has laboured with such patient industry on the history of Pembrokeshire. He has edited with sympathy and learning the writings of that George Owen whose father had " purchased " the Kemes barony and who seems to have originated this claim in the reign, as Dr. Owen puts it, of " that stout old Welshwoman, Elizabeth Owen—wrongly called Tudor. " But he has to admit that " the Kemes lords were unable to maintain their independence,"[2] and when George Owen tried to revive it, Elizabeth Owen's Privy Council made short work of the would-be Lord Marcher. Our island could not hold two 'sovereign princes'. The sheriff was ordered " to repeire unto the howse of the said

[1] See the instructions of ' Gerald the Welshman ' (*Giraldus Cambrensis*) to the clergy of his archdeaconry :— " *parochianos vestros, qui nimis proni sunt ad pejerandum*, consilium est diebus Dominicis... super his corripiatis ...Dicatis etiam, et cum assertione proponatis, quia qui super evangelia frequenter aut irreventer ex consuetudine, *sicut in partibus illis plus quam alibi faciunt* pejerare præsumunt, divinam ultionem gravissimam, " etc. (II. 157-8). Also his character of the Welsh :—" quicquid commodi, quicquid temporalis emolumenti, sacramenti transgressione provenire potest, passim perjurio parant" (VI. 206). As to plunder, " rapinis insistere, raptoque vivere, furto et latrocinio..... etiam inter se proprium habent "...... " *terrasque* modis omnibus vel occupare vel dilatare, gens præ gentibus aliis ambitiosa ". After explaining that they seek to grab for themselves the lands they rent, he sums them up as " tot peccatis vitiorumque voragini datos, perjuriis, puta furtis, latrociniis, rapinis " (VI. 216). *Cf.* his statement that " populi Walliæ fures et raptores erant rerum aliarum " (I. 39). *Cf.* Domesday, I. 179 :— " Si quis Walensium furat' hominem aut feminam, equum, bovem, vaccam,... De ove vero furata vel fasciculo manipulorum " etc. etc. It is interesting to trace these peculiarities in later times.

[2] Owen's *Pembrokeshire* (Ed. H. Owen), 1892-7, p. x.

Owens " (*sic*) and to arrest him and send him up to London, as accused of " forging of certen charter deedes etc. to the greate prejudice of the freeholders of the lordship of Kaymise. " [1]

I am not, of course, expressing an opinion on any legal matter, but I can at least affirm, on a matter of genealogy, that the barony of Kemes cannot, as alleged, have " passed by right of inheritance to the Owens of Henllys " [2] in the 16th century, for the reason that they were not the heirs of its lords, the Martins, whose true heirs are, at this moment, claiming their peerage barony. Dr. Owen, indeed, puts forward a pedigree which would make them such heirs, [3] but it is at direct variance with the statement of his author, George Owen, himself ; [4] it is directly opposed to record evidence ; and it is even opposed to the family pedigree as now given in *Burke's Peerage* ! It is the way of Welsh genealogists to be somewhat primitive in their methods, [5] but Dr. Owen's version involves such impossible chronology that I cannot accept as proved even a descent in blood of the Owens of Henllys from the Martins.

Nevertheless, Sir ' Marteine ' Lloyd, in his petition to the Court of Claims (1911), asserted his descent from Sir Martin ' de Turribus ', the Norman conqueror of Kemes, and claimed as ' Lord Marcher ' thereof " to carry the King's Silver

---

[1] *Acts of the Privy Council,* 1578-1580, p. 303; Owen's *Pembrokeshire,* pp. 510-512.
[2] " *Burke's Peerage,*" 1911.
[3] *Op. cit.,* p. 491.
[4] *Ibid.,* p. 454.
[5] See my remarks on Welsh pedigrees in *Ancestor,* V, 47-51.

Harp at the Coronation. " [1] His counsel is reported as stating that " the ancestors of the
petitioner on divers occasions attended at Coronations as bearers of the King's Silver Harp, " but
as admitting, in reply to the Lord Chancellor, that
" he had no documentary evidence in proof of the
claim, which rested on tradition " ! The Court,
therefore, naturally, " disallowed the claim as not
being supported by evidence. " [2] As I ventured
to observe of Welsh pedigrees some years ago,
" the miserable evidence of records on which we
English rely is swept aside by the champion of the
Welsh in favour of that of tradition. " [3]

Within a few weeks of the failure of this claim
' the only Lord Marcher in the kingdom ' again
figured in the public press. " A descendant of
kings " was the heading of some paragraphs in the
Daily Mail (22 Feb. 1911), [4] from which I cull
these statements :

In Mr. Lloyd's family are vested several curious
ancient privileges. He traces his descent from Martin
de Tours, who accompanied William the Conqueror to
England. His father claims to be directly descended
from Edward I, and his mother from Robert II of
Scotland.

The guarded word ' claims' is here quite unne-
cessary : it is needless to question a descent shared,
so far as the first Edward is concerned, with
thousands of others at the present day, while, as for

---

[1] I take all this from the careful report of the hearing in the *Morning Post* of 28 Jan. 1911.

[2] *Morning Post*, 28 Jan. 1911.

[3] *Ancestor*, V, 47.

[4] Repeated in the *Evening Standard* of that date.

Robert II, the father of a huge family,[1] his descendants are to-day a multitude beyond the power of computation.   In view, however, of this publicity one may respectfully suggest that 'tradition' is perhaps mistaken as to the silver harp, and that what the family was privileged to carry was, originally, a trumpet.

To return to the 'Barons' of the Cinque Ports. Mr. Charles Dawson's valuable paper on their coronation services,[2] which came to be known as their 'honours at court,' supplemented by Mr. T. Ross' paper, with its extracts from local records,[3] will be found to supply full details.   The 'Barons' were thirty-two in number, sixteen for the king's canopy and the same number for the Queen's. One canopy, in early days, was carried off by the Eastern ports, and presented by them to Canterbury cathedral ; the other by the Western ports, and presented to Chichester cathedral.   The service of the ports was regularly performed down to and at the last unabridged coronation, that of George IV, and the 'Barons' enjoyed the further privilege of sharing in the coronation banquet, which was recognised in 1236 as that of sitting at table on the king's right (*sedendi in mensis regiis eadem die a dextris Regis*).   Banquet and procession have passed away, but the loss of the latter has been regretted.[4]

[1] See the great Stewart pedigree, compiled for the Stewart Exhibition by Mr. W. A. Lindsay, K.C., Windsor Herald.

[2] *Sussex Arch. Coll.* XLIV, 45-54.

[3] *Ibid.*, vol. XV.

[4] " Greatest of these losses has been the solemn Liturgical Procession on a raised staging, from Westminster Hall to the Abbey... It would have been much to have that great ceremonial and constitutional ' Proceeding' given back to England and the Church." *Church Times*, 7 April 1911.

One may perhaps venture to express the wish that canopies could still be borne, in accordance with the ancient custom, over the King and Queen up the nave, at least, of the Abbey Church as of old.[1]

THE CORONATION SWORDS

Of the royal emblems by which an English king was surrounded on his Coronation day the swords, perhaps, can claim the greatest proved antiquity. In the Bayeux Tapestry a bared sword is held, the point upwards, before Harold at his crowning, and in the so-called " coronation of St. Edmund " in Captain Holford's MS. of the 11th Century [2] we are distinctly shown a bared sword on each side of the King, resting on the shoulder of its bearer.

As the right to bear these swords was somewhat keenly contested, and was at times alleged to be hereditary and at others claimed by tenure, they are entitled to a place in these pages.

It is shown by an entry on the Pipe Rolls that the swords were used in 1170 at the coronation of

---

[1] There is, in Waurin's Chronicle, a very curious statement that over the corpse of Henry V, when brought home in state to England, " in passing through the large towns, there was carried aloft over the chariot a rich canopy of silk, like that which is usually borne above the holy Sacrament. " This may point to the use of a canopy as marking the sacrosanct status of the Sovereign.

[2] It is styled " an eleventh century MS. " on the illustration of this scene in Mr. Legg's English Coronation Records, but in the " Notes on the Illustrations" (p. 385) it is spoken of as " this twelfth century Manuscript." Mr. St. John Hope, however, in his paper on " The King's Coronation ornaments " (Ancestor, No. 1.), gives it as illustrating a coronation temp. William the Conqueror " and speaks of it in his text (p. 130) as " nearly contemporary with the Bayeux Tapestry. "

Henry's son, Henry the young king.[1] In 1172 the Pipe Roll contains a charge for cleaning and adorning " the king's swords, " which are possibly the same,[2] and in 1188 the sheriff of Hampshire charges three shillings " pro gladiis thesauri fur-biandis. "[3] These treasury swords were clearly those we are dealing with, still preserved in the old treasury at Winchester. For, a year later, at the coronation of Richard I, Hoveden styles them " tres gladios regios sumptos de thesauro regis ". They were clearly among the *regalia*, and had scabbards covered with gold.[4]

He tells us that the middle sword was carried by John, Count of Mortain (the King's brother), and those on each side of it by David, earl of Huntingdon, brother to the Scottish King, and Robert, Earl of Leicester.[5] These are great names and imply the honour of the post.

It is usual, in tracing coronation practice, to pass from the first great precedent, that of Richard I (1189), to the second, that of Queen Eleanor in 1236.[6] But, in this one matter of the swords, the second crowning, or quasi-crowning, of Richard (1194) is, it appears to me, of very great im-

---

[1] " Et pro auro.... ad reparandos enses ad Coronamentum Regis" (filii Regis). Pipe Roll, 16 Hen. II, p. 16.

[2] " pro gladiis Regis furbandis (*sic*) et pro auro ad eosdem adornandos ; et ad puntos et heltos eorundem gladiorum " (p. 114). This may have been for the young king's re-coronation at Winchester (27 August, 1172), which is mentioned on the same page.

[3] Eyton, p. 291.

[4] " quorum vagine desuper per totum auro contexte erant. "

[5] It has been suggested that Earl Robert may have borne a sword as steward (see p. 71 above).

[6] Mr. Legg does so in the case of the swords (*Op. cit.* p. lxxiii). Mr. Wollaston begins his precedents throughout in 1377.

portance.   Indeed, without it we cannot understand the keen dispute on the subject in 1236.
Hoveden tells us that the three swords were borne
on that occasion by the King of Scots, with the
chief sword, Hamelin, Earl Warenne (*i. e.* of
Surrey), and Ranulf, earl of Chester.[1]   The King
of Scots thus replaced his younger brother David
(to whom he is said to have handed over the
earldom of Huntingdon), and probably bore the
chief sword as being himself a king.   Earl Hamelin
was the King's uncle[2] and had been loyal to his
cause.   The mention of the Earl of Chester is of
special importance, because it gives us, in my opinion, the origin of the later Lancaster claim to bear
" Curtana. "   There is no contemporary authority
for the earl taking part in the first coronation
(1189).[3]   Perhaps he was a minor or passed over
in favour of the Count of Mortain, who was now
(1194) in disgrace.   We cannot tell if he owed
the honour in 1194 to his recent exploits on behalf
of Richard against that rebel Count or—which is
a tempting view—to his tenure of the greatest of
English palatinates.[4]

At the Coronation of Queen Eleanor in 1236

[1] " Et tres gladio de thesauro regis sumpti gestabantur ante regem,
quorum unum gestabat Willelmus rex Scottorum, et alterum portabat
Hamelinus comes de Warenna, et tertium gestabat Ranulfus comes
Cestriæ ; medius autem illorum ibat rex Scottorum, et comes Warennæ a
dextris ejus, et comes Cestriæ a sinistris ejus " (III, 247).   The repeated
phrase " gladii dethesauro " should be obs erved.

[2] As a natural son of Geoffrey of Anjou.

[3] See my life of him in the *Dict. Nat. Biogr.* (under Blundeville).

[4] It is worth noting that Gervase of Canterbury writes as if the
nobler and greater English earls were the bearers :— " Tres vero
comites nobiliores Angliæ portaverunt tres gladios in vaginis aureis "
(I, 526).

we again read of the three swords ; but the right
to bear them was in dispute. John, son of earl
David (mentioned above), claimed to carry one of
them as earl of Huntingdon and also the one called
' Curtana ' [1] as, in right of his mother, earl of
Chester, and the latter claim was allowed. [2] We
have now seen that his uncle, earl Ranulf, had
actually borne the sword in 1194. But earl Warenne
we learn, claimed one of the swords. This also can
now be accounted for by the fact that his father
had borne one in 1194. The King, it is added,
to avoid a tumult, postponed the settlement [3] of
the dispute and decided that, without prejudice to
either, the Earl of Lincoln (John de Laci) should
carry one of the swords on that occasion (*ea die*). [4]
The third sword was then allotted to Thomas (de
Newburgh), earl of Warwick, who claimed it as
his right. [5]

As I understand this arrangement, the earl of
Lincoln merely officiated as appointed for that
occasion by the King. The hereditary claims were
four : *viz.* the earl of (1) Chester and (2) Hunting-

[1] This appears to be the first mention of the name.

[2] " Comite Cestriæ gladium S. Edwardi qui ' Curtein ' dicitur ante
regem bajulante, in signum quod comes est palatii, et regem, si oberret,
habeat de jure postestatem cohibendi " (M. Paris). The mention of
the sword as ' St. Edward's ' and the statement of the earl's right (as
Palatine) and powers are very noteworthy.

[3] " Rege instante, quievit contentio usque ad prædictum terminum
(Quindenam Paschæ sequentem), ne oriretur tumultus " (*Lib. Rub.*,
p. 756.)

[4] I do not gather that the earl claimed this as a right, but his wife
was a niece and junior coheir of the earl of Chester who had borne a
sword in 1194.

[5] "Tertium vero gladium gestavit Thomas, Comes de Warewic, suo, ut
dicebatur, jure " (*Lib. Rub.* p. 756.)

don to two swords ; the earl (3) Warenne (of Surrey) to one ; and the earl of (4) Warwick, to the third sword. This seems to be the origin of the statement in the *Liber Regalis* that the three earls who should bear the swords are :—

Comes quidem Cestrie qui primatum vendicat deferendi portabit gladium qui vocatur curtana.[1] Et alium portabit comes Huntyngdoun. Tercium vero portabit Comes Warewyk.[2]

Now the interest of this statement is that it does not correspond with the facts at any known coronation. It appears to recognise the claim of the earl of Chester and Huntingdon (in 1236) to two of the swords, as if that of the Earl 'of Warenne' had been subsequently disallowed, and it ignores the earl of Lincoln, who officiated in 1236, and whose successor officiated in 1308 (see below). It cannot represent the intervening coronation of Edward I (1274), for the earldoms of Chester and Huntingdon were then, if anywhere, in the Crown. On the whole, it appears to me to be based, as I suggested, on Queen Eleanor's Coronation (1236).

For the coronation of Edward II (1308) we have record evidence that the three bearers were " the earls of Lancastre, Lincoln, and Warwyk, carrying three swords, and the sword called Curtana was carried by the earl of Lancastre. "[3] The earl of Warwick,[4] it will be seen, again carried the

[1] This is actually the same phrase as that in the record of Queen Eleanor's coronation :— " vendicavit primatum deferendi gladium qui appellatur Curtana. "

[2] Legg, *op. cit.* p. 85. The Earl of Warwick's claim is practically the same as in 1236 (see note above).

[3] *Cal. of Close Rolls*, 1307-1313, p. 53.

[4] Now a Beauchamp, inheriting from Newburgh through Mauduit.

third sword ; there was no earl of Huntingdon to claim the second, which was obtained by the grandson of that earl who had borne it in 1236,[1] and the principal sword is now carried by the King's cousin, the earl of Lancaster. Why ? the explanation, I think, is that, the earldom of Chester having been annexed to the Crown in 1246 and granted to the future Edward I in 1254, the right to bear "Curtana" was held to have passed with it, and was made over to Edward's younger brother, Edmund, earl of Lancaster,[2] I have been thus particular in setting forth the facts because they are somewhat inaccurately stated in Mr. Legg's "Introduction." We there (p. lxxiii) read, of the sword *Curtana*, that at Edward II's coronation it was given to the Duke (*sic*) of Lancaster, although there were then no dukes, while his own foot-note has "*portabat Comes Lancastriæ*". We further read, of the second sword, that it was carried "at the coronation of Queen Eleanor in 1236 by the King of Scots as Earl of Huntingdon," although the King was neither present nor earl of Huntingdon, while the actual bearer was the earl of Lincoln !

For the coronation of Richard II we have the record of the Court of Claims, so that our information is exceptionally complete. John of Gaunt, who, as High Steward, presided over the Court, claimed for himself, as Duke of Lancaster, the right to carry "Curtana." His claim was allowed

[1] The earl Warenne is ignored.

[2] He may well have borne the sword at his brother's coronation (1274).

as tenant by the curtesy of England,[1] and he bore
the sword till other duties made him hand it over
to his son (afterwards Henry IV) as his deputy.
The earl of Warwick claimed and obtained the
third sword " come ses Auncestres as coronementz
des Rois Dengleterre ont porte la tierce espie."
There remained the second of the swords.   Had
there been an earl of Lincoln, he would doubtless
have claimed it ; but if that earldom then existed,
it was in John of Gaunt, who had already more to
do than he could manage.[2] Of the two com-
petitors for this sword the claims, at first sight,
puzzle us.   John, the infant son and heir of John
(Hastings), earl of Pembroke, claimed the right,
in virtue of his tenure [3] of Pembroke castle and
other lands.   And Richard, earl of Arundel and
Surrey claimed it as that " que lui appartient de
droit pur le Counte de Surrey.[4]   From what we
have seen above it is clear that this claim was a
revival of that by earl Warenne (of Surrey) in
1236.[5]   The earl's claim was disallowed, but we
meet with it again, in later days, at the coronation
of Charles II.   As for the Hastings claim, I find
its explanation in the extraordinary return made in
1325 on the death of his predecessor Aymer (de

---

[1] He seems to have deemed the earldom of Lancaster as represented
for this purpose by the Dukedom.

[2] He had successfully claimed, as Earl of Lincoln, to be carver.

[3] " Come il tient. "   He was not technically their holder, not having
had seisin.

[4] It should be observed that this claim is precisely parallel to the earl's
claim on the same occasion to the office of Chief Butler " pur le Counte
Darundell."

[5] See p. 340.

Valence), earl of Pembroke,[1] that "the county" (? *comitatus*) of Pembroke was held of the King by service of carrying the (*sic*) king's sword before the King on the day of his coronation," which county included the town, castle and Hundred of Pembroke, the town and castle of Tenby, etc. etc.[2] Here we have the same allegation as that made before the Court of Claims 1377. Its origin I will not guess.

The next coronation was that of Henry IV. in 1399. Henry, we have seen, had borne "Curtana," part of the time, as his father's deputy in 1377. He now made his own son, Henry, Duke of Lancaster, his deputy for the purpose. The third sword was again allowed to the earl of Warwick. For the second there was a fresh dispute. It was claimed by Lord Grey de Ruthyn, who was heir of the whole blood to John Hastings, but who did not inherit Pembroke castle [3] etc. in virtue of the tenure of which the claim had alone been made. His claim, therefore, was disallowed. The successful claimant was a mighty man, Henry, Earl of Northumberland, to whom the new King had largely owed his crown, and who, with other rewards, received the Isle of Man—

by the service of carrying at the left shoulder of the king or his heirs on the day of coronation the sword called "Lancastre sword," with which the King was girt when he put into the parts of Holdernesse. [4]

---

[1] John Hastings was his youngest coheir.
[2] *Cal. of Inq.* VI. p. 323.
[3] This had passed to the Crown at John's death.
[4] *Cal. of Pat. Rolls.* 1399-1401. p. 27. The actual patent is dated six days *after* the Coronation, though the claim was made before it.

It might be supposed that this sword would be borne in addition to the three which had been borne till then ; but the record of the Court of Claims shows that it was one of the three which were allowed. Moreover, Waurin tells us that Henry at his Coronation " had on either side the sword of the church, and the sword of justice.... and the sword of the church was borne by Sir Henry de Percy, Earl of Northumberland."   Now we know that at the Coronation of Richard III (1485) the sword borne on the left of the King was that of " Justice to the *Clergy* " and we may, therefore, infer that the " Sword of the Church " borne by the earl in 1399 was borne " at the left shoulder of the King " as required by the grant, in the old position of one of the three swords.

The contest on that occasion appears to have been the last, save for one or two stray claims ; but one notes that in 1485 " the second sword " was borne by the Earl of Kent, who was Lord Grey de Ruthyn.

The claim of Lord Hastings to carry " the second sword " at the coronations of Edward VII and George V, it is now decided by the Court, " has not been established. "[1]   This, it will have been seen, was clearly right.   For the successful claim in 1377, on which reliance was placed, was made solely in respect of tenure of Pembroke Castle etc. and was derived, I have shown, not from the Hastings family, but from the Earls of Pembroke.   Indeed one does not see why this claim should have been mixed up with that to carry

---

[1] *Morning Post* report, 28 Jan. 1911.

the spurs, for the two petitions were entirely
distinct in 1377.

With regard to Lord Huntingdon's petition and
claim to carry the Sword of State at the Coronation
of the late King, this Sword had been always
separate from the three coronation swords. It
appears to have been based upon the fact that earls
of Huntingdon, his predecessors, but not his ancestors, [1] had been selected for that honour at the
coronations of George II and George III. These,
at least, are the only actual precedents vouched in
the petition. It is extremely difficult, in this case,
to ascertain the facts. According to Bell's *Huntingdon Peerage* (1821), the seventh earl, " as lineal
descendant (*sic*) of the Beauchamps, Earls of Warwick, preferred his claim to the honour of carrying
the third sword, and of being Pantler, [2] at the
Coronation " of James II (p. 139), and his son,
the 9th earl, " carried the sword of state, an
honour now considered established as a prescriptive
and hereditary right, " at that of George II (p. 145).
According, however, to Doyle's *Official Baronage*
it was at the coronations of George I and George III
that the earls bore " the sword of state. " Lastly,
the *Complete Peerage* asserts that the earls bore
" the third (*sic*) sword of state " at the coronations
of George I, George II, and George III.

It was formerly with ' the Sword of State ' that
the King was solemnly girt ; but now " the Lord
who carries the Sword of State, delivering to the

[1] The earl of 1727 was erroneously styled in the petition " your
petitioner's ancestor. "
[2] See p. 341 above, and the section on ' The King's Pantler.'

Lord Chamberlain the said Sword... shall receive
from the Lord Chamberlain, in lieu thereof, another sword in a scabbard of purple velvet, provided
for the King to be girt withal ". [1]

THE GREAT SPURS

Although the office (or alleged office) of carrying the great (or gilt) spurs in the coronation
procession is neither held by serjeanty, nor is among
the offices of state, it is sufficiently akin thereto to
deserve inclusion here.

It is, of course, a well-known fact that the
coronation ceremony and the coronation ornaments
are survivals from a very distant past, and are rich
in symbolical meaning.   But, although so much
has been written on the subject, the point usually
emphasised is the consecration of the King in his
ecclesiastical capacity. [2]   Mr. St. John Hope, for
instance, in his most valuable papers on " the king's
coronation ornaments, " [3] observes at the outset
that

The ornaments which are put upon the king at his
coronation have likewise from a very early date been of a
peculiar character, closely resembling those anciently put
upon a bishop at the time of his consecration..... The
coronation order has also a striking resemblance to the
order for the consecration of a bishop. [4]

But he makes no mention of another striking
parallel, which seems, although of no less interest,

[1] 'Form and Order' (1911).
[2] See Legg's *English Coronation Records*, pp. xvi-xviii.
[3] *The Ancestor* (1902), Nos. 1 and 2.
[4] *Ibid*. No. 1, p. 127.

to have been generally overlooked. I refer to that portion of the ceremony which corresponds with the creation of a mediæval knight.

This portion is numbered IX in the official ' Form and Order ' of the coronation service (1911) and is headed " The Presenting of the Spurs and Sword, and the Girding and Oblation of the said Sword. "

It has, indeed, been vaguely recognised that the spurs are the emblems of knighthood, [1] but they only are so, it must be remembered, because they are *gilt* spurs. To cite Ducange :—

> Calcarea aurea militum propria erant, cum enim armis accingebantur, ipsorum pedibus aptabantur..... Calcarea argentea scutifcrorum erant.

Of such antiquity is this distinction that he quotes the case of Bernard, King of Italy, son of Pepin, who was formally given the gilt spurs, [2] while Geoffrey ' Plantagenet ' of Anjou, when knighted by our own King Henry I in 1127, had gold spurs bound upon his feet. [3] It was from this distinction that the knight in later times was styled *eques auratus*. It may be that the presence of the spurs among the English *regalia* was an imitation of the practice in France, where the spurs similarly figured in the coronation procession and were known as " the spurs of Charlemagne. " [4] They are, it seems, first heard of at the coronation of Richard I, that knight-errant of chivalry, when

---

[1] The idea survives in the phrase that a man has ' won his spurs.'
[2] " Bernardi pedibus ita calceatis aurata induerunt calcaria."
[3] "Calcaribus aureis pedes ejus astricti sunt." (John of Marmoutier).
[4] In England they were styled at one time " the spurs of St. Edward."

they were borne in the procession by John the
'master' Marshal.[1] Under his successor, Mr. Hope
has shown, they are named among the *regalia* in
1203 and 1207 and are described in the latter year
as of gold (*aurea*).[2] A fresh pair of golden spurs
was made for the coronation at Westminster, in
1220, of the youthful Henry III, at the cost of
£6.13.4, and given by him towards the building of
the new chapel of St. Mary there.

It is not, however, on the spurs alone that the
parallel with knighthood rests, although it has
been so supposed. I claim the sword with which
the King is girt as in truth the sword of knighthood. This, indeed, is not the meaning which is
usually assigned to it, but 'belting' with the sword
of knighthood [3] was no less essential to the knight
than his investiture with the gilt spurs. [4] Perhaps
it is not generally known that even at so recent a
date as 1837, when the last " writ of right " was
tried and the procedure of the 'Grand Assize' [5]
followed, the " four knights " required by it, to
choose the twelve " recognitors, " [6] " appeared in
court, each girt with a sword...... The attendance
of the four knights girt with swords is indispensably

---

[1] See below.

[2] The " Order of the Golden Spur " is still among the distinctions
conferred by the Pope.

[3] *Cingulus* (or *balteus*) *militaris*.

[4] William of Malmesbury makes Alfred confer knighthood on
Æthelstan by investing him " chlamyde coccinea, *gemmato balteo, ense*
saxonico cum vaginâ aureâ," which shews at least what the chronicler
considered to have been essential. All the things he mentions are
included in the coronation ritual.

[5] Instituted by Henry II.

[6] " per quatuor legales milites de comitatu et de visineto eligantur
duodecim milites," etc. *Glanvill*.

necessary, " [1]—or that, at least as late as 1868, newly-elected knights of the shire were still, as such, girt with the sword. [2]

The reason why the girding or " belting " with the sword has not been recognised, in this case, as emblematic of knighthood is, no doubt, that it was also an essential element in the creation or investiture of an earl, both in England and in Scotland, from very remote times. [3] It was not, therefore, so distinctive of knighthood as were the gilt spurs. But that the sword and spurs were indissolubly connected is particularly well seen in the ancient English ceremonial for creating knights of the Bath. High above those modern distinctions that are now so freely scattered there stands, still unsullied, that " Most Honourable Order, " which wealth cannot purchase or the trade of politics procure. The gilt spurs of its Knight Commanders testify to its mediæval origin, even as its ancient device takes us back to days when religious ritual and the mystic bath proclaimed that high ideal of the knight, on his creation, riding forth to war for God and for the right. It was one of the essential ceremonies at the crowning of an English king that he should create Knights of the Bath, and the culminating act of that creation was when in front of the neophyte, as he rode to receive the

[1] As a matter of fact, two of them were baronets. See the newspaper report quoted in Pixley's *History of the Baronetage*, p. 233.

[2] The repeated insistence of the Crown, in the 14th century, that the knights of the shire should be real knights, " *milites gladiis cinctos,* " and the difficulty of enforcing this condition, will be found dealt with by Stubbs in *Const. Hist.* (1878) III, 397-402.

[3] It was afterwards extended to Marquessates and Dukedoms when these dignities were introduced.

honour, there were brought and presented to the king the spurs hanging on the sword. The order prescribed was this :—

And there must be provided a young Esquire, courteous, who shall ride before the Esquire, bareheaded, and carry the Esquire's sword, with the spurs hanging at the handle of the sword...... And the youth shall hold the sword by the point...... and so soon as they come before the hall dore, the Marshalls and Huishers [1] are to be ready to meet him, and desire him alight : and, being alighted, the Marshall shall take the horse for his fee, or else c s.

And when the King is come into the hall...... he shall aske for the sword and spurs, which the chamberlain shall take from the youth, and shew to the King ; and thereupon the King, taking the right spur, shall deliver it to the most noble and gentile person there ; and shall say to him : 'Put this upon the Esquire's heel ; ' and he kneeling on one knee, must take the esquire by the right leg, and putting his foot on his own knee, is to fasten the spur upon the right heel of the Esquire ; and then, making a cross upon the Esquire's knee, shall kiss him ; which being done, another knight must come and put on his left spur in like manner. And then shall the King, of his great favour, take the sword and gird the Esquire therewith...... And the King, putting his own armes about the Esquire's neck, say : 'Be thou a good knight,' and afterwards kiss him.

The new knight is then led to the altar, where he kneels with his right hand on the altar and promises to maintain the rights of Holy Church.

And then he shall ungird himself of his sword, and with great devotion to God and Holy Church, offer it there, praying unto God and all his saints that he may

[1] See p. 83 above.

keep that order which he hath so taken, even to the end.[1]

The swords thus offered up in the king's chapel were, in prosaic practice, the fee of the Dean of Chapel (*Liber Niger Domus*, Edw. IV).

That this ceremony was actually performed, in the case at least of the spurs, is proved by the narrative of the knighting of the young Duke of Buckingham by Henry VII at his accession.

The same day (28 October, 1485) before dinner the banes [2] *(sic)* was prepared in a great Chamber in the ...... as of old tyme hath bene accustomed, and when it was night, the King himself of his benigne goodnes, nobly accompanied with the Duke of Bedford, the Earle of Oxford, the E. of Derby, the E. of Devon, with many other Noble Lords, Knights, and Esquires... them in the bayne *(sic)* the advertisement of the order of knighthood and after him other Lords and Estates, etc. On Saturday when the Esquires which had been in the baynes and after other observants *(sic)* as of old tyme accostomed were come into the Hall, the King in a rich gowne entred into the Hall and stood under the Cloth of Estate, to whom the Duke of Buck : was presented by two Estates, and the Henchmen that bare the Sword and the Spurs presented them to the Earl of Oxford. And he tooke the right spur and presented it to the King, and the King tooke it to the Duke of Bedford commanding him to putt it upon the Duke of Buck : heel of his right legg, and in likewyse the Earle of Darby the left spurre, and the King girt the sword about him and dubbed him Knight. [3]

Here the King chooses his own uncle, the newly-created Duke of Bedford, and the newly-created

---

[1] From " The order and manner of creating Knights of the Bath in the time of peace, according to the custom of England, " printed in Dugdale's *Warwickshire* (1730), p. 708.

[2] *i.e.* the baths (*bains*).

[3] *State Papers (Domestic)*, vol. 8.

Earl of Derby, to whom he chiefly owed his throne, as the noblest persons present, to place the spurs upon the duke's feet. It is remarkable that, although the spurs were eventually fastened to the King's feet by the Lord Great Chamberlain, yet, at our earliest example, the coronation of Richard I, the office was performed by " two earls." [1]

Now if the creation of a Knight of the Bath be compared with the coronation of the sovereign, we observe a parallel procedure.

THE KNIGHT	THE KING
(1) is invested with the spurs.	(1) is invested with the spurs.
(2) is, immediately afterwards, belted with the sword.	(2) is, immediately afterwards, belted with the sword.
(3) subsequently ungirds the sword.	(3) subsequently ungirds the sword.
(4) offers the sword upon the altar.	(4) offers the sword upon the altar.

Mr. Legg's description runs thus :—

Over the *supertunica* is put the girdle or swordbelt [2] so that the sword may be put on. The sword is that which is known as the sword of state, which is carried in the procession and laid upon the altar. It is now blessed by the Archbishop with the prayer *Exaudi quæsumus Domine...*

[1] " Deinde duo comites calciaverunt ei calcaria quæ Johannes maresallus portaverat."

[2] Mr. St. John Hope, at the outset of his monograph, claims the girdle as part of the bishop's gear, observing that a ' belt or girdle ' was put upon the King as upon a Bishop (p. 127), but on p. 150 he speaks of " the sword and its girdle " as put upon the King, which is, clearly, the right view. The jewelled belt (*balteus*) was among the *regalia*.

The sword is then taken from the altar and brought by the bishops and given into the King's hands.

The Lord Great Chamberlain girds the King with it, while the Archbishop says *Accipe gladium per episcopos* (p. xli) [1]..... the King ungirded his sword, and went to the altar, where he offered the sword (p. li.) [2]

I have quoted Mr. Legg's version of the ritual that I may not be supposed to have adapted it to my theory. Should it be objected that the sword of knighthood is conferred by the Primate, this, one replies, is but a survival of a very early practice ; William Rufus had received knighthood at the hands of Archbishop Lanfranc,[3] and so had Henry I in 1086. [4]

The point, however, that I wish to make is that the spurs, the gilt spurs, [5] though the most distinctive emblems, were not the only emblems of the King's investiture as a knight. One cannot separate the sword and spurs. Even in the days when ' the Gothic revival' flourished with the side-whisker they were still deemed essential to the dignity of a golden knight (*eques auratus*).

In 1836 that egregious person Mr. Richard Broun claimed the right to be knighted as the eldest

[1] The full prayer was : " Accipe hunc gladium tibi conlatum in quo per virtutem spiritus sancti resistere et ejicere omnes inimicos tuos valeas et cunctos sancte Dei ecclesie adversarios regnumque tibi commissum tutari atque protegere castra Dei per auxilium," etc.

[2] " super altare deo offerat " (*Liber Regalis*).

[3] " Eum ...... militem fecerat." (Will. Malms.)

[4] " Hunc Lanfrancus, dum juvenile robur attingere vidit, ad arma pro defensione regni sustulit,...... eique, ut Regis filio et in regali stemmate nato, *militiæ cingulum* in nomine Dei cinxit " (*Ord. Vit.*).

[5] Giltspur Street, London, preserves their name, and a pair of gilt spurs was a frequent render for land in the Middle Ages. For this purpose they were valued in 1197 (according to the Pipe Roll of 9 Ric. I.) as the equivalent of sixpence.

son of a baronet. [1]   An official refusal, grimly referring to his " alleged ancestor, " did not disconcert him.   The 'Committee of the Baronetage for privileges,' of which he was honorary secretary, was at length stirred to action ; in 1842 they claimed that the eldest sons of baronets were entitled to " be inaugurated knights (*Equites Aurati*), " and Mr. Broun was " required, " as " a knight *de jure*, as the eldest son of a Member of the Order of ancient creation, " to " vindicate this fundamental and unalienable privilege..... by henceforth using, taking, and enjoying the ancient chivalrous dignity of a knight (*Eques Auratus*). "   Mr. Broun was not reluctant.   He at once " formally assumed knighthood, throwing the responsibility of his doing so upon the Lord Chamberlain and the Prime Minister who sanctioned the Lord Chamberlain's conduct. "   In the full flush of his new dignity, he compiled an account of his family, the following year, as " Sir Richard Broun, Eq[ues] Aur[atus], K. J. J., [2] hon. sec. of the Committee of the Baronetage for Privileges. "   He had also produced a pamphlet on " British and Continental titles of honour, " which Mr. Pixley treats as anonymous,

---

[1] His father, a Dumfries solicitor, had assumed the baronetcy of Brown of Coulston (1686) in or after 1826.

[2] These mystic letters stand for Knight of St. John of Jerusalem. Kemble, the historian, wrote in language of not unnatural scorn, in his preface to Larking's " Knights Hospitallers in England " (1847) :— " Least of all shall I vouchsafe a word either of ridicule or indignation upon a number of persons whom one meets with in various European Courts ; and who are Knights of St. John of Jerusalem by virtue of a white cross upon a black coat, and the nomination of some king or other, who claims to be Grandmaster of a non-existent order, which once was a great truth, and not a *sham* and a matter of ribbons. " (p. xiii).   But the title doubtless appealed to Mr. Broun's chivalric soul.

but the authorship of which is betrayed by its insistence on the nobility and antiquity of the house of Broun. Grateful for his vindication of their rights and of his " natitial dignity, " the baronets' committee resolved to present to " Sir Richard Broun " the " insignia appertaining to the degree of Eques Auratus, " including, of course, the spurs. They comprised also a sword and ring and, actually, " a golden collar of S.S " ! Mr. Pixley candidly admits that the right to this collar is " exceedingly doubtful. " [1]

The reason for insisting on the close connection of the gilt spurs with knighthood is that it seems to me to offer a possible explanation of their being borne in the procession, when we first hear of them, by the Marshal. The Court of Claims which sat in 1901-2, after hearing three conflicting claims, arrived, if I may say so, at the perfectly proper decision that

Because no sufficient evidence has been adduced as to the nature of the said office or hereditary privilege, therefore the court considers and adjudges that no one of the said petitioners has established a claim to perform the said service on the day of their Majesties' Coronation.

It is a most extraordinary fact that, according to Mr. Wollaston's report, [2] the all-important evidence that the spurs were carried by John the Marshal at the coronation of Richard I, when they are first mentioned, was not brought before the court.

On that occasion, and again in 1911, there were

---

[1] See, for this Broun episode, Pixley's *History of the Baronetage*.
[2] *The Court of Claims : cases and evidence* (1903).

three claims to carry the spurs in the coronation procession. Although the whole matter is clear enough to an expert, it is exceedingly difficult to convey clearly to the reader what were the questions at issue. The starting point for all three claims [1] was the record of the first Court of Claims in 1377. It was admitted by that Court that John de Hastings, then a minor, son of the deceased John de Hastings, who was Lord de Hastings and Earl of Pembroke, was entitled " of right " to carry the spurs. Had he left lineal heirs, they would probably have had their right recognised, without dispute, ever after. He was, however, slain at a tournament, still a minor and without issue, twelve years later. There thus arose a question, at that time not unfrequent, as to who were his right heirs. But here we are only concerned with his right to bear the spurs. Broadly speaking, the point to be decided, in 1901-2 and again in 1911 —if the Court was prepared, as apparently it was, to investigate the question *de novo* without being bound by the precedents,—was whether he derived that right through his great-great-grandfather, Joh ., Lord Hastings, or through that John's *first* wife, Isabel de Valence, youngest co-heir of the earls of Pembroke (through whom that earldom had come to him). In the former case, the rightful heirs would be the representatives of Sir Hugh Hastings, that John's son by his *second* wife ; in the latter case, the rightful heirs would be the representatives of Elizabeth de Hastings, that John's

---

[1] Except, it will be seen, to some extent, that of Lord Grey de Ruthyn.

daughter by his *first* wife, who married Lord Grey de Ruthyn. [1]

Unfortunately, the claim made in 1377 was not in respect of either of these two descents, but was based on the wholly false allegation that William Marshal, who had carried the spurs at the coronation of Edward II (1308), was the earl's " ancestor " ! It leaves us, therefore, wholly in doubt as to the real source of his right, which was recognised as based on " records and evidences. "

That the allegation was false is not a matter of dispute, but I may add that the real heir of this William Marshal, in 1377, was Lord Morley, the son of his daughter and sole eventual heiress, who had succeeded to his office of hereditary marshal of Ireland, but who made no claim to bear the spurs. I would point out further that this erroneous allegation is by no means so strange as counsel seemed to imagine. On this same occasion Margaret ' Marschall, ' as Countess of Norfolk, claimed to execute the office of marshal " come Gilbert Mareschall Comte de Strogoil fist as coronement *le Roy Henri Second,* " and thereby threw the whole history of the Marshalship of England into hopeless confusion until I put it right by explaining that the occasion when earl Gilbert officiated was at the coronation of Queen Eleanor in 1236. [2]

---

[1] I pass over the additional complication that, owing to the doctrine of the half-blood then accepted, this Elizabeth and her heirs were wrongly supposed, down to 1641, to be entitled to the earl's barony of Hastings.

[2] So also, in the case of the Earls of Oxford, one of them obtained the Great Chamberlainship by a demonstrably false allegation, and another tried to obtain the Chamberlainship to the Queen (*q. v.*) by one no less false (see pp. 122, 139).

It will make the matter simpler if we begin by disposing of the claim of Lord Hastings. In the first place, it is difficult to understand what that claim really was. Did his lordship claim as heir of Sir Hugh Hastings,[1] or in respect of his holding the dignity of Lord Hastings? If the former, he could not claim the office for himself alone, for he was only the junior co-heir of the junior co-heir of Sir Hugh. Yet he presented his petition " as representative of and successor to his predecessor, " the earl of 1377. His counsel's argument, however, according to Mr. Wollaston's report, was based not upon heirship, but upon the allegation that " The right to carry the spurs is attached to the Barony of Hastings, " and that, as that barony had remained dormant or in abeyance till 1841, no one since 1389 had been in a position to advance the claim at a coronation before.[2]

Mr. Wollaston, who ably argued the case for Lord Loudoun, appears to have been as much in doubt as myself as to the real basis of Lord Hastings' claim. As he observed, with perfect truth :—

Lord Hastings' claim is based on suppositions which are entirely contradicted by fact. He contends that the right is attached to the Barony of Hastings ;... yet at the Coronation of Edward II, the spurs were carried by William le Marshall, and not by the second Baron Hastings [3]......

If Lord Hastings rests his claim not on the Barony, but

---

[1] See above.

[2] Wollaston, *op. cit.*, p. 119.

[3] This argument might have been strengthened by pointing out that at the coronation of Richard I (then so strangely overlooked) they were carried not by a Hastings, but by John the Marshal.

on the ground that he is the representative of the male line, as opposed to the female, he is confronted with the difficulty that the succession has twice gone through coheirs, and that he is descended from the youngest branch ; so that he cannot truly say that he is the representative of the male line. [1]

Nevertheless, the claim was renewed in 1911 with the same allegation that Lord Hastings was " representative of " the earl of Pembroke, the assertion being also made that he was " heir (not ' co-heir ') of John Earl of Pembroke. "   Although it was not possible to produce any evidence whatever that the right was in the Hastings family, as claimed, before 1313, an extraordinary pedigree " was put in evidence, " [2] in which the house of Hastings was traced back to the Conquest, presumably on the supposition that this had a bearing on the issue.

The beginning of this precious pedigree is enough to betray its character.   It starts thus :—

Robert de Hastings, Lord of Fillongley, Portgreve of Hastings, Dispensator or *(sic)* Steward to William the Conqueror. [3]

On this my comment is :—that no such person as Robert de Hastings was either Lord of Fillongley, or ' Dispensator, ' or ' Steward ' under William the Conqueror.

---

[1] *Ibid.*, pp. 123-4.

[2] It faces p. 124 of Mr. Wollaston's book.

[3] Mr. Paley Baildon, reviewing Mr. Wollaston's book, observed :— " In the sheet pedigree accompanying this case we are somewhat surprised to see our old friend ' the Portgreve of Hastings ' sitting in his wonted pride of place at the top ; we thought that he had decently retired to the limbo of myths some time ago " (*Ancestor*, VII, 138).

Let us take the Fillongley story first. In the *Testa de Nevill* Henry de Hastings is found holding as an under-tenant a quarter of a fee in Fillongley of the fief of Robert Marmion. [1] Now Marmion and Beauchamp had shared between them the great fief of Robert the Dispenser (*Dispensator*) [2] in Domesday, Marmion receiving Tamworth castle as the *caput* of his portion. Following this up, we duly find half a hide in Fillongley, in 1086, held by Robert ' Dispensator ' in the Warwickshire portion of his fief. [3] Robert, of course, was a well-known man, brother to the dreaded Urse d'Abetot, but, it will be seen, he is here converted into a Robert " de Hastings, " with whom he had nothing in the world to do, exactly as his brother Urse d'Abetot has been converted into a Hanbury in order to provide an ancestor for the Hanbury family. [4] Thus was evolved the statement that Robert " de Hastings" was "Dispensator or Steward to William the Conqueror " ! From which statement it is further evident that those who make it imagine ' steward ' to be the meaning of ' dispensator. ' The steward (*dapifer*) was, of course, always and essentially distinct from the dispenser (*dispensator*), but to those who concoct or repeat pedigrees such as this they are doubtless all the same. [5]

[1] " De Filungeleg de feodo Marmen H. de Hasting pro quarta parte j militis " (p. 84) ; " de quarta parte unius feodi Henrici de Hastinges de baronia Roberti Marmion " (p. 90).

[2] See my *Feudal England*, and compare the section on ' the king's champion ' (p. 381).

[3] *Domesday*, I, 242b.

[4] See my *Peerage and Pedigree*, II, pp. 145-6.

[5] It is to the credit of Dugdale that in the Hastings pedigree in his *Baronage* (I. 574) he ignores this Robert altogether.

As to Robert being " Portgreve of Hastings," historians would be thankful for proof of the fact, but the town, unfortunately, is one of Domesday's omissions. A Robert " de Hastings " is entered as a holder of two and a half hides on the abbot of Fécamp's great manor of ' Rameslie ' or Brede, which extended into Hastings, but his connexion with other men of the name, if any, is unknown. The origin of the later baronial house is still a matter of speculation.[1]

It seems, however, to have been overlooked that there was a family of Hastings who were among the chief tenants of the lords of Hastings and its Rape, the Counts of Eu. In 1207 Robert de Hastings was claiming against Simon de Etchingham " the stewardship of the Count of Eu's Honour in the Rape of Hastings," which, he alleged, William his father had received in frank marriage with Yda, daughter of the Count of Eu.[2] This Robert was holding seven knight's fees of the Count in 1212.[3] William the father was probably son of Robert de Hastings, who held in 1166 half a fee (of the new feoffment) under the count [4] and who seems to have been, with the counts, a bene-factor to the abbey of Foucarmont.[5] He also appears, under Sussex, on the Pipe Roll of 1168

---

[1] Mr. G. T. Clark professed to have solved the problem in his paper on "The Rise and Race of Hastings" (*Arch. Journ.*[1869], Vol. XXVI), but his conclusions, as on some other matters, do not inspire conviction. Indeed, I have torn his theory to pieces (*Ancestor*, No. 2, pp. 91-2).

[2] *Rot. de Fin.* (9 John), p. 376.

[3] *Lib. Rub.*, pp. 554, 623. They were held by a later Robert in 1242-3 (*Testa*, p. 223).

[4] *Ibid.*, p. 203.

[5] See my *Calendar of Documents preserved in France*, No. 186.

(pp. 195, 197). And he, again, may have been the son of that William de Hastings who is found, with tenants of the Count of Eu, attesting charters of Henry I in 1130-1131.[1] Earlier still (1107-1116) there was Enguerrand (*Ingelrannus*) de Hastings, who is found in charters of the Counts of Eu,[2] and who was doubtless the ' Ingelramnus ' who is found in Domesday holding of the Count at several places in the Rape, especially on the manor of Wilting, which is found in far later days held of the house of Hastings.

To return to the pedigree ' put in evidence ' before the Court of Claims, we find that Robert is succeeded by Walter (*sic*), " Steward to Henry I, Owner of Manor of Ashill, Norfolk, by Grand Serjeanty, ' to take care of the Naperie (*sic*) at the Coronation '." The phrase is obviously derived from Dugdale,[3] who, however, gives the man's name as ' *William* '. ' Walter ', indeed, fulfils the function of a marked coin, for it proves that the compilers of this pedigree cannot even have gone to Dugdale, but must have reproduced his statement through the medium of *Burke's Peerage*, where ' Walter ' is carelessly given for ' William '. Moreover, the ' Naperie ' business does not emerge till more than a century later![4] ' Walter ' has a son Hugh and grandson William, each of them, like their predecessor, ' Steward to Henry I '. But the last is also ' Steward to Henry II ', to whom, by

[1] *Ibid.*, Nos. 122-3.
[2] *Ibid.*, Nos. 232, 1417.
[3] *Baronage*, I, 574, citing Glover.
[4] See p. 223 above.

the way, in authentic records he was 'Dispensator'.
A son of the same name is followed by "Henry
Lord (*sic*) Hastings," who made the great match
with the Earl of Huntingdon's daughter, and he
by "Sir Henry de Hastings, 1st Baron (*sic*) Hastings," the common ancestor of all the claimants.
If he was "1st Baron Hastings," how can his
father have been "Lord Hastings"? And why,
moreover, is either of them styled 'lord' or 'baron',
when the Lord Chancellor, in the Hastings case
(1842), rejected even the son as a proved peer, and
dated the peerage from the next generation (1290)?[1]
Here we may leave this pedigree : it is always instructive to learn what lawyers mean by ' evidence '.

Having thus disposed of the Hastings claim,
which, indeed, was rejected by the Court in 1911,
we may turn to that in respect of Elizabeth, Lady
Grey de Ruthyn,[2] which was represented in 1901-2,
and again in 1911, by two rival claimants.   Lord
Loudoun claimed to be entitled alone, as her senior
co-heir, or, alternatively, to be entitled jointly with
her other co-heirs.   Lord Grey de Ruthyn, the
second co-heir, claimed to be entitled solely, as
holder of the barony of Grey de Ruthyn, to which
the right, he alleged, was annexed.[3]   The question,
as between these claims, really turned on whether
the Court would consider itself bound by the decisions of its predecessors in 1820 and 1831, which
favoured Lord Grey de Ruthyn's claim, or would
examine the question *de novo*.   If the latter, there

---

[1] See my *Peerage and Pedigree*, I, 251-2.
[2] See p. 358.
[3] Wollaston, *op. cit.* pp. 101, 107, 109, 115-119.

was no doubt, as Mr. Wollaston clearly showed, that the right was not annexed to the barony of Grey de Ruthyn ; for the right could only have been brought by Elizabeth Hastings to her husband, Lord Grey de Ruthyn. Therefore the holders of that barony could not have had the right before this marriage; nor, indeed, did they claim it at the accession of Richard II.[1] We have here, indeed, but a further illustration of the error and confusion arising from the practice of former Courts of Claims in looking only to the person in whom a right had been allowed, without investigating the source from which that right was derived.[2]

There remained the claim of Lord Loudoun, as the eldest co-heir of Elizabeth Hastings (Lady Grey de Ruthyn), to exercise the office solely, or, alternatively, to be jointly entitled to it with the heirs of the other four sisters between whom the representation had fallen into abeyance in 1868. This was a very interesting claim, for it raised at once the question, so long and keenly discussed in the Great Chamberlain case,[3] whether in the case of offices—or of dignities savouring of office—the right, in virtue of *esnecia*, descended to the eldest co-heir alone, or was inherited jointly by all.

But, unfortunately, this point does not appear to have been discussed in 1911. The Gordian knot was cut. Counsel for Lord Loudoun was asked by the Lord Chancellor :

[1] *Ibid.*, p. 122. It was doubtless upon this account that the petition of Lord Grey de Ruthyn (*Ibid.*, p. 101) ignored the decision of 1377 and significantly began with the coronation of Henry IV (1399).

[2] See p. 152 above.

[3] and affecting also the Lucas case.

" You share with Lord Grey de Ruthyn, if you get rid of the claim of Lord Hastings ? "

Counsel, without waiving the possible prior right of his client as senior co-heir, admitted that Lord Grey de Ruthyn " was a (*sic*) co-heir. " The result was a strange decision of the Court, delivered by the Lord Chancellor :—

Having heard further evidence the Court adjudges that the Earl of Loudoun and Lord Grey de Ruthyn have established their claim to perform the service of carrying the Great Spurs, and that it be referred to the pleasure of his Majesty how such service shall be performed. [1]

' A strange decision, ' for it certainly did *not* allow the claim of Lord Grey de Ruthyn, which was that he possessed the sole right in virtue of his holding that barony; nor did it allow Lord Loudoun's claim as eldest co-heir, to the exclusion of Lord Grey de Ruthyn ; nor did it allow his alternative claim that the right was vested in *all* the co-heirs. What it allowed was, apparently, a claim which they had not made—and which, in law, they could not make—namely that the right was vested in their two selves jointly.

It is to be hoped that, at a future Court, the other co-heirs will claim their rightful share in the privilege.

It will be observed that this decision speaks of " further evidence. " This would seem to refer to Mr. Wollaston's statement that " since the petition was disallowed in 1901-2 on the ground

---

[1] I take all this from the *Morning Post* report, which was specially full and clear.

of insufficient evidence, they had been able to
establish a new fact, that the Great Spurs had been
borne by the Marshall family. " [1]   But this " new
fact " appears to have been only what has always
been common knowledge (although as I have said,
overlooked in 1901-2) namely that they were
borne by John (the) Marshal at the coronation of
Richard I. [2]   The fact is duly given in Dugdale's
Baronage (1675) under Marshal (' Mareschall '),
and the right authority cited, which authority is
discussed in my paper on ' The coronation of
Richard I. ' [3]   And, needless to say, the same fact
prominently figures in Mr. Legg's " English Coronation Records " (1901).

Historically, therefore, the position is this : at
the coronation of Richard I (1189) the spurs
were borne by John (the) Marshal ; at that of
Edward II (1308) by William Marshal. [4]   We
have no other precedents previous to 1377.   Can
we find a consistent explanation of these two
facts ?

Clearly the case was not one of hereditary right,
for William Marshal, though descended from a
brother of John, was not his heir.   A chart pedigree is absolutely necessary to make the matter
clear.

[1] *Morning Post* report.
[2] See p. 356 above.
[3] *The Commune of London* (1899), pp. 201 *et seq.*
[4] *Cal. of Close Rolls.*

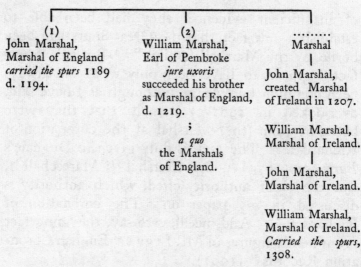

(1)
John Marshal,
Marshal of England
carried the spurs 1189
d. 1194.

(2)
William Marshal,
Earl of Pembroke
jure uxoris
succeeded his brother
as Marshal of England,
d. 1219.

;
a quo
the Marshals
of England.

....
Marshal

John Marshal,
created Marshal
of Ireland in 1207.

William Marshal,
Marshal of Ireland.

John Marshal,
Marshal of Ireland.

William Marshal,
Marshal of Ireland.
Carried the spurs,
1308.

John, created marshal of Ireland in fee, 12 Nov.
1207,[1] received with that office certain Irish lands
(as five knight's fees), but, his chief possessions
being in England, he and his heirs were allowed to
execute the office by deputy.   He was an intimate
counsellor of his uncle, the great earl,[2] and it was
doubtless through his uncle's influence that he
obtained a moiety of the Rye barony with his wife
in or before 1211, besides receiving grants from
the Crown of Hingham and other forfeited lands.
His son William[3] was a great supporter of Simon
de Montfort and was grandfather of that William
Marshal who officiated in 1308 and who was
summoned to Parliament as a Baron in 1309.

Why was this William chosen to carry the spurs
in 1308?   The answer I suggest is that the right

[1] Charter Roll, 9 John.
[2] *Histoire de Guillaume le Maréchal.*
[3] Dugdale wrongly interpolates another John between them.

(if we admit that there was a right) was not hereditary, but *official*. The Marshal family, on this
hypothesis, carried the spurs *ex officio* as Marshals
of England. When the male issue of the great earl
became extinct in 1245, the marshal's rod, as is
well known, passed to the Bigods, as his *eldest*
co-heirs, and remained with them until the death,
in 1306, of Roger, earl of Norfolk, when it passed,
under his surrender, to the Crown. There it
remained till 1316, when it was granted to the
king's brother, Thomas of Brotherton, in tail male. [1]

It was precisely in this interval that Edward II
was crowned (1308), and, on my hypothesis, the
question would naturally arise—who was to carry
the spurs ? The Crown would have to appoint
someone, and what appointment could be more
fitting than that of the hereditary marshal of Ireland, the only one remaining, who represented,
moreover, the cadet line of the marshals of England? [2]
It is, I think, a noteworthy fact that in that
'recension' of the coronation service which is
represented by the *Liber Regalis* and is believed to
have been first used on this occasion, the direction
runs :—"unus de magnatibus *ad hoc per Regem
designatus* portans calcaria magna et deaurata." [3]
It was the King's right to appoint.

In 1377 there was again no hereditary marshal,
as Margaret, daughter of Thomas of Brotherton,
unsuccessfully claimed the office on the false allegation that it was her 'droit heritage,' though it

---

[1] *The Commune of London*, p. 308.
[2] I made this suggestion in the *Commune of London* (1899), p. 307.
[3] Legg's *English coronation records*, p. 85.

was limited to the male issue of her father. How the privilege was obtained for the earl of Pembroke we do not know, but I suspect that the argument was this : — it was held by his ancestors the Marshals, Earls of Pembroke, whose earldom of Pembroke he held (though only their junior co-heir), and should therefore be held by him. This would be exactly parallel to the claim (also successful) of the FitzAlan earls of Arundel to the butlership of their ancestors the D'Aubigny earls of Arundel, though they were only the junior co-heirs. In the one case the Marshals had held *as marshals*, not as earls ; in the other the D'Aubignys had held as D'Aubignys, not as earls. But this distinction would be too abstruse for the 'rule of thumb' methods of a Court of Claims.

After the successful claim by Lord Grey de Ruthyn as heir to the earl of Pembroke, in 1399[1], there would seem to be no claim recorded as allowed till 1685,[2] and during this interval of nearly three centuries it is known that the spurs were carried at the coronation of Richard III by the (Herbert) earl of Huntingdon,[3] at that of Henry VII by the Earl of Essex,[4] at that of Henry VIII by the Earl of Arundel, at that of Edward VI by the Earl of Rutland, at that of Mary by the Earl of Pembroke, at that of Queen Elizabeth by the (Hastings) earl of Huntingdon.[5]

[1] " en manière comme le dit Johan de Hastings nadgairs conte Pembrooke, et ses auncestres, a qui heir le dit suppliant est de tout temps ont fait."

[2] See the table in Mr. Wollaston's book.

[3] Legg's *English Coronation Records*, p. 195.

[4] *Ibid.*, p. 227 ('Little Device').

[5] State papers and Privy Council Records.

and at that of Charles II by the Earl of Pembroke and Montgomery. [1] From 1685 the right of the Lords Grey de Ruthyn was allowed, but the long breach of continuity and the absence even of claims on their part, so far as our evidence goes, would seem to betray a consciousness on their part that they could not prove their right. [2]

The object, however, of this paper is to advance the theory that the king's chief marshal would be, as such, the most likely person to carry the great spurs at a coronation. Although I cannot *prove* that this was the marshal's function, he was certainly the officer more especially associated with the horse.[3] Etymologically, *marescallus* is derived from an ancient word for horse, and, according to Stubbs, " the *mariscalcus* " of the Salian law answers " to the *horsthegn* " of the Old English court.[4] In France, of course, the word *maréchal* retains, in the sense of farrier, the association with the horse. Now the knight (*chevalier*, *eques*) was essentially a *horseman*, and it is at least significant that when a knight was created, his horse was the marshal's fee. [5]

[1] *Cal. of State Papers*, 1661-2, pp. 584-5.

[2] Counsel's opinion in 1685 was that it was an office in gross held in fee and could not be entailed.

[3] " Mareschall," writes Madox, in his *History of the Exchequer*, " was a general name for several officers that were employed about horses." In France " Johannes marescallus domini Ludovici regis " notifies " me super sacrosancta jurasse ipsi domino regi quod non retinebo equos nec palefridos nec roncinos redditos ad opus meum ratione ministerii mei " (*His Grace the Steward*, p. 139). See also p. 85 above and Addenda.

[4] *Const. History*.

[5] In 1236, at Queen Eleanor's coronation, the marshal's fee is thus given :— ' Recipit de quolibet barone facto milite a Rege et quolibet comite palefridum cum sella ' (see my *Commune of London*, p. 312). In

It is, indeed, of an ancient past that the great golden spurs speak to Englishmen to-day. When knighthood has become the frequent guerdon of the pushing trader or the party hack, it is well to think of that distant age, eight hundred years ago and more, when the knight's spur was buckled to the heel of count and duke and king. In the hour of his crowning the sword of knighthood is still girt about an English king ; the spurs of knighthood touch his heels ; and the great dream of the Middle Ages is brought before our eyes to-day when the holder of Lanfranc's see delivers to the king his sword—to " use it as the minister of God,"—" by the hands of us the Bishops. " For even so had Lanfranc girt the king that was to be " with the belt of knighthood in the name of God. " [1] With this sword he is still bidden to " protect the holy Church of God " : for the

1377, at that of Richard II, Margaret ' Marschall ' spoke of the marshal as " pernant de chescun Baron et Conte faitz Chivaler au cel jour un palfrey ove une sele " (*Ibid.*, p. 303)   And at the creation of knights of the Bath the marshal took the horse (see p. 351 above).

[1] See p. 354 above. As Hallam justly observes, " the purpose for which men bore arms in a crusade so sanctified their use, that chivalry acquired the character as much of a religious as a military institution. For many centuries, the recovery of the Holy Land was constantly at the heart of a brave and superstitious nobility ; and every knight was supposed at his creation to pledge himself, as occasion should arise, to that cause. Meanwhile the defence of God's law against infidels was his primary and standing duty. A knight, whenever present at mass, held the point of his sword before him while the gospel was read, to signify his readiness to support it. Writers of the middle ages compare the knightly to the priestly character... and the investiture of the one was supposed analogous to the ordination of the other. The ceremonies on this occasion were almost wholly religious ;... his sword was solemnly blessed ; everything in short was contrived to identify his new condition with the defence of religion, or at least of the church. " (*Middle Ages* [1860], III, 396.) See also p. 350 above.

ancient dream lingers yet; the Church that made
the priest made the knight also;[1] and the sword
that She had given him he did not bear in vain.
It was " in defence of the church, " and at the
Pope's command, that Simon de Montfort, with
his knights and priests, stormed the walls of Beziers
and put her ' heretics ' to the sword. It was as
the champion of the church, fighting beneath her
banner, that William, duke of the Normans,
triumphed on the hill of slaughter,[2] and taught to
men the grim meaning of knightly sword and spur.
The swords the Church had blessed were red with
English blood.   For ' the great spurs ' are witnesses to-day to the true title of our ancient kings, to
that bitter day when Edward's abbey was guarded
by Norman horse while a trembling primate set
the crown on their victorious chief.

THE GLOVE AND SCEPTRE SERJEANTY

Although this is one of the very few serjeanties
of which the service is still performed at the coron-

[1] It has been pointed out that the *Ordo Romanus*, most ancient of
coronation rituals, directs that the Emperor should be " crowned, in
St. Peter's, at the altar of St. Maurice, the patron saint of knighthood "
(Bryce's *Holy Roman Empire*, 1871, p. 250).
[2] Freeman wrote, of the banner sent to William by the Pope :—
" Rome was already beginning to practise her characteristic arts under
their greatest master.. Slaughter, robbery, devastation, all the horrors
of an unprovoked war against an unoffending nation, were to be held
as nothing when the interest of the Roman See was in the other scale. "
In view of her obstinate demand for the lost ' temporal power, ' history
may, in Italy, repeat itself.

> Nè sa quando una simile
> Orma di piè mortale
> La sua cruenta polvere
> A calpestar verrà.

ation of the sovereign, there is a singular lack of early evidence for its existence. The manor of Farnham Royal, Bucks, was held by the Verdons from the Conquest, as is proved by Domesday Book, and yet, neither in the *Testa de Nevill* nor in the *Red Book of the Exchequer*—those two great repertories of serjeanties—can we find its tenure mentioned. It is not, apparently, till the death of Theobald de Verdon in 1316 that we find the manor returned as " held of the King in chief by service of finding a glove for his right hand on the day of the King's coronation for supporting the King's right arm with his said gloved hand whilst the King shall hold his sceptre. " [1]

It should be observed that this service is quite different from that which is now performed. Theobald, if it is correctly rendered, is to find a glove for his own right hand and " with his said gloved hand " to support the King's arm. Dugdale's version of the same return gives the service, on the contrary, as identical with that which is now performed :—

" by the service of providing a glove, on the day of the King's coronation, for his [2] right hand, and to support his right arm, the same day during the time that the Royal sceptre is in his hand. [3] "

As the official translation, given above, is somewhat obscure,—the " his " being ambiguous, I have had the original Latin independently examined. It runs thus :—

[1] *Cal. of Inq.* VI (1910), pp. 36-7.
[2] *i.e.* The King's.
[3] *Baronage*, (1675), I, 471.

.....de domino Rege in capite per servicium ad inveniendum ad manum suam dextram die coronacionis domini
Regis unam Cirotecam et ad subportandum dextrum
Brachium domini Regis eodem die dum Regalem virgam
in manu sua tenu[er]it cum predicta manu sua cirotecata.

The text, it must be admitted, is itself ambiguous,
but the official rendering seems to be right.   It is
the lord of Farnham who has to support with *his
own* gloved right hand the King's right arm.   On
the other hand, Walsingham describes Richard II
as receiving a red glove and holding the sceptre
" in manu chirothccata. "   As this was but some
sixty years after the above return, it seems unlikely
that the service can have thus changed and one can
only say that the return may have been inaccurate
in detail.

Farnham passed, with Theobald de Verdon's
eldest daughter and co-heir Joan, to the Furnivals,
by whom the service was claimed and performed at
the coronation of Richard II and at those of
Henry IV and V.   From them it passed with an
heiress to Nevill, and through another to the
Talbots, Earls of Shrewsbury, till, in 1541, Francis,
Earl of Shrewsbury exchanged with Henry VIII
the Manor of Farnham Royal for " the site of the
late Priory or Manor of Worksop " and other lands
in the parish of Worksop, his service for all which
was to include the finding, " at the date of every
coronation, to the King of England for the time
being one glove for his right hand, and the same
day of his coronation to bear up his right arm as
long as his Highness the same day beareth in his
hand the Sceptre Royal. "   In accordance with this

arrangement, Gilbert, Earl of Shrewsbury performed the service in respect of the ' manor' of Worksop,
at the coronation of James I.   He died in 1616,
leaving no son, and his daughter Alethea brought
the ' manor' to the Howards, afterwards Dukes of
Norfolk, who thenceforth performed the service up
to and at the Coronation of Queen Victoria. [1]

Not long after that, viz. in 1839, or thereabouts,
the lands in virtue of which this service is rendered
were sold by the Duke of Norfolk to the Duke
of Newcastle, with the exception of some small
portions sold off to other owners.   For the coronation of Edward VII, the Duke of Newcastle
claimed the service as holding " substantially the
precise lands of the Priory of Worksop which
were possessed by the Duke of Norfolk in 1838." [2]

A long counter-petition was presented by the
Earl of Shrewsbury, who contended, on the one
hand, that the alienation of a small portion of the
lands broke the integrity of the serjeanty, which
had therefore " lapsed and become extinct, and has
reverted to the Crown, and is in the absolute
disposal of his Majesty, " and, on the other, that
he himself had a preferential claim, in that event,
to a grant de gratia of the privilege.   The latter
proposition was supported by a strange array of
arguments.   It was firstly assumed that William
the Conqueror had granted the privilege to Bertram

---

[1] It is to be observed that on that occasion, according to the official
report, the glove presented by the Duke was embroidered with the arms
of Howard.

[2] From statement on his behalf drawn up by his counsel, Mr. W. A.
Lindsay, K.C. and printed in Mr. Wollaston's valuable report of the
proceedings.

de Verdon, with Farnham " in support of the maintenance of the said service ; " secondly, that it " was a hereditary personal service granted to the said Bertram and his heirs, " and not exercised in respect of the manor ; thirdly, that his " ancestors, the ...... Lords de Verdun performed the said services at the coronations of the Kings and Queens of England, providing the said glove embroidered with the arms of de Verdun until ...... 1316, " (for which there does not appear to be any actual evidence at all) ; fourthly, " that he is the heir in direct descent to his ancestor, Bertram de Verdun, " which he most certainly was not, being neither his heir male, nor his heir general. [1] As a climax his Majesty was to be petitioned

" of His especial grace and favour to restore this honourable privilege to the family of De Verdun [2] (sic), who alone are entitled to bear the arms of De Verdun, which have immemorially been embroidered on the said glove, [3] and to grant to your Petitioner and his heirs the right to execute the said service at his ensuing Coronation. "

The Earl's counsel argued that " the grant of this privilege was originally made to Bertram de Verdun...... and his service was a personal one, and descended in the blood of the de Verduns...... Inasmuch as the original grant was to the de Verduns to descend in their blood, and has now reverted to the Crown, the Earl of Shrewsbury, as

[1] The heirs ' in direct descent ' of the Verdons, through the Furnivals, are Lord Mowbray, Segrave and Stourton, and the infant daughter of the late Lord Petre, for the latter of whom the barony of Furnival is now being claimed.

[2] The family of *Talbot* must be meant.

[3] But compare p. 376, note 1 above.

representing the blood of the de Verduns (!), has the best right to have it regranted to him by the Crown. " [1] This extraordinary claim reminds one of those 17th century Earls who, though their baronies were inherited " through a lass, " would not admit that they should " go with a lass. "

The Earl's claim was " disallowed " and that of the Duke of Newcastle, as Lord " of the Manor of Worksop, " allowed by the Court. [2] Appropriate, perhaps, in the case of an old or a feeble monarch, the claim to support the King's arm must seem, for the coming coronation, singularly out of place. Himself bred in that great service which is, before all, a maker of men, the King needs no " support " of man. The arm that wields his sceptre needs no other's help. Even though a Duke be the proffered prop, the protest rises to the lips :— " Non tali auxilio ! "

THE KING'S CHAMPION

There is probably no feature of the ancient coronation ceremony that is more familiar to the public or on which more nonsense has been written than that of the champion's challenge. Few of those who have pictured to themselves a performance, which, before it was abandoned, had already verged on the grotesque, realise that it was merely

[1] See, for all this, Mr. Wollaston's report of the proceedings (*Op. cit.* pp. 144-5.)

[2] The one point, as it seems to me, that Lord Shrewsbury was able to make was that the Priory lands were not a true " manor, " and that, therefore, there were no manorial rights to remain intact and unaffected by the sale of part of the actual lands.

a survival of Anglo-Norman law. It was, in the highest sphere, that ' proof by battle' which was still, theoretically, part of our law till two years before the champion's challenge was last heard in Westminster Hall. In the words of the learned authors of the *History of English Law* :—

The Anglo-Norman judicial combat belongs to a perfectly regular and regulated course of proceeding, is as strictly controlled as any other part of it, and has no less strictly defined legal consequences. [1]

The demandant in the Writ of Right " offered battle by his champion's body ", which champion must, in theory, have become his " man " by homage. But the champion usually swore falsely,[2] and was frequently but a hireling.[3] I have myself calendared a businesslike agreement, in 1272, duly sealed and witnessed, by which a champion was to receive £8 if he proved his employer's right by the combat, the agreement to be void if the parties came to terms before he " shall have struck one blow with the horned staff ". [4] Even so, the king's champion was only entitled to his fee, as of right, if his challenge were accepted and the combat were actually fought. [5]

[1] Ed. 1895, I, 16.

[2] " pur ceo que rarement avient que le champion al demandaunt ne seit perjurs" (Statute Westm. I, c. 41).

[3] " For civil causes professional pugilists were shamelessly employed. Apparently there were men who let out champions for hire....... there was much talk of fighting, but it generally came to nothing." See the same invaluable work, II, 630.

[4] *Calendar of Duke of Rutland's manuscripts* (Hist. MSS. Commission), IV, 49.

[5] This is best seen in the *Inq. p.m.* on Alexander de Frevill, the unsuccessful claimant, 24 June 1328. He was returned as having held (with his wife) Tamworth Castle by the service ; " and if no one shall

It was justly pointed out by Taylor in his *Glory of Regality* (pp. 315-6) that an *Inq. p. m.*[1] of 1333 (7 Edw. III) returns a tenement as held of the manor of Scrivelby, " which is held of the king in chief by grand serjeanty, namely by finding on the day of the king's coronation an armed knight on horseback, to prove by his body, *if necessary*, against whomsoever that the king who is crowned on that day is the true and right heir of the kingdom. " It is evident, therefore, that an actual combat was originally contemplated as possible. With regard to the champion's gauntlet, this also was a survival of the old legal practice. I have discussed " the glove as gage " in another work,[2] and have cited passages from *The Song of Dermot and the Earl* (12th century),[3] in illustration of Prof. Maitland's remarks in his Introduction to *The Court Baron*.[4] It figures also in the scenes between the King and Williams and Fluellen in Shakespeare's ' Henry V '.[5]

oppose him, the arms and horse are the King's (*i.e.* return to the king), but if anyone shall oppose and engage in combat (*congressum faciat*), the arms and horse shall remain to the aforesaid tenant " (*Cal. of Inq.* VII, No. 134). So also, for the coronation of Henry IV (1399) Sir Baldwin de Frevill petitioned that he might perform the service " armis regiis de liberacione Regis universaliter (*i.e.* 'cap-a-pie') armatus, super principalem dextrarium regium sedens,.... cui si nullus contradixerit, sint arma et equus domini Regis, si autem aliquis se apponat et congressum fecerit, remanebunt equus et arma predicto Baldewino." Sir John Dymoke's petition, for the coronation of Richard II, expresses this more obscurely, but admits that if his challenge were not taken up, he could only obtain the fee by grace, not by right.

[1] See *Cal. of Inq.* VII, No. 439, and Taylor (p. 385) for the Latin text. I take this opportunity of again insisting on the excellence of Taylor's work.

[2] *The Commune of London*, pp. 153-4.

[3] Ed. Orpen.

[4] Selden Soc. publ. IV, 17.

[5] Act. IV, Scenes 1, 7, 8.

K. Hen.   Soldier, why wearest thou that glove in thy
            cap ?

Will.   An't please your majesty, 'tis the gage of
            one that I should fight withal, if he be
            alive.

The King's champion pledged himself by his
glove to fight either on the spot or on any future
day selected.[1]

It is not my intention to supply the reader with
the *crambe repetita* on the championship, with
which the public has been fed in books and in the
newspaper press.   It is rather my wish to dissipate
some of the delusions on the subject.   Of these the
worst and the most persistent is the statement that
Robert Marmion, champion of Normandy, received
Tamworth and Scrivelsby from the Conqueror, to
hold by the 'champion' service in England.   Even
the admirable Dugdale (owing to the silence of
Domesday) believed that Robert Marmion received
Tamworth from the Conqueror and had seen there
in "an antient window" William "in his Robes of
State" handing it by charter to Robert.   As to
Scrivelsby, however, he made no such assertion.
That Tamworth with its castle was held by Robert
'Dispensator', a great Domesday baron, is proved
by a charter which I printed in *Geoffrey de Mande-
ville* (pp. 313-5), and I have dealt fully in *Feudal
England* with the early pedigree of Marmion (pp.
190-195).   It is clear that the lands held by Robert
'Dispensator' were shared between Marmion and
Beauchamp (of Elmley) under Henry I and that

---

[1] "ou a quel jour que lem affera."   This became in the English
challenge "on what day soever he shall be appointed."

Tamworth and Scrivelsby fell to the former's share. The ludicrous idea that " this Robert " was " the first English Champion " and that his *alias* was " Sir Robert Marmion, the Sire or Lord of Fontenay " [1] is on a par with the assertion that " the family of Marmion enjoyed the peculiar privilege of acting as Champions to the Dukes of Normandy, and they held their lands on feudal tenure by knight (*sic*) serjeanty subject to the performance of this particular service," [2]—an assertion for which no evidence is vouchsafed.

All such statements are due to foolish attempts to carry back an ancient and interesting tenure further than evidence permits. Even Mr. Wollaston, to whom we owe a valuable work on coronation claims, has written of " the owners of the manor of Scrivelsby — the ancient knightly house of Dymoke who have held that manor since the time when, to use the quaint legal phraseology, ' the memory of man runneth not to the contrary '. " He must have forgotten for the moment, although himself a barrister, that the limit of legal memory was 1189, [3] and that Scrivelsby had no Dymoke for its lord till 1350.

It is recognised by all those who have written on the subject that the first recorded recognition and performance of the service was at the corona-

---

[1] Lodge's *Scrivelsby, the Home of the Champions* (1893), pp. 34-5. This work makes some parade of ' accuracy '.

[2] *Ibid.*, p. 30. So also we read in Hazlitt's *Blount's Tenures* (1874) that " Robert de *(sic)* Marmion, Lord of Fonteney in Normandy, and hereditary champion to the dukes thereof, was by King William the Conqueror, for his services rewarded with the Castle of Tamworth " (p. 268).

[3] *History of English Law*, I, 147.

tion of Richard II (1377), after a keen contest between two claimants. These were Freville and Dymoke, representatives respectively of the elder and the younger co-heirs of the last of the Marmion line, who had died in 20 Edw. I, and from whom they had respectively inherited Tamworth Castle and Scrivelsby. We may safely *infer*, no doubt from their claims that the office of champion had belonged to their common ancestor, Marmion, although we have no direct evidence of the fact. One turns, therefore, to the 'Inquisition' (8 Jan. 1291/2) on Philip, last of the Marmion line, to learn the tenure of the two estates. This Inquisition I have had examined,[1] and, though it is now damaged, we find Tamworth returned as held by knight-service[2] and Scrivelsby as held " by Barony."[3] Of the 'champion' service, or even of serjeanty, there is nothing.

The earliest mention of that service which has yet come to light is, apparently, in an inquisition of 18 July 1326, which returns a messuage in Coningsby as "parcel of the manor of Scrivelsby, which is held of the King in chief by grand serjeanty."[4] Just after this, Edward II died (20 Jan. 1326/7), which brings us to the new fact. This fact is that Henry Hillary, then tenant of Scrivelsby, claimed to perform the service at the coronation of Edward III, that

---

[1] Chanc. Inq. p. m. Edw. I, File 62.

[2] " tenuit castrum de Tamworthe de domino Rege in capite per servicium militare faciendo et inveniendo (tres) milites sumptibus suis in guerria Wall' per quadraginta dies." The text is eked out with the help of Dugdale's *Baronage*.

[3] "tenuit manerium de Scryvelby cum pert. de domino Rege in capite per Baroniam."

[4] *Cal. of Inq.* VI (1910), No. 734.

the King dispensed with its performance and that Hillary thereupon petitioned that his proffer might be recorded and his fee paid him, in consideration of the expense he had incurred. His petition is here printed, I believe, for the first time.

A nostre seigneur le Reye e a son counseil prie Henr' Hillary tenaunt del Maner de Scrivelby per resoun de quel Maner il ceo deit profrer de fere son service alen corounement de cheschun Rey, set asaver sil ieyt nul home qe vodra dedire q'il ne seyt dreiturel Rey, il est prest a defendre per son corps q'il ne dit ne bien ne verite, epur cel profre fere nostre seigneur le Rey ly durra le meillour destrer q'il ad sauve un [1] e les meillours armures estre un per son corps demeigne. [2]   De puys q'il ne pleet mye a nostre seigneur le Rey q'il face le profre a sete feche, [3] q'il veille comaunder q'il seit entre en recourt q'il est prest de fere le service avauntdit per le dit Maner issi q'il ne chcte en damage de ly ne des tenauns de Maner avaunt dit per temps avenir e q'il veille comaunder qe son fee ly seyt paye de sicom . . . . . . ment despendu per son atir purvere [4] e apareiller.

This document is now ' Ancient Petitions, File 265, No. 13230.' That careful antiquary, Mr. Joseph Bain, saw it in 1887, when it was ' Privy Seals, 1 Edw. III, File 3 ' and had still attached to it the " writ ordering the Chancellor to pay the petitioner his fee." This, which, I am informed, cannot now

[1] i. e. the king's second-best charger.
[2] i. e. except one (reserved) for his personal use.   In the petition of Margaret, widow of John Dymoke, to Richard II the claim is to " le melliour destrer ove trappure et le mellior armure du Roy forspris un."
[3] i. e. cette fois.
[4] Miss Stokes, the very capable record agent, read this word as ' purnere ', but, as I think the sense requires ' purvere ', I have ventured to change the ' n ' to ' u '.

be found, is of great consequence, if accurately given, as a recognition of the claim.

It is difficult to explain the king's decision to dispense, on this occasion, with the performance of the service, unless he was in doubt as to the right, owing to the rival claim of Alexander de Freville of Tamworth. Alexander died shortly afterwards and his *Inq. p. m.* returned Tamworth castle as held

by service of coming to the king's coronation, armed *cap-à-pié* (*universaliter*) with royal arms delivered by the king, seated upon the king's charger (*super principalem dextrarium sedens*), offering to make proof, etc. etc.[1]

This return was accepted and recited by the King in letters close of 25 August, 1328.[2] It was evidently relied on by Sir Baldwin Freville in the great contest of 1377 before the Court of Claims, for, only twelve days before Richard's coronation, he obtained an exemplification of the inquisition and of the letters close.[3]

The claim, however, of the lords of Scrivelsby was asserted at the same period no less confidently, in Inquisitions relating to that manor.[4] And though the question was fought out at the next coronation, the contest was renewed at that of Henry IV.

In 1377 Sir John 'Dymmok' petitioned that he might be received to perform his service on coronation day, "que lui appent come de droit Margarete sa femme de lour Manoir de Scryvelby come les Auncestres le dit Margarete ont fait et

---

[1] *Cal. of Inq.* VII, No. 134.

[2] *Cal of Close Rolls*, 1327-1330, p. 313.

[3] *Cal. of Pat. Rolls*, 1377-1381, p. 4.   This proves that such documents were then accepted as evidence.

[4] *Cal. of Inq.* VII, Nos. 110, 439, 464.

clayme." The actual wording of his petition is of
sufficient interest to be quoted.

C'est la demande que Johan Dymmok Chivaler de-
maunde a nostre sieur le Roi qil lui soeffre son service
certein avoir que a lui appent de fee et de droit le jour
de son Coronement . . . . . . cestassavoir que le Roi lui face
avoir le veille de son Coronement un des bons destrers
que le Roi eit ove le sele et ove touz les harneys bien
covert de feer, ensement ove touz les armures quappen-
dont au corps le Roi ansi entierment come le Roi mesmes
le duist avoir sil dust aler en un bataill mortell, En
ycell maner qeu le dit Johan doit venir arme de mesmes
les armes, et mounter mesme le destrer bien couvert le
jour de son Coronement, et chivaucher devant le Roi al
procession, et doit dire et crier al poeple trois foitz joint,
en audience devant tout le monde, qeu sil y a null
homme, haut ou bas, que dedire voille que son seignour
liege, sire Richard, Cosyn et Heir le Roi Dengleterre
Edward, que darrein morust, ne devie estre Roi Dengleterre coroune, qil est prest par son corps a darreiner
meintenant qil ment come faus et come tretre ou a quel
jour que lem lui affera. Et si nulle le dedie, et il face la
darrein pur le Roi, le chival ove touz les harneis lui
demurra come son droit et son fee. Et si nul le dedie
tanque come la processioun dure, apres la tierce heure
meintenant apres la processioun et que le Roi soit enoint
et coroune, descend et soit desarme, et puis soit a la
volonte le Roi si le destrere et les armes lui devient
demurer ou noun.

The rival claimant, Sir Baldwyn de Freville, recited
his *senior* co-heirship of the Marmions [1] and alleged
that he held Tamworth castle, his share of their
inheritance—

---

[1] "Heir a Leynesse file le dit Philip" (Marmion). Here we have
again the 'esnecia' *(aînesse)* claim. Taylor, who did not understand
it, read the word "Lionessæ" (p. 137).

par les services destre a la Coronement nostre dit sieur le Roi en ses armures et sur un des dexstrers le Roi, si nul voleit contredire son dit Coronement, de la deffendre come a lui appartient.

He asked, therefore, that he might be 'accepted' to perform his service.

After keen and long dispute and hearing of evidence,[1] the Court decided that Dymoke had produced "more and better records and evidences" than Freville, and, as sundry magnates had testified before it that both King Edward (III) and his son the Prince had constantly asserted that Dymoke should perform the service for Scrivelsby,[2] it resolved, by the king's wish and direction, that he should perform it on that occasion, reserving to Freville the right to prove his case, if he could do so within a limited time. No allusion, it will be observed, is made to the recognition of the Scrivelsby claim at the coronation of Edward III, but that king's expressed opinion may be accounted for by the fact.

From 1377 the right of the Dymokes as lords of Scrivelsby has been invariably maintained; but the abolition of the 'banquet' (after 1821) has put an end to the service.[3] There was, however, a general feeling that a tenure so ancient and so famous should still be recognised in some way at

---

[1] "habita super serviciis predictis inter prefatos Johannem et Baldwinum gravi et prolixa contencione, auditisque hicinde quampluribus racionibus, recordis, et evidenciis."

[2] "dictum servicium pro dicto manerio de Scryvelby de jure facere deberet."

[3] It should be observed, however, that Sir John Dymoke's petition contemplates his riding, as challenger, in the coronation *procession*.

the crowning of the king.   By a singularly happy
thought (attributed to His late Majesty), Mr.
Dymoke, as the lord of Scrivelsby, was assigned the
duty of carrying 'the Standard of England'—a
keenly coveted honour—in 1902 and is to perform
the same service at the coming coronation.

It is peculiarly fitting that the only standard
which has come down to us without change from
medieval times should be borne in the procession
by one who is himself a survival from the Middle
Ages, as the champion of England's king.   Five
banners were flown by Edward king of England,
as he marched north against the Scots in the
summer of 1300, and he planted all five on
Carlaverock's walls.   Two were those of the lions
of England—the standard which the champion
will bear in the Abbey—and the other three were
those of St. Edmund, St. Edward, and St. George.
Five banners were flown by King Henry at
Agincourt : on one were seen his royal arms ; the
others were those of the Holy Trinity, of Our
Lady, of St. Edward, of St. George.   Among the
ten standards that will be borne in the Abbey,
in addition to that of the Royal arms, will be seen
those of the Sovereign's Kingdoms, Empire, and
dominions, and also one that is oddly supposed to
represent certain counties in the west of his English
realm.[1]   We shall see such modern heralds' con-
coctions as the standards of India, of Canada, of
Australia ; but for the ancient banner of our nation

---

[1] This standard is an innovation.   At the coronation of George IV,
the standards were those of the three kingdoms, England, Scotland,
and Ireland.

we shall look, alas, in vain. It was under the emblem of St. George that our fathers fought and conquered ; but, save in the glorious 'white ensign,' it is to-day merged and, practically, swamped in that deplorable heralds' mess, the ' Union ' flag.[1]

Up through the crowded ranks of a newly-gilt nobility the standards of England and of Scotland will be borne by country gentlemen, beside whose ancient dignities their own are things of yesterday. If I do not venture on the same assertion in the case of 'The O'Conor Don', it is because that tribal title must be borne at the present day under the strange impression that it descends, like a modern peerage dignity, to heirs male of the body. Its existence, of course, was inseparably connected with the Irish and rival system of 'tanistry'.[2]

As to the third standard, that of Ireland, Mr. Fox-Davies, even as I write, has come forward, once again, to enlighten the public on heraldic matters. The head-line " Triple Crowns of Sovereignty, " in large type, caught the eye,[3] and under it one found an article beginning :— " There seems

---

[1] The excellent persons who delight in explaining this composition (*i.e.* disentangling its elements) do not realise that the necessity for such explanation is itself the condemnation of the jumble. As a flag, perhaps, it is worthy of a people which appears to imagine that its 'national colours' are those of Republican France.

[2] " These chieftainships, and perhaps even the kingdoms themselves..... followed a very different rule of succession from that of primogeniture. They were subject to the law of tanistry, of which the principle is defined to be that the .... dignity of chieftainship descended to the eldest and most worthy of the same blood ; .... the preference given to seniority was to be controlled by a due regard to desert ...... it was not unusual to elect a tanist, or reversionary successor, in the lifetime of the reigning chief." Hallam, *Constitutional History.*

[3] In the *Daily Express,* 19 May 1911.

to be so much confusion with regard to the Irish flag that perhaps it will be well to put the real facts upon record." As the writer's "facts" are often amusing, and his "real facts" more so, we turn hopefully to those which prove his vaunted "fulness of knowledge."[1] And we are not disappointed.

The original arms of Ireland were "azure, three crowns or." That was the coat of arms granted by Richard II as the arms of Ireland to be borne as an augmentation with his paternal arms of De Vere by Robert de Vere, Earl of Oxford, when he was created Duke of Ireland.

Such are the "real facts." Unfortunately, "azure, three crowns or" was *not* "the coat of arms granted," for it had a bordure argent, which made all the difference;[2] it was *not* granted "as the arms of Ireland;" and it was *not* granted to the Earl of Oxford "when he was created Duke of Ireland," but more than nine months earlier.

But even this is not the worst. With his usual confidence, Mr. Fox-Davies informs us that

This coat of arms with the three crowns appears upon some of the old Irish coins...... The change from the crowns to the harp was made by Henry VIII, who disliked the papacy and any suggestion of the triple tiara of the Pope.

Now in what the writer terms "the original arms of Ireland", granted by Richard II, the three crowns were "two and one" (in the language of heraldry),

---

[1] This phrase is taken from the prospectus of his latest edition of *Armorial Families*.

[2] Therefore a belief, in later times, "yt (*sic*) ye (*sic*) three crownes were the armes" of Ireland cannot refer to this differenced coat.

which could not possibly suggest the Papal tiara. So we turn to " the old Irish coins "—which the writer, evidently, cannot have seen—and discover that what, in his loose way, he styles " the three crowns " are a totally *different* design ; *viz :* three crowns *pale-wise !* This coat—if it *was* a coat, which is doubtful, as no shield is shown,[1]—would be that attributed, in those days, to King Arthur, " gules, 3 crowns or pale-wise " (though he may not be aware of the fact), and is certainly suggestive of the Papal tiara.[2] Only one who was ignorant of heraldry or singularly careless of the facts could possibly confuse the two coats.

From " real facts " we pass at once to the writer's quaint beliefs. As to the three crowns of the coat granted by Richard—

King Richard II, like his father Edward III, was styled King of England and France and Lord of Ireland, and it seems to me more probable that the triple crowns signified the triple sovereignty than that they originated from the arms attributed to St. Edmund.

Does it indeed ? Apart from the fact that our sovereigns then were 'lords', not 'kings' of Ireland, and could not, therefore, claim a third kingly crown, a knowledge of that mediæval heraldry which is so distasteful to Mr. Fox-Davies would have taught him that the arms of 'St. Edward' and 'St. Edmund' were familiar, in the Middle Ages, on the banners of our kings in war, and that, as Richard allowed his nephew the Duke of Surrey

---

[1] These coins had the royal arms, in a shield, on the obverse.
[2] Fynes Moryson wrote, in his *Itinerary :*—" they had silver groats, called Cross-Keale Groats, stamped with the Pope's triple crown."

to impale the arms of St. Edward with a bordure ermine, so he allowed his favourite, Robert, earl of Oxford, to quarter the arms of St. Edmund with a bordure argent.[1] The arms, of course, attributed to St. Edmund (" azure three crowns [2 and 1] or ") were familiar then and long afterwards; in a roll of arms under Henry VI they are entered as those of " Sainct Edmond Kynge of Yngelonde of old tyme ",[2] and even at so late a date as 1485 there were made ready for the coronation of Henry VII " trappours " (*i.e.* horse-trappings) of the ' arms of St. Edward ' and ' arms of St. Edmund ', which were still associated *ex officio* with the sovereign of this country as they were in the days of Edward I[3] and of Richard II; as they were in the days of Henry V, on whose great seal they were held by angels, and who stamped them on his golden bowls; as they had been since Henry III, in 1232, had ordered St. Edmund and St. Edward to be painted in his chapel at Woodstock and had, some years later, bestowed on his own sons the names of these royal saints.

[1] I duly explained this in *Peerage and Pedigree*, II, 353-4.
[2] *Ancestor* III, 208.
[3] See p. 388 above.

INDEX

A

Abergavenny, Lord, claim of to larderer service, 241.

Abingdon Abbey, relations of Dispensers with, 189 *seq.*

— Cartulary account of Herbert the Chamberlain, 121.

Accatry, connexion of with larder, 237.

— , wages, 215 *n.*

— , Serjeant of the, duties of, 237.

Accountant of the bread, *(computator panis)* 201.

" Act for placing the Lords " regulates precedence of great offices, 122.

Adam, the queen's cook, lands of, 249, 250.

— , le Despenser, 196.

— , of Yarmouth, (a Gernemue), 192, 193.

Addington serjeanty, 8, 23, 243 *seq.*

Adeliza, queen, 142, 320.

Aguillon, William, sergeanty of, 23, 245.

Ailward the Chamberlain, 126.

Aislaby, Yorks, serjeanty of, 279.

Albertivilla, Hugo de, *see* d'Auberville, Hugh.

Alderbury, Wilts, serjeanty of, 288.

Alfred, Knighthood conferred by, 349 *n.*

Alienation from serjeanty, 17.

— , Aston Clinton case, 28.

Alington, family, 267.

Almeric, name, origin of, 195.

Almoner, claim to office of, 326 *seq.*

Alton Priors, serjeanty of, 10.

Alvescote, Oxon, serjeanty of, 108, 109.

Amauri the Dispenser, son of Adam, 196.

— , son of Thurstan, 193.

Ambrosden, Oxon, holder of, 141.

Ancaster, Lord, petition of, *see* Great Chamberlain case.

Andrewes, Lancelot, bishop, servile spirit of, 8.

Angortby, Lincs., serjeanty of, 284.

Angoulême, mayor of, robes made for, 261.

Anne, Coronation of, claims, 113, 119, 140, 241.

Anselme, Père, history of the grand Panetiers of France, 221.

Archbishop's chamberlain, 113, 114.

Arch-Butler, symbol of office. 140 *n.*

Arch-Chamberlain, duties of, 115.

Archer service, in Domesday, 13.

Argentine, family, lands of, 265

— , Sir William, claim, 266.

Arms of Ireland, Fox-Davies on, 390.

Arrentation of 1250, 17, 18-9.

Art de Venerie, 275.

Artington, Surrey, 102.

Art of hunting, The, 278.

Arundel, earls of, claims by, 147, 151 *seq.*, 170, 343.

— , — , Spurs borne by, 370.

— , William d'Aubigny, earl of, 142, 143.

— , Sussex, holders of, 142.

Ashill, Norfolk Serjeanty of, 223 *seq.*

Ashwell, Essex, serjeanty of, 254.

Aston Bernard, *see* Aston Mullins.

Aspland, family, 129.

Aston Clinton, Bucks, Serjeanty, 28 *seq.*

Aston Mullins, Bucks, Serjeanty of, 305 *seq.*

Aubrey the sapper, 16.

Austurcarii, *see* Goshawk-men.

Aylesbury, Bucks, Serjeanty of, 299.

B

Baa, John de. Serjeanty of, 289.

Bacon, making of, as serjeanty, 254.

INDEX

409

Pelisse, rendered by tailor to king, 258.
Pembroke, earls of, as spur-bearers, 370, 371.
— , Aymer de Valence, earl of, 264, 343.
— , Gilbert de Clare, earl of, claim to Catteshill Wardship, 104 *seq.*
— , Gilbert Marshal, earl of, marshalship of, 89, 358.
— , John Hastings, earl of, claim of, to bear sword, 343.
— , Wales, alleged tenure of, 344.
Pepper, tenure by render of, 249.
Petty serjeanty, 20, 33, 36, 197 *n.*, 252.
Petworth, Sussex, holders of, 156.
Philberts (Filberts), manor house of, origin of name, 178.
Philip Augustus, coronation of, 71, 72.
Philippa of Hainault, coronation of, chamberlain's fees at, 136.
Picot, family, serjeanties of, 127.
— , Laureta, holder of larderer serjeanty, 239.
— , Peter, serjeanty of, 128.
Pinel, the miner, 16.
Pipe Roll (1234) on Addington serjeanty decision, 23, 24.
Pishill, Oxon, change in tenure of, 227.
Pixley, Mr., on Broun case, 355.
Pleas of the Hall, 85.
Polechart, H. Hall's misconception of meaning of, 58.
Police functions, marshal's 86, 96.
Ponsard, family, serjeanty of, 256.
Porcel, Geoffrey, 99.
Porcherez, Thomas, origin of name, 285 *n.*
Port, Adam de, fees held of, 181.
Porter service, 14.
Portskewet, 80.
Prayers used at coronation, 325.
Prebende, meaning of, 84.
Privy Seal, office of, 161.
Punchard, family, *see* Ponsard.
Punsard, family, *see* Ponsard.
Purpyn, or pour-pain, 218 *q.*, 219.
Pytchley and Laxton service, 296.

Q

Queen's Chamberlain, 132 *seq.*
— , Basin and towel service, 114.
— , fees of, 113, 117, 133, 137.

— , Lands held by service of, 133.
— , office combined with great chamberlainship, 134.
— , office passes to earls of Oxford, 134.
— , claims for office at various coronations, 140.
— , Privy Kitchen, wages of head of, 215 *n.*
Quévilly, France, 183.
Quit rent, Sauser's render, 252.

R

Rainald, Abbot of Abingdon, 189.
Ralf, archbishop of Canterbury, 320.
— , the crossbowman, of Burgh, 14,
— , 'le Moyne', 235, 236.
— , 'Naper' or le 'Napier', 227.
— , the otterhunter, gift to, 300.
— , of Prestbury, 16.
— , Purcel, 99, 100.
— , the Sauser, grant to, 251.
Ramesey, Adam, Master of the harriers, 289.
Randulf de Broc, Catteshill in possesion of, 100.
Ratcliffe on Soar, Goshawk serjeanty of, 127.
Raynerius Taliator, record concerning, 259.
Raynham, Norfolk, serjeanty of, 310.
Re-coronation, ceremonial of, 325.
Red, favorite colour for robes, 261.
Red Book of the Exchequer, H. Hall's edition, 55.
— , Urri the engineer's land in, 15.
— , on Addington serjeanty case, (1234) 23, 24 *q.*
— , Addington serjeanty records, 245.
— , "Establishment of king's household" printed in, 54.
— , on divided Marshal serjeanty, 94.
— , Teversham Manor case, 95.
— , Catteshill serjeanty, 104.
— , hose serjeanty in, 177.
— , on meaning of *hosarii*, 177.
— , West Hendred serjeanty, 185.
— , Dispenser estates, 195 *n.*
— , incorrect edition of, 246.
— , entries of Adam the cook, 251.
— , on turnspit serjeanty, 256.
— , entries of tailor service, 259.
— , on king's tailor, 258.
— , on Wallbury serjeanty, 264 *n.*
— , on Hairez 285.
— , Bockhampton serjeanty, 287.

27

410 INDEX

INDEX